West German Leadership
and
Foreign Policy

West German Leadership and Foreign Policy

Edited by

HANS SPEIER and W. PHILLIPS DAVISON
The RAND Corporation

With contributions by

Gabriel A. Almond

W. Phillips Davison

John H. Herz

Henry J. Kellermann

Otto Kirchheimer

Hans Speier

Samuel L. Wahrhaftig

ROW, PETERSON AND COMPANY

Evanston, Illinois   White Plains, New York

Acknowledgments

Many political observers in both Germany and the United States have assisted in the preparation of this book. Government officials, university professors, businessmen, labor leaders, journalists, political party leaders, and many others have taken the time to enter into lengthy discussions and to answer a wide variety of questions. Without their kind co-operation these studies could not have been made.

Special thanks are due Professor Otto Kirchheimer of The New School for Social Research, New York City, who was generous with his time and advice during all stages of the manuscript's preparation, and to Dr. Ewald W. Schnitzer of the RAND Social Science Division, who provided extensive editorial and administrative assistance. The individual monographs were prepared for publication by Emmanuel Mesthene, Ian Graham, and Sibylle Crane.

These studies represent a part of a continuing research program of The RAND Corporation.

H. S.

W. P. D.

Contents

VIII. TRENDS IN WEST GERMAN PUBLIC OPINION, *continued*

ONE

Introduction: The German Political Scene

Hans Speier

From the establishment of the German Federal Republic in 1949, almost until the time of the third Bundestag elections in 1957, the basic orientation of West German foreign policy was determined primarily by factors beyond the control of political leaders in Bonn. The Adenauer government was in a favorable position to bargain about details, but its scope for making major foreign policy decisions was limited.

The studies assembled in this book represent an effort to increase our knowledge about the foreign policy decisions German leaders are likely to make as the range of possibilities open to them increases. To this end, the contributors to this volume have sought to ascertain the political views prevalent among those who control some of the major public and private institutions of West Germany, and to examine the characteristics of these institutions which are likely to affect future foreign policy decisions. The comprehensive nature of the subject matter has made it necessary to use a variety of approaches to it. But before describing the research procedures followed, it may be useful to sketch briefly the political background against which these studies have been made.

When Konrad Adenauer visited Washington in April, 1953, John Foster Dulles said in his welcoming statement, ". . . we are encouraged that the large majority of the German people are ready to unite their fate with the rest of the free nations. American hopes for the realization of unity and strength in Europe are largely due to the contribution which

EDS. NOTE.—The author is Chief of the Social Science Division of The RAND Corporation, which he organized in 1948 and has since directed. During the past decade, he has visited Germany many times for purposes of study.

you, Mr. Federal Chancellor, have made in the movement toward these objectives." [1]

Adenauer has often been praised for the staunchly pro-Western, anti-communist foreign policy which he has pursued ever since the creation of the German Federal Republic in 1949. To a generation living with the memories of World War II, into which another German chancellor had plunged the world less than twenty years earlier, Adenauer has been the symbol of sobriety and moderation. His firm adherence to the principles underlying Western civilization is beyond doubt, and his policies bear no trace of Hitler's nihilism and *hybris*.

While the Chancellor's single-mindedness of political purpose and devotion to peace and international order deserve the recognition and praise they have received, it is also true that various circumstances over which Adenauer had no control created for him the historic role that he has performed so successfully. To begin with, the Social Democratic opposition to his administration has, on balance, been a help rather than a hindrance to him. Unlike the French and Italian postwar governments, Adenauer's regime has not had to contend with resistance from a large communist minority. The German Social Democrats, although they have opposed the Federal Chancellor's foreign policy, are as anticommunist and pro-Western in their basic orientation as Adenauer himself.

Neither has Adenauer been plagued by rabid nationalism in any significant sector of the opposition. The nationalism of the Social Democrats, who have insisted that the problem of reunification rather than rearmament should be the main concern of German foreign policy, has been antimilitaristic in spirit. As opposed to the reactionary nationalists, who fought the Versailles Treaty after World War I and brought about the downfall of the Weimar Republic, the Social Democratic critics of Adenauer's foreign policy are staunch supporters of West Germany's democratic institutions. Antidemocratic nationalists on the extreme right of the political spectrum have so far remained few and are lacking in influence.

Moreover, for nearly seven years Adenauer has been able to use the socialist opposition at home to improve his diplomatic bargaining position. In negotiating with the Western powers about German rearmament —the central issue of his foreign policy ever since 1950—Adenauer has been able to exact many concessions by pointing to the opposition to rearmament at home. In yielding to one of Adenauer's demands, U.S. High Commissioner John J. McCloy once remarked: "All right, then. This is now the 122nd concession the Allies have made to the Germans." [2] This happened in the spring of 1952. Several more years passed and many more concessions were made to Germany before she furnished her first soldier to NATO. Early in 1957, the Federal Republic had about 70,000 men under arms—one-seventh of the figure talked about in 1950 —but a German general was appointed commander of the NATO forces in the Central European sector.

The German Chancellor has led his country away from the aftermath of crushing defeat in 1945 and has made it a politically rehabilitated, respected partner in the Western concert of nations. Germany's political comeback has been no less spectacular than her economic resurrection, and while the Chancellor can rightly claim credit for this feat, it should be borne in mind that the much maligned opposition has given him many of the means with which to accomplish it.

Another reason the foreign policy of the Federal Chancellor has been successful is because it has been pursued in a period of buzzing economic prosperity. The so-called "miracle" of Germany's economic recovery following the stabilization of the German currency in 1948 not only increased Adenauer's domestic popularity but also channeled the energies of potential political extremists into more profitable work. Full employment, expanding production and trade, high profits, and a rising standard of living did not provide the conditions under which either the socialists or right-wing nationalists could challenge Adenauer's foreign policy effectively. Socialist insistence on the priority of reunification over rearmament did not embarrass the Chancellor, mainly because many German voters associated Adenauer's leadership with economic well-being, and their prosperity with his pro-Western policy.

A third important factor contributing to the success of Adenauer's foreign policy has been the state of international affairs during the years of his chancellorship. The international scene has been dominated by the conflict between the United States and the Soviet Union. In 1949, this conflict led to the creation of the Federal Republic itself. Given the strong anticommunist leanings of the West Germans, the conflict of the two super-powers virtually forced a pro-Western policy upon the Bonn government. This policy obtained for Germany the support and protection of the Western powers, especially the United States, and facilitated the rapid political rehabilitation of the Federal Republic.

Sometime in the future German foreign policy may be less dependent upon the United States. Adenauer himself has taken steps leading in this direction. Throughout his chancellorship, he has shown a persistent interest in the possibility that a unified Europe might supersede the ancient division of the continent into sovereign states. In 1957, the groundwork was laid to extend West European co-operation from the field of coal and steel production to international trade and investment, and to the development of atomic power for peaceful ends. If, in the course of time, this economic co-operation results in closer political co-operation among the European powers, the independence of the new bloc of nations vis-à-vis the United States would probably be strengthened and, within the bloc, Germany's weight would be considerable. While Adenauer once denied that he was trying to walk in Bismarck's shoes, one of his successors might find the international scene inviting enough to try just that.

It is more likely, however, that an increase in the independence of German foreign policy will result from international developments beyond Germany's control rather than from the initiative of the federal government. In particular, the more reluctant the giant powers are to resort to nuclear arms in the pursuit of their national interests, the more freedom for political maneuver will Germany and other smaller powers enjoy. Further weakening of the NATO alliance as a result of diminished military contributions by Britain and France would also improve Germany's bargaining position, by increasing the relative importance of her armament and enabling the Federal Republic to put a higher price on her continued loyalty to the West. Finally, a revision of American military policy toward Europe would give the Federal Republic at least the illusion that she might then profit from maneuvering politically between East and West.

As the independence of German foreign policy increases, the demands on German statesmanship will become greater than those faced by Chancellor Adenauer from 1949 to 1957. The viability of democracy in the Federal Republic will then be put to a test considerably harder than any since 1949, and the commitment of the West Germans to freedom will be tried for the first time since 1933.

How well German democracy will survive the strains posed by an independent foreign policy is a difficult question to answer, since the political institutions of the Federal Republic lack tradition. All German voters are considerably older than the regime under which they live and which they are supposed to respect. In the last forty years, Germany has experienced two world wars, a period of runaway inflation, and another in which a barter economy prevailed. The Germans have had no less than five different regimes: monarchy, republic, dictatorship, an occupation regime, and again a republic. Berlin, Germany's former capital, has been partly absorbed by Soviet-occupied East Germany, and is partly a Western enclave in communist territory. Foreign troops are stationed on Germany's divided soil. The state of Prussia has been abolished, and many of the new *Länder* which form the Federal Republic are creations of foreign political planners. Under these circumstances, it is not surprising that German political traditions are feeble.

Continuity in German traditions and culture has been assured by a number of nonpolitical institutions—certain economic organizations, the class structure, the churches, and the family. These nonpolitical institutions, however, can not provide guidance in the field of foreign affairs, especially if foreign policy no longer is limited to bargaining over the conditions of carrying out decisions basically made by others.

To a degree, the absence of a political tradition in Germany has been compensated by the strong personality of Chancellor Adenauer, and there has been much speculation abroad as to what will happen to German foreign policy when Adenauer leaves the political arena. Foreign observers have asked how the German government would react to changes in the policies of her major allies, how German democracy would take the shock of an economic recession, how high a price Germany would be willing to pay the Soviet Union for reunification, and so on. None of these questions can be answered with certainty, but it is possible to improve one's ability to anticipate developments by a close study of the groups which are likely to be called upon to furnish the leaders who will make the political decisions of the future.

In the present volume six political scientists have collaborated to try to shed light on the political attitudes of German leaders in various walks of life in order to assess the viability of the Federal Republic both as a democratic regime and as a partner of the West. In four of the contributions, the views of politicians, civil servants, labor leaders, and businessmen have each been treated monographically. In addition, the press and other media of communication which form an important link between the elite and the mass of the population have been examined as a political institution in Chapter Seven; and Chapter Two reviews the postwar development of the institutions that are concerned with foreign policy.*

As a result of the popularity of public opinion polls, both with the Western occupation powers and with the Germans themselves, a great deal is known about mass opinion in Germany since 1945. By contrast, information on the political attitudes prevalent among German leaders is relatively scanty. The essays assembled in this book attempt to fill the gap. They are based to a large extent on several hundred interviews with German leaders which the authors conducted in various parts of West Germany and in West Berlin in the period 1952–1955. Only the last chapter, in which the political views of the West Germans are culled from public opinion polls, offers a general survey of West German

---

* The views of German military leaders have been treated in a separate volume. Cf. Hans Speier, *German Rearmament and Atomic War*, Row, Peterson & Co., Evanston, Illinois, 1957.

opinion at large. This chapter serves to throw into relief the more detailed findings on the political orientations of West German elites with which the rest of the volume is concerned.

The procedure followed by the contributors to this volume is statistically less reliable than that followed in public opinion polls, but it has several advantages over the quantitative surveys. To begin with, each of the authors has a general familiarity with German society and politics and is in addition a specialist on the particular social group he has studied. The authors knew something about the personality and position of each man they contacted, and in many cases had been acquainted with him long before he was interviewed for the purposes of this study. As a result, it was possible to conduct each interview in such a way as to take account of the background, interests, position, and special knowledge of the respondent. Moreover, the analysis of the data has been undertaken by the authors in the context of the institutional setting within which the interviewed leaders were located.

This book may be thus considered as belonging to the growing number of studies in political science in which "field work" supplements library research, and in which the study of "subjective" factors is added to the observer's customary concern with recorded events and the structure of institutions.

TWO

The Development of German Foreign Policy Institutions

Samuel L. Wahrhaftig

The machinery for the formulation and conduct of recent German foreign policy came into being with the organization of the Federal Republic. The precise origins of the current policies themselves can not be determined as easily. They can not be considered direct descendants of the so-called "traditional" German foreign policies. As far as foreign relations are concerned, the German collapse meant not only the physical dissolution of the Wilhelmstrasse foreign office, but also a revulsion, at least for the time being, from the mental attitudes of the past.

Nevertheless, the break with old patterns does not necessarily mean that past foreign policies and foreign policy objectives disappeared without a trace. These have remained in the German political consciousness at least as memories. Just as the campaigns of Caesar and Napoleon serve, though conditions of warfare have since changed, to sharpen the analytical minds of today's military strategists, so the past international strategies of the Wilhelmstrasse supply present foreign policy experts with standards of comparison. Thus, the years before 1945 provide criteria for arriving at decisions about current realities without governing the character of the policies pursued.

Eds. Note.—This account of the postwar growth of German foreign policy institutions was written during 1955 and revised during 1956. It is based partially on research done for this specific study, but also on Mr. Wahrhaftig's general familiarity with the German political scene since 1945.

The author is an American freelance journalist, currently working in Frankfurt. For several years he was an editor of the *Frankfurter Hefte,* a magazine widely read by German intellectuals, and prior to that time served on the staff of the U.S. High Commissioner for Germany.

Germany under Occupation

In the period immediately after World War II, efforts were made to formulate new international aims appropriate to Germany's changed situation. True, few of the ideas and theories proposed immediately after the capitulation can be viewed today as contributing to the outline of a foreign policy. Most of them were too opportunistic and too easily punctured by experience to serve as a basis for later policies. The absence of a realistic approach and even of an agency to carry out acceptable ideas, together with a complete lack of the power to back up such ideas, foredoomed the various proposals of those days. Nevertheless they contributed to the political atmosphere in which later ideas and plans developed.

The destruction of the Hitler regime and the complete occupation of German territory provided postwar planners and dreamers with a *tabula rasa* upon which to try out their ideas. Unencumbered by domestic political pressures or by the existence of voluntarily accepted foreign obligations, they sought to accommodate Germany or parts thereof in various international systems and blocs. Many of these schemes were highly idealistic. In no period of German history have plans for the reorganization of the nation and its participation in international arrangements been so free from the influences of materialistic interest groups as in the months following the capitulation.

Most of those ideas are today considered products of abnormal times and as such are disregarded. For instance, the efforts to establish an independent Bavaria or to create a Danubian confederation are now interesting but forgotten episodes of early postwar German history.

Some Germans, however, developed proposals in 1945 which anticipated in many respects those advocated and pursued today. An interesting example of this tendency can be supplied from the history of the National Democratic Party, formed in 1945 by the octogenarian Dr. Heinrich Leuchtgens. In 1945 and 1946, the group was regarded as belonging to the nationalist lunatic fringe. In due time, because of various political deals, it achieved its own self-elimination even on the local level. And yet, in the program it submitted to the American Military Government in 1945, this insignificant group advocated an alliance with the West—specifically, with the Anglo-Saxon countries; the organization of a German army under officers trained by the Anglo-Saxon armies; and a strong stand against Russia. Possibly Dr. Leuchtgens' insistence that the capital of the new Germany be Friedberg—the small town where he lived, near Frankfurt on Main—detracted somewhat from the seriousness with which his program was viewed.

Meanwhile, more stable political organizations, which were slowly developing, also began thinking about the eventual international role of Germany. The dominant notes in these first formulations by responsible political parties were the recognition of the nation's political ineptitude and the conviction that the Allies ought to bear the responsibility for Germany's foreign relations "for at least twenty-five years."

At the same time, two older concepts lingered in the German political atmosphere. Both of them dated back to before 1945 and were historically linked with the "traditionalists" of the German Foreign Office, as well as with some anti-Nazi circles. The influence of these concepts is still noticeable even today. The first is the so-called "bridge-building policy," which envisages Germany's mission as that of providing a link between East and West. In 1945 and 1946, nonsocialist political leaders of the Eastern zone and Berlin were especially fond of this idea which implied a static coexistence of East and West, in which the Soviet lion and the American lamb would lie down together, with Germany as the interpreter of each to the other. Basic to this policy proposal were the assumptions that both sides would respect the German bridge, would accept its services, and would not be interested in aggressive actions.

A more dynamic role for Germany—that of balancing and maneuvering between the two blocs—was at first advocated only by small groups, and views of this nature were aired for the most part in conversations and interviews. The ultimate goal of this policy was the re-establishment of a powerful Germany, through her position as a balancing force in the conflicts between East and West.

While this theorizing about foreign policy was going on Germany lacked all the prerequisites for active participation in international politics. Unconditional surrender and the actions of the occupation authorities destroyed the state machinery, including all agencies entrusted with the conduct and maintenance of foreign relations. Control Council Proclamation Number 2, dated September 20, 1945, deprived Germany of even a nominal claim to conduct her own foreign relations when it decreed that only the Control Council was empowered to regulate Germany's foreign affairs and to decide about the continuity, enforcement, and termination of all international agreements in which Germany participated. It also prohibited the exchange of diplomatic representatives between Germany and other countries.

Before Germany could return to the field of international politics it had to acquire greater political stability, and national agencies with at least limited powers to act for the German people had to be re-established. Only following some international consensus as to what Germany comprised and who represented it could the country, or any part of it, hope to become active diplomatically or to assume control over its own international position.

During the period between the German capitulation in May, 1945, and the establishment of the Federal Republic in September, 1949, Germans tried to arrive at an acceptable definition of their status and to chart a plan for national agencies which would represent them politically.

Neither the Berlin Declaration nor the Potsdam Agreement provided the German people with an answer about its future status as an ethnic, cultural, or political community.* At first the occupying powers concentrated on the annihilation of the past regime and its institutions, and postponed for the time being the construction of a new central governmental system.[1] The Potsdam Agreement envisaged the establishment of purely economic central agencies, but no four-power agreement of that period noted the need for a central political administration. On the contrary, by stressing the occupation objective of political decentralization, the implication was established that no such administration was desired in the near future. Individual zonal commanders could establish representative governments on a local or *Land* ("state") basis if the situation warranted it.

The mere emergence of local and *Land* administrations, however, posed the problem of the relationships among these various administrations. Not only academicians but also the executives of the newly formed agencies searched for an answer to the question about the status of the German people. Had Germany ceased to exist as a state? What had happened to German sovereignty?[2]

The academic discussion about the essence of the German nation is still going on today. By the end of 1946, however, the concept of German national unity and the continued existence of the German state were established firmly enough to provide a working basis for the discussion of the question of who should represent Germany in dealings with the occupying nations and who was competent to advise the Allies about German wishes.

Germany's international position at that time was often rationalized by German politicians who pointed out that, while Germany had no diplomatic missions abroad and carried on no international negotiations, her dealings with the occupation powers represented in many respects a limited German participation in diplomatic relations. According to this

* The Berlin Declaration was issued following a conference of Allied military commanders on June 5, 1945. It announced the assumption of authority by the four occupying powers, the formation of the Allied Control Council, and the division of Germany into four zones of occupation, with a special status for Berlin. The Potsdam Agreement, signed August 2, 1945, declared the aims of occupation to be the destruction of Nazi institutions and the establishment of a democratic system.

reasoning, the occupation powers could be considered Germany's diplomatic agents in dealing with other countries.[3] In spite of these rationalizations, the Germans realized that Germany had as yet no policy of her own.

Before Germany could take an active part in international politics, it was necessary that other nations be ready to accept German sovereignty in principle. The Stuttgart address by Secretary of State James F. Byrnes on September 6, 1946, gave the first official indication that the Western powers were prepared to do so.* It also made more pressing the question of who should represent Germany.

Efforts by the Minister Presidents to Establish a Body Representing Germany

On October 4 and 5, 1946, one month after Byrnes's Stuttgart speech, the chiefs of the *Länder* in the British and American zones met in Bremen to consider ways and means of following up the Secretary of State's recommendations. The initiator of this conference, Bremen's mayor Wilhelm Kaisen, invited the *Länder* chiefs from all four zones. The Soviet zone Minister Presidents informed Kaisen, however, that in view of the election campaigns then in progress in the five Soviet zone *Länder* they could not spare the time. The Minister Presidents from the French zone were prevented from attending the conference by administrative difficulties caused by the French Military Government.

The discussion at the conference, as well as the decisions reached by the participants, indicated that the chiefs of the *Länder* still thought in provisional terms. Organization of the four zones into a uniform administrative system was the major theme, but the Minister Presidents still did not ask for anything which approached a sovereign and independent state. The representative bodies which they envisaged were to be appointed by the *Land* governments or by the *Land* assemblies. The Minister Presidents still feared the possible effects of general elections for the proposed interzonal parliamentary bodies and asked for them only advisory powers. These agencies were to advise the Allied Control Council and to acquaint it with the German viewpoint about pending Military Government actions.

In 1947 another effort was made by the Minister Presidents. On June 6, the Bavarian *Land* chief, Dr. Hans Ehard, convoked a conference of Minister Presidents from all four zones in Munich. This time the Soviet

* Byrnes proposed that Germany should receive a provisional government composed of the Minister Presidents or other chief officials of the German states in the four zones. This provisional government was to direct central administrative agencies and provide for drafting a German constitution.

zone officials appeared but, apparently in response to orders from the Soviet Military Government, they left almost immediately on the pretext that their demands for the democratization of the conference had not been met. In an official statement they said that the German problem could not be solved by a conference of Minister Presidents, but rather by a popular vote to decide on the structure and role of the central German government and on the functions of the *Länder*.

Both of these conferences reflected the foreign policy aspirations of the existing German administrations. Their primary objective was to gain the support of the occupying powers for a normalization of the economic life inside the four zones. To this end, the Minister Presidents asked that the decisions of the Potsdam Agreement of July, 1945, with regard to the establishment of central economic agencies be carried out; that Germany be allowed access to international markets; that occupation expenditures be regulated; and that reparations and dismantling not be carried to a point at which they would reduce Germany's industrial capacity below the minimum required for national subsistence.

The Minister Presidents addressed themselves also to international public opinion. They claimed that, while a disarmed Germany represented no danger to world peace, an impoverished Germany would hinder the reconstruction of Europe. They insisted that it was contrary to the principles of international law to deny a democratic Germany a chance for peace and means of existence. They also asked for the regulation of the occupation burdens in accordance with international law.[4]

The state administrations, and specifically the Minister Presidents, found it difficult to make a whole out of the sum of Germany's parts. Though the German *Länder* added up to an entire Germany statistically, they could not be added together politically.* The doctrine of the unity of the German people and of all parts of Germany made governmental and political leaders reluctant to accept the creation of any national body representing less than the whole nation. But the division between the East and West and the uncertainty about Germany's geographic boundaries made it impossible to establish any agency that could speak in the name of all German areas. German representatives from the *Länder* in the British and American zones were disinclined to act in the name of Germany, for fear of prejudicing future German claims.** Furthermore,

* By 1948 the stream of expellees from the German areas under Polish administration had ceased. Thereafter, substantially the entire German nation lived in the *Länder* of the four occupation zones, in Berlin, or in the Saar, even if geographically the "whole Germany," according to German opinion, included additional areas.

** Until 1948 the French Military Government discouraged political co-operation of the *Länder* in its zone with those of the other zones.

the Minister Presidents were unable to transcend the administrative limits of the *Länder*; nor could they reconcile the competitive vested interests of the various *Land* bureaucracies. Even while joining in larger functional agencies, such as the *Länderrat* (council of Minister Presidents in the U.S. zone) and later the Bi-zonal Administration (a body formed in 1947 to provide a common economic direction for the U.S. and British zones), the *Länder* remained merely an aggregation. It proved impossible for them to create a national political entity.

Efforts by the Political Parties

At the same time, the political parties began to exhibit a greater interest in trying to influence the occupation powers, and the still comparatively weak party bureaucracies vied with the Minister Presidents for the right to present the German point of view. The party organizations insisted that the Minister Presidents were merely administrative officials and not competent to speak ex officio for the German people. Since most parties were loosely organized, however, their objections were easily ignored. Only the critical voice of the Social Democrats was noted, because by 1948 they had built up an effective organization that covered almost the whole of West Germany.

Ideological preparations for a German foreign policy and for representation of German interests abroad were carried out during this period primarily by the Social Democratic Party (SPD). In spite of, or perhaps because of, the fact that the country was divided into four zones, the special nature of the division between East and West Germany was not as yet generally realized. All zonal boundaries at first hindered normal contacts and hampered economic life. Even in 1947 and 1948 special licenses and passes were required for trade and transport between the economically merged British and American zones on the one hand and the French zone on the other. In view of this, the restrictive measures affecting the Eastern zone were not immediately seen in their true perspective by the population. They were regarded simply as more stringent and more repressive than those prevailing in the West. It was only after the beginning of the Berlin blockade and after currency reform that the West German public became more fully aware of the depth of the division between East and West Germany.

As early as the spring of 1946 the SPD had become aware of the deep cleavage between East and West, when Soviet authorities in East Germany forced the communists and socialists there to merge their parties. Activities of the SPD as such were forbidden in the Soviet zone. Thus the SPD acquired a special status among the political parties, in that it had no East German branch. Both the Christian Democratic Union (CDU) and the Liberal Democratic Party (LPD) * still maintained the illusion that their East zone namesakes were able to represent substantially the same principles in East Germany as they were in West Germany.

Kurt Schumacher, Chairman of the SPD, was probably the first German political leader to introduce the claim for German rights into postwar international political discussion. On the whole, existing German agencies on the *Land* or zonal levels accepted the "sovereignty" of the occupational authorities. They tried merely to weaken Allied restrictive measures and to carve out for the German administrations as much self-determination as was possible under the circumstances. Schumacher, however, insisted that Germans could claim certain rights deriving from international agreements, specifically the Potsdam Agreement, and that these rights should be respected by the occupation authorities. He also argued that the Allies had occupied Germany not merely in order to carry out punitive measures, but ultimately to restore German unity and to create an effective central administration.

Though the SPD defined the prerequisites for the formation of a central German administration, it expected the occupying powers to take action to bring these conditions into being. For example, in May, 1947, SPD leaders rebuffed representatives of the Christian Democratic Union when the two groups met in Hanover to discuss national representation.** The CDU leaders asked the SPD to view matters realistically and implied that the socialists should temporarily close their eyes to the forced merger in the Eastern zone. Schumacher insisted, however, that the SPD could participate in any national body only when it was in a position to function freely throughout Germany. He insisted further that the political prerequisites for a unified Germany were the establishment of political freedom, civil equality, and the rule of law throughout the four zones.

This meeting represented the last serious effort on the part of the two largest German political parties to establish a common platform. Subsequently, each of the parties acted independently.

Thus, while the Minister Presidents could not bridge the divisions among the *Länder,* the political party leaders could not eliminate basic differences among the parties. The Social Democratic Party represented that portion of the German people throughout the Western zones who, regardless of *Land,* accepted the party's principles. The Christian Demo-

* In 1949 this party became known as the "Free Democratic Party" (FDP).
** Jakob Kaiser, Ernst Lemmer, Dr. Friedrich Wilhelm Holzapfel, and Dr. Joseph Müller for the CDU; Dr. Kurt Schumacher, Erich Ollenhauer, and Fritz Heine for the SPD.

cratic Union, though not centralized, represented another country-wide cross section of the population. The same could be said for the Liberal Democratic Party. Each one of the parties claimed to represent a portion of the German people.

In spite of efforts by various political leaders to reach interparty agreements with regard to the manner in which German interests should be represented, a basis for unity and an institution giving expression to it were never achieved. Only the decision of the 1948 London Conference —to proceed with the establishment of a German state—finally induced the West Germans to create the basis on which they could unite as a nation and the institutions through which they could act as a nation.*

Other Groups Interested in Foreign Policy

Before 1949 the political parties and the existing *Land* and zonal administrations sufficed, by and large, to provide scope for the political activity of politically acceptable and public-minded Germans. A few, however, could not accommodate themselves in the framework of these recognized organizations. They therefore formed circles (*Kreise*) of their own, in which they could discuss current problems in their own fashion. As centers for discussion, the *Kreise* had advantages over both the political parties and the *Land* administrative institutions. Being informal and nonofficial, the *Kreise* could include personalities who for various reasons were not as yet politically acceptable, and also they could work independently without fear of going counter to established party or *Land* policies.

Decisions were rarely reached in the conferences of the *Kreise,* but the discussions themselves were often sufficient to influence government action eventually, since a considerable number of the personalities in these *Kreise* also held important administrative positions. *Kreise* such as the Königsteiner Kreis or the Ellwanger Kreis, in which the Christian Democratic Union members played the dominant role, contributed appreciably to the crystallization of German opinion about a number of issues—in particular the issue of a German governmental structure.

After the split between East and West became more apparent, neutralist *Kreise* made their appearance. The most important of these was the

* The London Conference, which took place between February and June, 1948, was attended by representatives of the United States, Great Britain, France, and the Benelux nations. Having become convinced that the Soviet Union would not permit German unification except on her own terms, the Western powers agreed at this conference on a series of measures known as the "London Recommendations." These measures included the following: economic policies in the three West zones were to be co-ordinated, West Germany was to be included in the European Recovery Program, and German *Land* authorities were to be authorized to arrange for the drafting of a constitution for a German Federal Republic.

Nauheimer Kreis, which for about two years influenced at least the news coverage about German political opinion, even if in fact it did not at that time exercise any serious influence over German political action.

The Nauheimer Kreis was organized by Professor Ulrich Noack, and succeeded in attracting considerable support from the ranks of German industry during 1948 and 1949. Its program of German neutralism and political nonalliance was applauded in those industrial circles which traditionally had close contacts with the economies of Eastern Europe. In addition, the contention of this group that a neutral Germany might form the basis for eventual understanding between East and West, and that a proposed four-power agency to control German military potential might eventually lead to an international arms control authority, appealed to the romantic sentiments of certain German circles. The group's final failure in 1950 resulted more from the lack of understanding which it encountered in the East zone than from West German opposition. Though Professor Noack was at first acclaimed by the communists as a true German patriot, they reacted brusquely when in 1950 he demanded that the Soviet zone permit freedom of political activities and free elections. The Nauheimer Kreis expired as an organization shortly thereafter, but its theories have lingered on and at times have influenced important political groups.

The concern of some Germans about the unity of their country brought about still more informal kinds of activity, called "talks" (*Gespräche*). These *ad hoc* conferences of German political figures did not assume a permanent organizational pattern. Nevertheless, some *Gespräche* contributed appreciably to the growth of neutralist sentiments in highly conservative circles which included certain persons who have continued to play influential roles in West Germany down to the present.

In November, 1947, for example, a number of West and East German political and cultural leaders met in Berlin to formulate German wishes regarding the cultural and political unity of the country on the eve of the four-power Foreign Ministers' Conference, which was to meet in London in December. Among the participants were Dr. Ferdinand Friedensburg (CDU) from Berlin; the late Professor Karl Geiler, former Minister President of Hesse; Dr. Walter Strauss, now State Secretary in the Federal Ministry of Justice; the late Dr. Otto Lenz, an influential adviser of Dr. Adenauer who performed many of the functions of a campaign manager for the Chancellor in the 1953 election; Dr. Alfred Weber, Professor from Heidelberg; and Paul Loebe, dean of the Social Democratic parliamentarians. The resolution adopted by the group culminated in a series of demands:

. . . The participation of responsible and expert representatives of the German people in the preparation and conclusion of a peace treaty is indispensable. The German people demand that they be regarded as a political entity. They demand that a statute be adopted to regulate the relationships between the occupation powers and Germany as a whole. Furthermore, it appears that the creation of central administrations in the important fields of state activity is most urgent. The German people also consider the cultural division, as it now exists, unbearable. . . .[5]

On the eve of the formation of the Federal Republic the number of such talks increased. Some attracted widespread attention and the attendance of influential public figures. This was the case with the Bad Godesberg *Gespräche,* for instance, initiated by Rudolf Nadolny, former German Ambassador in Soviet Russia. The first of these discussions took place in March, 1949, and dealt with the role of Germany as a "mediator" and "bridge" between East and West. Among the participants were Dr. Franz Blücher, now Federal Vice-Chancellor; Professor Ludwig Erhard, now Federal Minister of Economics; and Andreas Hermes, at that time leader of the German agricultural and farmers' organizations.

Uncertainty in some quarters as to whether there really was a conflict between German unity and Western orientation was partially allayed by the work of groups which favored European integration. By 1947 a number of such groups had already sought official recognition, and by 1948 these were joined together in the *Europa Union,* which in turn was affiliated with the Union of European Federalists, and was represented in the European Parliamentary Union. The European unity movement of 1948 and 1949, though numerically insignificant, paved the way for the acceptance of certain concepts by the German public. It laid the basis for European policies later formulated by the Bonn government, and for the incorporation in the German constitutional system of a number of principles designed to enable Germany to merge part of her sovereignty in supranational bodies.

The desire for European integration did not stem only from political considerations. Economic motives led some German circles to the conclusion that European unity might solve the problem of Germany's inferior status. They envisaged an integrated Europe to which Germany could bring her curtailed sovereignty and within which she would function as an equal partner with nations hitherto fully sovereign. Those who could raise their voices with impunity asked the world not to leave Germany in the status of an invalid. They warned that Germany, as a permanent sick man of Europe, would infect the political climate of the world. Rejecting the principle *si vis pacem para bellum* ("if you want peace prepare for war"), they pleaded for the idea of European solidarity within the framework of an international community and insisted that only a healthy Germany could make its contribution to the world.[6]

West Germany's De Facto *Relations with the West*

Germany's final attachment to the West was determined less by the superiority of the arguments advanced by pro-Western circles over those advanced by the neutralists than by the personal contacts which grew up between Germans and the Western world. These contacts, which the occupation made necessary, served as a substitute for foreign relations. They widened and deepened as a result of the German desire to escape from a miserable state of enforced economic self-sufficiency, and the increasing value placed by Allied foreign policy planners on German cooperation in the struggle against Soviet expansionism.

While formal diplomatic relations between Germany and other countries were prohibited by Control Council order, certain forms of foreign consular representation were established in West Germany by several foreign governments, including neutrals. These consulates were accredited to the occupation powers and not to any German agency, but their mere presence brought them into contact with the German population.

There were also what might be called domestic foreign relations. Until 1949 the German administrations had little to say officially about international affairs. But in solving domestic problems they actually became involved in foreign relations, for these problems required negotiations with the Allies about every phase of Military Government activity. German officials opposed the requisitioning of homes and attempted to halt plant dismantling. After the currency reform German agencies began maneuvering, within the framework of Military Government restrictions, to obtain easier access to foreign markets and sources of raw materials.[7] By persevering in their demands they succeeded in increasing the autonomy of the German administrations and reducing the severity of some occupation measures. At the same time, however, they acquired the habit of dealing with the West. The German economy thus developed Western heliotropic tendencies, which were accelerated by Soviet reparation policies and by Moscow's delay in releasing German war prisoners.

Furthermore, Germans—especially the Minister Presidents—had opportunities to participate in foreign policy discussions. These officials were in a better position to transmit German wishes to the occupying powers than were the representatives of political parties or other groups.

The Minister Presidents could make use of the *Land* bureaucracies to prepare and formulate German proposals. In view of their position they were more frequently called upon to present their views to the Military Governors than were other German leaders.

On the eve of the four-power Moscow Conference, which met in March and April, 1947, the Minister Presidents of the British and American zones decided to form a Bureau for Peace Questions. This office was to prepare material and studies reflecting German viewpoints for submission to the occupation powers. In view of prevailing policies a German agency could function only on a zonal level. The German Bureau for Peace Questions was therefore established within the framework of the *Länderrat* for the U.S. zone at Stuttgart.

After 1947 there were also other contacts, not directly involving the occupying powers, which strengthened German inclination toward the West and tended to weaken the effectiveness of neutralist appeals. By 1949, for example, all three major noncommunist parties in Germany had established touch with similar parties in other European countries. The Social Democratic Party was the first to find its way into the international arena and, by 1948, was working with the Committee for International Socialist Co-operation. A number of SPD leaders were also active in the *Mouvement Socialiste pour les États Unis de l'Europe,* a Social Democratic group working for European integration. The Christian Democratic Union co-operated with similarly oriented groups in other European countries, as did the Free Democratic Party, at that time still going under various names such as the Liberal Democratic Party and the People's Democratic Party.

Formation of German Governmental Agencies

When, through the London Recommendations, the Western Allies forced the Germans to take steps toward formation of a West German state, skeleton central agencies already existed as part of the Bi-zonal Administration for the British and American zones. This administration had undergone several changes since its inception in 1947. By 1949, it was composed of a bicameral legislature and an executive. The legislature included an Economic Council, whose 104 members were delegated by the parliaments of the eight *Länder* in the British and American zones in proportion to their respective populations, and a bi-zonal *Länderrat* of two delegates from each *Land* government. Executive functions were performed by an Executive Committee consisting of the Directors of the six bi-zonal departments of government under a General Director. Decisions of the Bi-zonal Administration, which were strictly limited to economic matters, required the approval of the occupation authorities before going into effect.

In their search for German representatives with whom to discuss procedures for the organization of a West German political structure, the Military Governors ignored the Bi-zonal Administration almost completely and turned instead to the Minister Presidents. Until the elections to the first Bundestag in August, 1949, the Minister Presidents were the highest German administrative officials whose tenure of office depended directly on the confidence of popularly elected parliamentary bodies. Nevertheless, as the discussion about the form of the German state entered its final stage—from June, 1948, to August, 1949—the political parties increasingly challenged the position of the Minister Presidents as spokesmen for the German people. In the course of the discussions, the eleven Minister Presidents of the British, French, and American zones were forced to pay more heed to the wishes of the parties, although in substantive matters there was, in fact, little difference between the views of the party leaders and the *Land* officials.

German governmental and political leaders were still unwilling to take steps which might be interpreted as official recognition that the East-West division of the country was more than temporary. Up to the last possible moment German representatives fought to disguise the fact that a constituent assembly was to be convoked and that the document to be prepared was basically a constitution. They carefully avoided the use of such terms as "constitution," "German State," "German Parliament," and so on. They opposed direct election of the constituent assembly and ratification of the constitution by a popular vote. Instead, they favored preparation of a basic law by a body not directly responsible to the people and ratification of this law by the *Land* diets. This procedure, they believed, would avoid a document that looked too much like a permanent constitution and would give it the appearance of a mere administrative agreement. A vote by the people of West Germany alone, they argued, would underscore the political division of the nation and make subsequent unification all the more difficult.

The Parliamentary Council, as the constituent assembly was finally called, convened in Bonn on September 1, 1948. It consisted of 65 members, chosen by the *Land* legislatures. Berlin was represented by an additional five nonvoting delegates. After the Minister Presidents, as well as the political parties, had made it clear by their semantic discussions that they did not want to create a state which could claim full sovereignty and therefore organize itself independently of the rest of Germany, the Parliamentary Council proceeded to create a constitution suitable for such a state. The Basic Law, finally adopted by the Council on

May 8, 1949, and subsequently approved by the three Military Governors, defied in most of its articles the contention that the document was provisional. In addition, the Parliamentary Council began to regard itself, rather than the Minister Presidents, as the legitimate spokesman for the German population on political matters.

In spite of self-imposed restrictions on its area of competence, the Council could not remain blind to developments in the Soviet zone. On September 15, 1948, it temporarily forsook its constitution-drafting functions and passed a resolution protesting the action of a Russian military court in sentencing each of five participants in a Berlin freedom demonstration to twenty-five years' hard labor. This was the first time that representatives of West Germany had officially designated the fourth occupying power as a repressive regime and, by inference, had called for the support of the other three powers. The Council also asserted its rights as spokesman for the German people: "As the only organ which has the right and the function to speak freely for all the German people, the Council feels justified and called upon to raise its voice in questions concerning the life of the German people even before it has been able to complete its actual task." [8]

On May 12, 1949, the Military Governors approved the draft of the Basic Law as adopted by the Parliamentary Council, subject to certain interpretive reservations. The Germans of the Western zones were thus provided with an instrument which would enable them to establish political agencies to represent their interests.

New Forces Take Over

Formation of the German Federal Republic in September, 1949, proved to be more than merely another step in the construction of a German administration. It introduced new currents into German political life and placed political influence in new hands. First, establishment of the Bonn government produced a new set of German policymakers with whom the Western powers had to negotiate from then on. Second, it drew into the political arena a number of groups which up to then had kept aloof or lain dormant. Third, it shifted West Germany's center of political gravity to the Rhine-Ruhr area.

The Bonn government can not be regarded as an outgrowth of the governmental agencies which preceded it, although it did inherit certain portions of their jurisdictions and administrations. On the contrary, the new government followed new forms and was staffed by new personnel. This meant the relegation of the *Land* governments to positions of less influence. It also meant a restriction on the influence of the so-called "1945'ers," that is, those Germans who had been responsible for the reconstruction of their country in co-operation with the Allies.

This development was presaged by the conflict between the parties and the Minister Presidents, to which reference has already been made. The Social Democrats desired the replacement of the Minister Presidents as spokesmen for the German people and as negotiators with the Allies, because they felt that a more efficient and more German-minded leadership was needed. The right wings in the CDU and FDP also desired this, but for different reasons.

To understand the reasons why many elements in the CDU and FDP desired to see the Minister Presidents and *Land* bureaucracies superseded as spokesmen for the German people, one must turn back to the period from 1946 to 1948. In its postwar rejection of Nazi ideology the West German electorate turned politically left-of-center. At the same time, generally miserable economic conditions deadened individual initiative and induced even middle-class groups to favor socialization schemes. All of the *Land* diets of West Germany were elected during this period, and their composition reflected the political mood of the times. Those elements which opposed this trend were unable to assert themselves either politically or economically before the Western currency reform of June, 1948.

The currency reform and resulting economic improvements awakened private property interests. Relaxation of Military Government political controls encouraged former passive and active supporters of the Third Reich to re-enter politics. Both these groups were inimical to the *Land* administrations, as then constituted, and reasoned that a federal government, staffed from the personnel rolls of the *Land* administrations, would be equally dangerous to their interests.

The right wing of the CDU, therefore, pressed instinctively for a complete structural change in the German administration and, although completely at odds ideologically with the SPD, gained its support on the working level. While the Parliamentary Council was meeting, both the Social Democrats and conservative elements in the CDU favored a change in the policy-making elite. Since the CDU won the 1949 elections, its right wing reaped the benefits of the common efforts.

In the government which Konrad Adenauer formed in 1949, only one member was an active *Land* Minister at the time of his appointment. Several members had previously held posts in *Land* cabinets, but almost all of them had been swept out of office as a result of the first Landtag elections. The leading members of the cabinet were opposed to co-operation with the SPD, the favorite post-1945 political formula.

The Bonn government also made it clear that it did not consider itself to be merely a more advanced stage of the Bi-zonal Administration. Of the six Bi-zonal Directors only three were included in the new cabinet, and only one—Professor Dr. Ludwig Erhard—was able to transfer his prestige to the new administration. The chief of the bi-zonal "cabinet," General Director Dr. Hermann Pünder, was shunted to a political sidetrack. Other leading officials of the Bi-zonal Administration were accommodated in diplomatic posts away from Bonn.

Formation of the Bonn government started a number of far-reaching developments on the German political scene. First, the elements which had been responsible for the organization and reconstruction of German political and social life after the Nazi collapse became isolated on the *Land* level. The SPD, which had been conspicuous in the reconstruction work after 1945, was forced into playing the role of the opposition in national affairs and was excluded from participation in the formulation of national policy. Isolation of the SPD also implied a restriction on the effectiveness of the left wing of the CDU. Since 1949 this wing, though utilized at election time, has exercised little influence on policy-making.

Furthermore, the change in the German political leadership led to a change in relationship between German officials and the occupying powers. The SPD had been inclined to sympathize with Great Britain under its Labour government. Conservative German circles always suspected these sympathies, however, and considered them dangerous to the future of free enterprise in Germany. The pro-American attitude of the Bonn government was certainly encouraged by the German suspicion that the British Labour government favored the opposition party at Bonn, while the United States was expected to show a more active interest in re-establishing and preserving traditional property rights in Germany.

A third result of the institution of the Bonn government was to accelerate the organizational development of the two major government parties. Before 1949 neither the Christian Democratic Union nor the combination of liberal parties known from 1949 on as the Free Democratic Party had reached an organizational and ideological stage at which their various regional branches could agree on a uniform platform for domestic affairs, let alone for foreign policy.

The CDU was organizationally decentralized; ideologically it was held together merely by somewhat vague feelings of religious unity and social responsibility. The party's views about relations with the occupying powers, with the outside world, with Russia, and so on varied not only from area to area but also within each area. In December, 1947, for example, Jakob Kaiser and Ernst Lemmer, who were about to be removed by the Soviets from the leadership of the East zone Christian

Democratic Union, asked the West German CDU for aid, but the latter could not present a unified front. A few leaders rushed to Berlin, but none of them had a mandate to speak for the whole organization.

In the Free Democratic Party (to use the designation later adopted by the liberals) the situation was no different. While this party maintained better contact with its various *Land* organizations and favored greater centralism in government, it was unable to build a strong national organization. The *Land* organizations remained fairly independent, both organizationally and ideologically. This party, too, proved unable to muster strength when called upon, and failed to protest effectively against the communist campaign to subjugate its East zone counterpart, the Liberal Democratic Party.

After 1949, however, both parties strengthened their national leadership. In the CDU this process led toward domination of the party's organizations throughout Germany by the conservative wing. Both parties fully dissociated themselves from their former East zone affiliates.

There were several other significant developments after 1949. The refugees, who previously had been prevented by Military Government regulations from organizing themselves politically, now appeared with their own party. In some *Länder* they were able to carve out a position of influence for themselves. Various other groups with special claims also made their appearance, bringing pressure to bear not only on the administrations, but also on the various political parties. Some of these groups, in turn, provided a breeding ground for new radical parties.

Former Nazis and militarists now came forth with views that they had been unable to publish under Military Government restrictions. They contended that Hitler's Germany had opposed the Bolshevization of the world and that the Allied victory over Germany had only weakened the Western position. On the eve of the establishment of the Federal Republic the proponents of this approach gathered in such groups as the *Deutsche Reichspartei* or in associations such as the *Brüderschaft*. The publications and arguments of these groups were crude, but they planted seeds from which later developed more refined ideas about Germany's role as a "third force" between East and West. In 1949 they usually argued that Germany should maneuver between the Eastern and Western powers and that, in spite of differences between the nationalists or neo-Nazis and the Russian Communists, the latter could be utilized to promote Germany's interest.

By the time the federal government was finally established, most German political circles were fully aware of the fact that Germany was no longer merely a pawn in the hands of the occupation powers. The increasing conflict between East and West reduced the influence of both and allowed Germany greater space for tactical moves between the blocs. From the very start, however, the Federal Republic chose to ally itself with the West.

The new Bonn government did not have formal jurisdiction over the conduct of German foreign affairs, since the Occupation Statute * specifically reserved this right for the occupation agencies, but one of its principal tasks was in the realm of foreign relations. This was to expand German jurisdiction to a point where it would burst the narrow confines of the Occupation Statute and lead to the establishment of direct contacts with the other nations of the world. The broader the powers of the Bonn government became, however, the greater was the pressure of domestic influences on the formulation of German policy. An evaluation of current German foreign policy therefore requires an analysis of the processes by which it is formulated and of the influences to which it is subject.

Decision-Making in German Foreign Policy: The Constitutional Framework

While the most desirable foreign policy for Germany is a subject for dispute, the mechanism through which this policy is to be officially determined and carried out is established in general terms by the Basic Law. The executive branch, consisting of the administration (headed by the Chancellor) and the Federal President, is charged with the conduct of foreign affairs. The legislative branch, consisting of the Bundestag (lower house) and Bundesrat (upper house), participates in the treaty-making process, and the Constitutional Court may at times be called upon to determine the constitutionality of certain phases of foreign policy.

The language of the Basic Law even provides certain guide lines, as well as some restrictions, for the actual conduct of foreign policy. In particular, the document envisages Germany as playing an active role in both international co-operation and European unification. The preamble begins: "Conscious of their responsibility before God and before men, inspired by the resolve to preserve their national and political unity and to serve world peace as an equal partner in a united Europe, the German people. . . ." The first paragraph of Article 24 is more specific. It declares that the federal government may, by legislation, transfer

* The Occupation Statute, which went into effect when the Federal Republic was established, defined the relationship between the new German state and the Western powers. It reserved certain rights to the Western powers, including "control over foreign trade and exchange" and over "foreign affairs."

sovereign powers to international institutions. Article 25 is even more specific, and provides that the general rules of international law form part of the federal law, that they take precedence over local laws, and that they create rights and duties for the inhabitants of the federal territory. These articles can be regarded largely as an indication of German readiness in 1949 to renounce parts of her national sovereignty if only the other powers would do the same.

Both government and opposition have accepted without controversy the constitutional provisions urging international co-operation. The constitution's references to German unification have been cited periodically, especially by the opposition, as proof of the constitutional duty of the administration to promote a foreign policy leading toward the unification of Germany.

The language of the Basic Law leaves some doubt about the permanence of the document and some question about for whom it is intended to speak. The preamble modestly claims that this document is "to give a new order to political life for a transitional period." It also insists, however, that the German people in the *Länder* of the three Western zones of Germany "acted on behalf of those Germans to whom participation [in the Parliamentary Council] was denied." This claim of the Parliamentary Council to represent the entire German people is somewhat weakened by Article 146, which states that the document "becomes invalid on the day on which a constitution adopted by the German people by means of a free decision becomes effective."

In the light of these questions about permanence and competence, German constitutional experts, as well as political leaders, have been trying to harmonize the dicta and admonitions in the Basic Law about international co-operation with those about German unification. They ask how present-day Germany, under Article 24, can "transfer sovereign powers to international institutions," or "accept international arbitration for the settlement of disputes among nations," if Article 146 (providing for the invalidation of the document) is also to be accepted at face value. Will international agreements concluded by the Federal Republic remain binding on a unified Germany?

Thus far, not even government supporters have given clear answers to these questions. It is usually argued that "international co-operation" strengthens the federal government's drive for "German unification," or that some treaties will require re-ratification by the legislature of the unified Germany, and so on.[9] The debate is carried on at the political rather than the judicial level.

Differences of opinion about the constitutional intent with regard to direct and indirect foreign policy-making and administration are of a less theoretical nature. The Basic Law clearly indicates that foreign policy is to be directed by the executive branch of the government, that is, by the Chancellor, but subject to a certain amount of parliamentary control. Some experts argue that while traditional foreign policy may be primarily in the hands of the cabinet, a number of issues, such as unification, can not be described as traditional. On this issue, they say, all Germans have a right to participate and to be heard, since it is the primary right of a people to seek national unity and self-determination.

So far the government's foreign policy and the legislation required to implement it have been relatively little affected by the constitutional disputes. The Bonn government, however, if it had been forced to rely on a weaker majority in the Bundestag to back it up, would not have been in a position to interpret the Basic Law as it did, and the execution of its foreign policy would have been hampered even more than it has been up to the present time.

The Executive and Foreign Policy

Both the government and the Federal President participate in the actual conduct of foreign affairs. The government, acting through the Foreign Office, controls all operational actions. In theory, policy is initiated by the Chancellor and the Minister for Foreign Affairs and agreed upon by the cabinet. The Federal President, in addition to the ceremonial functions which he performs in connection with foreign relations, also performs certain tasks in connection with the promulgation of international treaties and agreements.

Formally, the executive alone directs foreign affairs. That is, it initiates policy, pursues and administers it. No other branch of the government can initiate foreign policy, negotiate treaties, and so on. All the Bundestag can do is to announce a wish, or to declare its determination. It cannot force the ratification of a treaty. The government must submit the bill providing for ratification.

The Minister for Foreign Affairs administers that phase of government action which involves intercourse between governments. All other ministries of the Federal Republic must use the Foreign Office as the channel to other governments. The extent to which the Minister for Foreign Affairs can determine policy has not yet been clarified by practice. Article 65 of the Basic Law states that the Federal Chancellor determines and assumes responsibility for general policy, but that within the limits of this policy each federal minister conducts the business of his department independently and on his own responsibility. While during the past seven years almost all ministries have established a degree of administrative independence from the Chancellor, the Ministry for Foreign Affairs still remains closest to the Chancellor's interests. Furthermore, since Adenauer himself served as Minister for Foreign Affairs during the first four formative years of the Ministry, his influence within it is still strong. At present both the Chancellor and Dr. Heinrich von Brentano, who was appointed Minister for Foreign Affairs in 1955, participate actively in the initiation and execution of foreign policies.

While one may clearly recognize the Chancellor's influence on the formulation of foreign policy, it is difficult to define the ideologies, groups, and personalities which in turn influence and aid him. This is due not only to the ability of the Chancellor to keep his own counsel, but also to the fact that he is both the chief of government and the active leader of a political party which controls a majority in the Bundestag. During his tenure as Minister for Foreign Affairs, party and clique politics frequently exercised a decisive influence on his policies. The individualistic Chancellor had little faith in the policy judgment of the formal administrative branches of government and on key issues preferred the advice of special experts and advisers. Today, accordingly, while he utilizes the facilities of the Foreign Office, he leans heavily on personal politics and on men in whom he has confidence, regardless of the position they happen to occupy. For a time he depended largely on Undersecretaries Herbert Blankenhorn and Professor Walter Hallstein to perform his foreign policy staff work. The latter was presumed to be an expert on America. As far as personnel and administrative controls are concerned, the two men closest to him are Dr. Hans Globke, State Secretary in the Office of the Chancellor, and Dr. Josef Löns, the Personnel Chief of the Foreign Office.

The strength of the Chancellor's influence depends largely on the control which he exercises over the personnel policies of the various ministries and especially over those in which he is interested. Almost all of the personnel chiefs are members of the Christian Democratic Union (CDU), are Catholic, and come from the Ruhr area. Dr. Hans Globke, his State Secretary, can best be described as the Chancellor's "man Friday." No doubt he has aspirations of his own, but none of these conflicts with the use which the Chancellor makes of him. Globke does not make policy, but he controls the government organization and ensures that the state machine is responsive to the will of the Chancellor. Globke was the only person connected with the government or with politics who had daily access to the Chancellor while he was seriously ill in 1955.

Dr. Josef Löns, Personnel Chief of the Foreign Office, performs a similar function, although the personnel policies in this ministry have not as yet become so intricate as to involve foreign policy directly. For a time, Löns's task was to find the right type of diplomat and, if possible, to limit the number of those whose claim to a position in the Foreign Office was based on past political services.

Appointment of Heinrich von Brentano as Foreign Minister dimmed the stars of Herbert Blankenhorn and Walter Hallstein and removed them from the vicinity of the Chancellor. Though both still claim the right to report directly to Adenauer without going through the Foreign Minister, it is clear that they have not done much reporting since Dr. von Brentano's appointment.

Inside the cabinet the men who have carried the most weight with the Chancellor are Dr. Fritz Schäffer, the Minister of Finance, and Professor Ludwig Erhard, the Minister of Economics. Because of the functions of their ministries they are also involved in certain limited aspects of international relations, but they do not appear to participate in the initiation of broad policies.

Franz Josef Strauss, on the other hand, especially since his appointment as Minister of Defense, has fought his way into the cabinet circle which is concerned with foreign affairs. Although as a Bavarian he has the disadvantage of coming from an area which is politically atypical, his influence on foreign policy formulation, both inside and outside the cabinet, is expected to increase with the expansion of the German armed forces.*

From time to time other ministers have exhibited an interest in foreign policy, but they have been kept fairly distant from the firing line. This is true of Dr. Franz Blücher and Jakob Kaiser, whose ministries deal with matters touching on foreign affairs. The position of Blücher, who heads the Marshall Plan Ministry, has been weakened by past uncertainties inside the Free Democratic Party, to which he formerly belonged, and by the weakness of the Free People's Party, which he now heads.

Jakob Kaiser's Ministry for All-German Affairs has been relegated to propaganda functions. He is the sexton of the shrine of German unity, which is what his ministry actually is. His ministry is permitted to plan for the day when unification will be achieved, but it is not permitted seriously to plan policies intended to promote unification. Nevertheless, he has achieved some influence because of his control over the extensive propaganda apparatus at the disposal of his ministry.

The present chairman of the Bundestag Foreign Affairs Committee,

* Minister Strauss's own position inside Bavaria is made easier by the comparatively strong Bavarian influence in the new army as well as in its civilian control agencies. The Chairmen of the Bundestag and Bundesrat Defense Committees, Minister President Dr. Wilhelm Högner and Dr. Richard Jaeger, are both from Bavaria.

Kurt Georg Kiesinger, as well as the past chairman and current President of the Bundestag, Dr. Eugen Gerstenmaier, have been continuously pressing for a larger role in the formulation of German foreign policy. Though the Chancellor has confided in them more than in other members of the Bundestag, with the possible exception of Dr. Robert Pferdmenges, he has not given them an active part in the development of foreign policy. He has merely utilized them to advance policies which he had already enunciated; for instance, from time to time they have been consulted about techniques in the presentation of policies to the Bundestag and to the German people.

Though insisting that the formulation and execution of foreign policy is almost solely a prerogative of the executive and that the Bundestag has at most only a right to ultimate control, the Chancellor has on two occasions utilized Bundestag prestige to enhance his own position in diplomatic negotiations. The first such occasion was on the eve of the Chancellor's negotiations with Premier Pierre Mendès-France in 1954, after the defeat of the European Defense Community (EDC) in the French parliament. The Chancellor summoned several Bundestag deputies to Paris, where their presence was supposed to strengthen the Chancellor's hand and also to give him an indication about the political thinking in German parliamentary circles. At the same time it enabled him to show the French negotiators how difficult it would be for him to make certain concessions. His subsequent actions clearly indicated, however, that in consulting the parliamentary representatives he did not attempt to disclaim sole responsibility for the conduct of German foreign affairs and for shaping German foreign policy.

On his visit to Moscow in September, 1955, the Chancellor again flanked himself with representatives from the German parliamentary bodies. This time, unlike the previous occasion, the cabinet had, in Dr. von Brentano, a separate Minister for Foreign Affairs. Nevertheless, the Chancellor rigidly kept the leadership in his hands and again made his own decisions. The parliamentary representatives were clearly designated as members of the delegation and therefore subject to his leadership. In this case apparently it seemed advisable to him for political reasons to let the other members of the delegation unwillingly assume some responsibility for the burden of unpleasant decisions which had to be made.

The Ministry for Foreign Affairs

Up to 1955 the Ministry for Foreign Affairs functioned as an administrative annex of the Chancellor's office. The Chancellor insisted that in the first formative years of the German Federal Republic he must have full control of foreign policy. It is therefore difficult to determine the degree of influence exercised by the staff members of the ministry during this period.

Following the appointment of Dr. von Brentano as Minister for Foreign Affairs, the ministry acquired greater scope for initiative. For a time Dr. von Brentano seemed to have captured the imagination of the press with his alleged independence from Adenauer, his greater frankness, and his more conciliatory attitude toward the opposition. These characteristics of the new Foreign Minister, however, were noted during a period when the Chancellor was either on vacation or sick, and they should not be taken to imply that Brentano was at this time primarily responsible for the shaping of German foreign policy. As Minister for Foreign Affairs, Dr. von Brentano moved cautiously.

Thus far he has not sought to dramatize his independence and has refrained from antagonizing the circles close to the Chancellor. He has improved administrative operations in the ministry without resorting to drastic personnel changes and has attempted to integrate and harmonize the various elements composing the present German diplomatic bureaucracy.

The present Foreign Ministry is similar structurally to the old German Foreign Office of Weimar and imperial days. Little has been done to alter its traditional organization or the jurisdictions of its various divisions. Some structural innovations have been attempted but have thus far failed to take firm root.

The ministry has seven divisions: Organization, Political, Foreign Relations, Economics, Legal, Cultural, and Protocol. Of these, the Political Division is considered to be the most important and influential. It is here that the closest approach to a formulation of foreign policy is made. The Economics Division is relatively weak and has remained limited in size in spite of the efforts of the Foreign Office to expand and to develop it. The reason for this is the competition from the Division for Foreign Trade of the Ministry of Economics. In international trade negotiations, economic negotiations, and so on, the Foreign Affairs Ministry is nominally in charge, but it has to lean heavily on the Ministry of Economics, which has a number of experienced officials who came originally from the old Wilhelmstrasse Foreign Office. The influence of these people on the economic side of foreign policy is understandably considerable.

Other ministries, especially the Ministry of Finance, also supply members for delegations engaging in international negotiations. The Foreign Office readily admits that there is a limited number of qualified persons available for duties involving negotiation. Those in government service are frequently augmented by experts from industry and banking. Thus economic interests are able to make their influence felt on foreign policy, at least during negotiations for trade and commerce agreements.

Their influence extends to the Ministry for Foreign Affairs through yet another avenue, for many professional civil servants in the Foreign Office have had previous experience in industry. Industries with extensive interests abroad frequently used to employ former Foreign Office officials, and at times the Foreign Office gave diplomatic appointments to executives from certain industries. Some members of the Foreign Office who went over to private industry before 1945 and represented leading German firms abroad—usually chemical, machinery, or electrical firms—have now found their way back into the Foreign Office and hold leading diplomatic positions.

The German Foreign Office has surpassed its prewar numerical strength. In spite of the fact that the Federal Republic does not maintain diplomatic representation in the communist area, except at Moscow, the ministry already employs about five thousand persons.

The Foreign Office Bureaucracy

By and large, the old stock of the Foreign Office managed to survive not only the Third Reich, but also denazification procedures. A small proportion of the present officials suffered persecution of one type or another under the Nazis. Some had been dismissed because of foreign wives, others because of international ties, and some presumably because of connections with the bomb plot of July 20, 1944. This group fared comparatively well in the new Foreign Office, as long as they did not run afoul of the principle of maintaining numerical parity between Protestants and Catholics. Most of them obtained good appointments, usually abroad. Of the majority who had been able to retain their positions during the Hitler era, only a few were actually rejected because of concessions they had made to National Socialism. On the other hand, very few of the officials who had been brought into the diplomatic service by the Nazis were accepted in the new ministry. To these older officials must be added a large number of younger ones who have been recruited since the war.

During the early organizational stages of the present Foreign Office much ado was made about the recruitment of new blood and the injection of new types into the Foreign Service. Efforts were made to attract some candidates for Labor Attaché posts from trade-union ranks, and candidates for the so-called "social and cultural" branches of the service were sought from other than the traditional "diplomatic sources."

This trend has now almost stopped, and with it the importance of the branches of the service for which these new personnel types were destined. The only exception probably is the Press Section of the Foreign Office, where outsiders are still welcome. This receptivity may be due in part to jurisdictional competition between the Foreign Office's press branches and those of the Federal Press Office. It may be worth noting, however, that the Foreign Office did recruit, although primarily for subordinate positions, some persons who had been employed formerly by the occupation agencies.

There is no doubt that the government has used diplomatic positions as a means of repaying political debts. In consequence, some foreign posts have been filled by parliamentary figures rather than by persons with traditional diplomatic training. During the early years of the Federal Republic such positions were also offered to opponents inside the coalition parties whom the Chancellor found uncomfortable, or for that matter to officials who had to be taken over from the Bi-zonal Administration and for whom no place could be found in the Bonn government.

Training for the Foreign Service has, on the whole, undergone the same shift in emphasis as training for other civil service positions. The academic requirements remain, but there is less stress on legal education and other qualifications are given some consideration. As noted above, however, the nonprofessionals are one by one being withdrawn and replaced by regulars.

The failure of the efforts to include noncareer diplomats in the present Foreign Service is primarily due to lack of co-operation by the professionals within the bureaucracy. The noncareer man has remained an outsider. Even today, frictions in certain German embassies—for instance, in Bern and previously in London—go back to cleavages between nonprofessional heads and the professionals at lower levels.

Recent German foreign policy has not been appreciably influenced by the career diplomats. One reason may be that, though some of them can claim "historical experience," few of them can qualify as "current experts." The new problems and the new tone in international relations are apparently still foreign to them. Moreover, their role in maintaining international ties has tended to shrink with the increasing use of special emissaries, visiting high officials, and various conferences at which large numbers of delegates appear.

Diplomatic representatives in the smaller countries are, paradoxically, in a better position to influence German policy toward these countries than are the German ambassadors in the United States, France, Great Britain, or other major powers. There seems to be a feeling in the Foreign

Office that German representatives in the more sensitive capitals are not as yet in a very good position to provide Bonn with correct analysis and information. The diplomats in these spots, it is said, must be careful not to give the impression that they are trying to find out too much. They are also burdened with a "lack-of-equality complex," in spite of the fact that the Federal Republic has been raised to full sovereign status.

The Minister for Foreign Affairs and the Chancellor attempt to exercise close control over diplomatic personnel, especially those in sensitive positions, not only by detailed instructions but also by direct contact. It is customary for German ambassadors in the leading world capitals to visit Bonn once every three months or so. In addition, the Foreign Office has tried several times to organize general and regional ambassadorial conferences.

The dearth of experts on Russia became apparent on the eve of the Chancellor's trip to Moscow. There were, of course, a number of officials who had previously held various positions in Eastern Europe, for the most part during the war. Though almost none of these could qualify for the trip, obviously being *persona non grata* to the Soviets, it was soon discovered that most were not even qualified to perform the necessary staff work. Their estimate of the situation in Russia, in the opinion of members of the delegation, was so completely off-key that it may have been one explanation for the Chancellor's sudden agreement to trade the establishment of a Soviet embassy in Bonn for the return of Germans held in Russia.

Responsible officials in the government are concerned about the shortage of qualified personnel for service in communist areas. The present government is not inclined to dispatch personnel who, although very conservative on domestic issues, may become influenced by the Soviet point of view in matters of foreign policy.

Not that the Foreign Office bureaucracy is in a position to make policy, for its functions include merely such tasks as research, writing drafts, and providing information. Policy-making is left to the so-called "political heads" of the ministry, and possibly to one or two of the highest career civil servants.

But it was not always so. Before 1933 the bureaucracy of the Ministry for Foreign Affairs did make policy. The political instability of the Weimar governments strengthened the position of the bureaucracy vis-à-vis the responsible heads of government. It was during this period that the so-called "Rapallo concept" developed with the support of the career diplomats. Today, German professional diplomatic circles still regard the Rapallo treaty as a classical example of diplomacy. Some add that the

Hitler-Stalin Pact of 1939 is another classical example of secret diplomacy and the advantages it can offer. It can link disparate political groups without requiring any of the participants to make concessions in his social philosophy or domestic policies. Many in today's Foreign Office still believe this to be the major goal of diplomacy and see the Weimar Republic period as the Golden Age of the professional diplomat.

There is no doubt that today's Foreign Office, and especially the professional diplomats, were glad to accept as chief a man who was "their own Minister." Through Dr. Heinrich von Brentano the Foreign Office bureaucracy now feels that it is represented in the cabinet and that it can count on protection inside the government. It now feels equal to other ministries and can, as one official said, work out the basis for new policies, rather than merely seek justifications for policies already decided upon.

The Federal President and Foreign Policy

The functions of the Federal President in matters of foreign affairs are defined by Article 59 of the Basic Law: "He concludes treaties with foreign states on behalf of the Federation. He accredits and receives envoys." This has been interpreted to mean that the President can not initiate or participate in negotiations. Such actions would conflict with the right of the Chancellor to determine policy. The Federal President does, however, have the right to be informed, and in practice the Chancellor reports to the President about important policies, international negotiations, and important state visits. The Federal President may also ask for information from the branches of government directly, although up to now he has rarely made use of this right. He does not have a foreign affairs staff of his own, but utilizes the Foreign Office apparatus for such duties as receiving the credentials of accredited foreign diplomats. Neither does he enjoy the right to send his own emissaries or "personal ambassadors" abroad.

In theory the government depends on the good will of the President, since his signature is required to promulgate legislation and to authenticate treaties. If the President should refuse to sign the documents, they presumably could not go into effect. In such a case the government could either ask the legislature to impeach the President or could apply to the Constitutional Court for a writ ordering the President to sign. But the latter possibility is doubtful in view of the fact that the court does not consider itself authorized to interfere in jurisdictional disputes among the branches of government. In the absence of any clear constitutional provision for arbitration in case of conflict between President and Chancellor, it is clear that good relations between the head of the state and the head of the government are imperative.

At times the office and personality of the Federal President have been drawn into political disputes on foreign policy. The government was eager, for example, to have him complete the ratification procedure for the EDC agreements, while the opposition asked him to delay action. President Theodor Heuss succeeded in keeping his independence without offending either side. Indeed, he has managed to stay out of political feuds and has established his claim to be the President of all the Germans. He has also been able to utilize his prestige to calm down overheated debates without, however, decisively taking sides.

It should be noted that the Federal President, although not officially authorized to initiate policy, can and does inject suggestions into the discussion at least of nonpartisan foreign policy issues. His office ensures an attentive reception of his ideas, but not necessarily their acceptance by either government or political parties at large.

The Legislature and Foreign Policy

The federal legislature participates only indirectly in the formulation of foreign policy. Its participation is based primarily on two functions assigned to it by the Basic Law: to pass legislation and, in the case of the Bundestag only, to select the Chancellor. Article 59 of the Basic Law states that international treaties which pertain to political questions or to matters governed by federal laws require the approval of those bodies which are competent to pass federal legislation. Moreover, it is obvious that the Bundestag offers a platform from which propagandistic statements intended to influence domestic or foreign opinion can be made.

The Bundestag can not initiate foreign policy; nor can it oblige the government to do its bidding without overthrowing it and replacing the Chancellor by one more amenable to its will. It may, however, pass resolutions, exercise its rights where its concurrence is specifically required by the Basic Law, and ask the government for information. But the amount of information which the government is required to give is not defined clearly. The Bundestag can not order executive officials to disclose all the information they have on a given question. Nor does it have any recourse to action if it is dissatisfied with the information given, unless it wishes to overthrow the entire government. Similarly, while the Bundestag has the right to investigate the composition of the Foreign Ministry, there seem to be no provisions which make it mandatory for the government to act in accordance with the findings or recommendations of the Bundestag investigating committees. So far, the legislature has not attempted to achieve its wishes through attaching "riders" to foreign treaty ratification bills or to the bills implementing them.

While the Bundestag is powerless to initiate foreign policy, individual deputies have used every opportunity to see influential members of foreign governments and to acquaint them with "the true situation in Germany" or "the true wishes of the German government." Such visits, however, have remained unofficial. In 1955, Erich Ollenhauer, chief of the SPD, tried to arrange conversations with Nehru even before Nehru had met Adenauer. Similarly, SPD leaders have attempted to meet the heads of the Scandinavian governments independently of the Chancellor. These contacts probably did no more than gain some sympathy for the opposition's point of view. Their significance was that they represented an effort of the opposition to promote an alternative foreign policy which was counter to the one being followed by the German government.

Another way in which the Bundestag is now beginning to participate in foreign relations is through the European Council in Strasbourg and, more indirectly, through some of the other European agencies. The Bundestag is not represented in the European Council as a unit, but by delegates from each of the principal parties in the parliament. Other European countries are similarly represented and there is a tendency in the Council for voting to follow party lines. All European Socialist parties tend to vote together, as do the Christian Democratic parties. But it is not so much the voting pattern as the form of voting which is important. In the European Council the individual Bundestag members have a forum in which they can formulate and initiate action on certain phases of foreign policy. Though these phases may not necessarily pertain to Germany directly, they do affect it as part of Europe. Another international forum before which the delegates may present political views is the Assembly of the European Coal and Steel Community. This body is, however, far less active than the European Council.

On several recent occasions, specifically during the Berlin and Geneva four-power conferences, the Bundestag party fractions established "liaison headquarters" in the city where the conferences took place. Though in theory it was not the Bundestag deputies who acted as observers, but rather the parties which they represented, it is noteworthy that only Bundestag members did the "observing." At the second Geneva four-power conference in 1955, every party fraction of the Bundestag, with the sole exception of the German Party, was represented outside the conference rooms. The Bundestag representatives came to Geneva, as well as to Berlin, on behalf of their respective parties, acting on the theory that in questions pertaining to the unification of Germany they had powers and rights which exceeded those of the Chancellor. The actual functions of the party observers at such conferences, however, were limited to consultations with subordinate delegates, efforts to establish other contacts, and the issuance of statements to the international press.[10] In contrast, at the 1954 and 1955 conferences in Paris and Moscow, the Bundestag representatives were summoned either to consult with the Chancellor or to join the official delegation.

To impress its opinions on the executive the Bundestag may make use of its budgetary authority, but experience has proved that the fiscal powers of the legislature are usually inadequate for this purpose. Budgetary reductions undertaken or suggested by the Bundestag have been circumvented without curtailing programs of the executive. The construction of buildings for the federal government in Bonn is a case in point. The annual budget contains so many undefined funds that the Bundestag can not easily starve the executive into submission.

The Foreign Affairs Committee of the Bundestag has, of course, no more power than the Bundestag itself, although its members enjoy a privileged position in regard to foreign affairs. The Chancellor and the Minister for Foreign Affairs inform the committee about certain confidential phases of foreign policy, but committee members are, as a rule, not supposed to use in Bundestag debates the classified information they obtain in this manner. The chairman and vice-chairman of the committee have at times performed certain functions in the formulation of foreign policy or in support of foreign policy, and members of the committee are sometimes consulted by the government. SPD members insist, however, that these consultations are very superficial and that neither the committee as a whole nor the individuals on it have any decisive influence on foreign policy. Nonetheless, it is to be noted that the chairman and vice-chairman of the Bundestag Foreign Affairs Committee, as well as the chairman of the Bundesrat Foreign Affairs Committee, were included in the delegation which traveled with Adenauer to Moscow.

The most important function of the Bundestag Foreign Affairs Committee is to report to the plenum. All legislation regarding treaties is referred to this committee after a first reading. The committee can, therefore, slow down ratification, and it can also prejudice decisions through its reporting. Since reporting is done in open sessions of the Bundestag, the committee has a certain ability to mold public opinion on foreign policy.

It is probably still too early to pass judgment on the extent of Bundestag influence over foreign policy. It can be argued that the relationships between the government and the Bundestag during the past seven years have been abnormal, in that they have been greatly influenced by pressing political considerations which, in turn, have strengthened discipline within the party fractions. During the first Bundestag all the original government parties—and during the second, at least the Christian Democrats and the German Party—remained solidly behind the Chancellor. Their solid majorities prevented a real test of strength between government and legislature.

The Parliamentary Council decided to create a strong executive for reasons of domestic policy. The framers of the Basic Law wanted a strong Chancellor because they visualized the opposition as made up of radical, basically antidemocratic groupings. The lessons from Weimar were before their eyes; they remembered the persistent offensive of the Communists and National Socialists against the government. The Basic Law, therefore, was written in such a way as to deprive the Bundestag of effective influence on the policies of the executive, unless its members can agree on a replacement for the Chancellor.

The foreign policy role of the Bundesrat—the upper house of the legislature in which *Land* governments are represented—is still indefinite. Its claim to participate in foreign policy formulation is based primarily on procedural aspects of the German legislative system. For example, Professor Hans Ehard, former Minister President of Bavaria, contended that the Basic Law required Bundesrat approval of the laws providing for the EDC treaties, because the duties which Germany assumed under them touched upon rights involving the *Länder*. Such a broad interpretation of the Bundesrat's jurisdiction has been challenged by the Bundestag and has not been fully recognized by the executive.

Although the Bundesrat has tried to shed some of its political complexion, at times it has been torn in two by political conflicts raging in the neighboring Bundestag corridors and at the headquarters of the parties. In other instances, such as the EDC laws, the Bundesrat lost face because of its procrastination and inaction.

In general, however, the Bundesrat has used its powers with great caution and has protected its political independence. It has usually been able to reduce its objections to a level at which they will be acceptable to a majority in the Bundestag. On only six occasions during the first parliamentary term from 1949 to 1953 did the Bundesrat refuse to approve legislation passed by the Bundestag. In four cases its disapproving votes were responsible for failure to enact the proposed legislation.

The Bundesrat's functions in relation to foreign affairs, like those of the Bundestag, flow from the general rights granted it by the Basic Law.

It has an advantage over the Bundestag, however, in that it has behind it the various state bureaucracies, which are in a position to support it in the event of a conflict with the executive. On several occasions political parties have used their positions in the *Land* governments to influence the Bundesrat in matters of foreign policy. The Social Democrats have tried to bring pressure on the *Land* governments to oppose certain government policies under discussion in the Bundesrat. The government, on the other hand, has tried to muster a two-thirds majority in the Bundesrat, in order to ensure the adoption of the constitutional amendments required in connection with German rearmament and certain other aspects of its foreign policy. Recently, in view of the absolute majority enjoyed by the CDU-CSU in the Bundestag, not only the Social Democrats but also some of the minor parties have threatened the government with adverse action in the Bundesrat unless their rights as minorities in the Bundestag are respected by the all-powerful majority. Efforts to use the Bundesrat to further the purposes of party politics have, however, come from the outside. As a body, the Bundesrat seeks to avoid emotional political disputes.

The upper chamber is determined to defend its jurisdiction and to ensure that its work has an effect on the conduct of governmental affairs. To achieve this, it feels it must be more efficient and more expert than the Bundestag. It insists, for instance, that its committee chairmen devote themselves to their work. A case in point is that of Minister President Wilhelm Högner (SPD from Bavaria), who failed of re-election as chairman of the Bundesrat Foreign Affairs Committee because he had not actively participated in the conduct of the work of this committee, leaving the task to subordinate officials. The Bundesrat felt that its claim to participate in foreign policy-making depended in part on having a strong Foreign Affairs Committee and therefore selected Karl Arnold, formerly Minister President of North Rhine-Westphalia, to replace the inactive Högner.

It is no wonder that Adenauer has tried constantly to assure himself of a reliable following and a comfortable majority in the Bundesrat. While the present majority may suffice to support comparatively insignificant bills on which government and opposition may differ, experience has shown that the majority is not stable enough to support the government in instances where constitutional questions are involved, and where the executive's interpretation of such questions implies a restriction of the rights of other branches of the state structure, including the Bundesrat. Nevertheless, as far as foreign policy is concerned, the degree of power possessed by the upper chamber remains to be established in practice.

Up to the present a head-on collision between the Bundesrat and the executive has been avoided.

The Constitutional Court and Foreign Policy

The Constitutional Court has attempted to avoid becoming entangled in foreign policy questions. This is probably one aspect of the court's effort to keep out of politics and to establish its independence and objectivity.

Because of the manner in which the court was first set up, a reputation for political independence could only gradually be achieved. The judges were selected by the Bundesrat and Bundestag on the basis not only of their legal and judicial qualifications but also of their party membership or political inclinations. Furthermore, there is no doubt that during the first years of the court's existence each party looked upon "its" judges as party members. While as good democrats they expected judges to be independent in their judicial decisions, as party men they wanted this show of independence to follow party lines. In cases under adjudication each side was usually certain that party interests, democracy, and judicial independence would all be well served by the decision it favored.

On several occasions the court was asked to pass judgment on the constitutionality of legislation necessitated by international agreements. This provoked a series of debates about the jurisdiction of the court: that is, to what extent and under what circumstances it was competent to rule on the validity of international agreements. Some of these debates also degenerated into discussions of whether the court, in view of its party composition, could be trusted to render an objective opinion, and politicians shrewdly weighed the chances in a given case by taking stock of the number of "black" or "red" judges in whichever chamber of the court was to hear it.

This controversy at first made it difficult for the court to assert its authority. In the course of time, however, it succeeded in casting off the political influences under which it was originally created and it now tends not only to judicial but also to personal independence. The parties, too, have now ceased to look upon the judges as loyal members from whom judicial assistance can be expected when needed. To achieve this state of affairs the court practiced patience and forbearance, but above all it let time work in its favor.

The most controversial questions which the Constitutional Court has had to handle arose from SPD complaints challenging the constitutionality of five moves made by the government in the realm of foreign policy: the Petersberg Agreement, 1949; the Franco-German Economic Agreement, 1950; the Kehl Agreement, 1951; the EDC, 1953; and the Saar Agreement, 1954.* In the first three cases, the basic question was whether these agreements required ratification by the Bundestag. In the fourth case the question was whether a two-thirds majority of the Bundestag was required to ratify international agreements directly affecting the territory under the jurisdiction of the local administrations. The Basic Law does not clearly define the limits of the sphere of "foreign affairs" entrusted to the federal government or define what is meant by treaties regulating political relations. This appeared to be an area in which gaps in the constitution would have to be filled by the court.

Without going into detail, it may be said that the decisions of the court have not been startling from a constitutional standpoint. In the conduct of foreign affairs it has upheld the responsibility of the executive branch, although in the most important case, that of the EDC, the issue was never resolved because of the failure of the EDC in the French Assembly. The court's decisions have left the authority of the Chancellor and his cabinet in the field of foreign relations largely unimpaired.**

Pressure-Group Influences on Foreign Policy

Groups and associations whose *raison d'être* is to be found in grievances resulting from the effects of a lost war are inclined to concern themselves with foreign affairs. Seldom, however, has any one of these groups attempted to chart a general foreign policy. Instead, they concentrate on specific issues which affect their grievances or interests, a course that tends to limit sharply their influence on major aspects of foreign policy.

In practice, the main interest-groups have made opportunism their only political line, and those which advocated largess from the state have

---

* The Petersberg Agreement, concluded between Dr. Adenauer and the Allied high commissioners in November, 1949, provided for the first steps toward the Federal Republic's admission to international organizations and assumption of consular services. The Franco-German Economic Agreement laid the groundwork for the so-called "Schuman Plan." The Kehl Agreement dealt with the French "bridgehead" on the German side of the Rhine, opposite Strasbourg.

** Eds. Note.—Since this was written, the court decided a case involving a conflict between the authority of the *Länder* to regulate education, as provided in the Basic Law, and the educational provisions of a concordat between Nazi Germany and the Vatican, which the Adenauer government sought to uphold. While the court confirmed the validity of the concordat, it declared that there was no constitutional obligation forcing the individual states to fulfill the treaty. Because of the special issues involved, it is not likely that the effects of this decision will be to increase the influence of the *Länder* in the area of foreign policy.

ordinarily been successful. Their price has usually been within the reach of the government, especially since so far the latter has always been in a position to determine the date and amount of the concession.

The various veterans' organizations can claim that, due to their efforts, the honor of the German soldier has been restored, almost all former servicemen have been accepted as eligible for duty with the future armed forces, and almost every former professional soldier can now realize his pension rights. Even *Waffen SS* * officers are now "not necessarily disqualified" for service in the future army, "if otherwise politically reliable."

On the other hand, the point of view expressed by these organizations on other issues has had relatively little impact. During the first years of the Federal Republic and the early days of the rearmament discussions it was frequently said by veterans' spokesmen that no self-respecting former officer would serve in an army organized along the lines proposed by the EDC agreements or by NATO, or for that matter as advocated by Adenauer. They insisted on full equality for German officers, and made special demands with regard to the war criminals, troop location, and other matters. Much of what they demanded was eventually achieved by the German state, but even before this time numerous qualified veterans were applying for positions in the new army. As formation of German military units actually began, the veterans' point of view received less attention and was expressed with less vehemence. The few political illiterates among the old military who could not read the signs of times and persisted in extreme demands are now outside the main stream of developments.

The same is true of the refugees' organizations. They, too, failed to develop a consistent ideological line and have failed to influence foreign policy. In the early days of the Federal Republic the various refugee groups made certain demands about the eventual peace treaty and the reintegration of Germany. Some of them even clumsily theorized about the reorganization of Europe in a manner which would safeguard the economic and political claims of refugees. Their point of view, however, is reflected scarcely at all in the day-to-day foreign policy of the Federal Republic. Outside the refugee organizations the question of the Oder-Neisse Line is rarely mentioned. And who today thinks about the claims of the various Germanic groups which were driven out of Rumania, Hungary, Yugoslavia, and so on?

The political organizations of the refugees failed to develop an ideolog-

* *Waffen SS:* Literally, "armed protective units"; those units of Hitler's elite guard which served with the regular armed forces.

ical program in part because they had pressing demands of an economic nature, so that their allegiance could be bought most easily by immediate financial concessions. For some time the prevailing motto in refugee circles was *"Konzeption ist Konzession,"* implying that the formulation of clear ideas meant playing down immediate economic demands.

Even more important is the fact that the refugee organizations (with a few exceptions) lacked the traditions and experienced leadership of older bodies. Those among the refugees who possessed political experience of which they did not have to be ashamed in a democratic state accommodated themselves within the existing political parties. Those who had held positions in the Nazi Party or similar groups could scarcely claim experience in democratic leadership.

The economic needs of the refugees did not continue indefinitely. More and more refugees, after satisfying their economic demands, assimilated their political views to those of the native West Germans. They became more interested in defending and expanding their new economic positions than in regaining their old ones.

All these factors have reduced the importance of the refugees in German politics. This group, despite early fears that it would press explosive foreign policy demands, has remained on the whole ineffective and has not appreciably influenced German foreign policy. The weak efforts on the part of the refugees to have the Bundestag seat representatives from Germany's Eastern territories have not even aroused editorial comments, let alone parliamentary attention. Attempts of some refugee groups to establish working agreements with other national exile groups have been equally unimpressive.

Such plans as refugee organizations have made to reshape Europe have served only to produce embarrassing situations. The *Sudeten Landsmannschaft* ("organization of Germans from the Sudetenland"), for example, through its spokesman Dr. Lodgman von Auen, has tacitly allied itself with Otto von Hapsburg's restorationist efforts and his plans to reorganize Europe along clerical and authoritarian lines. The Hapsburg organization, the European Information and Documentation Center, maintains its own radio outlet in Madrid. Part of the West German press has felt called upon to warn the refugee leadership against such hazardous schemes in the field of international relations and foreign policy.

In 1945 the German public almost instinctively turned for help to those groups which still retained a residue of international good will and still enjoyed international contacts. Trade-unions and church organizations seemed to meet these specifications best. During the early years of the occupation the trade-unions were among the first to present the

German point of view, very modestly of course, at international conferences.

The unions were also called upon to perform other tasks affecting international relations. Thus, in the struggle against Allied dismantling of German industry, trade-unionists were utilized to provide the German opposition with mass support, and labor was sometimes mobilized to protect the interests of individual employers and firms, as in the case of Röchling and Krupp. Later, trade-union voices were synchronized with the general expressions of approval for international policies which seemed to advance the interests of the nation and of the West.

These developments produced many misunderstandings. Trade-union leaders began to believe that they were actively helping to formulate foreign policy.[11] In reality they were merely being used to prepare the ground and lend support for policies formulated by others, and to increase German respectability abroad.

Industry is more interested in foreign policy than are the trade-unions and is actively concerned with molding public opinion on given foreign policy issues. For instance, part of the European Union movement is financed by a group of industrialists and bankers.

In the general competition between executive and legislature industry is more on the side of the executive, partly because, as industrial leaders frankly admit, the Bundestag is sometimes forced to seek popular support by measures pleasing to the political left. For example, the Christian Democratic Party in the Bundestag frequently has to heed its left wing by considering social legislation and even such matters as codetermination.* In contrast, the executive can be trusted to limit economic reforms to a rate which is less likely to endanger the economic principles of the present system.

Industry is not widely represented in the Bundestag. Its representatives there may be regarded as observers, who tend, interestingly enough, to be either politically nondescript or socially progressive. A real conservative of the type exemplified by the Ruhr industrial baron Hermann Reusch can hardly be found in the Bundestag.

By and large, industry trusts the government in matters of foreign policy. It leaves policy formulation to the executive and rarely criticizes governmental diplomatic actions. It is remarkable that Chancellor Adenauer, who enjoys the confidence of industry, is relatively immune to pressure from industrial groups. If he does anything which coincides with industry's thinking, it is because he has arrived independently at the same conclusion.

* Codetermination is a system under which labor is able to participate along with management in determining plant or industry policies.

The activity in Bonn on the part of economic associations, pressure-groups, and lobbyists has been so intense of recent years that at one point a federal minister, not necessarily one of the most popular, even threatened to resign unless these groups ceased to bring pressure on the government.

In 1952, according to one authority, there were in and around Bonn approximately two hundred and seventy offices representing various groups and associations.[12] No doubt this number has by now increased considerably. A closer look at the functions of these offices indicates that most of them are engaged in specific tasks which exclude serious efforts to formulate and advance long-range policy. The major task of most of the offices is to provide information to the members of the organization in question. That is, they seek to gain advance information or specialized information about prospective governmental or legislative action which is likely to affect the interests of group members.

Only a handful of the organizations represented in Bonn take even a remote interest in foreign policy, and still fewer seek to influence it. Even industrial or employers' associations, organized specifically for the promotion of "better government," have rarely interested themselves in foreign policy matters. They seek to strengthen the government's position against the trade-unions; they urge opposition to codetermination; or they support the economic theories of the Ministry of Economics. But almost never (except in the case of the Schuman Plan) have they conducted propaganda for or against a given foreign policy.

Of the few associations specifically interested in foreign policy, two enjoy an influence which extends beyond their own membership: *Das Kuratorium für ein Gesamtdeutschland* ("Trustees for a United Germany") and the European Movement. The former is a nonpartisan group, including leading citizens of all political shades, and has been instrumental in keeping the unification issue alive. Its proposals for the promotion of unification have sometimes embarrassed the Bonn government, as when it suggested that the government transfer more agencies to Berlin to dramatize the city as the real capital of Germany. The second of these bodies, the European Movement, is an association of groups both inside and outside Germany. It can take little credit for developing new ideas about European integration. Most of the programs for European unification have originated elsewhere and have been adopted by the German branches of the movement. The association, however, has helped to popularize the concept of European integration in Germany. Another body, the *Europa Union,* which is a unified organization within Germany, has supported the Chancellor's policies, aided by its youth division.

Regional Interests and the Land Administrations

The *Länder* of the German Federal Republic officially play an insignificant role in the formulation of foreign policy. The Basic Law provides that when certain direct interests of a given *Land* are the subject of a proposed international agreement, this *Land* must be consulted. The *Land,* however, can not hinder the conclusion of the treaty.

Unofficially, the *Länder* do exercise an influence on foreign policy, since their administrations provide channels through which regional interests make themselves felt. Political parties and groups which are in disagreement with Bonn's policy sometimes use the *Länder* as strong points from which to attack it. Furthermore, the Bundesrat, to which each *Land* sends two members, is a favorite platform from which *Land* interests are defended.

Thus for tactical reasons the traditionally centralist SPD opposition has insisted on strengthening the role of the Bundesrat in foreign policy matters. Somewhat surprisingly, CDU and CSU officials of the *Land* governments have taken a similar approach. In 1952 Karl Arnold (CDU), Minister President of North Rhine–Westphalia, insisted that the *Länder* were not only masters of their own domestic policy but were also interested in federal policies, both domestic and foreign.[13] Arnold complained that the Bundesrat, which represented the *Länder,* did not participate in certain international bodies, such as the Coal and Steel Community agencies, although the Bundestag and the government did. He suggested that the Bundesrat was interested in the work of such bodies because of the direct effect which their decisions had on the individual *Land*. The Schuman Plan, for instance, primarily affected North Rhine–Westphalia, which produces about 98 per cent of the coal and 80 per cent of the iron and steel of the Federal Republic. And yet, Minister President Arnold complained, no effort was made to associate this *Land* formally with the implementation of the plan.

Arnold's views, however, did not convince the majority in the Bundesrat that the Constitutional Court should be asked for a ruling on whether the *Länder* would have to be consulted. Instead, North Rhine–Westphalia's interests were protected through a tacit agreement with the federal government, which provided for consultations with the *Land* where its interests were concerned. In addition, North Rhine–Westphalia was represented informally by the personnel actually operating the Schuman Plan agencies, since most of the experts on the industries affected come from that *Land*. North Rhine–Westphalia, in spite of the fact that it does not participate formally in the Schuman Plan agencies, can be said to speak for Germany in these agencies through the allegiance of individual Germans in their employ.

Some *Land* governments have recently claimed that they should be consulted on certain points in cultural treaties which affect matters for which *Land* governments are responsible. For instance, a cultural treaty may contain provisions for the promotion of a foreign language and culture in the German educational system, which is administered by the *Länder*.

The effect of West Germany's federal structure on foreign policy can be noted most clearly in the case of Bavaria. It is from there that proposals for special alliances and special friendships usually come. Aside from the fact that Bavaria is interested in the southern parts of Europe, Bavarian leaders and the Bavarian state are more concerned with religious issues than are other Germans. In recent years Bavarian Catholic politicians have frequently mentioned the possibility of maintaining *Land* representatives at the Vatican and have pressed for closer alliances with southern Catholic countries, notably Spain. It is Bavaria, rather than North Rhine–Westphalia, which calls for closer cultural and diplomatic contacts with Madrid, while it is North Rhine–Westphalia which has the closer economic relations with Spain.

Bavaria is cooler than other areas of Germany toward the issue of reunification and toward Berlin as the German capital. Bavarian politicians and commentators frequently get into hot water because of their outspoken insistence upon the relegation of the unification issue to a secondary position on the political agenda of the Federal Republic. Thus Bavaria supports the Chancellor in his determination not to follow the SPD urgings for a more passionate unification campaign and for greater support for Berlin.

Hamburg and Bremen, because of their strong commercial interests, take a lukewarm attitude toward both the government's and the opposition's foreign policy positions. Socialist-controlled Bremen has supported without enthusiasm the SPD position in the Bundesrat, and at the same time has praised the Chancellor's policies for bringing about an expansion of its trade and port facilities. Hamburg, which had a socialist government up to the end of 1953 and is now under a coalition administration similar to the one in Bonn, has also shown a lack of enthusiasm for either party's proposals. The former SPD city government mildly supported the opposition's position while the present administration just as mildly supports the government's.

Schleswig-Holstein's dispute with Denmark about the treatment of the Danish minority in South Schleswig provides an interesting case history, because on the one hand the issue involved a *Land* and on the other it disturbed the relations between Denmark and the entire Federal Republic. The dispute was brought on by a Schleswig-Holstein election law and a decision by the Schleswig-Holstein parties to the political right of the SPD to unite in a single bloc. These two developments made it impossible for the Danish minority to gain representation in the Landtag. While the German parties in Schleswig-Holstein appeared determined to deny representation to the Danish minority, the Bonn government, which set great store on maintaining friendly relations with all Western European countries, deplored the adverse effect of this course on Danish opinion. It therefore used its influence and power, especially the power of the purse, to persuade the Schleswig-Holstein government to settle the dispute and even to accept a temporary, extralegal solution, namely, to admit Danish "observers" to certain committees of the Landtag.

A somewhat similar situation arose in the Rhine Palatinate, where the population felt strongly about certain border questions, especially those dealing with the Saar. This feeling was enough to induce the local *Land* government, completely dominated by the CDU, to support the position of German unionists in the Saar. Bonn, however, was able to prevail on the Palatinate government not to come out officially against the federal government's more gradualistic Saar policy. Both these cases indicate that, at least as far as small *Länder* are concerned, the federal government is able to impose its will in foreign policy matters.

Some *Länder* enjoy relatively great influence on federal domestic and foreign policies due to their representation on key executive and legislative bodies. Men from the Rhineland and from South Germany occupy most of the key positions in the West German government. Four key positions in the cabinet are occupied by South Germans: the Ministries of Foreign Affairs, Economics, Finance, and Defense. Baden-Württemberg dominates the leadership in the Bundestag, and members from this area hold more than their proportionate share of the leading committee positions, especially on the Foreign Affairs Committee.

The Rhineland is represented not only by the Chancellor himself but also by many members of the bureaucracy, particularly among the higher officials. The Rhineland has furnished almost all of the leading personnel chiefs in the government. It might be said that, while South Germany retains the formal political leadership, the Rhineland holds the administrative and bureaucratic controls.

By contrast, North Germans participate relatively little in parliamentary or in cabinet affairs. They occupy the less important posts in the cabinet, while in the Bundestag—with a few outstanding exceptions such as SPD leader Erich Ollenhauer—North German representatives are seldom heard. Dr. Ehlers was probably the last leading CDU official from this area.

Berlin is not an active agent in international politics. It remains an asset in German foreign policy in so far as it can be used to win Western support. It helps to involve the Western powers in German matters and may prompt them to support Bonn's aspirations. But Berlin is also something of a liability. Neither its public opinion nor its political leaders support the "realistic" politics of Bonn. As an enclave belonging to the Federal Republic the city has its value, but it becomes a dangerous burden when it insists on being treated in the same way as the rest of the Federal Republic. This could mean, for example, that all the defense measures which apply to the Federal Republic would also have to apply to Berlin.

During the years that Bonn has been the German capital, Berlin's pride and aspirations have been whittled down. The financial dependence of the city on the federal government forces the city administration to keep a civil tongue and not to exaggerate its foreign policy demands. But the city is a catalyst in the movement for unification and for ties with the Soviet zone population. Many of the economic links between West Germany and the Eastern countries now run through Berlin. Furthermore, some German enterprises still hope that the communists in the Eastern zone, being Germans after all, may sometime be in a good position to do a good turn for their Western brethren. Hence, in spite of bitter propaganda warfare and the official rejection of "technical contacts" with the East, there are contacts on the industrial and commercial level, partially justified by the interzonal trade agreements.

The political leadership which Berlin once gave Germany seems to have vanished, especially since Mayor Ernst Reuter's death. In spite of tradition and experience, neither Berlin nor Berliners now play a significant role in the formulation of federal policy, whether domestic or foreign. The native sons of the West German *Länder* are in full control of the various branches of the government and also of the institutions which help frame public opinion. Following the death of Minister Tillmanns the former capital was represented in the cabinet only by a naturalized Berliner, Jakob Kaiser, whose influence was not large. Another Berlin CDU leader, Ernst Lemmer, has been recently appointed Minister of Posts and Communications.

The opinions presented by Berlin's spokesmen in Bonn are always listened to attentively but with caution. As much as the West German population admires the Berlin spirit and is willing to bask in the reflected glory of the Berlin blockade, it does not want to be given the opportunity of becoming as heroic as Berlin. It fears that some of the proposals coming from Berlin, especially suggestions on how to deal with the Russians, may be too risky.

Political Parties

The strongest nongovernmental factors in the formation of policy are, of course, the political parties. Through their parliamentary representation the parties indirectly participate in the official initiation and formulation of foreign policy. Through their organizational and publicity machinery they can interpret government policy to the public and shape public opinion on the issues involved.

Most parliamentary deputies are heavily dependent on their party organizations. The individual Bundestag member who does not adhere to the party line has little influence in Bonn, and still less hope of making his position clear to the electorate and winning in the coming election. In spite of voices demanding a greater show of independence by the deputies, the electorate as a whole has no ears for political differences which may lead the individual Bundestag member to deviate from his party's position. When he appeals directly to the electorate for support over the head of his party, he is likely to appeal in vain.

This generalization is almost uniformly true in the case of the two major parties, the CDU and the SPD, and possibly also in the case of one smaller party, the German Party. It is less true in the case of two other smaller parties, the FDP and the BHE (League of the Refugees and the Dispossessed).

The Free Democratic Party has undergone a marked sociological change during the past five years. Though originally considered the party of conservative industry, in the course of the years it has moved toward the center. While it has not lost industrial support completely, it has become more a party of the Protestant middle class. Up to now the Free Democratic Party has not succeeded in developing an efficient party machine. This means that its representatives in parliament are in a position to formulate party policy, but in spite of the weakness of the party machine the parliamentary leaders never were able to gain full control over it. Until 1956, when the FDP split on the question of whether or not to continue supporting Adenauer, there was an important difference of opinion between the party's Bundestag fraction and its national board. The latter, composed of the functionaries and officeholders of the party on the *Land* level, was more opposed to the Bonn government's foreign policy than was the Bundestag fraction.

Most of the FDP's organizational leaders maintain that the CDU aspires to "one-party rule," that it is scheming to eliminate all other parties except the SPD, and that the *Deutsche Partei* ("German Party") was "smothered by love" into submission and almost complete political identification with the CDU.

On domestic issues there are few differences between the CDU and FDP. The CDU includes various economic groups, some of which share the FDP's approach to social and economic issues. As far as cultural questions are concerned, there are differences between the two parties, but these are argued within the confines of *Land* politics. It is, therefore, only in matters of foreign affairs that the FDP has been able to establish a line of demarcation between itself and the CDU-CSU.

The indecisive thinking of German business is reflected in those FDP members who mistrust Adenauer's pro-Western orientation and do not wish to burn the bridges to the East. The FDP considers itself a guardian of the German national interests and insists that these interests not be forfeited through sacrifice to the West and a deterioration of relations with the East.

Regional political interests within the FDP add to the party's internal disharmony. The Baden-Württemberg organization was, until recently, mostly concerned about the Saar. In North Rhine–Westphalia, FDP leaders would like to utilize European integration schemes to achieve for Germany greater equality with other nations and the ability to bargain with East and West. The FDP in Lower Saxony is especially concerned about unification, while in Bremen and Hamburg the party is interested in cultivating closer relations with the West and increasing commerce with the Far East.

Some of the economic elements which support the FDP financially regard this party as an insurance policy against the possibility that the CDU may become uncontrollable and let its religious inclinations run away with it. Fear of an unduly powerful CDU, not dependent on any group to maintain itself in government, is strongest in the Rhine-Ruhr area. Although these circles are willing to bear with the Chancellor for the time being, they are greatly concerned about what may happen after his death. They are fully aware that even now strong elements of the CDU parliamentary fraction are emotionally inclined toward the left and might ally themselves with the SPD. The continued existence of the FDP is therefore required in order to provide a lever with which to bring pressure on the CDU, to strengthen its right wing, and to exercise some influence on its foreign policy views.

The FDP's inability to solve its internal problems finally led to the split in the party's Bundestag fraction. The proponents of a more distinct FDP policy on the national level gained a majority of the 51 deputies and, under the leadership of Dr. Thomas Dehler, frequently issued statements criticizing coalition policies, especially with regard to rearmament and unification. The Chancellor proved unable to make the FDP, as a member of the governing coalition, toe the line. When the showdown came, only 15 members of the FDP fraction advocated continued support of the Adenauer policies, although the party's four cabinet members were included in this minority. This small group then split with the party and formed the *Freie Volkspartei* ("Free People's Party"). Though financially well off, the FVP has failed thus far to build up an effective organization, and obtained only an insignificant percentage of votes in the various local elections held in 1956.

Like the FDP, the BHE (Refugee Party) has also been unable to overcome internal differences resulting from varying attitudes toward the Chancellor's policies. Adenauer's efforts to tie the BHE more closely to the coalition resulted in the open rebellion of 18 deputies in the 26-member fraction. This majority decided to oppose the government on certain issues—such as rearmament and unification. The remaining deputies, including the party's two cabinet members, left the BHE and eventually joined the CDU.

The influence which party bureaucracies exert on policy-making, and specifically on foreign policy, appears to be declining, while more and more of the various parliamentary fractions have come to speak for their parties, especially in matters of foreign policy. On domestic issues, because of the more immediate social and economic issues involved, the regional party organizations are still influential.

The party representatives in the *Land* governments, because they control an official structure of their own, have frequently managed to follow lines different from those laid down by the central party organization or by the party's representatives in the Bundestag. This remains true in spite of the fact that both Chancellor Adenauer and the SPD leaders have at times been successful in forcing *Land* governments to act in conformity with party interests at the national level.

Contributing to the declining influence of the party organizations has been the continuous drop in membership in all parties, which means in effect that the party has a direct influence over fewer people and ordinarily has less money to spend on organization. Hence the party Bundestag fraction has become more influential in policy formulation than the party bureaucracy. Yet the parliamentary deputies still depend on the bureaucracy for organizational and logistic support. Election campaigning is costly, and the large contributions flow almost exclusively to party chests and rarely to the campaign funds of individual candidates. The effect of this network of relationships is usually to ensure fairly strict discipline in the parliamentary fraction.

The indirect influence exercised by the opposition on the formulation and conduct of foreign policy should not be underestimated. This influence is naturally stronger when the opposition enjoys strong leadership. Especially during the earlier years of the Federal Republic, the opposition forced the coalition and the government to present better and clearer justifications for their actions, and to report more frequently to the Bundestag. In his lifetime Dr. Kurt Schumacher, the first postwar chairman of the SPD, was hated by Dr. Adenauer. Yet the Chancellor's current assertions that he misses his former opponent are not merely digs at Ollenhauer, the current SPD leader. They contain a great deal of sincerity. Schumacher not only led his own party, he also forced the coalition leaders to think through the actions they were about to take. For Schumacher gave them real opposition, and as a personality he could compete with Adenauer.

Even now the opposition performs valuable, although indirect, services on behalf of the government's foreign policy. Since there is no serious communist problem in the country, the German government can not influence Western nations by telling them that the internal communist danger will increase if Germany gives in to Western demands. It can, however, use the "opposition threat": that is, it can argue that the Chancellor can not undertake measures which would give the opposition an opportunity to weaken the government. Ironically enough, the success of the CDU-CSU in the 1953 Bundestag election dulled this argument somewhat and weakened the bargaining power of the Chancellor. With a clear majority of his own, reinforced by the vote of the coalition partners, he was deprived of the "opposition threat."

The opposition has served the government's goals also by presenting to the public certain policies which the government at first rejected, but eventually incorporated into its own program. Thus the question of relations with the Soviet Union, various problems of unification, and the issues involved in several four-power conferences were first aired by the SPD. The government naturally denies that its acceptance of policies which previously had been urged by the SPD represents an admission that the opposition was right. The governing coalition, however, finds the public prepared for measures regarding unification and relations with the East, which would have taken people by surprise if the opposition had not discussed these issues first. The strong disinclination in dominant government circles for a bipartisan foreign policy is based in part on the fact that the latter would preclude the above advantages, and would mean that the Social Democrats could claim some credit for the international successes of the government.

From time to time elements of both parties have hinted at the desirability of a common foreign policy, or have openly urged it, especially after the Geneva conferences of 1954 and 1955. But influential elements in the CDU argued vigorously against co-operation with the SPD,[14] and both government and opposition again began stressing their differences.

Konrad Adenauer as a Personality and a Party Leader

Any analysis of the influences shaping German foreign policy would be incomplete without consideration of Dr. Konrad Adenauer, not as Chancellor but as a personality and a master of party politics. As Chancellor he enjoys constitutional rights, including the right to initiate and determine policy. But as a political leader he is in a position to organize the necessary political support for his policies, and his personality is an important factor in German politics.

The present strength of the government and the support which it enjoys among the electorate are not necessarily based on conscious support by the voters of Adenauer's policies. It is not so much what Adenauer says which is now important, and which provides copy for the newspapers, as the fact that the eighty-one-year-old Chancellor manages to stand straight for half an hour in the Bundestag, or that he manages to sit through its sessions, or that he can say that his sixty-year-old State Secretary is getting on in years.

During the past six to seven years the German public has been trained to have confidence in the Chancellor and, at the same time, not to ask too much from him. It is now widely accepted that the Chancellor can do no wrong, because an eighty-one-year-old man is simply beyond evil. As a result, when the press links him with scandals or when the government takes unpopular positions, as in the Saar question, the position of the Chancellor is scarcely affected. Attacks on him by the press have little or no effect on his public standing.

It is not only the Chancellor's personality, at first artificially built up abroad, and later by domestic public relations as well, which explains his almost uncontrolled influence on policy determination; it is also the combination of offices which he holds.

Most important is the fact that he is the head both of the government and of the strongest party in Germany. There probably is no democracy in Europe where the fusion between party chairman and government chief is so close and effective as in this case. As chairman he can not only determine party policy but, what is more, he can control the finances of the party. This is important, for it is the party that decides which campaign is to be emphasized, how much financial support various candidates are to receive, and so on.

Dr. Adenauer's strong position inside the CDU and his domination of the government have tended to circumscribe informed discussion of foreign policy or attempts to influence it. Even progovernment papers complain about the lack of information on foreign policy, and the Bundestag itself fares little better than the press. Since tight party discipline assures the government of the loyalty of an absolute majority in the Bundestag, even on issues which have not been fully explained, the Chancellor does not find it necessary to provide the parliament with more than a minimum of foreign policy information.

It would be both unjust and mistaken to refer to the present government of Germany as one-man rule. Nevertheless, because of the country's constitutional system, the extra-constitutional political practices which have grown up in the postwar period, the distribution of seats in the Bundestag, and the personality of the Chancellor, there is no question that Adenauer exercises not only the strongest single influence on the formation of West German foreign policy but, in fact, the dominant influence. While the same constitutional system and most of the same political practices might be expected to continue under another Chancellor, they would unquestionably function in a very different way.

THREE

Party Leaders and Foreign Policy

Henry J. Kellermann

It is well-nigh impossible to find a person in a position of public responsibility in the Federal Republic who will not volunteer the remark that Germany is a "Western nation" and can always be counted upon to remain a member of the "occidental community."

As a rule, such pro-Western professions are quite sincere, but they may spring from different motives and may have different meanings for different political leaders. To the leader who is identified with the Adenauer coalition, Western orientation means a political commitment to the West, and indicates support for the Atlantic community and for Europe. To the opposition leader and the neutralist, it may not mean this at all. To them, and in fact to a very large number of Germans, Western orientation does not necessarily have political implications. It stands for cultural affinity, and its primary relevance is to moral principles, aesthetic tastes, and social habits. Some politicians will argue with disarming naïveté that, since culture has a spiritual quality, Germany's basically Western orientation can not possibly be affected by any agreements concluded for reasons of political expediency, even if these agreements sup-

EDS. NOTE.—In 1953 RAND invited Mr. Kellermann, then in the State Department's Bureau of German Affairs, to prepare a monograph on the foreign policy views of German political party leaders. The State Department kindly granted him leave, and he spent the period from September, 1953, to March, 1954, in Germany, where he interviewed several hundred party leaders, including numerous members of the Bundestag and the state legislatures. These interviews were supplemented by conversations with other civic leaders and with Germans who visited the United States during 1954 and 1955.

The full report which emerged from this study early in 1956 ran to over a thousand pages and covered many specialized aspects of German foreign policy. An abstract, by E. W. Schnitzer and W. P. Davison, of several sections of the complete report is presented here, and is intended to provide a brief, nontechnical introduction to the foreign policy views of Germany's party leaders.

Mr. Kellermann is currently U.S. Permanent Representative to UNESCO in Paris.

port the interests of the East more than those of the West. Germany—so they say—will always remain "Western," no matter what the external form of her association with the East or the West.

This kind of reasoning typifies the dilemma of a nation which, although tied culturally to the West, has found it necessary throughout its history to seek various compromises with the East, mainly because it straddles the dividing line between the two realms. The conflict between culture and politics is especially pronounced in the views of those who feel that national unity is attainable only at the cost of a major political compromise with the Soviet Union.

Germany's Cultural Orientation

As understood by most leaders of the two major West German parties —the CDU and the SPD—Germany's cultural ties with the West contain a number of clearly identifiable elements, of which anticommunism, democracy, and Christianity are the principal ones. Of these, anticommunism is the most important, both in its emotional intensity and in its political effects. Indeed, an anticommunist attitude is often considered the most significant test of Western orientation, if not the only reliable one.

In contrast to the attitude of German leaders toward democracy, which is essentially rational and often academic, their anticommunism is highly emotional and concrete. To most of them, anticommunism signifies not the repudiation of Marxism or Leninism but hostility to Soviet Russia. In most cases, it is intensified by such personal experiences as military service at the Eastern front or life as a prisoner-of-war in the Soviet Union. Communism also stands for the atrocities charged to Soviet troops and for Soviet policy in East Germany. Anticommunism is thus primarily a rejection of something that is by nature and origin foreign. It is "Russophobia." As such, it is shared by leaders in all important portions of the political spectrum, and is to be found among the Social Democrats no less than among the coalition parties.

The second major element in Western cultural orientation—democracy —is becoming a household term in German public life. Professions of interest in "the democratic way of life" from politicians of all shades are legion. Even leaders of the now defunct *Deutsche Reichspartei* (DRP), on the extreme right, at least paid lip service to the democratic form of government.

Different political leaders interpret democracy in different ways, and it is difficult to generalize without being unjust. Nevertheless, it would not be too wide of the mark to say that, in both major parties, democracy is conceived of predominantly as a system of government whose chief characteristic is the observance of procedures safeguarding majority rule. For example, a high government official named the Bishops' Conference, the German universities, and the Prussian officer corps as prototypes of democratic institutions in German life, because, as he pointed out, in all three instances decisions required a majority vote.

Another common attitude toward democracy, found in all major parties, is that it is a convenient device for delegating responsibility to the "expert," meaning the professional politician and the government official. In the words of a former German general, "Democracy is understood by us as the voter's way of passing the responsibility to the government, simply by dutifully electing every four years the representatives to the diet." Democracy has a social content only to a slowly growing minority of German politicians, who associate it with the concept of citizen participation in public affairs.

Frequently, also, democracy is regarded as a system of minimum authority. This interpretation is popular with many politicians, since a government that places few restrictions upon the individual citizen is agreeable to an electorate most of whose members are deeply absorbed in private pursuits and anxious to keep their public obligations to a bare minimum, particularly as long as the state of the nation is "normal" and the economy sound.

References to democracy as a political system that lacks color are frequent among politicians, and are often accompanied by expressions of disdain for a government that has little use for ceremonial display of power and prestige in the daily exercise of political authority. To the conservative, in particular, the absence of a political etiquette that discriminates according to status and rank makes democratic government appear as a system of drabness, which depreciates the personality of the leader and makes for social egalitarianism. The importance that democracy attaches to majority rule is regarded as a weakness, since creativeness and leadership rest with great individuals like Goethe or Schweitzer, not with the masses.

One attitude, which is often expressed in the form of a question, is whether the new German democracy has enough strength and resilience to meet the test of internal or external crises. The implicit suggestion is that, if conditions were to change, it might have to be modified, or perhaps exchanged for a more efficient type of government. Memories of the "Weimar system," which proved too weak to weather the crisis and to turn back its enemies, have produced attitudes among political leaders ranging from honest skepticism to cynical distrust.

Nothing, probably, has been more prejudicial to the development of a positive German attitude toward democracy, as political leaders will point out time and again, than the ominous set of circumstances that surrounded the genesis of democratic government in Germany. In both the twenties and the forties, democracy bore the stigma of defeat, and was even less palatable for being allegedly imposed by the victors. Democracy in Germany seems to be the type of government that always arrives in the wake of national disaster. Yet, since it now appears to be there to stay, Germans conclude that it will have to be adapted to German conditions and tastes. Right-of-center politicians, who seem particularly disturbed by what they consider the foreign and the "collectivistic" aspects of democracy, insist that Germans must yet devise the kind of democracy that is "most appropriate" to them. Extremists of the radical right make no bones about the fact that they regard the present order of things as provisional. They say that the current regime, and the provisional constitution on which it is based, will be superseded by the "real" one at some appropriate time—by which most of them mean the time when Germany is reunified.

Nevertheless, German democracy is slowly but progressively losing its abstract and formalistic character. A majority of the German political elite no longer think of it as an alien form of government, even if certain aspects of it have a foreign flavor. Political leaders proudly point to precedents in German history, as, for example, the self-administration of the Prussian cities under Stein in the early nineteenth century. On the legislative, executive, and judiciary level, reforms have been instituted which attest to the growing strength of democratic convictions and practices. And, above all, politicians are aware of increasing public support for civil liberties and for institutions that guarantee freedom of expression, including the privilege of criticizing public authorities.

Yet even those leaders who are most sincere in their desire to encourage the growth of a healthy democracy in Germany do not show unqualified satisfaction with the increased concern about civil liberties. They point out that these have frequently been used as a convenient excuse by the individual who wishes to shirk civic duties, rather than as a guarantee of the citizen's right to take part in public affairs. Worse yet, in Germany the privilege of free speech and assembly has often been most loudly championed by extremists of the right and left, who have found it expedient to invoke the issue of civil rights to protect themselves while they seek to destroy the existing governmental system and to liquidate the very liberties whose violation they protest.

Concern about the creation of a proper balance between the exercise and the abuse of the basic freedoms has harassed German lawgivers and policymakers for more than a century. Failure to reach a satisfactory solution in the twenties helped seal the doom of the Weimar Republic. Today, responsible politicians on both the right and the left are well aware of a similar danger. Social Democrats are somewhat more likely to mention the problem of defending freedom, while leaders of the CDU are more apt to stress the need to prevent license, but both groups have good grounds for concern.

On balance, one must conclude that the German "bill of rights," as embodied in the Basic Law, is gaining the respect of German political leaders, and the exercise of the democratic rights is taken seriously by both government and opposition. In a few critical cases, certain proposed constitutional reforms, suspected of being an infringement of those rights by the authorities, unleashed a storm of public protest, and the government decided to desist from its plans. The defense of basic freedoms is often cited by German political leaders as evidence of a growing political affinity between Germany and the Western democracies.

Christianity is the third major force which Germans often mention as tying their country culturally to the West. Many political leaders interpreted the heavy vote for the Christian Democratic Union in the federal election of September 6, 1953, as an indication of growing religious loyalties on the part of certain segments of the population. Dignitaries of both the Catholic and Protestant churches, on the other hand, doubted that such trends as were discernible constituted a religious revival.

Nonetheless, the influence of organized religion among the political elite is conspicuous. Both Catholics and Protestants play an influential role in the CDU. The Catholic Church seems to have achieved predominance within the party, but Protestant leaders are also found in important positions, particularly in Southwest and Northwest Germany. Of particular importance is the work of the "Evangelical Academies" which, under the leadership of Protestant lay and clerical leaders, are bringing together representatives from all areas of public life in meetings devoted to a serious diagnosis of political and social developments. The academies have played a major part in introducing ethical considerations into political discussion.

All major parties are trying to establish a positive, or at least a non-antagonistic, relationship with organized religion. Critics as well as friends of the Social Democrats mention a growing disinclination among SPD officials to accept their party's traditional agnosticism and antagonism toward organized religion. Religious groups have been formed in the party, and these are said to demonstrate the compatibility not only of socialism and Christianity but also of active membership in both the SPD and the Church. Even the anticlerical leadership of the Free Democratic Party (FDP) is emphatic in its public espousal of Christianity. FDP Chairman Thomas Dehler has stated that Christianity must be the spiritual foundation of all those interested in the welfare of the national community. The affirmative attitudes of the Christian Democrats and the Christian Social Union toward religion are clearly indicated by their names.

Yet it would be erroneous to assume that the use of Christian terms in the daily vocabulary of the political leader constitutes proof of a religious revival, either genuine or spurious. A likelier and simpler interpretation is that, after the national collapse, organized religion emerged as one of the few elements of social continuity. And, at a time when most secular ideals had disintegrated, Christianity stood as one, if not the only, value which retained validity. To a people with a strong proclivity for ideological commitment and organizational affiliation, religion thus offered the much-needed point of orientation. For the politician, then, Christianity is one of the facts of political life. Since it is a heritage shared with other Western nations, it becomes one of the important cultural forces that tie Germany to the West.

Foreign Relations: Germany and the Big Four

While her cultural affinities place West Germany clearly in the Western camp, German history furnishes ample evidence that cultural considerations exert only a limited influence in the forming of political alliances. *Realpolitik,* that is, politics shorn of idealistic and romantic notions, is a term which has enjoyed a vogue among German politicians since the days of Bismarck. For example, former Chancellor Heinrich Brüning recently called the treaties of Rapallo, Locarno, and Berlin "masterpieces of German diplomacy," and stated that in foreign policy every kind of dogmatism must be rejected. What was needed, he said, were "broad views" which would permit quick seizure of opportunities and a sudden change of position.

While Brüning's statement is undoubtedly extreme, the attitude toward politics which he expresses is not uncommon among German political leaders. Hence, we can not assume that their adherence to the cultural values of the Western world will necessarily determine their political orientation.

The Image of Soviet Russia

German leaders seem to be torn between rational and emotional reactions toward the U.S.S.R., and it is difficult to describe their attitudes toward the Soviets without becoming involved in seeming contradictions.

One attitude is fear. A majority of political leaders, the neutralists always excepted, see Russia as an ever-present threat to German independence and, indeed, to European culture. This point of view is summed up in a much-quoted book by a Protestant theologian:

It is an illusion to believe that any country under Soviet control could maintain the kind of independence possible under British, American, or other control. Integration into the Soviet sphere of power means—not in one fell swoop but with irresistible certainty and within the foreseeable future—to become Sovietized and Russified. If Europe were absorbed into this power sphere, it would lose its traditions and its very identity and become but an insignificant annex of the Greater Russian Empire. I cannot see why the moral strength of the European nations to resist successfully the pressure of communist control should be greater than the strength of the nations already subjugated proved to be. . . .[1]

Distrust is another characteristic attitude. Politicians who claim to "know" Russia and the Russian people warn against measuring Soviet motives or actions by Western standards of rationality. The Russians, many political leaders say, are "inscrutable," they are "Asiatics." As one put it, Soviet politics rely on the methods of "fraud, prevarication, and silence."

In their analyses of Soviet policy and their predictions of things to come, many Germans differentiate between the Russian people, who are believed to be the unhappy victims of a despotic regime, and Soviet leadership, which is regarded as a group of ruthless, power-mad doctrinaires. Indications of conflict within the Soviet leadership have German politicians puzzled. The death of Stalin, for instance, and the first measures taken by his successors, produced a host of speculations about the "fundamental" versus the "tactical" significance of Malenkov's "new course." Many leading politicians interpreted Malenkov's emphasis on consumer goods as evidence of internal strains and weaknesses that would force the new leaders to slow down the pace of external expansion and would reduce the danger of aggression. Hopeful comparisons were drawn between the "realist" Malenkov and the "dogmatist" Stalin. These optimistic interpretations, however, found relatively little currency among government and coalition leaders; they were circulated chiefly by members of the opposition and in groups which favored a resumption of diplomatic and commercial relations with the Soviet orbit.

Hope for a change within the U.S.S.R. gained momentum with the four-power Berlin Conference of January, 1954. But, even then, nearly all responsible politicians expected at best tactical shifts and accommodations rather than fundamental changes.

The political leaders of most parties agree on the nature of Soviet long-range policy objectives. Essentially, the U.S.S.R. is believed to be an expansionist power bent upon pushing its frontiers as far West as possible. Germany, with her natural and industrial resources, is thought to be the prize most highly coveted. Possession of all of Germany would assure the control of Ruhr and Belgian industries, or would at least deny them to the Western powers. It would also afford the Soviet Union access to the Atlantic seaboard, thereby providing a natural staging area for further conquest.

German images of the methods of conquest likely to be used by the Soviet Union are less uniform, but it is generally agreed that the choice of method will be determined less by dogmatic considerations than by expediency. Political leaders officially concerned with the defense effort are inclined to assume that Soviet policy is shaped by strictly military considerations and that the influence of the Red army is strong. Rightist politicians forecast the eventual use of force and insist that war with the U.S.S.R. is inevitable. Yet, while few leaders of the coalition parties would be prepared categorically to deny the possibility of war, the majority seem to feel that Soviet leaders prefer methods short of war as long as they yield satisfactory results. This view is occasionally linked with expressions of a fairly high regard for Soviet diplomacy, which some German politicians consider superior to that of Downing Street or the Quai d'Orsay. By contrast, no such laurels are accorded Soviet propaganda, which is considered too obvious and clumsy to be effective.

As to short-range objectives, German politicians tend to agree that the first and minimum goal of the U.S.S.R. is to maintain its hold on the territories now under its political and economic control. The second Soviet objective is said to be the prevention of any move by the Allies which would alter the *status quo* to the disadvantage of the U.S.S.R. The third and most ambitious aim of the U.S.S.R. is believed to be that of improving its position through a systematic reduction of Allied strength.

Elevation of the German Democratic Republic to the level of satellite statehood is cited as an example of a move toward the first objective. The attempted frustration of EDC, and now of Western European Union (WEU) and NATO, through tactics designed to split the Western allies is an example of the second. The persistent attempts to subvert the government of the Federal Republic illustrate the third. The remarkable feature of these objectives, in the German view, is that all may be accomplished without resort to force.

According to a theory that German political leaders express with mounting frequency, Soviet policy toward Germany is governed by Russian fears or, at least, by a very real need for military security. As to what, or whom, the Soviets fear, German opinion varies. Conservatives and nationalists will say that the Russians have not forgotten their encounter with the German *Landser* ("foot soldier") in World War II. And if there is anything the Russians dread more than a German in arms, it is a German in American arms. German military prowess and American technological skill and resources are thought to constitute an unbeatable combination, which Soviet policy must prevent from ever fully materializing.

Social Democratic leaders will admit that the Russian fear is understandable in view of two German invasions within less than thirty years. Neutralists will add that this fear is justified not only in the light of past history but, above all, in the face of the progressive "encirclement" of the Soviet Union by the Western allies. In neutralist opinion, it is the U.S.S.R. which is on the defensive, and the West which, by its aggressive conduct, generates fear and insecurity. In the words of one of the leading neutralists, the establishment of a Western defense system with German participation constitutes in Soviet eyes "an expansion of the U.S. atomic bridgehead in Europe." This, of course, is an extreme view, rarely heard outside neutralist circles. But whether or not Soviet fears are believed to be justified, leaders of both the opposition and the coalition have felt for some time that the sincerity of the professed Soviet interest in security arrangements with the West ought to be tested.

With this in mind, the coalition parties, in 1954 and 1955, produced a variety of security schemes, some of which found their way into official policy statements. The government also endorsed Western plans for European security as developed in connection with the four-power Geneva Conference in 1955. Nevertheless, many political leaders close to the government have remained skeptical of Soviet readiness to achieve a *modus vivendi*. Convinced that the U.S.S.R. pursues an essentially aggressive policy, they have found it difficult to reconcile that belief with the Soviet quest for security. Coalition leaders, therefore, have tended to place little stock in Churchill's and Adenauer's earlier proposals of security guarantees to the U.S.S.R., and to regard them, rather, as shrewd psychological moves.

Whatever the differences in German interpretations of Soviet Russia's political course, there is general agreement that the danger of military conflict, which only a few years ago appeared inevitable, has lessened. Politicians of all major parties point out that the Korean invasion has not been followed by similar attacks elsewhere. German students of the military situation see the race for atomic supremacy as having bogged down in a strategic stalemate. News of internal changes in the Soviet Union has provided further relief. Arguments that "the Soviets do not want a war and can't afford one" could be heard frequently from German politicians in 1954 and 1955.

The trend toward relaxation of international tension caused some concern in official circles. Leaders of the government and of the coalition parties remained convinced that fundamentally nothing had changed, and least of all Soviet policy. In the Chancellor's opinion, the German people—and not they alone—were dancing on a volcano. The Soviet threat, though less overt, was still there. Or, as a prominent member of the Bundestag put it, civilization was living "on borrowed time," with the chances of survival only slightly improved. Coalition leaders admittedly were afraid that large parts of the population were being pulled into a false sense of security and that, as a result, German interest in an alliance with the West might lose momentum.

Relations with America

Since 1949 an amazing *rapprochement* between Americans and West Germans has taken place. Political leaders of all shades often express astonishment about the extent to which the memories of the early occupation phase, with its repressive and punitive features, have been forgotten. "Ami go home" inscriptions on German walls have all but disappeared, and the few that can still be detected are due to communist agitation.

The Berlin airlift, the currency reform, Marshall Plan aid, and the McCloy Fund are most often cited as causes of this change in public attitude. Much credit is also given to the "America Houses," libraries and information centers designed to promote a better understanding of the United States, and particularly to the exchange program of the Department of State, which facilitates direct contact between Germans and Americans. It is probably correct to say that Germans today are better informed about, and more sympathetic toward, the United States than ever before.

The climax of this development may now have passed. But in 1952 and 1953, the United States was without any doubt the most popular of the occupation powers, and friendship with America was an accepted goal of German policy. Political leaders, who a few years earlier would have thought twice before associating themselves with American policy, now felt free to express solidarity with and gratitude to the United States in public as well as in private. On the nonpolitical level, manifestations of friendship extended far into the ranks of the opposition.

One also hears today tributes to American progress, cultural as well as technological. Criticisms of American materialism, gadgetism, and sensationalism are, of course, still frequent, but they come from only a minority of political leaders. Higher-ranking politicians, who are likely to be members of the intelligentsia, have changed their attitude. The idea that America is peopled by cultural barbarians is decidedly on the wane. The American book, the American play, and the American motion picture have scored a considerable success among German intellectuals. Some are naturally more articulate in their appreciation than others, but the impact is not limited to any one group. A leading nationalist, known for his flirtation with the radical political right, remarked that his most ardent desire was to visit the country of Thornton Wilder and Eugene O'Neill.

Interest of German leaders in American culture is accompanied by an interest in American political forms. Rightist politicians, for instance, are prone to advocate administrative reforms modeled after the American type of "presidential" (as against parliamentary) democracy, with heavier responsibility placed on the executive branch of the government. Liberal leaders, who deplore the doctrinal structure of the German party system, point with envy to the American system made up of two nonideological, "liberal" parties. Political leaders to the left-of-center appear to be especially impressed with the American democratic process as it operates on the local community level. At the same time, they are critical of certain social and economic inequities in the United States, but show a keen interest in American efforts to cope with these problems.*

As spokesmen of the opposition party and custodians of the socialist tradition in Germany, SPD leaders suspect that American policy is weighted in favor of the CDU. Their suspicion was greatly strengthened as a result of pro-Adenauer statements by U.S. officials prior to the German elections of 1953. In spite of the *modus vivendi* that has been achieved between the SPD and U.S. representatives in Germany, many Social Democratic leaders have never fully dropped their guard in dealing with American officials, and continue to suspect an American bias in favor of the upper middle class, industry, and the high bureaucracy. A Social Democratic deputy attributed American lack of favor for the SPD to distrust of the poor man's party and favoritism for the idle rich.

In the heat of election campaigns, some Social Democrats have gone so far as to suspect U.S. representatives of complicity with the ruling circles in bringing about the defeat of Social Democratic candidates.

* Opinion surveys conducted among exchange visitors upon their return to Germany confirm that they are likely to be most impressed by political institutions and attitudes, and least so by existing social conditions.

Others have gone beyond expressing suspicion and have accused American authorities of backing reactionary forces, including militarists and Nazis, in an effort to gain support for the U.S. rearmament policy at the expense of the workers and the lower middle class. Social Democrats have been particularly distrustful of the sincerity of any American interest in reunification.

Leaders of the coalition parties, as a rule, approve of America's influence on German policy. While they are inclined to keep their expressions of friendship and assertions of identity of interest within the limits appropriate to representatives of a sovereign nation, many of them have made use of Germany's close relations with the United States to shore up their own political position. In the election campaign of 1953, the CDU pointed repeatedly to the Chancellor's successful visit to the United States, an emphasis that also earned Mr. Adenauer much derogatory comment from Communists and rightist radicals.

"Americans," Adenauer once said, "are the only true Europeans." This statement was meant as testimony to the identity of interests between America and Europe, but it also was an acknowledgment of American leadership even in matters that are basically the concern of European nations. To leaders of the government coalition parties, America's interest in EDC, WEU, or EURATOM has appeared, not as "meddling," but, rather, as a much-needed stimulant to the European Movement. However, what these government leaders welcomed as assistance was resented by leaders of the opposition as interference in German—or European—internal affairs.

While leaders of both major political parties are, on the whole, favorably disposed toward the United States, less positive attitudes toward specific aspects of America and American policy can be found among politicians throughout the political spectrum. A frequent charge is that American policy has a schizophrenic quality. A leading political analyst has characterized this quality in the following terms:

> To the German, the image of America floats in a kind of eerie dusk. America, the gigantic world power, is also America, the island that clings to isolationism. America with its tendencies to hegemonial expansion is also America, the insular continent that prefers to sulk and to retire from its European responsibilities.[2]

A related criticism is directed at the youthfulness of America. This trait, while often admired and envied, is also held accountable for a naïveté that is believed to lead America into frequent diplomatic and political blunders. Hand in glove with this naïveté, it is said, goes a tendency to entwine diplomatic and political issues with lofty idealistic or moralistic purposes. America's missionary urge to re-create the world in her own image has been most severely criticized by certain neutralist politicians, who fear that the idealistic approach to policy may eventually involve America and her allies in military adventures on moral grounds.

At the same time, the critics maintain that the tendency of American policymakers to sermonize or moralize is an attempt to conceal the lack of clearly defined concepts and adequate policy-planning. For instance, political leaders of all shades have applauded the U.S. position on the problem of reunification, but have found it wanting in realism and practicability.

It is also suggested that the doggedness with which the United States pursues certain objectives, e.g., the nonrecognition of Red China, results in a dogmatic quality in American foreign policy that is apt to deprive the United States and its allies of the flexibility necessary in international relations. This type of criticism is found primarily among political groups to the left-of-center. It is not shared by middle-of-the-road and right-of-center politicians, who welcome vigorous assertions of American leadership and, by the same token, deplore America's indulgence and lack of firmness in dealing with certain nations, notably France.

The proverbial urge of Americans to produce tangible results in short order is believed to cause them to disregard or belittle obstacles which by their own standards are trifling, but to which Europeans, and especially Germans, attach considerable significance. One such case was the problem of the Saar which, Germans suspected, was of only peripheral interest to Americans in comparison with the larger issues of European unity and defense. There are frequent complaints that the United States has little understanding of foreign idiosyncrasies, and displays impatience with those who, for reasons of their own, refuse to fall in promptly with American policies.

One also hears charges of "American fickleness," which is said to lead to the sudden abandonment or reversal of American policies. Some politicians attribute this alleged instability of U.S. policy to constant experimentation, springing from both an incapacity to accept failure and an addiction to change. German politicians believe they understand these tendencies, but they nevertheless find them exasperating. They argue that the perennial search for new approaches is justified in a society with a flexible structure and an economy of abundance, but that it will cause severe strains and dislocations if applied to the rigid European system.

American technological accomplishments come in for criticism as well as praise. Some politicians have voiced the fear that American infatuation with technological progress may shake off the constraints of religious, ethical, social, and political standards. They do not, as a rule, go so far as one German newspaper which, on the occasion of a hydrogen-bomb test, demanded that a stop be put to the efforts of fanatical American scientists who showed nothing but indifference to the fate to which they were exposing mankind.

There is still much ridicule of the American "gadget craze." Although the advantages of the washing machine and the refrigerator have not been lost on Germans, some politicians propound the view that habitual reliance on labor-saving gadgets has "softened" Americans to a degree where they no longer could withstand the strain of a real emergency. A prominent member of the Bundestag expressed serious doubt that the American soldier would be able to endure the hardships of a winter campaign in Russia. The German soldier, by contrast, is believed to possess greater stamina. Recent opinion polls show, however, that the record of the GI in the Korean war has increased German respect for his combat qualities. The GI, in fact, appears to be gradually catching up to the Russian soldier, although both still rank far behind the German *Landser*.

The present importance of these negative attitudes should not be over-rated. Whether they lose or gain in strength will depend ultimately on the way American-German relations develop in the coming years. In general, these German views do not manifest a basic hostility to the United States. They do, however, spotlight existing psychological blocks on the road to fuller mutual understanding.

Rapprochement *with France*

A prominent leader of the CDU confessed recently that he had first been won over completely to the Chancellor's policy by the latter's statement, in a public address in 1953, that Franco-German understanding was the key to European unity. "From that day on," he said, "I have been an 'Adenauer man.'"

Understanding between Germany and France has been called a key-stone of German postwar policy, especially in view of the need for European integration. "Europeanization and European co-operation," Dr. Heinrich von Brentano said in 1950, "are not possible and never will be possible unless the two nations, France and Germany, which form the core of this continent, overcome the obstacles dividing them. . . ."[3] The same general idea has been expressed in countless variations by other leading politicians and seems, in fact, to be one of the few basic principles in German foreign policy on which government and opposition find themselves in almost complete agreement.

And yet, nothing could be more complex and contradictory than

German attitudes toward France. What makes them so complicated is the fact that rational motivations and sober reasoning seem to be forever in conflict with sentiment and emotional bias. In the words of a political analyst close to the cabinet, "in contrast to the relations between Germans and Anglo-Saxons, the German-French relationship is preponderantly emotional." [4]

The long history of Franco-German conflict has, of course, left its mark on present-day attitudes of German politicians. "The road from Washington to Bonn," says Schütz, "is marked by power, the road from London to Bonn by prudence, the road from Paris to Bonn by memories." [5] The German memory, no less than the French, is excellent, and, like that of the French, highly selective. Unfortunately, the memories which the French and Germans have in common are characterized more often by friction and conflict than by harmony and co-operation; recollections of Versailles and Compiègne are more vivid than memories of Locarno.*

On the other hand, aside from occasional outbursts by rightist elements, the chauvinism of earlier days is no longer in evidence. References to France as the traditional archenemy have practically disappeared from the vocabulary of the German politician. One reason for this change may be that, when the balance is drawn, Germans have fewer grievances to remember than the French, and what grievances they have are more deeply buried in history than those of the French.

Nevertheless, French claims to the spoils of victory after World War II are regarded with ironical indignation. In German eyes, France was the only major power which suffered unmitigated defeat at the hands of the Wehrmacht; there are few who do not have a vivid recollection of the swiftness of the French collapse in 1940 and of the triumphant German columns marching down the Champs Elysées. Many German politicians, even those of moderate leanings, are irked by France's present claim to the title of a world power. The thought of having been governed by French authorities, of having the vanquished French sit in judgment over German policies and help determine the future of their former conquerors, has been a source of constant irritation to political leaders, but especially to politicians to the right-of-center.

This resentment often colors the judgment of German politicians when they discuss the ups and downs of French politics. It also accounts for the serious doubts which Germans, particularly conservatives, have about France's potential value as a future military ally. Rightist politi-

* A sole exception to this common observation can be found in Bavaria. Particularist leaders there remember with mild relish the days when Bavaria was allied with France against the "archenemy Prussia."

cians, who are traditionally inclined to gauge national virtues in terms of military capabilities, do in fact suggest that France's military potential should be neither feared nor relied upon.

The cultural aspects of Franco-German relations are far more complex. German intellectuals have always admired French philosophy, literature, and fine arts, and the postwar triumph of French art, motion pictures, and writers such as Sartres, Camus, and Anouilh has reinforced this predisposition.

In contrast, German attitudes toward the French way of life are negative and often reflect moral disapproval. German politicians on the highest level can be heard to comment scornfully on French "superficiality" or "frivolity," and on the effeminacy of French social habits. The word most frequently applied to the French character and French culture is "decadence," and references are often made to the soft living and working habits of the French, as well as to their permanent state of political irresolution and prostration. French cultivation and refinement of leisure, ranging from aesthetic to gastronomic pleasures, remain the subject of constant criticism, and the sacrosanct French lunch hour epitomizes to Germans the internal weakness of a society that places leisure above work. French "levity" is contrasted unfavorably with the solidity of German tastes, and yet, ironically, it is the very feature of French life that has attracted successive generations of German tourists to Paris, and which even today prompts German intellectuals and politicians to confess privately that they would not mind making France their second home.

German prejudices about France are most pronounced in the field of politics. They revolve around three central issues: French domestic conditions, French foreign relations, and European integration.

Political leaders of all shades are more or less in agreement that postwar France is suffering from a chronic malaise, which keeps the nation from assuming its full share of responsibilities as a major power and has made it heir to Turkey's role of "the sick man of Europe." Diagnoses of France's illness vary. To some German leaders, it is but a figment of the French imagination, a neurosis attributable to the trauma of defeat. To others, it is inherent in the very structure of the French body politic, constitution, party system, process of policy-making, and social habits. The French presidential elections of December, 1953, were repeatedly cited by German politicians as a symptom of France's internal debility, a "sorry spectacle," offering a pathetic contrast to the glamour and dignity of the British coronation. The attitude of condescending sympathy toward France may have its political usefulness. The knowledge that other nations, even in the camp of the victors, are weaker than Germany may have done almost as much to raise German morale and to restore political self-confidence as have the impressive statistics of German postwar recovery. Informed leaders admit that this knowledge imbued many Germans with a sense of equality, and even superiority, vis-à-vis the French long before German sovereignty had been attained.

Responsible German politicians have no desire to curb France's influence or to keep her in a state of weakness. The Chancellor himself has repeatedly stated that he would prefer a strong France in Germany's back to a weak one. Other CDU leaders have deplored French weakness as being just as harmful to Germany as it is to France. Remarks of this sort bespeak a realization that an effective defense system will require co-operation with a strong and friendly France, and that, so long as there remains a military vacuum in the West, Germany's own military position is bound to be problematical.

German politicians, on the whole, believe that their country has done its part in promoting the establishment of friendly relations with France. However, they often complain that their feelings are not reciprocated and that their intentions, far from being appreciated, are actually suspected and misjudged by the French. They do not deny that the French have legitimate cause for bitterness, but they are becoming increasingly resentful about continuing manifestations of French distrust. German exasperation reached new heights when, early in 1954, the French government threatened to veto the new German defense law then under debate in the Bundestag. A leading conservative politician put France on notice that Germany's patience was "not inexhaustible." His warning was couched in language that had long been absent from political discussions.

The "Ernst case," in which a former mayor of Strasbourg was first indicted on charges of war crimes, then released, and subsequently rearrested before he had reached the German border, caused a similar flurry of excitement. It prompted a leading member of the CDU to remark that, if the French persisted in irritating the German people in this vein, they would eventually succeed in rekindling the flame of German nationalism.

Many political leaders believe that this persistent French antagonism is prompted by fear, not of any imminent German aggression, but of the possibility that a renascent Germany might use her newly-gained strength to establish German hegemony in Europe and, subsequently, to harness the power of her allies to a policy of revisionism.

As a result, Germans suspect that, despite public assurances, the French are not really interested in German rearmament or in German reunification. Instead, most Frenchmen are believed to prefer a policy that would delay Germany's full recovery and vitiate her legitimate aspirations. Worse yet, some French politicians are suspected of being ready to join forces with nations that have an interest in keeping Germany disunited or, if united, in a permanent state of weakness and isolation. Carrying this reasoning to an extreme, some German political leaders have predicted that France, if she were faced wih the choice between an alliance with Germany and one with Soviet Russia, might gravitate toward the latter. "After all," a prominent party politician said, "a Frenchman much prefers shooting a German to shooting a Russian."

During the early 1950's, fear of a French-Soviet "deal" existed among leaders of practically all political groups. It reached its climax before the four-power conference in Berlin in 1954, which, German politicians suspected, would be used by the French as a convenient occasion to "sell out" Germany. A high German official intimated that, to his mind, the conference was the product of a "Franco-Soviet conspiracy." When Bidault made his eloquent appeal in defense of Western and German interests, these charges were temporarily dropped, and France was granted the benefit of the doubt. Yet a number of German leaders, especially those to the right-of-center, appear to have remained distrustful of French intentions.

Responsible politicians, in general, are deeply concerned lest fear of Germany become the central motive of French policies. "The French," a leading member of the CDU complained, "do not see the Russian forest for the German trees." To them, 12 German divisions appear as a menace more formidable than the Red army. As a result, it is feared, France may not only jeopardize her own security but also that of her neighbors, indeed of all Western Europe. What the French would like, many Germans say, is a German army stronger than that of the U.S.S.R. but weaker than that of France.

Some of the bitterest statements about French policy have come from those German leaders who staked their hopes and, in some cases, their political careers on Franco-German *rapprochement* within the framework of European integration. "The French," said a leading member of the CDU, "are re-erecting the walls which were leveled to the ground after the war." This remark was typical of the attitude of many German politicians and intellectuals who, after having honestly fought for Franco-German understanding and European union, felt stabbed in the back by what they regarded as French national egotism and political myopia.

Long before EDC was formally rejected by the National Assembly, leading German officials expressed the suspicion that France did not want a European Defense Community, because, as some pointed out, it would compel France to abandon her national army, a sacrifice which would not be matched by Germany. In general, German politicians appreciated the French dilemma but pointed out that postponement of the decision, rather than solving the problem, would only demonstrate the need for alternative solutions that might prove even more painful to France.

In 1953 and 1954, annoyance and impatience with French conduct became so intense that, for once, leaders of the coalition and of the opposition saw completely eye to eye in their condemnation of French irresolution. The climax of German indignation was reached when the French Chamber of Deputies rejected the EDC on August 30, 1954. A statement issued immediately afterwards by the federal government was eloquent in both what it said and what it left unsaid. It called for the continuation of the policy of Europeanization and for early negotiations with the United States and Great Britain, but made no reference to France. In his broadcast of September 4, 1954, however, the Chancellor adopted a more conciliatory tone. "An understanding between France and Germany," he said, "is the foundation, the necessary prerequisite, of any European integration. The great historic design of European integration will not be killed by a vote on the procedural handling of the EDC treaty in one of the parliaments involved."

In spite of the hopeful and even generous words of the German Chancellor, the ups and downs in French policy have confirmed many German leaders in their feeling that France is politically untrustworthy. It is said, among other things, that a nation in which the Communist Party is a major political force can not qualify for membership in a system of mutual defense. In this connection, many Germans have criticized America's indulgence toward the whims of French politics and have asked how long the United States would continue to make "charming gestures" toward her vacillating ally.

France, it is generally felt, must be made "to see the light"; but there is little agreement as to the means to be employed toward that end. A leading member of the SPD recommended a "shock treatment," meaning the withholding of American economic aid to France. Another Social Democrat suggested financial bribes. In both cases, the United States rather than Germany was to try its hand in making France mend her ways.

With the exception of a minority group, which favors more drastic measures, most political leaders are opposed to any action which would eliminate France permanently or even temporarily from membership in the common defense system and the European community. This moderation is probably the result of long-range practical considerations.

Whatever concepts German politicians may hold of the future organization of Europe and of collective security, they generally include France as an indispensable partner. Thus, it is ultimately national self-interest, combined with a sincere admiration for French cultural achievements, which makes German political leaders advocates of Franco-German *rapprochement.*

A New Look at the British

Relations between Great Britain and Germany, by contrast, are characterized by cool and sober reflection. Moreover, until recently, Great Britain and her politics did not occupy a central place in German thinking. German political leaders rarely referred to Great Britain with the same emphasis with which they spoke of France, the United States, or Soviet Russia. Above all, relations with Great Britain were seldom thought of in terms of friendship and, prior to the London and Paris conferences of 1954, hardly ever in terms of military or political partnership.

To some extent, German indifference toward Great Britain is caused by British indifference toward Germany. Most Germans are convinced that the British attitude is dictated not so much by hostility as by a general aversion to any concern with continental affairs. British aloofness, while not welcome, is more or less accepted as a traditional feature of the British character and of British policy.

A mutual lack of understanding seems to be particularly marked among conservative politicians, both in Germany and in England. In discussing the differences between German and British notions of conservatism, a prominent member of the Conservative Party said: "Conservatism has a derogatory sound for many Germans today, particularly for young people. Time and again we have to explain to them that British conservatism, contrary to the German variety, is not nationalistic and not bourgeois." A conservative member of Parliament seemed convinced that the vast majority of Germans were incapable of finding a proper relationship with Great Britain out of sheer ignorance of the British character. German conservatives, on the other hand, are attracted by their British counterparts, but aware of the British lack of response. "The British don't like us," concluded a leading member of the German Party.

On the political left, relations between German Social Democrats and British Labourites, while far from intimate, are considerably closer than those between other parties. A number of leading Social Democrats, including party chief Ollenhauer, are "remigrants" from Great Britain, having spent the Hitler years in England in close contact with the Labour Party. As a result, cordial personal relations still exist between the leaders of both parties. But Social Democrats and Labourites do not see eye to eye in the field of foreign affairs, and some leading Labourites are openly critical of the SPD's foreign policy stand, and especially of the "nationalism" with which the SPD agitates for German reunification.

The principal issues which German leaders see as causes of friction between their country and Great Britain lie in the economic sphere. It is generally assumed in Germany that the chief aim of British postwar policy has been the recovery of lost markets and that, in order to achieve this aim, the British have tried to restrain foreign competition. Many German leaders argue that dismantling of German industries after the war afforded a convenient device for keeping a formidable rival at bay. The Allied ban imposed on German shipbuilding, and later restrictions on trade with the East, were seen as yet another effort of the hard-pressed British to eliminate undesirable competition.

Rallying to the counterattack, German politicians have supported an economic free-for-all that includes the invasion of markets which have previously been the domain of Great Britain. "If the British cannot get along with the Arabs," a right-wing political leader said, "why shouldn't Germany move in and fill the gap?"

Leading Germans are aware of unfavorable British reactions to these trade policies, but they do not seem appreciably disturbed by them. The fight is on, they say, and it is nothing to be ashamed of, since it is a respectable and legitimate struggle fought by equals with equal chances for all.

While German relations with Britain, on the whole, are cool, they are not encumbered, as are those with France, by a mortgage of animosities going far back into history. There are no living memories of territorial conflicts or of questioned defeats and victories. Germans know full well that they did not win the Battle of Britain. They have a fairly high regard for the British soldier, especially if his fighting qualities are compared with those of the French.

During the last few years, British popularity has risen steadily. The change of climate is due in part to the recovery of German self-confidence, and in part to a growing conviction that the decline of the British Empire is just as real as was the fall of Germany. The British, too, as one of Germany's leading figures put it, have become "small fry." The attitude of many German politicians toward Great Britain is one of unsentimental sympathy. Unlike their condescending pity for the

French, it is the appreciation, based on respect and even admiration, for the able competitor who has succumbed to odds due partly to no fault of his own.

The deeper roots of this attitude were revealed during the coronation ceremonies of Queen Elizabeth. The British display of power and pomp left a deep impression upon millions of Germans. Political leaders—liberals, as well as conservatives—enviously and nostalgically compared the regal spectacle with the paleness of their own political existence. In German eyes, Britain's loss of power has not impaired her status as a spiritual force and as a partner in world politics. On the occasion of Churchill's eightieth birthday, Chancellor Adenauer called Sir Winston outstanding among the statesmen of Europe in his influence on the destiny of Europe, and one "whose birthday the German people have good cause to observe in gratitude."

Adenauer's statement was a tribute to Churchill the European, as well as to Churchill the British Prime Minister. The idea of British partnership in a broader European community has introduced a new element into German-British relations; it has created a basis on which a more positive relationship between the two nations may be built. In the past, many German politicians associated Great Britain's traditional role in Europe with the concept of the "balance of power." Today, the moderate politician, from the conservative on the right to the Social Democrat on the left, sees this concept of a balance between antagonistic powers abandoned in favor of a new union, in which age-old conflicts of interest will be resolved through a system of collective security. Political leaders close to the government believe that Great Britain's move toward the European commonwealth will ultimately remove certain psychological blocks which now retard the process of European integration. According to a prominent member of the Chancellor's entourage, it will deliver the French from their fear of being "left alone" with the Germans; it will contribute a needed element of political stability; and it will broaden the political and cultural horizon of the new Europe.

In the months preceding the collapse of EDC, many political leaders expressed concern that Great Britain might miss her historical chance of becoming a co-sponsor of European union. Yet none of the coalition leaders went so far as to maintain that the new Europe was unthinkable without British participation. Leaders of the SPD, on the other hand, insisted on the inclusion of Great Britain as a *sine qua non* for European unity, and opposed what they called the Chancellor's "Little Europe." They have consistently declined to accept a concept of Europe without Great Britain and without the Scandinavian countries. The British pledge, made at the London Conference in the fall of 1954, to continue military support for a united Europe was welcomed by both coalition and opposition leaders in Germany as a significant advance for the cause of European unity.

Some German leaders support their case for closer relations between Germany and England by pointing to strategic necessity and the requirements of *Realpolitik*. Great Britain and Germany, they say, need each other. A close association with Germany is believed to offer Britain two advantages: a continental shield from possible Soviet aggression and a guarantee of her independence in the face of America's magnetic pull. By the same token, an Anglo-German association would give Germany a greater measure of independence from the United States, as well as protection for her interests in the Atlantic and overseas areas. Some German politicians say they would welcome close Anglo-German co-operation in view of Britain's record as a moderating influence in world politics and as a master of the diplomatic game.

The concept of a full-fledged German-British alliance is considered premature so long as the obstacles to close mutual understanding are as great as they seem today. The Germans suspect that the British are still afraid of Germany's hegemonic aspirations and that, furthermore, England's insular situation and her pride in her Empire and sovereign status will continue to preclude any genuine integration with continental powers. However, it is undeniable that, as Germany's hopes for a close alliance with France have faded, German politicians have begun to look with growing expectation toward Great Britain.

Germany and the New Europe

In the ten years since World War II, there has been general agreement among leaders of all major parties that Germany's future is bound to that of a unified Europe. Indeed, the idea of a "new Europe" has captured the imagination of most of Germany's leaders to an extraordinary degree.

The European movement in Germany and German policy toward European union are motivated by a variety of reasons. Some of these reasons reflect idealistic aspirations; others derive from Germany's postwar pragmatism. Chancellor Adenauer's own position shows a blend of high-minded idealism and strategic realism. He sees European unity as having two major purposes: to save Europe from political and physical destruction, and to give German policy a new idealistic perspective. The German people, the Chancellor has pointed out, need a goal, something worth living for. The concept of Europe meets this need.

Most of the "pro-Europeans" hold that, in the twentieth century, nationalism no longer offers a sufficient guarantee of security. In a world divided into two major spheres of power, they argue, individual nations do not stand a chance of survival unless they seek security in supranational agreements. Chancellor Adenauer, in a personal remark to the author, referred to a disunited and isolated Europe as a fragment that could neither live nor die, and as a natural hunting ground for political adventurers. In a statement before the Bundestag on March 19, 1953, he said:

> We must free ourselves from thinking in terms of national statehood. The last war, and developments in the field of armament and modern technology, have created entirely different and new conditions in the world. . . . West European countries are no longer in a position to protect themselves individually; none of them is any longer in a position to salvage European culture. These objectives, which are common to all, can only be attained if the West European nations form a political, economic and cultural union, and, above all, if they render impossible any military conflicts among themselves.

The need for a larger loyalty and for the establishment of supranational European authorities has been frequently stressed both in statements by individual leaders and in resolutions of the Bundestag.* The supreme goal, in the words of Dr. von Brentano, must be "the establishment of a European Political Community on the broadest possible basis," with the Coal and Steel Community (Schuman Plan) and European defense arrangements constituting merely the first two phases of total unification.[6] A number of political leaders, particularly in the ranks of the Social Democrats, have deplored the fact that military unity was planned to precede political union. They argue that military agreements will hinder establishment of a solid European political framework. Others, making a virtue out of a necessity, express the hope that the supranational military system will smooth the way for political union.

In the annals of German foreign policy the concept of supranationalism is practically without precedent. That political leaders in Germany could publicly propose such a course without provoking cries of protest and charges of treason attests to the radical change of the political climate in Germany. It also highlights the disillusionment of the German people with nationalism as a system that has brought them defeat and disgrace.

* A resolution adopted by the Bundestag on July 26, 1950, advocated the conclusion of a European Federal Pact in the following words: "Convinced that the present division of Europe into national sovereign states tends to lead the European nations into ever-increasing misery and to deprive them of their freedom, the Bundestag of the German Federal Republic, established by free elections, declares itself in favor of a European Federal Pact. . . ."

Although agreed in principle that the nations of Europe should be more closely associated, Germany's political party leaders differ widely on the following basic questions: Of what should the new Europe consist? How is the new Europe to be achieved? What should be Germany's place in this new Europe?

Some of the setbacks that protagonists of European union have suffered can be attributed to their failure to develop a clear and commonly-acceptable definition of what they mean by "Europe." This was well illustrated during a round-table discussion of German politicians and publicists in 1954. A young intellectual, for example, confessed that an attempt to define Europe confused him:

> You will find that each of us will give a different answer when asked to state what Europe means. As far as I am concerned, it means a cultural rather than a geographic notion; to me it is the point of origin of occidental culture but it includes the marginal areas across the seas. . . . For many of us, Europe is a kind of substitute ideology.

Another participant declared that "Europe is the West, the West of Europe, both politically and culturally." A member of Germany's nobility insisted that Europe must be regarded as a "spiritual" ideal, "the expression of a human attitude." As such, he felt, it could not be confined to the West: "If Europe means anything, it must mean all of Europe, and, one day, it may extend to the Ural Mountains and the Volga River." The integration of Europe, in another's opinion, meant a progressive amalgamation of ethnic and national groups:

> Whether the Oder-Neisse area will come under Polish or German administration . . . will be of no significance whatever. The Sudeten Germans will move to Prague and will live there under Czech rule, and the Czechs will move to Nuremberg and will reside there under German administration.

All participants in the discussion agreed that their image of Europe did not necessarily tally with that of the man-in-the-street, to whom European union was an alternative to a narrow national existence. They agreed also that European union signified a *modus vivendi* for Western Europe: to some, it meant the establishment of the European Defense Community, while others regarded it simply as a slogan, and still others as a short cut to German rehabilitation and political respectability. According to a leading Social Democrat, "Europe" meant an escape, a refuge where one might avoid the great conflicts of our time. It was also sarcastically said that to an increasing number of people—but especially to the so-called *Speseneuropäer* (literally: "per-diem Europeans")—the promotion of the European idea offered a convenient source of income.

Adenauer's leaning toward an association of West European states has exposed him to criticism from Social Democrats and from some of his own coalition supporters who fear that his policies will lead to another "Holy Roman Empire" of predominantly Catholic nations, in which Germans would find themselves a relatively small cultural minority. (These objections have been partially stilled by Great Britain's decision to join the West European Union.) Socialist leaders have been particularly dissatisfied with another aspect of the Chancellor's plans for what they call a "Little Europe," for they fear that this would mean the truncation not only of Europe but of Germany herself.

Opinion has been sharply divided also on the way in which European unity is to be achieved. Socialist leaders insist that German reunification should precede European union, and therefore have opposed not only European defense agreements but also many of the moves toward European co-operation in the political and economic sphere. However, their opposition being one of approach rather than of principle, it is not stubbornly upheld once the chips are down. SPD leaders point out that, although they fought the Coal and Steel Community as long as it was in the debating stage, they accepted and loyally supported it after it had been ratified. SPD leaders have followed a similar course in the case of EURATOM and the common market.

A majority of coalition leaders have adopted a "functional" approach to European integration. This involves the delegation of successive governmental functions to supranational bodies, rather than the adoption of an all-inclusive federal plan. The European Coal and Steel Community was the first step along these lines, the Paris agreements on European defense were another. Since then, there have been the attempts to establish a common program for atomic development and a common European market. In general, however, conservative politicians favor retention of the basic prerogatives of sovereignty.

As to Germany's place in the new Europe, all politicians agree that she should be a leader, but opinions differ about the manner in which such leadership should be exercised and about the degree of preeminence that Germany ought to enjoy. In the larger Europe envisaged by the Socialists, Germany would be one of the principal powers, but she would not attempt to dominate the others. It would be enough to have the economic strength, cultural eminence, and numerical weight of a reunited Germany ensure her a respectful hearing in all European councils.

Many of the more liberal CDU politicians and other coalition leaders share this view, but, as one moves toward the right of the political spectrum, one finds that a united Europe is frequently regarded merely as the tail of the German kite. Conservative nationalist leaders privately express the opinion that political, economic, and military leadership in a united Europe will of necessity devolve on Germany, not because of any German desire to dominate but because the facts of postwar Europe require it. To the very small neo-Nazi fringe, a united Europe is merely a convenient cover for nationalist ambitions. Indeed, members of this group are likely to point out that the most successful approach to a united Europe in recent times was made by none other than Adolf Hitler.

An Alternative: Neutralism

Among the major German parties, the SPD is usually thought of as representing the strongest neutralist tendencies. To most SPD leaders, however, the term "neutralism" is repugnant. SPD chairman Erich Ollenhauer, indeed, chose the occasion of the conclusion of the Austrian treaty to register his and his party's objection to any form of neutralization, including the incorporation of German territory in a *cordon sanitaire*.

It is fairly obvious why the SPD has repeatedly been suspected of aiding and abetting the cause of neutralism during the postwar years, despite assurances to the contrary by its leading spokesmen. The party consistently fought the government's rearmament policy in its formative stage on constitutional and political grounds. It has resisted Germany's participation in EDC, in the Coal and Steel Community, in WEU, and in NATO. After the signing of the Paris Pacts, it made efforts to achieve a modification of the agreements, and many SPD leaders seem prepared to trade membership in NATO and WEU for concessions by the Soviet Union which would ensure the reunification of Germany in freedom.

Many individual SPD leaders give the impression of having strong neutralist inclinations. Some do not hide the fact that at heart they are pacifists and are averse to military commitments and to a "policy of strength." Others are afraid that by endorsing a military alliance with the West they would help to perpetuate the cold war. In addition, many believe that a close military alignment with the West is the main stumbling block on the road to German unification.

In order both to secure the peace and to attain German unity, SPD leaders have proposed the establishment of a multilateral security system which Germany should join in preference to one-sided military alliances. The following declaration of the governing bodies of the party, issued after the collapse of EDC, expresses the SPD's position:

The restoration of German unity and the abandonment of German integration into a military system either of the West or of the East would constitute the basis on which to establish a European system of mutual and collective security guaranteed by and binding upon both the United States of America and the Soviet Union within the framework of the United Nations.[7]

SPD leaders have repeatedly affirmed that they respect the validity of treaties already concluded with the West, but they have also continued to call for "adjustments to changing conditions."[8] Moreover, they have urged the government to persuade the Western allies to take up negotiations with the Soviet government again with a view to replacing the Paris Agreements by a "collective security system."[9] In the system they envisage, the antagonistic military alliances now existing would be merged into a comprehensive pact. (SPD leaders seem to prefer to disregard the practical difficulties of implementing such a policy.)

This proposal has the virtue of aiming to achieve all the major objectives of the SPD leadership. According to leading spokesmen, its adoption would reduce the danger of armed conflict and would obviate the need for costly military preparations, so that public funds could be diverted to civilian production and services. By meeting the security requirements of both East and West, it would help remove some of the major obstructions on the road to German reunification. It would eliminate the danger of an East-West *détente* on the premise of a continuing division of Germany and, by making Germany an integral part of a security system, would forestall potential distrust and conflict over the international status of a reunified Germany. Finally, the Federal Republic would be able to shake off its "dependence" on the Western powers, notably the United States, which to many SPD leaders appears incompatible with the dignity and freedom of a sovereign nation, although at the same time they expect Germany to continue to receive American protection.

Somewhat against their wishes, Social Democrats are forced to admit that the ratification of the Paris Agreements has made German membership in WEU, as well as in NATO, a legal obligation. They will abide by these agreements until the latter are changed by regular diplomatic negotiation, for they consider themselves, as it were, a "loyal opposition" within the Western camp.

Opposition to the Bonn government's policies of rearmament and integration with the West is expressed not only by parties on the political left, but also by nationalist groups on the right. There is, however, a basic difference between the opposition of the left and that of the right. SPD opposition to the government may be strong and at times irritating, but, as indicated above, it supports in principle the present political order in Germany and is often motivated by considerations which transcend the limits of selfish national interest. Most of the nationalist groups, on the other hand, refuse to recognize the government's political obligations and commitments and oppose any infringement of national power. The restrictions which supranational plans place on political, economic, or military prerogatives are regarded by them as offensive and intolerable and therefore subject to defiance and outright violation.

Nationalists in Germany do not present a united front. Not even the radical fringe is united; it vegetates outside the margin of political respectability. While the extremists have little numerical or political strength, they deserve attention as a potential element of trouble. Their resistance to official policy is unrestrained and totally irresponsible. Their return to power—and power is what they want—presupposes the collapse of the present order. Consequently, they have nothing to gain from compromise or "loyal" opposition. In foreign policy it is their aim to restore the German Reich to the ranks of the great powers.

The most radical of these elements clustered around the German Reich Party (DRP) until 1956, when the party was outlawed by the constitutional court. They fought furiously against Adenauer's policy of association with the West. They rejected EDC, not only because they found the restrictions imposed on Germany insufferable and the intimate company of France distasteful, but also because they saw in it an obstacle to reunification. In August, 1953, *Reichsruf,* the DRP organ, declared that "EDC means the abandonment of Eastern Germany. . . . Reunification and integration into the Western military system are incompatible." [10] These radical rightist elements are opposed to the Chancellor's policy of "Little Europe," because, in their view it is paving the way for another "Holy Roman Empire." To them, Europe comprises not only the German territories to the East of the Oder-Neisse line but also the Soviet satellite countries, Yugoslavia, and European Russia.

In the ultranationalists' concept of Europe, a reunified German Reich would form the center of the continent rather than a protecting glacis for countries to East and West. This "new European order" would make Germany not merely the geographical, but also the political and strategic, heart of Europe. Spokesmen of the DRP have insisted that Germany can not fulfill her historic mission if arrayed against either East or West. The real interests of Germany, they have declared, lie in the creation of a "third force" bloc, strong enough to permit her "to shape her own destiny" and to turn back any invasion, from whatever direction it may come.

The radical rightists favor neutrality, but an armed neutrality. They have called for the creation of a German national army under the command of generals who can be trusted to inspire military loyalty and enthusiasm among German youth. By the same token, a European army is rejected.

Rightist agitation in favor of neutrality was intensified after "Operation CARTE BLANCHE," NATO's atomic maneuvers in the summer of 1955. Always somewhat disdainful of the military value of twelve German divisions and the presence of American troops, the ultranationalists now insisted that the NATO maneuvers had demonstrated how hopelessly archaic was any defense concept that entrusted security to a number of ground divisions. Under the heading "Get Rid of the Military Bases on German Territory," *Reichsruf* called for the liquidation of both Eastern and Western bases, which in the event of war would become the primary targets of air attack.[11]

The foreign policy of the ultranationalists is in a stage of fermentation. But it is quite obvious that the neutralism of the DRP and of related groups is not an end in itself, nor is it intended as a bridge of reconciliation between antagonistic powers. It is instead a device to create a third power aggregate in which Germany will play an important, if not the dominating, part.

While extreme nationalist pronouncements are rejected by the major political parties, there is a growing inclination among some politicians to heed certain of the nationalist demands; for instance, that a more critical attitude should be adopted toward the Western allies, notably the United States, and that a greater sense of objectivity should be displayed with regard to the "legitimate" or "real" interests of the Soviet Union. There also appears to be an increasing tendency among a number of political leaders in middle-of-the-road parties to use nationalist arguments against an extension of existing commitments and in favor of exploring the possibilities for their modification and even cancellation. Existing treaties, like those involving WEU or NATO, have been regarded increasingly as objects of barter that can be abandoned in exchange for agreements which appear more attractive from the point of view of the national interest.

The significant fact about such views is that their proponents are not limited to any one political group but transcend party lines, and that some can be found even among leaders of the parties which are represented in the government coalition. The difficulties in reconciling German interests with Western security requirements have reinforced these tendencies, and external factors such as Operation CARTE BLANCHE have contributed toward their growth. The NATO maneuvers demonstrated to many German leaders for the first time the nature of the risks inherent in a military alliance with the West, risks which some decided were not worth taking. While views tending toward neutralism are thus gradually entering the political center from both the left and the right, they have not so far affected the policy of the CDU.

The Problem of Reunification

For the past few years, the German political scene has been dominated by controversy over two problems: the reunification of Germany, and her integration into the European or Western community of nations. From some aspects the two aims appear incompatible. Yet the controversy is not one between advocates of two mutually exclusive policies. With the exception of a few dyed-in-the-wool defenders of regionalism, there is not a single political party leader who has openly come out against the restoration of German unity. At the same time, a great majority of politicians are advocates of one or another form of European or Western integration. The dispute has raged largely over the relative priority to be assigned to each problem and over rival methods for achieving German unity.

Common to practically all political leaders who favor reunification are strong humanitarian feelings of kinship and sympathy with the people in East Germany. Both Protestant and Catholic churches have endeavored to give the issue of unity a spiritual meaning, and have sponsored conventions of East and West German churchgoers under the motto: "We are brethren, after all!" Since most of the population of East Germany is Protestant, it is often said that Protestant leaders are more serious in their work for German unity than Catholics.

Certain economic arguments are advanced in behalf of unification. West Germany needs her traditional bread-and-potato-basket of Pomerania and East and West Prussia. It also needs the industry of Saxony and Thuringia, and the lignite mines of Central Germany. Reunification would restore a national economy with an integrated system of production and distribution. In addition, impoverished East Germany needs West German products, particularly consumer goods, and represents a large potential market for West German producers. The city of Hamburg, in particular, badly needs the restoration of its economic hinterland. In spite of Hamburg's remarkable economic comeback, its present mayor, Sieveking, points out that half of the city's prewar trade was with the Prussian provinces of Mecklenburg and Saxony, both now in the Soviet zone.

Demography is called in to support the case for reunification. For several years political leaders of all major parties maintained that West Germany's territory was simply not large enough to support some sixteen million German refugees and expellees from the East. In view of the present boom and an incipient manpower shortage, arguments of this nature have lost much of their currency, but they are likely to be revived the very minute that the present wave of prosperity should stop or recede.

Government officials and party leaders usually stress that they consider these practical reasons for reunification to be secondary. Above all is the desire of Germans to become a nation again and thereby to recover a sense of national identity and coherence. In the words of a political leader of national-liberal persuasion, "Each piece by itself is nothing; it is something that today is associated with Germany in name only—but it is not Germany, it is only a fragment." Expressions of this sort can be heard from political leaders in all major parties.

A great variety of political arguments for unity may be heard in political circles. Members of the SPD leadership, for example, argue that the unity of Germany is a matter of enlightened self-interest for all nations, because it will remove one area of international friction and make a positive contribution to the cause of international peace. At the same time, many observers believe that the SPD looks to a Social Democratic majority in East Germany to tip the scales in its favor in any all-German election.

Some politicians of the extreme right intimate that they regard reunification as necessary to enable Germany to conduct an independent course in international power politics. These and the leaders of expellee and refugee groups consider reunification of the Soviet zone with the Federal Republic merely as a step toward the recovery of other territories, which may or may not have been included within the German boundaries of 1937.

Few politicians are willing to stress publicly the arguments sometimes heard *against* reunification, yet these do exist. For a while there was a widely-spread apprehension that the low economic level of East Germany would tend to drag down the standards of prosperity of West Germany. The development of the East will require a large capital investment which, some argue, the Federal Republic can ill afford in view of its own insufficiency of investment capital. Reunification might also bring shortages of consumer goods in the West and possibly even higher taxes. Many leaders of the coalition parties, and even a few Social Democrats, express the apprehension that a headlong drive for reunification might necessitate concessions on the part of the Federal Republic which would compromise its security. A related but less common fear is that a substantial number of East Germans, particularly young people, have now been "Sovietized" and that they would increase the power of the Communists in a unified Germany.* But the vast majority of political leaders maintain that communism has made almost no impression on East Germany and, indeed, that it is immunizing the people there against radical appeals.

Mention has been made of the political hopes which some Social Democrats seem to associate with reunification. As a corollary, some coalition politicians seem to be apprehensive about the high proportion of potential Social Democratic voters in East Germany, although they can hardly be expected to admit this publicly. We have noted, too, that the Protestants have a special interest in German unity. Conversely, Roman Catholic leaders are accused of being secretly quite satisfied with the present situation in which over a third of Germany's Protestants are cordoned off in East Germany and Berlin. South German politicians sometimes express apprehension about the increased power the "Prussians" would enjoy in a unified state. Neither the special interest of particular groups in avoiding reunification, however, nor the more popular reservations about it are sufficient to elicit public declarations against German unity. They are adduced merely as grounds for proceeding cautiously or for ranking reunification below other national objectives.

How to Achieve Reunification

Discussions with German politicians during 1953 and 1954 showed that, at that time, the majority favored one or more of four principal approaches, which were expected, singly or together, to accomplish reunification.**

The first and most innocuous of these, often labeled the "magnet thesis" by politicians close to the government, proceeded on the assumption that the progressive recovery of West Germany and the increasing strength of Western Europe were bound to attract the dissatisfied and disaffected inhabitants of the Soviet orbit. This suction process was expected eventually to cause such strains in the Soviet-controlled areas of Germany and in the satellite countries that the orbit would gradually

* This argument has also been turned around and used in favor of speedy reunification. Since the Russians are making progress in Sovietizing East Germany, it is sometimes said, no time should be lost in reunifying Germany and arresting this Sovietizing process before it goes any farther.

** As a result of subsequent events, especially the inconclusive conferences in 1954 at Berlin and in 1955 at Geneva, some of these approaches have lost much of their currency; yet advocates of each can still be found among politicians of various parties.

disintegrate. The "magnet thesis" did not require of the Federal Republic the development of any specific plan of action beyond a vigorous program of internal recovery and, possibly, the promotion of external alliances designed to increase Germany's strength and prestige. Following the abortive East German revolt of June 17, 1953, however, the "magnet thesis" lost much of its attractiveness. To be sure, West German freedom and security have continued to draw large numbers of refugees from the East, but their defection has not had the wider effects expected of it.

A second approach to reunification lay in the theory that the prevailing stalemate could be terminated only if both sides were prepared to pay "a reasonable price." The hypothetical Soviet concession was more or less fixed, and consisted essentially of allowing free and democratic elections throughout East Germany and withdrawing Soviet occupation forces. Views on the price to be paid by the West varied. Leaders of the SPD favored relinquishment of all military commitments prior to reunification, and subsequently a guarantee that Germany would stay out of alliances binding her to either side. Both Social Democrats and leaders of the government coalition frequently suggested that the West might make concessions in other areas; for example, the United States should recognize Red China. The common feature of most of these interpretations of "a reasonable price" was that in each case the price was to be paid by a third party, by the Allies rather than by Germany.

The third approach mentioned by political leaders might be called the "thesis of agreement through strength." Like the "magnet thesis," this required a systematic build-up of political and economic strength. It called for the acquisition of sufficient military power to enable Germany to press her claims effectively. The essence of this thesis has been defended by many leaders of the coalition parties. But a minority of SPD leaders, too, has mentioned it as a logical sequel to the payment of "a reasonable price," should the latter fail to achieve results.

Finally, there was the "calculated risk" approach, which called for the employment of pressure or force to gain political advantages. Those who advocated this approach were not necessarily suggesting resort to war or military action, but usually maintained that the Soviet bluff could be called through a mere demonstration of force. Adherents of this thesis, however, have always been few in number and of limited political significance. They are usually identified with extreme right-wing parties.

These four major alternatives did not exhaust the list of suggested courses of action. Of the minor proposals, many amounted merely to supplements to or variations of these formulas. Several political leaders suggested, for instance, that the West German build-up of strength should be accompanied by systematic attempts to weaken the political, economic, and military structure of the Soviet zone by undermining the morale of the population, thus making the zone an ever-increasing liability to the U.S.S.R. Other suggestions concerned the interpretation of what constituted "a reasonable price." Some politicians proposed a token withdrawal of Allied troops to the West bank of the Rhine. Others favored a new system of security guarantees to take the place of existing arrangements and designed to afford assurances against aggression to both the Western allies and the U.S.S.R. Finally, there were a very few politicians who favored unity even at the expense of acquiescence in Soviet demands. Extremists who will pay almost any price for unity still exist and are either outright Communists or pro-Communists disguised as neutralists or nationalists.

Approaches of the Major Parties to Reunification

It is the Social Democratic opposition that has made the greatest political effort, especially during the election campaigns of 1953 and 1954, to monopolize the cause of German unity. Its program is largely a sustained attempt to achieve "unity now," if necessary at the expense of all other objectives. Inasmuch as the major alternative has been integration into the community of European nations, the stand of the opposition has often been criticized as anti-Western, neutralist, or intemperately nationalist. The charge seems paradoxical in view of the history of the SPD as a champion of international socialism, tolerance, and peace. Yet it is undeniable that SPD leaders, when addressing themselves to the problem of German unity, have frequently resorted to language the vehemence of which recalls the nationalists of the Weimar Republic.

The ardor with which SPD leaders espouse the cause of reunification is caused in part by their wish to avoid the ignominy of Weimar days, when the SPD's participation in the revolution of 1918 and its subsequent pronounced internationalism made it "the party of treason" in the eyes of its opponents. The SPD leaders, in spite of their vigorous appeal to nationalist sentiment, do not permit themselves the kind of vulgar prejudice, aggressive provocation, and active interventionism which have characterized German nationalism in the past. Thus the SPD may be said to have aided in preventing mass movements on the extreme right or the extreme left.

Notwithstanding their adamant and sometimes polemic pursuit of the unity issue, SPD leaders have always insisted that a solution can be found only through patient negotiations among the four major powers.

Their perennial criticism is that the four powers, at each of the conferences in recent years, have failed fully to exhaust the possibilities for agreement. Every concession offered by the Western side has been followed by SPD comments that it did not go far enough or that it skirted the core of the problem. SPD leaders insist that the major powers who created the problem of a divided Germany can and must settle it. Germany's role is to prod the four powers, especially the three Western allies, to resume negotiations whenever they are broken off. The logical conclusion of this argument is that Germany can do little to contribute to the problem's solution. True, the Soviet Union will have to be compensated for relinquishing the Soviet zone, but it will be the Western allies, not Germany, that will have to make the payment. The sole suggested concession from the German side has been Germany's military neutrality.

The SPD leaders, when pressed for details about the price to be paid for German unity, offer a variety of suggestions, ranging from recognition of Red China, through agreement on Korea and Indochina, to recognition of Soviet annexation of the Baltic states. Until EDC collapsed, its abandonment was the favorite *quid pro quo*. It was also suggested that the Soviet Union might be "bought off" at the Berlin Conference by an attractive offer of trade or by an outright loan. More recently, modification of the Paris Agreements has been put forward as the West's logical contribution to the bargain.

None of these "price theories" is exclusively sponsored by the SPD leadership; other party leaders favor similar or even identical approaches. But where the others suggest them in combination with some form of pressure, the majority of the SPD leaders make the payment of a price the chief, if not the exclusive, device to break the deadlock. This attitude is thoroughly in keeping with the tradition of an internationally oriented party which includes a considerable number of pacifists among its leaders and in its rank and file. But the SPD position is also strongly influenced by practical political considerations, such as the need to avoid any move that might reflect on the party's patriotism.

Critics of the SPD, in explaining the party's recent electoral defeats, have pointed out that the party leadership has repeated the error of 1918, only this time in reverse. In 1918, it is said, Social Democratic leaders misjudged the temper of the times: they anticipated a decline of nationalism and therefore went all out in promoting the cause of democracy, peace, and international co-operation. They were tragically disavowed by events. In 1945, they erred again, this time by banking on a revival of nationalism and electing to champion a "national" cause, German unity. Once again, say the critics, they were proved wrong. Either German unity was not the vote-getting issue it was expected to be, or the SPD did not succeed in persuading the voters that it was the proper trustee of that cause.

In contrast to the directness and single-mindedness of the SPD's approach to reunification, that of the coalition parties is circuitous. A prominent member of the Adenauer cabinet once asserted that he would step out of politics the following day if he did not firmly believe that reunification would come in the long run. He added emphatically that, to him, reunification ranked first among Germany's foreign policy objectives. Yet the same high official identified himself completely with the Chancellor's thesis that reunification had to be achieved "by detour," that is, through the establishment of a position of strength which, at the time the remark was made, meant the creation of EDC.

This statement is typical of the position of government and coalition party leaders. It is next to impossible to find one who will not publicly pledge his support to the cause of German unity. At the same time, most coalition leaders, being in a position of responsibility, are realistic enough to recognize the great and practical obstacles to achieving German unity, and they therefore qualify their demands for reunification. One frequent reservation is that the time is not ripe. Many leaders of the CDU, for example, expressed the belief that the Berlin Conference had been called "prematurely." They feared that overenthusiasm for quick solutions, Allied "naïveté," and French "egotism" might combine to produce an agreement at the expense of Germany which would be a major diplomatic victory for the Soviet Union. At the time of the first Geneva Conference in July, 1955, too, fear of becoming "the Western boundary of Asia's sphere of influence," as a leading Bavarian official put it, caused many middle-of-the-road politicians to oppose any short-cut solution and to give priority to the integration of the Federal Republic into a Western system of defense. A military umbrella, they argued, would afford the strength to enter negotiations with a prospect of success and to protect West Germany against the consequences of concessions unfavorable to herself.

While a majority of the coalition leaders prefer "agreement through strength," they do not exclude altogether the payment of "a reasonable price." They are unwilling to bargain away Germany's membership in WEU or NATO, but are not opposed to concessions which maintain the bargaining position of the West. The range of acceptable prices for German unity resembles that mentioned by SPD leaders: concessions by the West in Indochina or Korea, a nonaggression pact which would include Moscow, or even outright economic aid to the Soviet Union. But the coalition leaders, unlike those of the SPD, usually realize and occasionally admit that Germany herself may have to sacrifice something for the sake of national unity. Some have intimated that Germany might be forced to abandon her territorial claims East of the Oder-Neisse line, if this should prove the only effective way to reunite with the eighteen million Germans in the Soviet zone. It can not be assumed, however, that this is the attitude of the majority.

Leaders of both parties generally view the Oder-Neisse line only as a *de facto* frontier and insist that the legal and moral claim to the Eastern territories must be upheld regardless of the prospects of realization. Since both major parties include refugee elements, both must tread warily on this issue in order to avoid losing support.

The Primacy of Domestic Politics

Almost without exception, politicians have personal opinions about the major issues of German foreign policy, but they do not necessarily vote or otherwise act in accordance with their personal opinions. This self-restraint can be explained partly as the result of party discipline and partly by the fact that in West Germany, as in most democracies, domestic affairs take precedence over foreign policy matters—except in times of crisis or national danger. The politician who wishes to retain his political position looks first to the domestic preoccupations of his constituents and only later at international affairs. Giving effect to his opinions on foreign policy seems less important to him than meeting the exigencies of domestic politics. The one notable exception to this general observation is Chancellor Adenauer, who has been known to risk unpopularity at home in order to achieve his foreign policy goals.

Foreign policy usually becomes a subject for popular discussion only when it affects the life of the citizen directly. German participation in the Western alliance, for instance, means that British and U.S. military forces continue to be stationed in the Federal Republic. This is welcomed by some elements of the population, such as shopkeepers and those with tourist interests, but is intolerable to others, especially those whose property has been requisitioned for use by the foreign military units. Reunification is another matter which directly affects many people: those who want to trade with the East, those who have relatives or property interests there, and those whose national pride makes it impossible for them to regain full self-respect while Germany is divided. But even the reunification issue apparently has taken a back seat to other issues when it comes to elections. Several opposition politicians, who used reunification as their principal talking point in the 1953 elections, expressed disappointment at the relatively small popular interest that the subject aroused. In their opinion, people were more concerned with taxes, pensions, and economic policies in general. As West Germany's economic situation continues to improve and the horizons of more voters widen beyond family and community, it may be that interest in foreign policy will increase. At present, however, it continues to occupy a secondary place among the concerns of the great majority of German political party leaders.

FOUR

Political Views of the West German Civil Service

John H. Herz

The impact of the bureaucracy on the life of Germany and of the average German is perhaps greater today than at any previous time. First of all, it is the only social group that has managed to maintain its control without interruption in spite of world wars, revolutions, and changes of regime. Just as after World War I German officialdom emerged as the embodiment and last refuge of state authority after the demise of the monarchy,[1] so in the years after 1945 a basically "unreconstructed" civil service remained the only indigenous group which continued to exercise power. Then, during the most severe crisis the German people has undergone in modern times, some groups and organizations which previously had competed with the bureaucracy for influence and control, such as the Junker class and the Nazi party, simply vanished; others, like the military, disappeared at least temporarily or, like the industrialists, were for the time being gravely weakened.

On the other hand, the bureaucracy was confirmed in its traditional position of control as soon as the occupation powers established their hegemony, despite certain attempts to conduct a political purge and a technical reorganization. It continued to function without interruption on the local level and after a slight pause regionally. Bureaucrats who

EDS. NOTE.—This study is based primarily on a series of 55 interviews with representatives of various levels of the German civil service hierarchy, conducted during the summer of 1953. A full report on this research appeared as a RAND Corporation Paper (P-528-RC) on June 2, 1954. The present, briefer version includes some material as of 1955 and 1956.

The author, Professor of Government at the City College of New York, has published several books and articles on problems of German government and politics.

had formerly worked for the national agencies were soon re-employed by the German departments working under the British Military Government, and from there many were transferred to Bonn in 1949 when a West German government was inaugurated.

A second reason why the influence of the bureaucracy, traditionally large in Germany, increased still more in the postwar years was that it was made responsible for innumerable tasks of reconstruction. These ranged from the establishment of new administrations (such as those for the new *Länder*) to the integration into German society of huge numbers of expellees from Eastern Europe and East Germany, refugees from the Soviet zone, evacuees, bombed-out persons, and others. West Germany has tried to solve this problem of integration, in part, by giving almost every imaginable group some manner of legal claim against the government, and some of the dissatisfaction and unrest which might otherwise have arisen in the postwar situation was thus deflected through the creation of what has been called a "universe of claims."[2] Since the bureaucracy (which, in Germany, includes the judiciary) has been entrusted with the task of adjudicating all these claims, it has emerged as the universal arbiter. This suggests that the state may run the risk of becoming, in the words of a recent German observer and critic, a *"Gefälligkeitsstaat,"*[3] that is, a state in which government and administration function chiefly to satisfy the wishes of many specific groups and individuals, possibly by giving them preferential treatment. It is clear that these increased functions can only add further to the power of the bureaucrat in West German society.

German Officialdom and Its Ideology

In studying the political views and attitudes of the present West German bureaucracy, one has to keep in mind not only that it is a group which "governs"—and thus stands apart from the rest of German society—but also that it is numerically large enough to qualify as an important segment of the German public and thus to reflect views and attitudes characteristic of Germans at large.* The officials share with their fellow countrymen a split in fundamental value judgments, which divides Germans intellectually, politically, and even in their personal relationships, and which affects their attitudes toward many specific issues of domestic and foreign policy. This split is characterized by

* The total number of civil servants in federal, *Land*, and local government is variously estimated between one and one and one-half million, depending on whether or not certain categories (public "employees" or "workers") are included. The exclusion of the latter groups reflects the maintenance in the postwar period of the traditional caste character and caste structure of the civil service.

sharply diverging views about what happened in Germany and to Germans during the last two decades.

One group of Germans—apparently the majority—reacts to events prior to 1945 by denying, so to speak, that they ever occurred. These people have developed a mental habit of negating or repressing what they prefer not to remember. They consider that any guilt or responsibility on Germany's part is compensated for by what "the others" have done to Germany—or to Germans, or Nazis, or Nazi "followers"— since the end of the war. History, for this group, begins in 1945. It would be wrong to believe, however, that all members of this group are Nazis or are outspokenly antidemocratic. There are such elements among them, to be sure, but the observer of the present German scene is struck by their relative numerical insignificance. More frequently the typical member of this group displays an absence of political interest, or a pronounced cynicism or opportunism. He refuses to embrace any new political value-system as a substitute for a shattered old one. He continues to vote, and—as recent election figures prove—usually not for one of the ultra-rightist parties. But his political activity should not be mistaken for genuine political dedication. It is precisely the precariousness and instability of their political convictions and affiliations that characterize most of these Germans today.

The second group is made up of those for whom history begins at least as early as 1933, a relatively small minority among present-day Germans. They possess firm value-standards and have strong views on political matters. The typical member of the second group is prepared to draw moral and political conclusions from the events after 1933, even though such conclusions may involve admitting guilt or responsibility. He is ashamed of many things that did happen, though he probably was not personally involved. He opposes totalitarian systems, trends, and habits. He tends to be liberal in a broad sense, humanitarian, and frequently pacifistic. But even when he is not these, he opposes the orientation toward power and the militaristic inclinations which characterized much of German political behavior even prior to Nazism. The member of this group is not found exclusively or chiefly in any one political party, although he is more likely to be on the noncommunist left than on the right. But the group cuts through almost every political alignment. It comprises not only victims of the Nazi regime, but also many others who are motivated chiefly by religious convictions or by humanitarian and democratic political principles.

If those members or adherents of political parties who have genuine convictions—as distinguished from the larger number of more "unpolitical" party followers—are divided into the same two groups, it can probably be said that, in the SPD, not all but most belong to the second group; in the CDU, not all but many do; and in the FDP, not many but some do.

With all that separates them from the remainder of the population in other respects, German officials are divided into the same two groups. A considerable number of leading positions in the civil service and the judiciary (even larger in local and state administration than on the federal level) are held by members of the "minority" group. This is not very surprising in the light of the post-Nazi reconstruction of the civil service. Despite its ultimate failure, denazification did at first involve the replacement of top-level Nazis by anti-Nazis. For two reasons, however, these senior officials have tended to become officers without an army. First, denazification never penetrated far into the rank-and-file bureaucracy. The former lower-level officeholders—not all Nazis, to be sure, but not all confirmed democrats either—stayed on or else returned after a relatively short absence. Secondly, the anti-Nazi top officials are growing old and are in danger of dying out; and the Germans of the younger generation, from whom new appointees are recruited, have not lived through the period of German history which divided the older ones, and have not had the standards and attitudes of the "minority" transmitted to them. In spite of attempts to infuse new ideas into German education, most schools and universities communicate to young Germans the old "majority" version of history, with its prejudices, distortions, and omissions.

Consequently (and paradoxically) it is at the top level of authority that one is most likely to find officials with anti-authoritarian, and even democratic, leanings and convictions. The farther down one goes, the more likely he is to find former Nazis, occasionally unreconstructed, and traditionally authoritarian-minded members of the caste. There are, of course, members of the "minority" in the middle and lower ranks, as there are authoritarians and Nazis (ex-, neo-, or pro-) at the top. But on balance the higher officials are the more liberal. At the risk of exaggerating only a little, it may be said that today it is the police commissioner who is likely to be the humanitarian, and the district attorney the democrat.

These top officials remain divided from the majority of their colleagues, who tend to reject them as too sophisticated or opinionated, or claim that they have been appointed for political reasons and hence do not really belong to the caste of career officials. And, indeed, these top officials are often replicas of those who, in the twenties, represented "the other Germany." Sometimes they even are the same people. They represent the liberal-democratic, republican opposition to the traditions of monarchical authoritarianism. Their political convictions are frequently based on a general and idealistic personal philosophy, and are the result of a good deal of reflection.

Thus there seems to be in the offing a repetition of what happened toward the end of the Weimar period, when top civil servants, by and large loyal republicans, were deserted almost overnight by the "unpolitical" rank and file which, either enthusiastically or with equanimity, went over to the Nazis. But while Weimar democrats were surprised by developments, present-day officials seem almost morbidly aware of the situation. Some agency chiefs warned the writer that none of their subordinates, up to and including the high-ranking officials immediately under them, shared their philosophy and opinions. Others felt that they were again, as under the Nazis, in a state of "internal emigration"; that is, in political and spiritual isolation not only from subordinates but, especially in rural areas, from the bulk of the population.

It is obvious, then, that the influence of such leading officials on the rank and file and on local populations should not be overrated. It is not the top-level officials who are the opinion leaders, but rather the lower-level officials who have roots in the local community. Thus, today there is more difference than identity of view between the group of policy formulators and decision-makers on the one hand, and the opinion leaders on the other. It is easy to see how this would render the position of the former precarious, even if it were a larger and more determined group than it actually is.

But the attitudes, opinions, behavior patterns, and value judgments of the "majority" group itself exhibit significant deviations from the somewhat stereotyped image of the traditional, conservative-nationalist, authoritarian, "Prussian-type" official. This old-fashioned type is vanishing, although still found here and there. What guided him was a positive, conservative system of values and ideals. In terms of the famous German "controversy over colors" (of the flag), he stood for "black-white-red," the old imperial colors. Today, few officials even remember those colors, but nothing has replaced the ideals they represented: certainly not the red of communism or the Nazi swastika; but also not the "black-red-gold," the official flag of present-day Germany, as it was of the Weimar Republic and the revolutionaries of 1848. The typical German official no longer identifies himself with a conservative outlook, movement, or party; but neither has he acquired a new philosophy in its stead. He is neither pro-democratic nor neo-Nazi—he is not pro- or neo- anything—he merely serves whoever happens to be in charge. From a genuine "estate" that knew what it wanted politically—and knew how to get and defend it in the face of hostile parliaments, parties, or other political forces—German officialdom has turned (one might even say, degenerated) into a group of functionaries who dare not have ideas or preferences of their own. They have no ideals and, apparently tough and realistic, sober and entirely unromantic, they suspect idealism. In this respect their attitude only reflects the general climate of Germany today. People who have a *Weltanschauung* * appear to them unpractical, utopian inhabitants of a cloudland. They reject not only democratic, pacifistic, liberal, or socialist anti-Nazis, but also Nazis, in so far as the latter have professed the ideals of race, nation, community, or what not. It is often said that such Germans now reject Nazism merely because Hitler lost the war. It would be more correct to say that they do so because the aims and ideals of Nazism turned out to be unrealizable.

Such a general attitude would seem all to the good because it discourages Nazi sympathies and because it may well ensure that officials will be neutral and effective instruments of government. But an official who is "neutral" may also be unreliable. Today he serves the more or less democratic parties and the groups they represent; tomorrow he may serve others. Undiscriminating serviceability—even servility—has been a common trait of traditional German officialdom; but it has been combined with the remnants of another Prusso-German tradition—the "rule of law" symbolized by the term *Rechtsstaat*—which occasionally made itself felt even against Nazism. One has the impression now that the latter tradition is almost gone, or that if it exists it is not likely to be maintained in the face of threats to the security of the average official. Having gone through nazification and denazification, the "new official" is unwilling to take risks. He won't be caught napping again: he does as directed and avoids responsibilities; he tries to maneuver himself into a position where he can join in with the developing majority opinion.

Any ideology to which an official might pledge allegiance could endanger his job security or otherwise threaten his personal interests. So he holds himself aloof from ideologies. In this he does not seem to differ from other Germans. To the majority of German workers, for example, especially to the young ones, socialism, the creed of the older generation, has paled; it represents the "myth of the nineteenth century." Instead, they want to acquire or maintain the living standard and prestige symbolized by possession of the ubiquitous motorcycle. The typical German bureaucrat, like his fellow-Germans and possibly like the average member of any society in which the individual is a cog in the organizational machine, wants a combination, perhaps unobtainable, of personal security and personal freedom. He wants security combined

* *Weltanschauung* has no satisfactory English equivalent. It is partly rendered by "ideology" or "set of guiding principles."

with a measure of individual freedom from the restrictions imposed by the regulatory machine of which he himself is a part.

Attitudes toward the Civil Service

In the light of this new character of the German civil servant, it is hardly surprising to find that the views of the average German official toward problems of domestic policy are colored by his preoccupation with questions concerning his own profession. These questions concern for the most part material things, such as salaries, additional emoluments, pensions, and so forth. True, he still pays lip service to the ethics and ideals of his profession; he still speaks of his vocation as an avocation, of the "servant of the state's" dedication to the common weal. But his words have a hollow ring when, for example—after opposing the idea that the civil service is a mere "interest-group" like others, and after emphasizing the difference between "ordinary workers and employees" on the one hand and civil servants on the other—he complains bitterly that his income has not kept up with that of the "better classes," not even with that of better-paid workers or employees in private industry. He frequently makes invidious comparisons, not only with respect to groups other than civil servants, but also among different categories within government service itself. With specific reference to American conditions, which the average German official still sees in terms of the "spoils system," he insists that his position is not a mere "job," but in spite of his rationalizations one finds that he is hardly less concerned with job security and all it entails than is his American colleague whom he considers a "jobholder." *

As a representative of the state, the German official used to view members of other social strata as people entrusted to his care. Now, in accordance with his new preoccupation with material things, they appear to him primarily as competitors in the general race for improved living conditions. He senses that the bureaucracy's former prestige has suffered somewhat in the eyes of the average German. But he rarely attributes this to the transformation of the bureaucracy into a group of functionaries. He prefers to see the cause in outward changes of income levels, relative losses which, so he claims, render the official unable to compete on an equal footing with members of other groups within what he considers his own social stratum. A local judge, or a *Landrat*

* Stung by such criticism, the *Deutsche Beamtenwarte,* official mouthpiece of a powerful civil service interest-group, explained: "When a worker fights for old-age insurance, he does so in his own or his family's interest; when the official defends the maintenance of his pension system, he thinks less of himself . . . than of maintaining the stability of government." (December, 1954)

("county executive official"), contends the modern bureaucrat, can no longer afford to maintain social contact with wealthier people, and these officials are thus no longer an elite group in the eyes of the people at large. If one remembers, however, that the income level of German officials has always been relatively low and that this has not affected their social prestige in the past, the present official's interpretation is probably incorrect. Nevertheless, this interpretation enables him to demand better emoluments to make up for lessened prestige.

The bureaucrat's increased concern with his security and his status in a competitive society is also reflected in the heightened importance he attaches to having his interests represented. As was already the case in Weimar times, not even the lower ranks of the bureaucracy feel very much affinity for the organizations and interests of other employee groups. Most officials who belong to any vocational organization at all join their own, the German Civil Servants Association (*Deutscher Beamtenbund*), rather than the trade-union-affiliated Union of Public Service Employees. The latter has attracted civil servants with non-professional jobs, for instance, postal and railway officials; and also a few who joined for opportunistic reasons—because their superiors happened to be Social Democrats, for example, or because they needed certificates of denazification. The *Beamtenbund* stands for, and voices, the views and prejudices of the caste. It rejects trade-union affiliation as "political" and, officially, maintains a nonpolitical (*überparteilich*) attitude. Nevertheless, by a variety of devices, such as the selection and emphasis of certain information in its journal, the *Deutsche Beamtenwarte,* the *Beamtenbund* usually makes it quite clear to its members which trends, parties, or deputies it favors.

Through its organization the bureaucracy is also amply represented in the federal parliament as well as in the *Land* diets. As under Weimar,[4] the *Beamtenbund* sees to it that its members are elected to these bodies on almost every party ticket, so that it is in a position to bring pressure to bear whenever specific interests of the group are affected. In such cases, the cry is: "Officials of all parties, unite! You have your salary claims to lose." But it is not only in connection with questions directly concerning salaries that the pressure is effective; it is also exercised in respect to more general questions which affect the official caste indirectly.*

The civil servant's present discontent does not extend, however, to the manner in which the civil service was restored and organized after the

* A recent illustration is offered by the debate on and enactment of a law governing the representation of employee interests in the federal agencies, where the *Beamtenbund* defeated attempts to conjoin officials with other public employees and have both represented by a single group in each agency.

war. On the contrary, there is general and sometimes gloating satisfaction with the restoration of the traditional professional civil service, which implies constitutional protection of the "vested rights" of officials (as under Weimar), and includes the other principal features of erstwhile German officialdom. None of the reforms dear to the hearts of the Western allies, and particularly the Americans, have been adopted by the Germans, even though the letter of the law pays lip service to a few of them. The German official is conscious of this, and he considers it a victory for a system in which he believes deeply, and which was temporarily threatened by demands arising from the "misled reforming zeal" of outsiders who did not understand or appreciate the merits of the German system. With the exception of the democratically inclined minority group, which favors liberal reforms even though they might affect vested interests of the caste, almost every official believes that what is referred to as the American policy of remaking the service in the American image was mistaken. They contend that this would have substituted a "political" service of inexpert job-hunters for the high standards of expert, professional officials.

This attitude is reflected in the position most officials take on the question of *"Aussenseiter"* (literally, "outsiders"), that is, on admission to the service of qualified persons who have not gone through the various stages of preparing for the career service and who have not achieved their positions through promotion from lower levels. It is hardly admitted that there can be such persons. Anybody from the outside can not, by definition, be qualified. There is general satisfaction with the fact that today there are fewer *Aussenseiter* in the service than ever before. Those that remain are ostracized as "1945'ers," that is, as persons who obtained their positions for political reasons in a time of defeat. Most of those who were chosen to replace Nazis in the civil service after the war had been former officials with all the civil service qualifications. However, a few did come to the service from the outside, for example, some trade-union functionaries and practicing lawyers, and a few of these inevitably proved to be unqualified or even corrupt. These exceptions are now cited as proof that the principle of hiring outsiders was itself unsound.

Another example of opposition to civil service reform is resistance to any attempt to break the hold which legal training has traditionally had over the entire service. Civil servants without legal training are considered amateurish, especially since the law has grown so complicated that even officials trained in it have a hard time understanding and applying it correctly. While such an attitude may be justified in the case of officials whose chief function is to administer laws, it ignores others who might benefit from a change of emphasis to training in public administration, public finance, or similar fields of social and political science. The universities are still organized as of old, and the political science departments which have cropped up here and there can not yet confer degrees which lead to admission to public service.

What has been called, since 1945, "restoration of the civil service" involves not only principles and structure but also personnel. Except for the younger new appointees, today's service is made up largely of pre-1945 officials. Restoration of the civil service has meant restoration of the service that existed under the Nazis, except for those few in certain leading positions who derive from the Weimar service. Though as we have indicated, this situation does not in itself imply "renazification," even some German officials are not so sure that it does not entail serious political dangers, especially in connection with another "number" group, the so-called "131'ers." This group includes both expellee officials from the East and officials dismissed or suspended after 1945 for Nazi connections or activities.* A federal law of May, 1951, based on Article 131 of the Bonn constitution, gave members of this group a legal right to reinstatement, regardless of their former position or activities under the Nazis. Only former Gestapo officials were still barred. Many officials who were never Nazis themselves feel that these "131'ers" are "career brethren" who do not constitute a political danger any more. Most of the latter, it has been said, were small fry who had joined the Nazis under pressure or for opportunistic reasons, and even those who formerly had been active were now unpolitical.**

In fact, it is the rare official today who voices Nazi views openly. Even among "131'ers" it is difficult to find anyone who admits that he ever was really connected with Nazism. In general, those who have been reinstated seem to have no major complaint against the present regime; in this sense it may be said that they are satisfied. After all, the new regime did treat them leniently. But this is far from a positive commitment, and to some officials, at least, it seems dangerous to have uncommitted former Nazis in policy-making positions, such as the Foreign Office, or to use them as instructors of German youth. Even those who play down this danger admit that the "131'ers" form cliques and try to promote them-

* Mixing these two categories, expellees and "politicals," itself created a condition widely exploited in order to obfuscate the political problem involved.

** The same caste spirit was reflected in the somewhat violent reaction of officials to a decision in 1953 by the Federal Constitutional Court, which declared that all employment relations of German officials had ended with the demise of the Nazi system, and that consequently all their rights and privileges had, in principle, been terminated by the same event. The decision implied that the civil service had lost its identity while serving the Nazi regime. German officials, it appears, resented the decision both as a reflection on their caste and as a threat to their status and vested interests.

selves and their comrades, meanwhile maligning those officials, such as the "1945'ers," who did not have to undergo "sacrifices" but "profited" by the temporary absence of the regular civil servants.

Some of the officials who had temporarily been removed for Nazi activities have not stopped at organizing themselves as "victims of denazification," demanding indemnification for "illegal detention," and trying to further their own interests by pressure-group activities. More ominous is the pressure they occasionally exercise on official policy. For example, when those in high positions mix into cases which they regard as having political implications—such as the prosecution of Nazi criminals—and thus try to intimidate the officials in charge, this intervention tends to undo the work which democratic officials still attempt to perform here and there.

In regard to recruitment problems it is difficult to obtain a balanced picture, especially in the elusive matter of motivations. The imperial service was characterized by the strongly conservative bias which governed the selection of candidates for leading positions; political and social influence were decisive in matters of promotion. Under Weimar there was added the influence of party affiliation wherever political parties were entrenched in certain ministries and branches of administration. Still, all in all, qualification played a decisive role in the general make-up of the service. When, under Nazism, political reliability became *the* overriding consideration, this antagonized an otherwise co-operative bureaucracy, and with the downfall of the regime there was thus a strong demand for return to previous standards of expert qualification. But restoration of the professional civil service, and the victory it implied for the idea of a "nonpolitical" career, did not mean that political or similar considerations ceased to play a role. Many officials contend that such considerations now play a bigger role than ever.

Thus German officials freely grant that political parties, and pressure-groups in or behind them, have a lot to do with appointments and even more with promotions. This is regretted not only by the adherents of the idea of a "nonpolitical" service but also by many among the "political" minority, who realize that most civil servants join a party out of pure opportunism. Some even change their affiliation with every change in the political coloration of the government or of the ministry in which they are employed. Others become entirely dependent on parties or interest-groups. This, in turn, strengthens the authoritarian and antidemocratic inclinations of the officials who consider themselves "nonpolitical," and who tend to identify party patronage with democracy. As a result, the present German bureaucracy tends on the one hand to emphasize that it is an independent caste and on the other to reflect the interests and desires of those to whom officeholders owe their positions or from whom they expect advancement.

Social connections also play a role in the recruitment and advancement of the civil servant. It is generally admitted that the reappearance of student fraternities of the traditional German "corps" type—promoting exclusiveness, snobbery, and political ultranationalism—was due to the initiative and interests less of the students themselves than of ex-members and alumni—the *Altherren*—who made it clear to all concerned that joining fraternities was the way to get on in life. Advancement due to such social connections seems, however, to prevail in industry and similar fields more than in government and administration, at least as far as the Protestant, dueling type of fraternity is concerned. The influence of the Catholic, non-dueling fraternities, on the other hand, is strong among government officials. This, in conjunction with the dominant position the CDU holds in many branches of government and administration, seems to indicate that the decisive influences among bureaucrats today are less those that spring from a conservative social milieu than those of a political or religious nature.

Attitudes toward Law and Justice

The average official's preoccupation with immediate personal concerns results in lack of interest in and information about anything beyond the narrow sphere of his professional activity. He frequently is unaware of the most elementary facts about government and politics. Indifference and, sometimes, an arrogant unwillingness to become concerned with political matters have long been traits of German officials, but their new "functionalism" seems to be yet another factor which accounts for their limited intellectual interests. Some of the officials who have more interest in politics insist that, even when given an easy chance to instruct himself, the average bureaucrat fails to make use of it. Those in charge of training young officials complain about the trainees' preoccupation with their narrow fields of specialization. They will not waste their time on things they consider impractical. Thus the citizen vanishes and the expert functionary emerges.

It is only where the organization and functions of the administration or judiciary are affected that one encounters more widespread interest in current issues. But even here a majority tends to be concerned with preserving "efficiency" rather than with any other goal or value. Conceptions of the rule of law such as that contained in the term *Rechtsstaat*, with which many an old official, otherwise authoritarian, used to be imbued, seem to have little impact today. This is apparent from the grumbling one hears about the restoration of an elaborate system of administrative jurisdiction and administrative courts where, as before Nazism, the citizen can sue the government if injured by official action. This, bureaucrats affirm, constitutes exaggerated liberalism and leads to "claim-happiness" (*Rechthaberei*) on the part of the man in the street.

Even more distrust is noticeable in reactions to a conspicuous innovation in German government, namely, the power of the constitutional courts to practice judicial review on the *Land* and federal levels. The Federal Constitutional Court, especially, has made vigorous use of its rather broadly defined jurisdiction. To many German officials these powers seem to interfere with efficient government. As one member of a local administration put it: "No sooner have they established a stable system of government than they create procedures for opposition, wrangling, and delay." Frequently objections are based on the allegedly alien origin of the innovation; it is construed as something imposed on Germans by Americans. Criticism of the Federal Constitutional Court is particularly strong among the ministerial bureaucracy. Some officials in the Bonn government departments are inclined to perceive in the Karlsruhe tribunal a "personal enemy" who, as one of them phrased it, "tries to set himself up as a third branch of the legislature next to Bundestag and Bundesrat." Their ire is to some extent understandable if one remembers the established German habit of having most legislative bills drafted in the ministries. Drafting officials claim that they no longer have means of knowing which bills, after they have passed the legislature and become statutes, will be found constitutionally valid and which not, especially since, according to them, the court tends to extend its jurisdiction to what they call "political questions."

The relatively minor role played by the concept of law is further revealed in connection with Nazi criminality, a problem that affects officials specifically concerned with the administration of justice. What to do about crimes committed by Germans under the Nazi regime has come to constitute the very touchstone for the German people's attitude toward its recent past. It has been pointed out above that in this as in other connections Germans are split into two camps: the relatively few who accept the problem and its challenge and try somehow to come to grips with it; and the majority who forget and repress if they do not apologize and excuse. The bureaucracy does not deviate significantly from this over-all picture. Since most of the present officeholders served the Nazi regime in one or another capacity, they apparently feel that they have to defend themselves and their own conduct by denying the necessity of punishing Nazi criminals. The failure of Nuremberg and the other Allied war crimes trials in their effect on the German people is nowhere more apparent than in the fact that the very term "war crime" (always used in quotation marks) has become synonymous with unfairness and miscarriage of justice, and "war criminal" with "victim of enemy revenge."

The Allies' attempt to distinguish between mere political error in siding with the Nazis, on the one hand, and commission of actual crimes, on the other, is dismissed or forgotten even among legally trained officials. Nazi or war criminals are thereby put into the same class to which most officials vaguely feel that they themselves belong, namely, the class of those who more or less actively supported the regime and its policies. As one official (not a Nazi) put it, almost everybody has succeeded in working out his own, personal philosophy of exculpation, so that even those who were formerly fervent Nazis are now convinced that they never were. They therefore readily believe that others were no different, and are genuinely surprised if one tells them that Nazi generals, for instance, were not tried and sentenced merely because they were generals, but that in each case they were indicted for specific crimes.

Even when this distinction is explained to them, most officials still try to evade the issue. "Why insist on stirring up the past?" they ask. Since any crime Germans may have committed can be considered as having been compensated for by corresponding crimes on the part of their enemies, they say, one should let the dead bury the dead and be ready to forgive and forget. One should now concentrate on the common job facing Germans and their former Western enemies alike. Nazism, after all, was only a "weak replica" of something more terrible: communism.

If this is the prevalent attitude among legally trained officials, one should not be surprised to find that they view indulgently the reluctance of *German* authorities to prosecute Nazi crimes. Courts, as one judge said, occasionally still have to take up the case of some member of the Nazi elite guard (SS) or storm troops (SA)—usually after the press has built up the case—but they do so reluctantly. The few prosecutors who still strongly believe in seeing that justice is done admit that it is almost impossible to get such cases prepared; legal niceties and other obstructions continually slow them down. On the other hand, where communists are charged with analogous crimes, such as the maltreatment of their fellow countrymen in Russian camps, the cases are processed in no time. In those rare instances where a Nazi crime eventually gets to trial, convictions are hard to obtain. There is no more forceful evidence of the weakness among German officials of the concept of equal justice under law than this refusal on the part of the very practitioners of the law to apply it to Nazi criminality, and the strange arguments proffered as pretexts for inaction. It is illustrative of a broad tendency among officials to display a "pro-rightist" and "anti-leftist" bias whenever a case occurs in which there are political implications, while avoiding any explicit and general commitment to a particular political philosophy. Communists and Nazis, in particular, are weighed with a different measure. As one official (who himself opposed such bias) put it: "If a Communist does something like attacking an opponent in a street brawl, it is 'sadistic terror' to the police, to the courts, and to public opinion as voiced in the press; if it is done by a rightist radical it is pardonable and pardoned." This is the same bias that characterized much of Weimar administration and adjudication.[5]

Attitudes toward Government and Internal Policies

With regard to more general problems of government and politics, one encounters much less pronounced and generally rather moderate views and attitudes. Indeed, when asked about their views on the constitutional structure of the Bonn regime and its governmental and political processes, most officials show surprise at being asked such uncontroversial questions: "Why, there is hardly any problem here. There is nothing wrong with the new government; it works as well as can be expected under the circumstances, doesn't it?"

The absence of any degree of marked hostility, criticism, or emotionalism is striking, particularly if one recalls how much controversy and argument pro and con prevailed in Weimar times. During that period officials commonly felt pronounced hostility not only toward specific features of the Weimar constitution but also toward the entire political structure of constitutional democracy. These attitudes reflected the existence, at that time, of strong opposition forces on both the left and the right, the latter being in a position to exert greater influence on the bureaucracy. Today such forces are insignificant.

Present-day bureaucracy no longer shows a tendency to develop its own political standards independently of the prevailing general climate of opinion; rather, it accommodates itself to the existing conditions. That this tendency does not imply any great degree of stable conviction or permanent commitment has already been stressed. Certainly it would not seem to exclude a general shift of standards and views toward a new rightist authoritarianism if political forces and parties of this stripe should ever increase in strength or assume power. But for the time being the bureaucracy tends to bolster the present regime and type of government, both of which are taken for granted as given factors, as it were, and whose orders and directives are, therefore, executed without much questioning—again in sharp contrast to the Weimar situation.

Whether in the case of a general shift toward the extreme left the bureaucracy would accommodate itself as easily, it is more difficult to say. Although the emotional reaction of the average German to communism is less pronounced than that of the average American, his knowledge of what communism stands for is better, and his rejection consequently at least as strong. Among officials—certainly those in the middle and higher brackets—there are no longer any Communists (if ever there were) and few, if any, fellow-travelers; and most officials would find it hard to conceive that they might embrace communism under any circumstances. However, in case of an actual assumption of power on the part of a Communist or communist-controlled regime, it is less hard to visualize that many German officials, concerned as they are with job security, might serve even communist masters, as they served the Nazis, if permitted to do so by their new masters.

The specific aspect of the Bonn regime which is most frequently acclaimed is the stability of the new government. This refers, of course, to executive stability, to the fact that the Bonn constitution has made it possible for one Chancellor, and practically the same cabinet, to stay in office since the inception of the new federal regime. This is contrasted with the "destructive," i.e., unstable, Weimar system, as well as with the traditional French condition. Stability implies efficiency, and this seems to be the major reason why members of the bureaucracy approve of the system. It gives them a feeling of being part of a machine which, undisturbed by partisan or similar interference, is permitted to work under the control of experts. There is hardly any apprehension that absence of such interference might also mean absence of controls, particularly democratic controls.

Fear of a new authoritarianism, owing to the strong position of the Chancellor in the structure of the new setup, is voiced occasionally, but chiefly in a personal connection, namely, in regard to Adenauer's own, well-known authoritarian habits, concerning which stories, probably apocryphal, are always being bandied about. One such story, for instance, concerns a CDU member of the Bonn diet, known as a strong backer of Adenauer. Asked whether he ever disagreed with the Chancellor's views, he replied: "When he is not present, sometimes; when he is there, never!" There is also one dealing with the way in which, prior to his chancellorship, Adenauer attained the chairmanship of the CDU. According to this account there was a meeting of regional party delegates who were supposed to elect the chairman from their midst. When they convened, the chair at the head of the table, which was reserved for the chairman-elect, at first remained unoccupied; then Adenauer, who was one of the delegates, entered and sat down in the chair. That settled it; there was no vote. In such stories, however, there is little hostile criticism; rather, there is admiration for the man who knows how to rule. It may be that there is some resentment at the very top level of the Chancellor's colleagues in the cabinet; it is hardly noticeable below that level.

Objections to the present system most frequently are centered on three aspects of it: the federal structure of the West German government; the election system; and the role of parties and parliament. The most outspoken and most general criticism concerns Germany's federal structure, and in particular the allegedly too broad powers and jurisdictions of the *Länder,* as well as their general geographical structure. It is perhaps not remarkable that the federal bureaucracy objects to the power of the *Länder* and their alleged intrusion into the field of federal administration, since this might appear as a matter of one vested interest defending itself against another. More significant is the fact that, with the one exception of Bavaria, there are hardly even any *Land* officials who would rise in defense of *Land* interests.

The two most frequently heard objections to the *Länder* are that their governments are top-heavy and that they are artificial creations. To many officials there appears to be a cumbersome and unwieldy organization at the top level of the *Länder.* They point out that formerly a handful of Prussian officials on the middle level of administration would manage a province; now, hundreds or thousands of *Land* officials man the ministries and other departments of a corresponding *Land.* Second, objection is raised to the artificial or synthetic character of the *Länder* as units, which, with the exception of Bavaria, have no roots in preceding political units and are frequently the chance result of the drawing of zonal lines by the occupation powers. Many of the resulting units are economically and otherwise too small to be viable. What officials regret above all is the lack of "large space" (*Grossräumigkeit*). This lack confines officials to action in a small and somewhat petty sphere and offers them little variety. Thus, most officials are in favor of strengthening the jurisdiction of the central government and of reforming the *Länder* in such a manner as to create a more streamlined system of fewer, larger states. Their criticism of the present federal system reflects the degree to which the hold of localism or regionalism has diminished even in the case of the very administrators of the local and regional units. It also illustrates the general tendency toward efficiency and streamlining, which in this instance means toward centralism.

On the other hand, some parties and officials affiliated with them may defend the *Länder* against the growing centralism. In doing so they show political realism, since the source of their own power and influence lies in certain *Länder* rather than at Bonn. The SPD is a case in point. Such a defense rarely signifies a real attachment to the federal principle. By the same token, the "unpolitical" (and usually antisocialist) officials object all the more strenuously to the present *Länder* system. They assert that it merely provides certain political parties with positions from which to fight their opponents, especially those at Bonn.

Similar reasoning can be found behind objections to another feature of the present governmental system, namely, the prevailing electoral law, even though interest in this problem is less pronounced than that in federalism. When interest is shown, however, the general attitude is one of criticism of what still is, in essence, a system of proportional representation. In the case of the politically interested and politically affiliated officials it is true that attitudes may vary, depending on their over-all philosophy or, more often, on whether in their view one or the other election system offers advantages to the party of their choice. Most other officials, however, favor the single-member-district system, for the simple reason that this system would tend to reduce the influence of the political parties on the executive branch, while proportional representation favors party bureaucracies and strengthens their hold on government, including their ability to dispense job patronage.

By the same token, with the exception of a democratic minority of officials who recognize that institutions and parties representing the various groupings and views within the public are needed in a democracy, most bureaucrats still adhere to a deeply ingrained German skepticism toward popular participation in government. Few of them oppose democracy outright, but they use the term "democracy" itself in an almost pejorative connotation. For example, "Western democracy" is blamed for almost anything that goes wrong or works badly, from party rivalries to traffic congestion. Furthermore, officials do not like those institutions and processes of democracy which are meant to ensure popular sovereignty, control, or consent. Parties and parliaments are still considered "elements of disintegration." Their positive role in a democracy is not appreciated. Their existence seems to involve a threat that outside forces may intrude upon executive affairs; that "inexpert talkers" may hamper the work of the experts.

Attitudes toward democratic institutions, however, are more mixed and varied than would appear from what has been said so far. In accordance with the ambivalent feelings of the present service toward politics most officials are critical of the influence of parties over appointments and promotions, or oppose the intrusion of parliament into administrative affairs, while at the same time they are not at all averse to joining these very parties in order to improve their professional chances; and they generally favor the election of officials to parliament so that officialdom will be strongly represented there. On the one hand, they voice apprehension lest officials who owe their position to the influence of parties, trade-unions, or churches become representatives of the interests of these groups. On the other hand, they are strongly in favor of acting as a pressure-group themselves in competition with the other social and occupational interests represented in parties and parliaments. There is now an additional reason for their desire to be represented and to exercise influence in all (or most) existing parties; namely, the absence of any one party which represents the particular material and prestige interests of the bureaucracy, as the Conservatives did in former times. Thus the civil servants, like many other groups in German society, are skeptical of democratic institutions in principle, while they utilize them fully where they promise to yield material benefit or political advantage.

In their attitudes toward economic and social problems and social groups outside their own, most officials betray what may be called typical middle-class biases. In this they are true representatives of the society they serve; West Germany, as it has now emerged, is neither proletarian nor in any way anti-bourgeois—not even in the feeble manner of Nazism. But West German society is decidedly *upper* middle class in regard to policies, people in control, and general atmosphere. Some officials, especially in the top ranks, share upper-middle-class attitudes; but since most officials do not belong to the higher-income groups and at present are particularly worried about their income and living standards, they tend to conform to lower-middle-class standards and views. They envy better-paid employees and workers; they emphasize that Germany after defeat can not afford too costly social welfare benefits; they indict the "power claims" of the trade-unions and in general draw a clear line between themselves and "mere jobholders." They stress the necessity of always distinguishing very clearly between "mere employees" who have "jobs," and "servants of the state" with their "calling"; even the idea of receiving bonuses, although recognized as beneficial in the material sense, was rejected because it tended to confuse the materialistic "wage," which the nonofficial gets, with the official's "salary."

Though the average official thus tries to draw a clear line between himself and the groups he considers as belonging to the proletariat, he is by no means always friendly to the businessman's cause. He often voices surprisingly sharp criticism of the present government's economic policy of *laissez faire,* and is afraid that the present boom, with its conspicuous expenditure and show of luxury, may turn out to be artificial and impermanent. There is much invidious comparison between the lot of an official and that of those who live "conspicuously": industrialists, small independents, and all those who have expense accounts.

And in view of the twenty years of continued farm prosperity uninterrupted by war and postwar conditions, and since protectionist policies have kept food prices high, "greedy" farmers come in for heavy criticism. Officials here react as urban consumers. They complain about the farmers' strength as a pressure-group and favor a common European market for farm products; this "would serve the peasants right and egg prices would be lower."

But there are also groups in relation to which the official still views himself as a protective administrator. They comprise the numerous elements for which the bureaucracy not only had to settle claims but had to provide shelter and food, clothing and jobs: the expellees and refugees, the victims of bombings and air raid evacuations, those who lost through currency reform, and so on. Officials take a considerable pride in the orderly and efficient manner in which they have solved these problems. The unbiased observer will admit that their pride is well founded.

Foreign Policy and the Official

German views on foreign policies can hardly be separated from attitudes toward domestic problems. The division of Germany lends the problem of reunification and all that is related to it a character which is at once international and internal. Other foreign policy problems, such as Germany's integration with a Western defense system, at once raise domestic issues, such as that of German rearmament.

For a variety of reasons, opinions voiced by German officials on these foreign policy questions and their domestic aspects can not be taken at their face value. The officials tend to be unfamiliar with some of the basic facts and are disinclined to voice outspoken views regarding a field in which the average official feels he is a layman. He expects to be asked questions about his own field, where he considers himself an expert, and thinks that foreign affairs should likewise be left to the appropriate experts, that is, the diplomats. One often receives such responses as: "This matter should be taken up with the competent foreign ministry officials." To the extent that views and opinions are voiced, they rarely give the impression of being the result of thorough reflection; answers often seem to be formed and formulated on the spur of the moment; they are vague, vacillating, or inconsistent. The stability of these attitudes may therefore be questioned. More critically inclined officials complain about the cloudy and variable nature of the opinions of their colleagues, who are apt, so these critical officials declare, to voice internationalist or supranationalist views today and ultranationalistic ones tomorrow, and who are pacifists of the "count-me-out" variety in one connection and militarists in another.

Such views as the average official has on foreign policy often seem derived, almost automatically, from the official's general party affiliation which, in turn, is usually determined by his private interests and the domestic program of the party in question, rather than by its foreign policy platform. A Catholic official, for instance, backing the CDU, also usually backs Adenauer's foreign line without much further thought. An official who favors the SPD usually opposes Adenauer's foreign policy as a matter of course. Incidentally, one finds an almost naïve overestimation of the importance of the "German question" in world affairs. Germany is believed to be the center of world politics, and very little interest is shown in any other world problem; the Near East is as far away as the Far East, not to mention problems of world organization and the United Nations. Though public opinion in all countries tends to be provincial, German self-centeredness seems to be above the average.

In so far as there *is* discussion and interest, it centers around the problem of Germany's "orientation"; that is, whether Western orientation in the comprehensive sense of Adenauer's policy, or a pro-Western policy without military ties, or demilitarization, or full-fledged neutralism is desirable. But, for the reasons just indicated, it is perhaps less important to analyze the details of the views expressed on this subject than to probe into the more basic approaches to international politics which they reveal, or conceal.

One of the more important impressions one gains from the study of officials' reactions to questions of foreign policy is that they depend, fundamentally, on whether the official belongs to the "majority" or the "minority" group referred to above. Thus those who adopt a certain orientation may do so on the basis of either one of two fundamentally different basic attitudes. If we take neutralism for an example, although the genuine neutralist is the exception among German officials today, we find that he and his fellows may differ fundamentally in their basic approaches.

One group of neutralists includes those whose values, from the point of view of liberal democracy, are the most desirable. These neutralists are impressed with the diabolic nature of totalitarianism, and are therefore unequivocally opposed to communism. This, rather than nationalism, seems to explain their desire to see the East zone liberated as soon as possible from its present communist control and reunited with the West. Rightly or wrongly, they believe that neutralization of Germany represents the only way of achieving liberation. They therefore advocate that the West renounce the policy of integration of Germany with the Western world in return for the Soviets' release of their zone. According to these neutralists, this course also offers the only chance of escaping war, not only for Germans, for whom such a war would be fratricidal and suicidal, but also for the world, because a neutralized Germany would serve as a buffer in a most sensitive area of world tension, and thus keep East and West apart. However impractical this approach may be, neutralists of this type undoubtedly are motivated by anti-totalitarianism, patriotism (as distinguished from selfish nationalism), and an abhorrence of war. These attitudes go hand in hand with antimilitarism and apprehension that Western integration, coupled with remilitarization, would lead to a revival of the authoritarian and un-democratic spirit of the past.

The idealistic nature of this approach contrasts with a widespread indifference in West Germany toward the East zone and toward re-unification. True, almost every West German official is for unification, as he is against sin. But some are so in a rather lukewarm fashion. Reunification, they fear, might create serious economic problems; it might even necessitate sacrificing present West German living standards in order to help the run-down East to its feet again. While West Germany prospers under the present setup, reunification might involve God knows what political and economic complications. By contrast the neutralist official impresses one as the keeper of the German conscience.

There is another type of neutralist, however, whose motives are of a different sort. He thinks of himself as a political realist and is interested in questions of power. For him a lineup with the West means that Germans would be asked to fight it out with the Russians at the front line, while Frenchmen would defect to the enemy or run away and Americans would quickly evacuate their troops and leave Europe to its fate. Why should Germans sacrifice themselves for others, especially for those who, since they destroyed Germany—the only bulwark against communism in Europe—are the ones really responsible for the present plight of the world? Members of this group believe that a policy of neutralism might not only enable Germany to escape fighting, but might also place her in a position to play an independent and powerful role again at some future time. Neutralists of this kind are less concerned about the fate of the East zone under totalitarian control; they are motivated not so much by antimilitarism or genuine patriotism as by nationalism of the traditional kind, which includes the belief that Germany is superior to other nations and should therefore again assume a leading, if not a predominant, position in world affairs.[6]

Similarly, those officials who favor a Western orientation for Germany may likewise be motivated by opposite considerations. There are those who feel that Germany owes a debt to the world, who, in contrast to the second type of neutralist discussed above, realize that it was Hitler and not "the others in 1945" whose policies opened the way for Soviet expansion into Central Europe. They believe that the Germans should now make up for this historic guilt by contributing their share to the defense of the world against the Soviet danger, even though this might entail the destruction of Germany in a new war, or, on a lesser level, at the risk that remilitarization might endanger the frail new German democracy. Thus this group favors German rearmament not for reasons of nationalism or militarism, but rather because of a feeling of responsibility in a common cause.

But the same outward Western orientation may be motivated by a quite different set of attitudes. Western orientation promises a revival of German political influence and German military might. Germany may thus hope to take its "rightful place" among the powers again. Conceivably, such a policy might lead to German hegemony in Europe West of the Iron Curtain, and eventually to reconquest of the lost territories in the East. This attitude, it is true, does not seem to be as popular among officials as among the population at large. Nevertheless, one can distinguish it in those officials who argue as follows:

1. The other powers are responsible for Germany's present plight. Reason: In 1945 America had a chance to solve the Russian problem by joining forces with Germans to defeat the Russians. This chance was lost, either out of pure negligence or because of a desire to destroy Germany. The Western powers even permitted the Soviet armies to penetrate into the heart of Germany by withdrawing from areas they had occupied first. There then followed a policy of oppression of Germany in pursuance of the Morgenthau Plan and the Potsdam decisions. No mention is made in this argument of a German share in responsibility for the situation of 1945 and after. On the contrary: "One cannot treat a civilized nation (*Kulturvolk*) like the Germans the way one treats Russians."

2. Therefore it is up to the United States, in particular, to solve problems of its own making. It should do this in a way which takes the interests of Germany into account and should make no arrangement at Germany's expense.

3. Since Americans, in contrast to their earlier postwar attitude, now

see the light and realize their responsibility, Germans are ready to forgive and forget, and co-operate in the common struggle. This does not mean, however, that essential German interests may be neglected.

In this connection, there is frequent reference to economic problems, such as the high costs of rearmament in relation to the present living standard of Germans. Germans, so it is claimed, have every right to insist on safeguarding these interests, for—and this is a widespread general belief—America today needs Germany more than Germany needs America.

Rearmament, Nationalism, and Power Politics

Within the larger problem of foreign relations in general, the particular issue of German rearmament usually elicits the greatest interest, straddling as it does the great domestic and foreign policy questions. Except for the out-and-out pacifist group, which includes some but not all of the neutralists and which rejects any kind of German remilitarization, there usually is agreement as to the necessity, if not desirability, of having some kind and measure of rearmament. But many officials are aware of the dangers that remilitarization entails from the standpoint of German democracy and peaceful development of international relations. The dilemma, according to one official, is that the widespread hatred of militarism and war is a matter for rejoicing as far as internal policies are concerned, but it is an obstacle to necessary foreign policies. Similarly, advocacy of rearmament is correct in foreign affairs, but it is dangerous because of its implications for domestic politics.

Because of this possible effect on the domestic scene even those who follow the Adenauer line often do so with misgivings. They express the fear that the training of new recruits will have to be entrusted to older officers who have militaristic and authoritarian inclinations, or even to those who became officers under the Nazis and who might "nazify" the trainees. Though civilian control of army and rearmament may be maintained and may lie in the hands of reliable democrats, these officials are afraid of a repetition of what happened under Weimar, when the generals in practice became independent of civilian control. They are also generally skeptical about the prospects of a more democratic spirit within the armed forces and assert that a few cases of insubordination might well serve as a pretext for demanding that "unduly soft" regulations be replaced by the discipline of former times. Many officials believe that the militaristic leanings of the German people, at present concealed behind an antiwar attitude, would quickly reassert themselves were Germans again given the chance to experience uniforms, parades, and martial music.

Not all members of the German bureaucracy, of course, take this anti-militaristic line. In accordance with the distinction in basic approaches pointed out above, there are those who stand for quick and comprehensive rearmament regardless of, or perhaps because of, its possible political consequences. Some believe that rearmament involves the risk of an early war, but believe this to be inevitable anyway. The majority concede the necessity of rearmament with reluctance, however, and many of them voice the hope that the actual process of remilitarization may be delayed or slowed down as much as possible.

This attitude on the part of a majority of officials contrasts strangely with the attitude one might have expected in view of their basic values and approaches. It would appear to be more consistent with the values of the group which we have called the democratic minority. It also contrasts sharply with past German attitudes and appears all the more unusual because of the absence, in the domestic sphere, of democratic commitments and leanings among the majority of officials. It might almost appear as if Germans had turned from worshipers of power politics and expansion into pacifists. For, even beyond the problem of rearmament, the older and seemingly so deep-rooted German nationalism seems to have vanished in so far as it was aggressive, expansionist, and intent on dominating others. One is struck by the almost complete absence of the typical Nazi ideas on race; these, like other more general Nazi ideologies, are frequently ridiculed, and militant nationalism, if not ridiculed, is rejected rather vehemently. If this were the attitude only of that minority group of officials who consciously embrace anti-Nazism and democratic values, it would not be surprising. What is surprising is that it extends to large segments of the "unpolitical" majority of civil servants as well. There is general insistence that war is discredited; that Germans have had their fill of adventurist foreign policies which might lead to war.

How can this new approach be explained? Can we conclude that the German people have at last been healed of nationalism, or at least nationalism in the extreme sense? There are some reasons for skepticism, or at least caution. It should be noted that the views described are those of officialdom, and although many officials claim that they share these views with most Germans, it would be unsafe to accept the claim too readily. For the rejection of militant nationalism is first and foremost the characteristic of a specific group. Civil servants, in contrast to other social groups in Germany which customarily have stood in awe of the military, have a certain tradition of "civilianism"; German bureaucracy has often boasted of its civilian point of view and, with all its authoritarianism, has sometimes opposed the military. In particular, it has often opposed the spirit of militarism which assigns priority to military concerns over the sober, peaceful, day-to-day administrative tasks of the average official. And when one recalls that under Nazism even military circles were fearful of and opposed to the adventurist policies of the political leadership, the anti-adventurism of officialdom can hardly be surprising. This attitude would also seem to conform to the general anti-romanticism, to the new sobriety, of the present-day official, who resembles the streamlined functionary of any big organization or enterprise more than a member of a group espousing specific policies or ideologies of its own. Finally, it would seem to reflect the prevailing spirit of retreat into privacy, if not egocentricity, which characterizes *all* German society today and encourages a general lack of interest in larger political questions.

The stability and durability of present antimilitaristic attitudes is sometimes questioned. One of their chief causes obviously is the impact which the war had on the minds of Germans. A certain amount of antiwar sentiment and even pacifism is a common result of defeat in war, and it took German nationalists and Nazis some time to overcome similar feelings among the German people after World War I. It is only natural to harbor doubts as to the strength and duration of today's attitudes, and they are raised not infrequently by officials themselves, who feel that the present prudence in the conduct of foreign policy might give way to a more aggressive course if Germany's weight in the power balance should increase again. Therefore the question remains whether present sentiments would prove stable enough to overcome the temptations of an environment more favorable than today's to national aggrandizement.

There is also the possibility that the decline of militarism on the national level may persist, but that it may appear again on an international plane. For example, one official, a self-styled pacifist with the usual views on dangers of rearmament, betrayed militaristic attitudes of a racist character in connection with the "white race's fratricidal wars," which rendered it powerless to resist "the tide of color" in other continents, the "claims of the Negro in Africa," and so on.

Germany's Place among the Nations

We may now ask how German officials view Germany's role as a power among other powers. First of all, there is a minority made up of those who refuse to visualize Germany as playing any role of her own, either because they think a uniform over-all German foreign policy is premature in view of the provisional nature of Germany's divided status, or because they are reluctant to see even a united Germany assume the role of a power again. They expect the Germany of the future to play the inconspicuous role of a small country outside the direct sphere of influence of the major powers, to retreat into privacy as a nation, as so many Germans have done on an individual level. This attitude, of course, is usually combined with neutralism.

But the majority of officials who express views on this matter concede, regretfully or otherwise, that Germany constitutes or will presently constitute a major power in international affairs. Some point with pride to the complete reversal of Germany's position within the short span of a few years. The economic miracle has been accompanied by a political miracle. The Germans have done it again, and this despite defeat and with only two-thirds of their territory and population. On the other hand, there are few who would indicate or even suggest that they regard Germany as a country which, actually or potentially, could or should claim first rank among the powers. Sober realism prevails here, too, and leads them to acknowledge that first-rank status in the world today has passed to the United States and the Soviet Union, and can no longer be claimed by others. Consequently, Germany can play her role only in alignment with other powers, and especially in co-operation with the West. Even those who plead for a policy of greater aloofness (except for the minority favoring German neutralization) do so for a period of transition only and usually come out for eventual Western alignment. Advocacy of a "go-it-alone" policy, designed to enable Germany eventually to choose between an Eastern and a Western orientation, or to play off one side against the other and line up with the highest bidder, is hardly noticeable among civil servants. If they think along these lines at all, they point out how impossible, or extremely improbable, it is that any country could line up with the Soviets without becoming a satellite. "There can be no new Rapallo."

Exactly as they concede leadership to the Soviet Union in the Eastern bloc, officials agree that in the Western camp the United States is and must be the leading power. There is little evidence of an expectation or wish that Germany might attain equal rank with America. This does not imply that they envisage a subordinate role for Germany. Feelings are outspoken as to her relative weight in comparison with other powers in the Western alignment. One expects Germany to be, and to be recognized as, senior among the second-string powers. In the eyes of most German officials the powers rank as follows: the United States and the Soviet Union are superior or "super-powers"; Britain, with the Commonwealth and Empire, is usually still admitted to be an equal of Germany, though somewhat reluctantly and in a spirit of invidious competition; France is looked down upon as an inferior power; and others, like Italy, are hardly worth mentioning.

Whether they are pro-Western, neutralist, or advocates of any other German orientation, officials consider the Soviet Union—or rather Russia, as the Soviet Union is generally referred to—to be beyond the pale. Russia is a different world, or *in* a different world, namely Asia, and the Russians are thought of as belonging to an inferior civilization. They definitely do not belong to the West, the Occident (*Abendland*), to which Germans feel they themselves belong. Not only do Russians have nothing in common with the West in their culture and civilization, but they do not share Western political institutions either. They have never known political freedom and can not, therefore, know what free elections mean; neither have they any comprehension of the rule-of-law and the like. To hear Germans, whose history likewise is not so amply graced with liberal-democratic experience, speak thus contemptuously of Russians seems strange; but none seemed to be conscious of or bothered by this. Looking down on the Russians, however, no longer seems to be based as much on contempt of Teuton toward Slav as it used to be. To distinguish other Slavic nations, such as Poles or Czechs, from Russians is not uncommon these days. The former are admitted to good society; they are not Asiatics, but Europeans; and for this reason many officials are not averse to a fair compromise on the question of future Eastern boundaries and the resettlement of expellees. For instance, they are opposed to driving out Poles or Czechs from lands to which Germans want to return.

Contempt for Russian civilization, however, does not detract from respect for Russian power. A healthy appreciation for Soviet military capabilities, and especially for the fighting capacity and stamina of the Russian soldier, is universally expressed. This seems to be a lasting impression of the Eastern war. Germans are rather anxious to impress this on Americans who, they feel, are likely to underestimate Soviet military power and potential.* A war with the Soviet Union, they say, would be a life-and-death struggle even for a united West, including the United States; the outcome would be by no means certain. This, in addition to Germany's geographical location and her partition between East and West, seems to be the chief reason why even Germans with a Western orientation consider almost anything short of communist control preferable to such a war. They prefer to see an indefinite prolongation of the cold war, in the vague expectation that something may happen to solve present problems peacefully; or they advocate continued talks with the Soviets, though more in order to delay fatal decisions than in the hope of

* In this connection, the alleged softness of the American soldier is regretted. According to many Germans, he lacks discipline, is pampered and spoiled, and "man for man" proved inferior to the German soldier. What showing would he make, so they ask, when compelled to fight Russians?

a genuine settlement. They would even countenance the conclusion of certain agreements with the Russians, although they consider such agreements to be of doubtful value, since the Russian, with his different mentality, can not be trusted. Russians are inscrutable; you never know what they are up to and (jumping to a somewhat sudden conclusion) you are not bound, therefore, to make agreements with them in good faith. Thus, should Soviet evacuation of the Eastern zone require in return Western recognition of the Oder-Neisse line, one should extend such recognition by all means, but with the mental reservation that it can be revoked on some later and more suitable occasion.

Fear of the Russian colossus has made many Germans accept the idea of closer ties between Germany and the West and, consequently, the idea of European integration. As a matter of fact, this term has become a slogan used so often and so broadly that its meaning has become somewhat blurred. In addition to military integration of German forces with those of the other Western European countries, the phrase encompasses everything from economic integration through the Coal and Steel Community, through integration of government agencies, to the more elusive aims of the Council of Europe.

Actually, discussion of European integration usually stays in the somewhat cloudy realm of generalities. German officials give the impression of not quite knowing what it implies. They will express their agreement with the idea that the various European countries should give up some measure of their sovereignty in order to establish a supranational, regional entity. They approve of the fact that in recent years citizens of various European nations have come to know each other better, that a good deal of traveling across boundaries, especially by children and students, has been going on, and so forth. But there is also much doubt as to how much all this means. While some officials believe that the idea of European regionalism has actually taken root in large groups of the population, others assert that the initial wave of enthusiasm has since yielded to less interest and more skepticism. Still others point out that "European enthusiasm," or whatever remains of it, is often linked with certain religious preferences. For example, the Catholic element of the CDU is sometimes accused of wanting to revive the Empire of Charlemagne through a union of the Christian-Democratic governments in Western Europe. Or it is claimed that the European idea is motivated by materialistic considerations, such as the job opportunities provided by European enterprises and the traveling opportunities they may afford. Some officials refer rather cynically to "professional Europeans" who already have a vested interest in Europeanism. Even those who feel that the European idea is popular with the people at large often question whether the various governments concerned are ready to take the necessary measures to turn an integrated Europe from an ideal into a reality.

But the very officials who favor European integration frequently do not wish to see Germany give up substantial elements of national sovereignty as long as they do not know how far "the others"—i.e., especially the French—are ready to go in this respect. From this point of view they claim that experience of the way in which the Schuman Plan organization functioned and of the handling of the Saar problem was not encouraging. True, most of them emphasize the outdatedness of old-fashioned nationalism, with its insistence on national sovereignties, the sacred nature of boundary lines, and so forth. But the older nationalist ideology has not been replaced by genuine internationalism, but at best by an unemotional, sober supranationalism or regionalism, to which the features of nationalism as it was previously understood are being partially transferred. It is now Germany-in-Western-Europe whose interests are to be defended. The question of whether this implies readiness to co-operate with and to respect the interests of other regions or combinations remains unanswered. One gains the impression that there are Germans who sincerely believe in the new regionalism as an instrument for peace and co-operation. But to others it may merely mean an up-to-date way of safeguarding German interests and of having them backed up effectively vis-à-vis the East, and possibly vis-à-vis the United States also. Just as, in 1871, the loyalty of Germans to their respective principalities was merged in a new national allegiance toward a Germany led by Prussia, so today this national allegiance is being transferred to a German-led Europe. It may turn out to be nothing more than nationalism on a higher level. France might then be relegated to the role of a non-German Bavaria.

The traditional German hatred of France has almost vanished; at least, it is hardly ever voiced by public officials. There are occasional exceptions in the case of unreconstructed ultranationalists of the old style, or neo-Nazis, but such cases are rare indeed among civil servants. To consider France as the hereditary enemy of Germany today seems as outmoded as are the "black-white-red" colors of the Empire under which that attitude prevailed. It would make sense anyway only if France were still seen as a major power with which Germany had to contend, but this is no longer so. On the other hand, France can not be completely ignored; France and the French problem play a considerable role in German political thought, and Germans return to it again and again in foreign policy discussions. It may be said to constitute the touchstone of a new German approach to international problems. Thus one need not be surprised to find considerable ambivalence in German attitudes toward France.

There can not be any doubt as to the sincerity of the ever-repeated sentiment of liking the French and things French. There has always been a good deal of German admiration for French culture, taste, and refinement; and quite possibly this feeling became stronger and more widespread when more Germans had a chance to know France during their occupation of the country, and to know Frenchmen through French occupation of a part of Germany. One German official nostalgically described how he had felt at ease and almost at home in a little French town where he had been military commander during the war and how he would love to visit it again. With France, as with the United States, Germans seem ready to "forgive and forget" and are almost proud of their magnanimity. But they are a little disturbed, too, because the French do not seem fully to reciprocate present German advances. It is a case of love unrequited, and Germans know it and feel a little hurt. But this has not yet dampened their ardor for France as a focus of European culture.

France as a power, on the other hand, is despised and discounted. After their experience of 1940, Germans apparently can not believe that a revival of French military power is possible. They consider France politically "degenerate," unpredictable, unreliable, a doubtful ally, and a vacillating collaborator in a regional organization. They view with a jaundiced eye her many neutralists and communists, and her persisting suspicion of German aims. Few admit that the French have any reason to be suspicious and those who do so add that the French should become more efficient in order to become stronger and not to have to fear Germans so much any more. Assertions that the French are too easygoing, that they do not make enough of an effort to compete with the Germans, that they just do not work hard enough, recur in almost every German discussion of the French problem. Thus the chief cause for German contempt of France as a power, apart from her military defeat in 1940, is her economic weakness and general inefficiency. To the German official, who is an idolizer of efficiency, the French are exasperating. The recent increase in travel and personal contacts has merely added to this feeling. "Travel through the French countryside, and you will see how inefficient the French farmer is; you do not observe a change for the better until you arrive in [German] Alsace." Sensing that they have something in common with efficiency-worshiping Americans in this respect, the Germans almost plead with Americans to admit that Germany has a claim to preference and that those American policies which, it is alleged, have favored France have been all wrong.

In contrast to this deep political interest and even emotional involvement in France and French problems, there is surprisingly little thought given to Britain. It is almost as if the Germans wished to reciprocate British aloofness, which found its most striking expression in the British policy of "invisible" occupation of their zone of Germany. If this mutual aloofness has curtailed the opportunities for Germans and British to learn to know each other, it has also meant that earlier adverse experience has been largely forgotten. For instance, Germans had tended to assign to the British most of the blame for the postwar Allied policy of dismantling German industry, since it was believed that the British wished to hamstring a major competitor. Officials still assert occasionally that it is British policy to suppress Germany as a business competitor, but there is comparatively little emphasis on this. Most officials feel that the British have only themselves to blame if they complain about the rise of German power and competition. England had a chance after 1945 to assume political leadership in a united Europe, but failed to do so; and as far as economic matters are concerned, the argument is the same as in the case of France: the British simply are not hard-working and efficient enough, and therefore should not complain about the rapid expansion of German production and foreign trade. Some officials, especially those who visited Britain in the postwar period, have considerable admiration for the way in which the British handle their domestic affairs. But in general, while there is hardly any remnant of the wartime, Nazi-inspired hatred of England, there is also little of the affection shown France. The British are considered as a nation still to be reckoned with and in many respects on a par with Germany. But there is hope and confidence that the Germans will outstrip them in due course and will then rank first among European countries, especially in the eyes of the United States.

Attitudes toward the United States

Even if the United States, through its personnel and policies, were not so visibly present in Germany, German-American relations would occupy a vital place in German thoughts and discussions on foreign affairs. As we have seen, Germans of today, including officialdom, are inclined to accept as a fact the proposition that the United States has become one of the two really decisive world powers. This was brought home to them through World War II and its aftermath. But the deep interest of Germans in America antedates even World War I, when American intervention proved similarly decisive. It is connected with what Germans refer to as "the problem of Americanism."

Since the political and economic disaster of the 1840's, millions of

Germans have settled in America. The attitude toward the United States of those who stayed at home has been profoundly ambiguous. On the one hand, America, as a land of freedom and equality, appeared attractive to German liberals. Even those Germans who were doubtful about its political and social system admired the technical achievements and efficiency of its new industrial civilization, from which they might learn something of value. For after 1870 the Germans, too, embarked on a vast program of industrialization. On the other hand, many Germans could not give an unqualified blessing to a New World civilization which, more and more, seemed to involve a threat to traditional standards of culture. Technological civilization seemed to debase or destroy many of the cultural values of which Germans, as Europeans, were proud, even though they themselves were relinquishing these values in favor of what they call *Vermassung*. Since Americans seemed to have initiated the trend toward technological mass civilization and to have advanced farthest on the road to it, Germans have tended to identify this worldwide process with "Americanism." While apprehensive of the effects of Americanization on their life and culture, Germans have been inclined to yield to them and even to accept them eagerly. Officials in particular, by their recent transformation from civil servants of the old school into functionaries, with their pragmatic or even materialistic approach, betray many a significant trait of what they refer to as "Americanism." Thus they themselves have become victims, perhaps unconsciously, of the selfsame "Americanization" of which most of them are severely critical.*

This ambivalent attitude toward the United States, and the general concern of Germans with German-American relations, are perhaps best reflected in the catalog of criticisms most commonly voiced by civil servants. These criticisms are sometimes contradictory, since they come from different groups with varying views; nevertheless, some of them seemed to be more or less common to all officials who were interviewed.

Among those who voiced criticism of American policies there was virtual unanimity on one point: it was difficult to find out what these policies were. American policies were criticized as vague, inconsistent, and given to sudden and unpredictable turns and changes. While German officials claimed at least to know where they stood in relation to France and Britain, they felt at a loss about American intentions. Since officials (like the rest of the population) are generally unaware of the

* Preoccupation with the problem of "Americanism" is reflected in the fact that the most widely discussed books on America in the last few years have been those which dwelt on the phenomenon of *Vermassung* almost to the exclusion of any other aspects of American culture; for instance, Robert Jungk's *Die Zukunft hat schon begonnen,* a Swiss newspaperman's report on the United States. Interviews with German officials suggested that most educated Germans drew their information on the United States from sources of this kind.

structure of the United States government and its policy-making procedures, contradictory or unco-ordinated statements by officials of the
executive branch, congressmen, and others tend to create confusion and
bewilderment. Thus in 1953 Senator McCarthy appeared to many to
wield more influence than any other single American upon his country's
affairs, including foreign policy. Others assume that the President is the
all-powerful maker of American foreign policy, and the difficulties
which he encounters in Congress or elsewhere are not understood. Most
of them, however, feel they do not know and can not find out how
American policies are made. Americans themselves seem not to know.

The question arises, therefore, as to how far Germany can rely on
continued American backing if she commits herself to any policy involving risks. Neutralists say that the United States can not be relied on,
and for this reason oppose tying Germany to the West. The relatively
few neo-Nazis among officials, and some others, are sure that in case of a
Soviet attack the United States would "fight to the last European" and
would be sure to leave Germany in the lurch, whatever American plans
may be now. Pro-Westerners, too, are afraid of a sudden turn in U.S.
policy, even though the United States may now be ready to give Germany all desired guarantees. Some suspect that American plans for the
defense of Western Europe provide for a strategic withdrawal as far as
the Rhine. Almost all the officials who were questioned, even full-fledged
backers of Adenauer's policies, had some misgivings in this respect and
were extremely anxious to learn whether their apprehensions were justified. What about a new isolationism? What about a deal with the
Soviets at Germany's expense?

But anxiety was equally strong regarding what was called the warlike
and crusading spirit of U.S. foreign policy. It was said that Americans
were too prone to consider preventive war against the Soviets. Such
fears were encountered not only among noncommunist leftists and
neutralists, but quite generally among the "unpolitical" run-of-the-mill
civil servants. A surprisingly small number of officials advocated a policy
of "roll-back," even though it might promise early liberation of fellow-
Germans in the East zone. The average civil servant, who blames Americans for the presence of the Soviets in the heart of Germany, does not
advocate a stronger policy than containment. Yet there was much
criticism of earlier American blindness to the communist danger and
forgetfulness of German interests, and the turn toward a more energetic
and forceful policy was hailed with relief. This reaction, however, has
not prevented Germans from pointing out frequently that Americans
were hoodwinked by the Russians for some time before they saw the
light. In a similar vein, some officials have affirmed that German interests

were unduly neglected at first in favor of a policy of pampering Britain and France. Others complain that too much preference is still being given to France. They feel that France should be compelled, if necessary through economic pressure, to cease her resistance to measures of European integration, and they accuse the United States of being "weak and sentimental" toward her. Strong-arm methods in dealing with France are sometimes recommended by the very persons who criticize the United States for an unduly "bossy" attitude toward Germany.

Not all the officials who were interviewed shared these views. In particular, the Socialists and the more democratic adherents of the CDU and FDP, among the politically conscious minority within the bureaucracy, warned against pampering Germany at the expense of France and Britain. This, they said, involved a risk of alienating those countries, the very thing the Soviets were banking on. A U.S. policy of establishing a rearmed Germany as its chief European ally involved not only the danger of a break in the Western camp, but might also increase the danger of an early conflict with the Soviets by provoking them into a preventive attack, or by encouraging those currently weak elements in Germany which favored revenge, reconquest, or crusade. They also pointed to the danger for Germany's domestic scene inherent in a policy which might be interpreted as a go-ahead sign to ultranationalists and neo-Nazis. These officials voiced openly what many Germans seemed to feel: an apprehension that Americans were inclined to subordinate any and all considerations to political and military expediency. This, in turn, was seen as one of the adverse consequences of American "materialism."

In regard to U.S. policies, not *toward* but *in* Germany, one may distinguish between the effect upon German attitudes of the mere presence of U.S. forces, personnel, and agencies in the Federal Republic and the effect of the *policies* governing these American elements. There is, as might be expected, a good deal of criticism that reflects no more than the irreducible minimum of friction between troops stationed on foreign territory and the people they live among. Officials whose work concerns areas where U.S. policies in Germany affect the population directly are outspoken in their criticism of what they call American intransigence and callousness in refusing to give proper recognition to civilian interests. In local government, housing, public health, and so on, complaints can still be heard that too many dwellings and hospitals are requisitioned. There are also complaints about red tape and overlapping or ill-defined jurisdictions of American authorities. Officials, like other groups, make complaints about the allegedly rude, loud, or otherwise uncultured behavior of individual Americans, especially soldiers. On the other hand, there is a good deal of ready recognition of the necessity of the occupation, as it is sometimes still called. Quite frequently there is even recognition of the benefits which American policy has brought to Germany and appreciation of the assistance rendered by America to a prostrate and starving erstwhile enemy in the early postwar period.

Criticisms of American policies toward the reconstruction of Germany often differ widely, because of the varied outlooks of the critics. There is some agreement about certain mistakes, such as those committed in connection with denazification, but even here Germans tend to disagree as to what was wrong. In other fields there is disagreement about the entire American approach. For example, while some officials admit that "re-education" * was necessary, and even regret that controls in this field were given up too early, the majority resent the entire policy. There is even more sweeping criticism of an allegedly persisting tendency to dictate to Germany, to keep her in tutelage, instead of treating her as a partner.

In other respects, differences in views more closely follow the line dividing the democratic, anti-Nazi minority from the "nonpolitical," or rightist, majority. Members of the latter group object to almost everything in earlier American policies: democratization, prosecution of war criminals, denazification, demilitarization, and so forth. By the same token, they express great satisfaction with the more recent change in American policy in all these fields. Officials belonging to the minority group, on the other hand, are profoundly apprehensive. They are disturbed not only about the international implications but above all about the internal impact of a policy which, so they say, tends to encourage the militarist, ultranationalist, antidemocratic forces in Germany. They assert that Americans are too little aware of how the sudden turn in U.S. policy has affected the average German. Even those Germans who had been inclined to give earlier policies the benefit of the doubt, and who had assumed an attitude of wait-and-see, now have come to believe that these policies never stemmed from principle or real conviction but, like the new policies, were adopted for mere expediency. German democrats, so these officials complain, have thus been discredited.

Members of this group object further that Americans quite generally have tended to oversimplify European, and particularly German, problems. This tendency can, they say, be seen in the American attitude toward genuinely democratic forces in Germany such as the SPD and the democratic trade-unions, both of which have often been confused with Communists. On the other hand, reactionary and authoritarian groups (the currently fashionable term to describe them is "restor-

* The term "re-education" itself is universally resented.

ative") have enjoyed American backing and are gloating like spoiled children. According to this view, workers and many others are disappointed and resentful. An America thus emerging as defender and promoter of reaction—economically as well as politically—ceases to be the representative of the free world in the eyes of many Germans. At best, it becomes a lesser evil; at worst, it encourages the latent neutralism characteristic of the frequently heard statement: "There is nothing to choose between the two systems."

In the early 1950's, apprehensions about American support of the reactionary forces in Germany merged with an even deeper and almost universal concern with, or fear of, what were believed to be fascist or totalitarian trends in America, collectively referred to as "McCarthyism." At this point officials of the "nonpolitical" majority usually joined the others in their anxiety. Not knowing much about American domestic affairs, Germans naturally tended to draw easy parallels, identifying all such tendencies, policies, and events with one man, in whom they saw the American counterpart of the European-type dictator—an American Hitler. The anxiety expressed during this period was revealing, and came as a surprise to one who believed that latent predilections for Hitlerism were still widespread in Germany. It is true that, here and there, one did encounter some malicious satisfaction at seeing the democratic "re-educator" in such a predicament. But in the vast majority of cases it was quite clear that there was genuine fear of what American developments might portend. In appraising this reaction it should be kept in mind that communist propaganda had, and has, very little bearing on West German opinion. To a large extent, the German reaction to McCarthyism may have been due to fear that U.S. foreign policy might turn to adventures into which Germans would be drawn willy-nilly. But to a higher degree than many foreign observers may have been willing to concede, it also seems to have reflected honest concern with the future of democracy or, rather, of constitutionalism and moderation. If civil servants are representative of more general opinion in this respect, then it may be said that Germans, who are in the main not yet democrats in the Western sense, at least show a strong distaste for any repetition of totalitarian experiments.

That attitudes toward the United States are so often critical does not imply that they are predominantly hostile or negative. That Germans are more critically inclined toward America than toward other countries may be due to two circumstances. One is that what so often disturbs or displeases them in America and Americans is felt to be related to something characteristic of their own development, so that such criticism in reality constitutes to some extent self-criticism. The other reason is their discovery of how decisive U.S. policies have become for the fate of Germany and for the life of the individual German. Though some may hate America, they would feel lost without it. As one (very critical) German publication put it: "The only thing worse than the presence of U.S. forces in Germany would be their absence."[7] What is said here about military forces might apply more generally to the American presence in Europe. Objections to U.S. policies do not necessarily spring from sentiments of antipathy at all. Rather, they often seem to reflect a friendly anxiety to warn and enlighten.

Conclusion

If there emerges from the foregoing a somewhat bewildering picture of the present German bureaucracy's approach to foreign policy problems, it may well reflect the fact that Germans in general are today uncertain and confused about the international situation in which their country finds itself. The question arises whether from such a welter of attitudes some broad general truths can be distilled—some composite picture which will sum up the views of the typical German official. To arrive at such a picture one must exclude the many and varied minority views which have been presented above, and to that extent must oversimplify in order to clarify. With this reservation and with some diffidence one may, perhaps, reach certain general conclusions.

Asked for his foreign policy views, the official first of all tries to avoid committing himself to specific attitudes or opinions. Even when he seems eager to talk, he indicates that these questions, after all, should rather be left to Mr. Adenauer, or to "the others" (meaning the former occupying powers). When pressed for his own views, his answers primarily reflect somewhat narrow personal interests and considerations. He hesitates to advocate bolder policies for fear of the risks they might involve for his position, career, or living standard. He stands, of course, for reunification, but he opposes steps which might entail the danger of international complications or a change in present West German economic recovery.

In the cold war situation, he stands for a policy of trying to "muddle through," but wants to be assured of Western backing in case of untoward developments in the East. He feels somehow that the West owes him such protection. He is, however, reluctantly willing to see Germany pay for protection by sharing in whatever closer alignments among Western countries—and particularly the Western European ones—are deemed necessary. He is therefore in favor of Germany's participation in the Schuman Plan and even of her rearmament in the framework of common Western defense, but he is hesitant in regard to the latter and hopes that it will not increase the danger of war. He insists that European integration, whether military, economic, or political, shall not involve neglect of German interests in favor of France.

He welcomes the growth of German power and prestige which he expects to result from rearmament, but he is suspicious of the old-style German militarism which, he fears, will revive with the rebirth of the German armed forces and lead Germany into adventurous foreign policies once more. While he would like to see Germany rank as a big power again—a rating he feels she deserves in view of her geographical location, her miraculous economic comeback, and the skills and cultural level of her people—he shrinks from advocating that she play the international role of an independent big power, because of the risks this would involve. At present he even seems ready to limit himself to making claims regarding the lost territories "for the record." * Realizing that even as one of the stronger European powers Germany can not at present compete with either the United States or the Soviet Union, he tends to be suspicious of the aims of both. He would love to see Germany established as another Switzerland outside the big-power spheres, and he would embrace any kind of neutralism, pacifism, or the like, were it not for his realization that this is impossible under present conditions. Thus the traditional concepts of "nationalism," "pacifism," and so forth hardly apply any longer to his attitudes. He is no old-fashioned nationalist, but neither is he a cosmopolitan internationalist. Rather, he soberly and unemotionally favors a supranational, regionalist spirit—a West European or "occidental" interest-community, a combination that will enable the West to withstand the power of the East. By the same token, he is neither aggressively militaristic nor an integral pacifist, but is characterized rather by a resigned "defense-readiness." He is no longer, if indeed he ever was, a racist in the sense of considering the German, or "Aryan," or "Nordic" race supreme or superior; but neither is he willing to concede the equality of all races or nations. Rather, he believes in the superiority of the West, or Europe, over Asia (to which Russia belongs) and the rest of the world. But he does not at present favor any kind of regional power politics, imperialism, or crusade. He would prefer to be left in peace to cultivate his own garden, growing red tape.

This picture may appear somewhat colorless, and thus disappointing, to those who expect more flamboyant attitudes from Germans. Perhaps it represents no more than a passing mood. But it may also indicate a

---

* The expression "lost territories" refers to former German territory in the East. Present German nationalism, or irredentism, does not seem to apply to Alsace-Lorraine or Austria any longer.

kind of "Americanization" which may have affected German officialdom more than any other group in German society. If this Americanization signalizes the acceptance of more pragmatic, sober views and standards in the place of romantic expectations and extremist aims, it may encourage moderate and peaceful developments in Germany. Here, as many officials point out, the time factor will play an important role. Much seems to depend on whether tendencies favoring peace and moderation, compromise and agreement, in both domestic and international affairs will be allowed a period of quiet growth.

By the same token, should developments deny the new Germany that minimum period of peace during which democratic institutions can grow into democratic habits, antidemocratic, authoritarian, militaristic forces might easily gain control again. Unduly hasty rearmament of Germany might have equally adverse effects; so might an economic depression. In either event German bureaucracy could hardly be relied upon to offer resistance to those who would advocate authoritarian solutions to German problems.* Its pro-democratic elements would prove too weak to contain the tendency of the "nonpoliticals" to follow and serve new masters, especially if these should enjoy the backing of America. The future attitudes of German officialdom, whatever its present views, will thus be determined in no small degree by American policies.

* In a much discussed publication, a German author (Herbert von Borch, *Obrigkeit und Widerstand,* Tübingen, 1954) draws the lesson from Weimar-Nazi experience that, once totalitarian movements have gained control, resistance comes too late. Therefore, he suggests that it is up to officialdom, through disobedience, to stop any nascent totalitarianism in its tracks. The fact that he suggests putting this responsibility upon officials, who are traditionally wont to obey superiors unquestioningly, may reflect the enhanced importance and power of the present German bureaucracy. But it would be too much to expect, and Borch seems vastly to overrate present German officials' readiness to take a stand involving risks. Their tendency to withdraw into an unpolitical sphere of privacy and security would seem bound to defeat all efforts to make them initiators of political action, especially action of such an unorthodox character. One should be glad if they merely abstain from actively furthering or promoting antidemocratic trends.

FIVE

West German Trade-Unions: Their Domestic and Foreign Policies

Otto Kirchheimer

German labor unions are presently passing through a critical period. The outward portents of the crisis are clearly visible. The membership of the *Deutsche Gewerkschaftsbund* (DGB), which climbed steadily until 1952, is now stationary, and may even be slightly on the decline. Union headquarters ring with controversies among factions and personalities.

These developments are taking place at a time of unprecedented boom, full employment, and a tight labor market; the critical state of the labor movement certainly can not be ascribed to economic difficulties. Rather, its causes are in part rooted in the history of many decades, and in part related to the configuration of political and social forces in the postwar era.

The Burden of the Past in Relation to the Present

The history of German labor is a history of high hopes and, more often, abject defeats. Its mainstream is closely linked with the history of the old Social Democratic Party (SPD) and its successor organizations. The assumptions, ideals, and goals of the SPD were shared by those actively engaged in elaborating the ways of German trade-unionism.

Eds. Note.—This study was written in the winter of 1955–1956, and is based in part on conversations with more than fifty West German union officials which took place during the summer of 1955. It was initially published, in a somewhat longer form, as a RAND Corporation Research Memorandum (RM-1673-RC), dated April 1, 1956. The present version includes a brief postscript, prepared in February, 1957.

Dr. Kirchheimer is Professor of Political Science in the Graduate Faculty of the New School for Social Research in New York City, and a former branch chief in the Division of Research for Western Europe, Office of Intelligence Research, U.S. Department of State.

Both SPD and unions believed that democracy and satisfaction of labor's justified claims would be automatically guaranteed when industrialization and concentration ended in transforming the majority of citizens into a class-conscious body politic. This belief was congenial to the orderly and disciplined mind of the German worker of pre-World War I days. Unionists also shared the SPD's rejection of the reigning trinity of army, big business, and semifeudal landowners. With the SPD, they went through the unrewarding experience of co-operating with the Kaiser's government during World War I as adjuncts of the official, patriotic, bureaucratic machinery.

After the war, both the unions and the party suffered serious splits over the problem of how to handle the increasing pressure from the ranks—and from resolute minorities within their own organizations—which demanded peace and favored labor initiative in changing the political order according to the old socialist image. The power thrust on them in 1918 quickly slipped through their fingers. As a consequence, the labor movement split into a rudderless conservative majority and a resolute minority with revolutionary aspirations; after 1923, however, this minority came increasingly under the control of Moscow, a liaison that bore no meaningful relation to the interests of German labor. This political rift dominated German labor throughout the history of the Weimar Republic, and weakened, from the outset, labor's chances to assume political and social importance commensurate with its numerical strength.

The majority, which had been induced to support creation of the Republic, defended the Weimar state on two grounds: It saw in the democratic order (1) the legitimate framework for the satisfaction of labor's claims, and (2) a shield against revolutionary onslaughts from right and left that endangered the very existence of the unions as free and independent organizations. Though continuing to appeal to its adherents under the guise of traditional socialist ideologies, this majority group took on many of the characteristics of a party of expediency. It was unable to assert itself over the Communist Party, which was its chief competitor for the favor of the working-class population.

The Communists' numerical strength varied according to the fortunes of the Weimar Republic, but even at the Weimar regime's high-water mark in 1928, their voting strength never fell below one-third that of the Social Democrats. This numerical relation expresses only incompletely the loss of energy, good will, and confidence that resulted from this fratricidal fight in which the hard-pressed majority often found itself aligned with the repressive forces of the public order.[1] The minority —whether it operated as a separate communist party or as an oppositionist faction within the unions—was more interested in charging the majority with deviation from hallowed labor tradition than in making a record of its own.

The majority, in turn, relied increasingly on props provided by the government machinery. Wherever appropriate opportunities existed in the complicated constitutional framework of German federal institutions, the official labor movement took an active part in the administration of police, social security, employment exchanges, and so forth. It did so in an attempt both to protect the Republic from its enemies and to secure patronage and benefits for its own members. The administration of justice, the army, and, by and large, the sphere of economic activities remained outside its reach. Yet official labor became saddled in the public mind with responsibility for the conduct of all public affairs. By the early 1930's, labor became a victim of its own *status quo* mentality, as well as of political and economic circumstances over which it had but little control.[2] The top leadership of the *Allgemeine Deutsche Gewerkschaftsbund* (ADGB) made some last-minute attempts to jettison its lifelong association with the SPD in favor of an arrangement with the new Nazi overlords, but these efforts were abortive.[3]

Ever since the days when a general strike was called to defeat the Kapp Putsch in 1920, both the SPD and the unions had shied away from mobilizing the active support of their followers. How the depression-haunted masses would have responded to a call to action in 1933 is not known. Since the early twenties, there had been developing an increasing gap between what the average worker hoped and expected, and what was being said and done by the reformist, government-affiliated bureaucracy of the SPD and the unions, or the pseudorevolutionary, Moscow-connected Communist Party machine. Yet, inveterate mistrust of National Socialism's intentions left the workers no alternative but to continue passive support of the SPD and the German Communist Party (KPD) at the polls. But worker estrangement from traditional labor organizations continued nevertheless. Dwindling union membership indicated progressive loss of confidence on the part of the rank and file. The governmental machinery, in turn, represented the workers insufficiently and ineffectively. Therefore, it failed to evoke loyalty or profound attachment, even though its services were not easily dispensable in a time of depression.

The workers' attitude during the Hitler era mirrors both the after-effects of the Weimar experience and the methods of the new masters. The new rulers guaranteed the workers full employment as a planned coincidence to the build-up of the machinery of aggression. At the same time, workers' representatives were barred from active political and social participation in public affairs. The workers adjusted to these conditions. As did everybody else, they drew some profit from the economic incidence of rearmament, but they felt neither responsible for nor sympathetic to the regime. There grew a trend toward passive obedience and protective withdrawal into privacy, which, however, did not rule out cautious preservation of a modicum of organizational contact with old friends. The SPD, the KPD, and the unions had been smashed by the Nazis. Only a few renegades from their ranks defected to the victors, however, and there were many heroes and martyrs. This relatively good showing of labor's leaders was due not only to the emergence of active resistance fighters from labor ranks, but also to the policy of the new masters who sought to destroy and eradicate rather than absorb the remaining nuclei of traditional labor organizations.

When the Nazi regime fell, labor, along with other persecuted and suppressed groups, expected and felt entitled to special consideration; it assumed that the occupying powers would give wholehearted support to its effort to rebuild free labor organizations as an integral and indispensable part of the reconstruction of German democracy.

The actual course of reconstruction, however, was determined more by the political needs of the occupying powers than by political and social images surviving among the remnants of pre-1933 labor leadership groups. Labor policies were increasingly dominated by the shadow of the deepening conflict between the major occupation powers. It was this conflict that shaped the framework of the different societies emerging in East and West Germany. Soviet policy brought about (1) the forced merger of the SPD and KPD into one official state party; (2) the use of the East zone *Freie Deutsche Gewerkschaftsbund* (FDGB) as a government auxiliary; (3) deportation of the German population from provinces detached from occupied Germany as well as from other parts of Eastern Europe; (4) wholesale dismantling of industrial plants; and (5) exploitation of production facilities for the benefit of the U.S.S.R.

All these moves contrasted unfavorably, in German eyes, with the policies of the Western powers, and especially those of the United States. Whatever picture of a future socialist society the older generation may have continued to have in mind, they were inevitably confronted with the realities of the East German society under Soviet domination. The comparison between East and West was bound to be ruinous for the Communists. From that time on, German labor's image of undesirable societies was to be dominated by East Germany's Sovietized condition no less than by the traits of Nazism, militarism, and war; the communist regime meant lack of political freedom, low living standards, and the rise of a new, utterly opportunistic upper crust. Careful and continuing

Soviet attempts to disguise this reality by deliberate use of concepts corresponding to the traditional imagery of the labor movement met with little success.

But, granted that German labor knows what it does not want, what about positive concepts? In conformity with both its tradition and its more recent experience, the German labor movement was conceived after 1945 as a democratically organized force working within the context of a democratically governed state. Secondly, it was to be a unified labor movement, embracing all the different shades of democratically inclined unionism that had existed under the Weimar Republic.

At the same time, new patterns of industrial organization were envisaged that would prevent future abuse of economic power for political ends. In the early postwar days, no one thought to deny that German industry, if it had not been solely responsible for Hitler's rise to power, had at least had more than its full share in establishing and running the regime both in peace and war.[4] Therefore, the demand for curbing the industrialists' economic power was more than just a traditional socialist call. It was, during 1945–1947, almost universally seen as the political prerequisite to establishment of a German democratic state. This was a self-evident truth to the SPD, and a basic tenet in all early program manifestoes of the Christian Democratic Union and its Bavarian affiliate, the Christian Social Union; it was also widely accepted by the Free Democratic Party, which otherwise advocated unfettered freedom of economic activity. Social Democratic, Christian Democratic, and unanimous union opinion also converged on the thesis that the introduction of planning patterns, and public controls, with active participation of the unions, would serve to prevent economic depression and unemployment.

Serving as supporters of, and partners in, the various Allied-installed *Land* governments, the unions enjoyed enough respectability and had enough time to plan the future economic and social structure, while Allied-appointed trustees and former owners and managers ran the factories with the active support of the works councils. There were to be, as the unions saw it, three major economic innovations: first, the traditionally advocated program of outright socialization of basic industries; secondly, participation of both works councils and trade-unions in the management structure of each industrial enterprise (codetermination); and, finally, institution of higher-level public agencies to coordinate and perhaps even regulate activities of individual industrial establishments in both the private and the public sectors.[5] If these plans had materialized, the unions, heavily represented on all three levels in addition to functioning as bargaining agents, would have assumed vast public functions. Whatever the possible conflicts between collective bargaining and the planning and managerial job, the combination of both would have given the unions a towering position on the German political scene while at the same time making them an integral part of the governmental structure.

Economic and political developments since the 1948 currency reform have made a shambles of these plans. Except for a problematic beachhead in the previously decartelized steel and coal industries, the unions have been thrown back to—some would even say behind—their Weimar position of a market party bargaining for wages and labor conditions. This outcome was the result of two closely related facts: the strength and success of the so-called "free market economy," and the establishment of a West German state under a government that excluded the Social Democrats—a government that won a resounding confirmation of its four-year record at the federal elections of September 6, 1953. Organized labor's present crisis in Germany must be seen against the background of this chasm between its postwar hopes and expectations and the actual developments of the last decade.

The present boom finds the German labor unions in an ambiguous position. They can not and do not deny that their members, along with everybody else, have profited from the economic upswing which has been occurring within the framework of a privately-operated capitalist society.* But they are not prepared, on that account, to renounce their constantly reiterated demand for a thorough transformation of the existing socioeconomic structure.

Some critics have intimated that the German union leadership is no longer in a position to evade a clear-cut choice;[6] it must decide whether the unions will confine themselves to operating within the framework of democratic capitalism and will concentrate on getting the most out of it for their members ("business unionism"), or whether they will continue to insist on a radical transformation of the present society, which would in reality prevent them from obtaining for their members the maximum share of the national product.

In fact, the union leadership has had no such choice. Union leaders may not always be able to make clear why they do not feel "at home" within the framework of the social and governmental structure char-

---

* The Research Institute of the DGB, however, contends that wage movements in recent years have been sufficient only to preserve the buying power of the wage and salary earners at their 40–41 per cent share in the net social product; cf. Bruno Gleitze, "Die Lohnquote im Spiegel der volkswirtschaftlichen Gesamtrechnung," *WWI Mitteilungen*, September, 1955, pp. 183 ff. These figures are considerably at variance with those cited in employers' publications; cf. F. Spiegelhalter, "Die westdeutschen Löhne im internationalen Blickfeld" in *Der Arbeitgeber*, August 15, 1955, p. 539.

acteristic of the Bonn regime, and their inability to formulate their position may make the union stand look ambiguous and confusing to many rank-and-filers. But this does not alter the fact that the union leaders' ambivalent attitude toward the type of social structure they live in has been to a large extent, as we have seen, historically determined.

The actual operating conditions of German society, as well as the shadow of the past, have militated against a clear-cut choice. Unlike their American or even their British counterparts, German labor unions do not really believe that they are operating within the framework of a safely established social order. The state itself is provisional and subject to important structural changes if and when reunification should take place. Moreover, in the light of both history and present experience, the unions lack confidence in the impartiality and neutrality of the state as between the interests of capital and of labor; hence their tendency to rely as little as possible on the governmental machinery. But such self-reliance presupposes a greater amount of self-confidence than exists in labor's ranks at present. Labor's prevailing feeling of insecurity and doubt about its power has increased since management returned to positions of predominance in state and society. This insecurity is heightened by the fact that management is not prepared to abandon the workers' mind to the embrace of the unions, but is fighting a tenacious and often successful battle for the loyalty of the workingman. This, in turn, fosters the inclination of the unions to press for new institutional safeguards (extension of codetermination privileges, institution of "economic chambers"), which would permit them to face the political and economic uncertainties of the future with greater equanimity. In all these endeavors, however, the unions are handicapped by the increasingly bureaucratic character of their organization and the accompanying lag in intensity of rank-and-file interest in union activities.

Both the historical burden and contemporary experience shape the present situation of the unions, and both must be kept in mind in evaluating labor institutions and policies in Germany.

Organizational Structure

The multifarious regional and functional unions which had sprung up under various Western occupation regimes since 1945 merged into the DGB in October, 1949, at the Munich convention.[7] Unionists were in a hurry to establish a united labor front as their gift of welcome to the newly-constituted Federal Republic. The accent lay on administrative centralization, maintenance of the principle of industrial unionism, and continuation of the by then well-established principle of independent and unified unionism as against politically or denominationally affiliated unions. The first emphasis led to a severe cutback in the prerogatives of the regional leadership, which had grown up especially in South Germany in response to the needs of the early occupation period. The second principle, adoption of uncompromising industrial unionism, had already been foreshadowed in various mergers of the Weimar days.

The new union organization was to rest on a federation of 16 industrial unions. But from the beginning—and much to the regret of many a district chairman—this plan led to the rise of dual unionism in the white-collar field. Unwilling to accept the *Deutsche Angestelltengewerkschaft* (DAG) as the sole representative of all white-collar workers, the leadership of the unions that were planning to federate—who were sworn to the fundamentals of industrial unionism—insisted on distributing the white-collar workers also among the various industrial unions. The DAG refused. As a result, the DAG, which by 1955 was to number 420,000 nonmanual workers among its members as against the 640,000 eventually organized in the DGB, found itself barred from the new federation.

But DGB chairman-elect Hans Böckler was determined not to brook another source of dual unionism. The practice of independent and unified unionism was to be based on a firm foundation. Delegates might fight on the convention floor over the person of the vice-president to be taken from the camp of the former socialist unions, but Böckler would not permit them to ignore the strength of the Christian union wing by allowing it insufficient representation on the executive board of the DGB. The executive board, as originally constituted, was made up of a president, two vice-presidents, and eight executive members (secretaries); Christian union representatives were elected to one of the vice-presidential posts and to one other seat on the executive board.

As for the distribution of functions between the Federation and the individual industrial unions, the Federation was charged with representing labor in all fields of common interest, especially in social and cultural affairs; specific negotiations over wages and hours, industrial disputes, and relations with individual union members were reserved to the constituent unions. The DGB's share in membership dues collected by the industrial unions was to be 15 per cent; in 1952, this share was cut to 12 per cent; a further reduction was voted down at the 1956 convention. While routine decisions were to be taken by the eleven-man executive board (which was reduced to nine members in 1952), more important matters had to be submitted to the Council of the Federation, where the members of the executive board were joined by the presidents of the 16 member unions. Since the DGB was formed, experience has shown that significant decisions require the open or tacit consent of the union presidents representing the metal workers, the public workers, and the miners, whose total of three million members constitutes about half the total membership of the DGB.

The Federation's strength rests essentially on two foundations: (1) the lower-level and medium-level officers' confidence in the top leadership (in both the industrial unions and the Federation), and (2) the continued willing co-operation of industrial union leaders with the Federation's executive board.[8]

The German Labor Federation operated successfully so long as its direction remained in the hands of a president who enjoyed undisputed authority and prestige both within and outside the organization. Moreover, Hans Böckler's two-and-a-quarter years of stewardship (preceded by two-and-a-half years as president of the DGB's precursor) coincided with the formative period of the new West German state, when social trends and definitive power constellations had not yet crystallized, and when the new governmental setup needed the prestige of the union leadership to help consolidate the authority of the emerging political system. When Böckler died in 1951, employer-employee relations had begun to deteriorate, and a growing intimacy had become noticeable between the administration and the business community. Neither Christian Fette, Böckler's immediate successor (who after one-and-a-half years' tenure was voted out of office by the dissatisfied convention majority), nor Walter Freitag, DGB President until the fall of 1956, was able to capture the public imagination, and neither was able to command more than grudging loyalty on the part of the Federation's staff or the executive boards and officers of the constituent unions. To some extent, the lessening prestige of the leadership—actually of the entire executive board of the DGB—symbolizes the political and psychological hardships under which the unions operate today; it also reflects the fragility of an organization welded together from many parts of differing strength and structure.

Bureaucratic squabbles at the Düsseldorf DGB headquarters have also contributed to a lessening of the Federation's authority. For a short while they served to catapult Viktor Agartz, the cochairman of the *Wirtschaftswissenschaftliche Institut der Gewerkschaften* (WWI) in Cologne, into the limelight as a policy-molder. The nucleus of this institute, which now employs more than sixty trained researchers, was formed in 1946 to service the union federation for the British zone. At that time, individual unions had no research personnel whatsoever, and even today their research departments are small and confine their work mostly to the everyday problems of the union to which they are attached. Hence the importance of the Federation's research center in Cologne.

Since the approximately two hundred officials at the Federation's headquarters are concerned primarily with the conduct of day-by-day business, the WWI from the outset loomed large in the formulation of union policy. The critical and sharply pointed utterances of cochairman Agartz of the WWI drew more publicity—and often hostile attention—than those of the elected union leaders. However, Agartz was only an appointed official; therefore, he was able to substitute for the absence of a Federation spokesman of undisputed authority only so long as he caused no embarrassment to the DBG board and the presidents of the major unions. When their confidence was withdrawn as a consequence of disputes within the Cologne institute, Agartz went into eclipse.*

For the time being, at least, the presidents of the big industrial unions not only enjoy complete autonomy in their own bailiwicks, but also have ample opportunity, if they so choose, to advance suggestions of a wider policy nature; thus DGB headquarters is more and more being relegated to the role of a clearinghouse of ideas.

Industrial unions compete with each other for prestige and power in the area of wage policies—where there is a lack of co-ordination, and where "first come, first served" is the practice—as well as by means of variations in union benefits.[9] Although, apart from strike allotments, union benefits (which merely supplement social-insurance payments in the event of sickness, old age, or death) are not substantial, they do constitute, from many a member's viewpoint, one of the union's most important attractions. The 1952 DGB convention voted on a motion to introduce directives for equalization of benefits among unions; however, the motion did not obtain the two-thirds majority necessary for statutory changes.[10] Attempts of financially less opulent unions to enforce some over-all benefit plan for all DGB affiliates, as provided for by the 1949 charter, have so far led to nothing more than the appointment of study committees. However, a well-developed system of arbitration serves to prevent differential benefits from becoming a lasting source of jurisdictional conflict. An individual union member is not free to shop around for the most "profitable" union; however, blocks of members may be shifted from one union to another on the strength of DGB-initiated arbitration decisions.

Financially solid unions—be they large or small—enjoy a great measure of administrative independence in building up union services and

---

* Dr. Agartz' contractual relation with the WWI was terminated on December 31, 1955. The present chairman of the WWI is Dr. Bruno Gleitze, who was appointed at the end of 1956.

facilities. Weak unions, such as the organization of farm laborers, have to rely on the Federation to help them carry on their collective bargaining or set up educational facilities. They are the ones who would most favor the re-establishment of a more effective and authoritative DGB leadership.

Until 1953 the membership of DGB-affiliated unions was on the increase, almost keeping pace with the rise of the labor force. About 39 per cent of the total labor force was unionized; union organization was highest among the miners (92 per cent) and lowest among farm laborers (10 per cent). Since 1953, some unions have been losing members; present membership figures no longer reflect the continuing rise in the labor force. Between September, 1952, and September, 1955, for example, total membership of DGB-affiliated unions showed only an insignificant increase from 6,004,000 to 6,104,000, whereas the total number of wage and salary earners during that period rose from 15,400,000 to 17,800,000. It may be assumed that today the percentage of unionized workers (including white-collar workers) has fallen to 35, with membership losses apparently heaviest among miners and textile workers. To some extent, this drop may be attributed to special problems, such as the changeover, in the miners union, from checkoff to dues collection by union officials, or the high turnover among textile workers (most of whom are women); the annual rate of admissions into and withdrawals from the textile unions is about 25 per cent of the union total, and is thus sufficient to impede the development of strong union loyalty. Yet, with all due allowance for specific situations, static or receding unionization in the face of an expanding labor force is indicative of growing skepticism on the part of workers about labor unions in general.

It has been traditional in Germany for union dues to equal one hour's wages per week. But when the checkoff system, unknown in pre-1933 Germany, was supplanted again by dues collection through union channels (save in a few major steel plants where the checkoff continued under codetermination), union treasuries were confronted with growing reluctance on the part of the rank and file to report actual hourly earnings. A good estimate of the dues actually collected by all the German unions would be 60 to 70 per cent of the sum expected on the hour's-pay-a-week principle. Some unions have instituted a more realistic dues scale, amounting to approximately two hours' wages per month.

Union revenues and expenditures vary with the income structure of the trade, the organization and efficiency of dues collection, and the members' frame of mind. As a consequence, there is considerable variation in the financial assistance that different unions can give their members. The richest of them all, the metal workers union, which collected

143,138,000 DM in dues during the two-year period ending December 31, 1953, was in a position to spend 28 per cent of its income from dues on worker benefits; and it still had 17.5 per cent of the dues left to put into the strike relief chest.[11] To be able to save a corresponding amount for the strike chest, the struggling textile workers had to be more frugal about benefits; they earmarked only 17.5 per cent of their income from dues for that purpose.[12]

Elected union presidents and board members on the national, regional, and local levels still are, by and large, men (and a few women) of the older generation. The youngest are now in their early forties; and the oldest of the presidents, head of the building trades, is well into his seventies. Most of today's union leaders acquired maturity as union men under the Weimar Republic, when they held union positions at a subordinate or medium level. Many of them were persecuted by the Hitler regime; all had been barred from public life during the Nazi era, and some spent the Hitler years in exile.

Among appointed officials, an increasing number are of the younger generation.* Most board members and appointed officials are members of the SPD. A minority, usually characterized by a high degree of activity and devotion, have graduated—in some instances as late as the mid-1940's—from the Communist Party or from smaller left-wing splinter groups, in particular from Leonhard Nelson's *Internationaler Sozialistischer Kampfbund* (ISK).

On both the Federation and the industrial union level, elective officeholders have to submit to new elections at biennial or, more recently, triennial conventions attended by elected delegates from lower-level units. A leader who is skillful and esteemed, even if he is not loved and admired, may expect to be re-elected, along with his entire slate. However, the 1952 DGB convention and the 1953 woodworkers convention surprised many by showing that re-election was not completely automatic. Still, except in cases of manifest dissatisfaction with the incumbent, or lack of authority and cohesion among board members (which seems to have been the case of the DGB leadership since the early fifties), open competition for union leadership is not unduly emphasized. In the majority of cases, election serves rather to bear out co-optation practices.

Christian unionists so far have been obtaining numbers of offices for their nominees by prearrangement with the Socialist labor leaders, although, in some instances, getting the delegates (most of whom were Socialists) to elect the candidates agreed upon was a tough job for the

---

* According to 1953 figures, 2.2 per cent of the 1,639 DGB employees were below 21 years of age; 55 per cent between 21 and 30 (*Geschäftsbericht DGB 1952–53*, p. 90). The average age of members of the public-service workers union was 39, and that of its elected board members 44 (*Geschäftsbericht ÖTV 1952–54*, p. 532).

union leaders. A minority of officeholders, accordingly, are full-fledged members of the CDU.

Communists were all but eliminated from officeholding on the federal and regional levels years in advance of the official banning of the party in 1956. On the local level, some industrial unions may be confronted with rank-and-file insistence on choosing or reappointing a known Communist. Occasionally, a Communist thus elected will be confirmed by union headquarters, and will be required to disavow Point 37 of the Communist Party Theses (which governs the true Communist's union conduct). But such confirmation does not protect the few communist officeholders from summary dismissal if they violate union policies. Also, while isolated communist officeholders might be tolerated, the same tolerance does not extend to well-organized clusters of communist officeholders. For example, the construction workers union recently dissolved its communist-controlled Rhineland district, ejected the incumbent officers, and started to reorganize from scratch.

As practiced by the unions, the system of co-optation of younger officials, later subjected to confirmation by election, ensures some measure of cohesion and unity of purpose, but it does so at a price. It does not make for a climate conducive to initiative and originality of thinking. The younger generation of union officials, now in their twenties and thirties, may well have less perspective than their elders, who saw (though they did not make) much history in their lifetimes; and it is too early to tell whether the more limited horizon of the younger generation will be compensated for by more steadfastness and efficacy in action.

Salaries of union officials as well as additional emoluments—such as housing allowances, per diem, and income from union-nominated membership on boards of directors—assure elected and some appointed officials of a comfortable, and at times (if they are allowed to accumulate many directorships and similar posts) even a considerable income. The old theory to the effect that remuneration of union officials should not exceed reasonably high workers' wages has generally been abandoned, though no attempt has been made to follow the American practice of raising the salaries of labor leaders to the income level of high-ranking members of industrial management. The union old-timer is still anxiously watching over the expenditure of union funds by the leaders. Unions might, and do, build spacious headquarters, but no union board would ever vote any sizable appropriation to help a union leader build a lavish residence.

Background and political ancestry have left a lasting imprint on the active unionist's analysis of the present situation, and on his understanding of the role he is to play in contemporary German society. Official, often elliptical, statements by union spokesmen to the effect that the unions represent the interests of all those employed in dependent positions manifestly refer to three fields of activity: (*a*) wages, hours, and working conditions; (*b*) social welfare; and (*c*) pressure politics.

From the late 1940's on, German unions have again been seeking the degree of control of the labor market that they had in Weimar days; to the bargaining and power position of private property and public administration, they oppose the bargaining and power position of organized labor in order to set the price of labor and to determine working conditions.

In the period immediately following the currency reform and during the early years of the Bonn regime, the unions, under Böckler's stewardship, still clung to the idea that wage demands should be de-emphasized in favor of a steady price structure, fuller employment, and increased investment. In part, this doctrine was based on the assumption that self-restraint might help labor obtain a larger share in industrial management and thus lead the way toward industrial democracy. To a greater extent, the policy had its roots in the obsessive fear of most union leaders that inflation might result from a wage-price spiral. In the mid-1950's, when there was full employment and a functioning market, this voluntary restraint in the exercise of normal labor-market functions was abandoned. There was substituted for it a doctrine inspired by Agartz. Union statements now argue that wage increases are necessary to underpin consumer demand and to secure labor's full share in the national product.[13] In advocating the reduction of the statutory work week from 48 to 40 hours, the cutting-down of actual weekly working time from an average of 50 to about 45 hours, and in urging adoption of a five-day week without loss of pay, the unions are exercising their labor-market function under especially auspicious circumstances.

As a rule, collective bargaining is industry-wide on the regional level. Thus, agreements that are arrived at extend to the most advanced as well as the marginal producers. This breadth of coverage deprives the agreement of much of its meaning, because exact conditions can not be prescribed for an entire industry. The setting of actual wages, which often run about 20 per cent above the contractual ones, becomes the subject of agreement between management and works council in particular plants. Whether the unions, facing determined employer resistance to a change, will be able to arrive either at more realistic bargaining units embracing smaller segments of an industry or at direct agreements with key employers, is open to question.

The union performs its functions in the field of social welfare in two ways: (1) it operates as a kind of mutual aid society extending benefits to its own members; and (2) it co-operates with governmental labor authorities and employers by serving as agent of the insured workers in the framework of private or public social-insurance institutions.

The third major area of union activity is in the political field. As every social group will do in the normal course of its activities, the unions bring pressure to bear on governmental agencies to ensure maximum benefits for their members. In addition, in the light of Germany's specific political history, labor organizations tend to arrogate to themselves the role of guarantors of the democratic process. Labor refuses to be considered just another group among many in a pluralistic society. As Alfred Weber, patriarch of "cultural sociology," and in recent years philosophical adviser to German labor, puts it, organized labor stands for specific human values not inherent in any other group.[14] It does not derive this role from the quantitative aspect alone, i.e., from the fact that labor, under conditions of advanced mass society, represents a larger part of the population than does any other group. Beyond the sheer impact of numbers, the labor leaders' analysis of past history and present trends in German society leads them to believe that they speak for the only group dedicated by virtue of conviction and self-interest to the maintenance and preservation of German democracy.[15]

This leads labor to view present-day parliamentary institutions with a great deal of skepticism. In its view, the working of these institutions depends on, and is impaired by, (1) the enormous power wielded by a huge bureaucracy of "experts," and (2) the close tie-in between the present administration, its parliamentary majority, and certain special-interest groups among which labor is conspicuously absent. The interplay of these factors, it is held, obstructs normal political channels and vitiates public opinion to the point of making parliament unrepresentative.

Given these views, labor's relationship to the government is necessarily ambiguous. In the immediate interest of those they represent, labor organizations participate in a number of public functions. Further, they defend and uphold democratic government against its communist and rightist detractors. But few union people identify themselves with the present governmental setup, because, in their view, it is not nearly democratic enough. This attitude is more than a fleeting displeasure with the actions of those who happen to be at the helm according to the rules of the parliamentary game. As far as devoted unionists—Socialists as well as most Christian Democrats—are concerned, the present Germany simply is not their state; it is the state of the others, of big bureaucracy, big business monopolies, big organizations of special-interest groups, and perhaps—as some might add in conspiratorial whispers—

the big hierarchy of the Catholic Church. These "Bigs," in the unionists' view, have gradually and methodically installed themselves in the machinery of government and are modeling it to their liking.

This feeling need not last forever. Adolf Kummernuss, president of the Industrial Union of Public Service and Transportation Workers, speaking at his union's convention in the spring of 1955, said: "If one day the function of the liberal-democratic *Rechtsstaat* should change, so would, too, the position of the labor unions within this state." [16] The feeling of the unions that they are facing a governmental structure usurped by "the others" is not in any way a manifestation of militant dissent inspired by the revolutionary image of a different state, a different government, and a different society; it is merely the mild expression of widely-shared reservations about the Bonn Republic's narrow social, psychological, and territorial basis. This attitude of muted reserve is accompanied by an almost mystical certainty that the future will rectify the congenital weaknesses of the West German State.

In spite of an occasional slip into the vernacular of former times, German unions reject as unrealistic any undifferentiated approach to the "bourgeois state," according to which (assuming the fiction of a homogeneous and united working class) there would be a fundamental change in social and political institutions as a result of labor's "conquest of political power." They are convinced that such "conquest," even if it were successful, would create conditions and problems much worse than the ones confronting the unions today. To this extent the arrangements of a pluralistic democracy predicated on the recognition of the needs of all social groups are accepted as final.

Expressing anxieties and apprehensions that are widespread among and deeply felt by the rank and file, union leaders voice grave doubts about whether present boom conditions will go on indefinitely, perpetuated by their own momentum. Nor are they convinced that those now in control of the German economy will be able to ensure industry's continuous and satisfactory operation. Moreover, they insist that, contrary to government propaganda, the German economic system, even today, is full of privately imposed or publicly decreed restrictive patterns.

Not that the union leaders believe in the desirability and practicability of a fully competitive system; they do not even oppose with any degree of consistency the restrictive patterns they decry. In fact, occasionally they themselves advocate measures favorable to restraint of trade, cartelization, and spread of monopolies. The miners union, for example, strives hard to prevent dismemberment of the tight coal-sales organization, on the ground that miners in many marginal mines would lose their livelihood if competitive prices determined the price of coal. Union leaders are not particularly inclined, either, in the present climate of opinion, to overemphasize the demand for transferring major sectors of industry into some form of public ownership; they seem to realize that such a move, besides lacking in popular appeal, would not essentially contribute toward furthering their objectives.

But again and again they argue emphatically that a basic pattern of industrial democracy—even on a limited scale—must be established; they urge action to this effect, eloquently pointing to the always latent and now once again manifest abuse of political power which is inherent in the present structure of industry, and to the urgent need of preventing the dangers of a new business slump. As spokesmen for those most directly affected by changes in the level of employment, the unions insist that the system of labor participation in management's economic decisions, which is now limited to the steel and coal industries, must be extended beyond these to comprise all major industries. In addition, they argue that economic stability requires the establishment of public agencies of economic control—jointly operated by representatives of management, labor, and public—that will have jurisdiction over entire industry groups, and that will supervise these groups and, if need be, correct managerial decisions on the plant level.

Union leaders add that monopolistic business, far from conceding these demands, does its utmost to turn the process of reconcentration now in full sway into a powerful tool for undermining and rendering meaningless what little progress in labor participation has been achieved in coal and steel. Management practically no longer objects to labor representatives on boards of directors, for these boards in individual corporations are rapidly losing their importance. On the other hand, the 1956 legislation regulating labor participation in the management of the newly-formed holding company restricts, far more than did the 1951 statute, both the number of enterprises subject to codetermination and, through election procedures, the influence of the union.[17] Labor leaders angrily brush aside industry's contention that there can be no functioning democratic society, nor exercise of labor market functions, unless the principle of private ownership of means of production remains intact, and unless the owners' responsibility for decisions affecting production and investments remains free of outside interference. Labor's spokesmen contend that that kind of democratic society has never existed in Germany, and that German industrial management has never at any time displayed a willingness to abide by its rules whenever they have run counter to the interests of those in control of economic power.[18]

The age-old antagonism between union and industry, after having subsided for at least part of the first postwar decade, has reappeared. It bears on principles rather than on concrete decisions. However, management and labor co-operation on boards of directors thus far has not given rise to any difficulties. Present boom conditions prevent more than an occasional full-dress flare-up of the basic antagonism; but when a clash does occur, all the bitterness of former days is unleashed, and labor and industry perform their traditional parts.

The much-discussed problem of the political strike presented just such an issue. Some political strikes had taken place during the occupation era; these had been directed against the public authorities and, still more, the foreign masters, rather than against the employers. Generally, they were regarded as patriotic demonstrations designed to bring the pitiable conditions of the people to the attention of those in power. Political strikes in the early 1950's were different, however. They were avowedly meant as acts of pressure to introduce, preserve, or extend labor participation in management. Some of the patterns of union participation in the coal and steel industries originally established by the British Military Government were retained under Bonn legislation, partly as a result of the strike threat issued by the unions and supported by a unanimous strike vote taken in the mines and the steel plants.

Union and SPD efforts to pass legislation extending the scope of codetermination were frustrated by the government and its parliamentary majority in 1952. This resulted in a political strike in printing, which, however, remained abortive. The latest political strike occurred in 1954; it was a one-day walkout in protest against a statement by industry leader Paul Reusch characterizing a 1951 strike as a successful attempt at blackmail.

Neither employers nor the overwhelming majority of the legal fraternity have been willing to acknowledge the ubiquity of pressure politics in a democratic society, and the consequent difficulty of differentiating between respectable economic activity and illicit political pressure.* The issue remains in abeyance. Meanwhile, as we shall see below, union attitudes toward rearmament have shown that labor lead-

* The legality of the "political strike" is affirmed in R. Schmid, "Der politische Streik," in *Gewerkschaftliche Monatshefte* (hereafter cited as *G.M.*), January, 1954, p. 1; and F. Bauer, "Politischer Streik und Strafrecht," in *Juristenzeitung*, 1953, p. 65. Schmid's article aroused a vehement controversy not only because of its content, but also because of Schmid's job. Many newspapers, members of the legal fraternity, and representatives of industry thought it improper for a president of an appeals court to utter opinions of such a nature. J. H. Kaiser, *Der politische Streik*, Berlin, 1955, thinks of the political strike as "a primitive weapon of self-help." *G.M.*, May, 1955, p. 326, gives an analysis of a public discussion between the Jesuit union theoretician, Nell-Breuning, and the vice-president of the Bundestag, C. Schmid. C. Schmid distinguishes between pressure on the parliament before a decision has been taken and the fact "that the trade-unions have no choice other than to accept a decision of parliament—as they have so far always done."

ers acknowledge the authority of the federal legislature and will not challenge political decisions which have become the law of the land.

The unions nonetheless continue to assert that political pressure in favor of broad legislative and political aims, even if it takes the form of political strikes, is as permissible as are the pressure tactics of management, which are no less effective for being applied behind closed doors. The irreconcilable views held by management and labor on the subject of the strike as a political weapon serve as another indication of the fact that, in Germany, political notions revolving around the state as a repressive authority never yielded to nor merged with those conceiving of it as a dynamic expression of community life with ample latitude for divergent social and political forces.

Unions in Politics

Unions, according to their leaders, are organized for political action; yet these very same leaders would immediately hasten to add that need for political action should not be mistaken for party politics. The distinction made by union leaders between neutrality toward political organizations (though they are never neutral toward communism or fascism) and neutrality toward political goals is of recent, postwar origin. The neutrality toward "political" organizations that is called for by all union charters primarily implies two things: (1) no union organizations shall take a stand on issues involving churches, religious beliefs, educational philosophies, or whatever else may be viewed as having a relationship to *Weltanschauung*; (2) unions will not subsidize or otherwise support "political" organizations.

However, in contrast to the practice in France, German union officers are not barred from running for political office. On the contrary, the unions want their officers to hold political office so that they can support union demands on whatever political bodies they might be elected to. Political neutrality thus becomes a difficult proposition for unions whose leaders and officers are in politics. There are strong tendencies afoot among both traditionally Socialist and traditionally Christian unionists toward reverting to the Weimar pattern, when all unions were more or less closely affiliated with specific political parties. Christian unionists constantly complain about disregard shown to their interests and personnel claims by the solid majority of SPD-minded unionists. Conversely, the more radical among the Socialists chafe under the DGB leadership's perennial efforts to ward off everything which might offend the sensitivities of or infringe upon the position awarded the Christian minority. One union intellectual who was interviewed in the course of preparation of the present study saw the Christian wing as an automatic brake that arrested progress whenever the unions were about to take a step forward, but which was immediately released whenever they decided to go into reverse.

In the parliament, labor's interests are the concern only of the SPD and the CDU. These two parties drew about 78 per cent of the total vote cast in Germany's last federal election.

The Social Democratic Party (28.9 per cent of the popular vote and 151 out of 487 Bundestag seats) is the group with the largest membership (over 550,000) and also the group that is the most homogeneous with respect to both traditional outlook and social composition. By and large, it represents the interests of wage and salary earners, the lower-level civil servants, and the urban consumers in general. Only occasionally do conflicts arise between the interests of these groups. From time to time, impelled by those who believe that a program favoring the independent middle class would improve the party's chance of shedding its minority status in the Bundestag, the SPD takes a few halting and generally unrewarding steps in this direction. But those in the party who see the prospects of a broader mass appeal in a more energetic and consistent representation of labor are likely to remain in the majority, as against those who urge that the party should try to appeal to the middle class.

Accordingly, the SPD is apt to uphold the union viewpoint on all major issues. Only in the few instances when organizations equally worthy of support from the SPD's point of view (such as the DAG and DGB) happen to be in disagreement does the SPD try to steer a neutral course, proffering its good services to both contenders. In view of the SPD's friendly feeling toward labor, the actual number of union officials among SPD parliamentarians matters less than do problems of adequate co-ordination, division of labor, and selection of qualified spokesmen for key political jobs. If there is, in the SPD, a nucleus of an interest-group that may pursue objectives not in line with union policies, it will be found in the ranks of present and past holders of political offices and government jobs, a group inclined to identify itself with "the state" or "the public order" as against the demands of any particular social group. In a number of instances, the wish to retain certain administrative positions may involve such officeholders in a public policy inimical to union demands. At present, this is, at worst, a problem on the lower level, in the *Land* administrations and municipalities in which the SPD is still firmly entrenched. The SPD's semipermanent opposition status on the federal level has not allowed much opportunity for such conflicts of loyalties, familiar to students of Weimar Germany.

The situation is quite different in the CDU-CSU, a loosely-knit federation of divergent interests that is kept together by ideological ties, a substantial share in the sinews of government, and the personality of the party leader. In contrast to its ancestor, the Catholic Center Party of Weimar days, the interdenominational CDU has acquired, all over Germany, a wide electoral following among both urban and rural middle classes, both Protestant and Catholic. Its labor vote, although very large in North Rhine-Westphalia, does not seem to have increased in the same proportion in other regions. While there is reason to assume that wage and salary earners accounted for possibly more than 50 per cent of the CDU's national vote in the 1953 election, it is not likely that industrial wage earners have ever provided as much as one-quarter of the total CDU vote. This, of course, makes it difficult for CDU union people to get a platform favorable to the unions adopted as official party policy.

Labor representation within the CDU-CSU consists of three distinguishable, though often overlapping, groups. There are, first, the officeholders and active union men from DGB-affiliated organizations. In the face of a conflict of loyalties, their allegiance in the past has generally gone first to the union from which they derived their power and status. Ever since the triumph of Hitlerism, these men have been opposed to every semblance of dual unionism. Therefore, they are in principle opposed to recent tendencies to set up rival Christian unions in various industries. Also, they would think twice before abandoning their jobs and pension claims, as well as those of their followers, for the sake of an uncertain future in a rival Christian union organization.

Secondly, there are, among labor's representatives in the CDU-CSU, full-time politicians who once came from the ranks of the pre-Hitler Christian unions, and who now hold strategic positions within the CDU either as labor experts or as political leaders and organizers. Their standing in the party often depends on the loyalty and response they may expect to evoke in the ranks of Christian unionists. Their attitude toward the prospect of a separate Christian union ranges from reserved to unfriendly.

Members of both these first two groups work together in the CDU's *Sozialausschüsse,* a skeleton organization which may be called the party's labor arm. They seek to keep Christian trade-unionists together, to enhance their influence in the unions, and to present labor's viewpoint to a wider Christian audience. They co-operate with the CDU's party machine, and they delegate about twelve organizers to the various party districts to take care of the party's working-class clientele. They distribute 20,000 copies of a newsletter, but the number even of nominal members of the *Sozialausschüsse* is much smaller. Active membership outside the circle of political and union professionals is restricted to younger people aspiring to a union or a political career. The *Sozialausschüsse* are more a breeding ground for Catholic labor politics than they are a labor organization.

The third group of CDU-CSU labor representatives may be said to include CDU parliamentarians whose main field of endeavor is in the *Katholische Arbeiterbewegung* (KAB), which is massed chiefly in North Rhine-Westphalia, the *Werkvolk,* which operates in Bavaria and the Palatinate, and the *Christliche Arbeiterjugend.* In all three of these Catholic lay organizations, major appointments are church-controlled; activities and personnel of these associations for Catholic workers are to some extent church-financed. Membership figures are not very meaningful, as they include wives and pensioners: for KAB and *Werkvolk,* together, they may be in the neighborhood of 200,000.[19]

From the end of the war to 1955, these organizations, which have a half-century history of disputes and rivalry with Christian labor unions, performed spiritual, welfare, and political functions, but were not engaged in union-type activities. Yet the recent drive for the establishment of a separate Christian union originated precisely within the ranks of this group.

A rival Christian union organization was officially called into being in November, 1955, under the name *Christliche Gewerkschaftsbewegung Deutschlands* (CGD). However, it met with but little success, and had claimed only slightly more than 20,000 members by the end of 1956. Its recent merger with the *Gesamtverband der christlichen Gewerkschaften des Saarlandes* ("Christian trade-union federation of the Saar"), whose chairman, Peter Gier, became president of the CGD, has brought the organization an additional 45,000 members, but has, at the same time, accentuated its regional, rather than national, character.

There is an important consideration which, from the outset, limits severely the chances of such a rival organization. After 1945, for the first time in recent German history, the long-standing barriers between the German labor movement and the Christian churches seemed to have been lifted. Many causes had contributed to this effect. The common background of hostility to the Third Reich had brought together many of the leading figures of labor and churches; both unionists and churchmen suffered at the hands of the Communists in the Soviet zone; and the decisive turn of the Protestant churches and, at least initially, of the Catholic Church toward emphasis on social responsibility, with the unions' de-emphasis of doctrinal points in the period after the war, as well as labor's willingness to lend an ear to the church's social program— all helped to minimize the area of ideological friction. Churches and labor have co-operated on many occasions, and the unions have not objected to the church's missionary forays into their ranks.

The consolidation of the Adenauer administration and the subsequent more conservative interpretation of Catholic social doctrine by the church authorities undoubtedly lessened the spirit of co-operation between the unions and the Catholic Church. Labor's coolness toward "political Catholicism" as an attempt to utilize religious issues as a pretext for political proselytizing tended to resuscitate some of the old cleavages. But relations with the Evangelical churches continued to be friendly.[20] Protestant Church authorities almost unanimously condemned the establishment of a rival union organization on a religious basis, whereas Catholic authorities were lukewarm and circumspect toward the new venture.*

In the long run, the strategic position of the Christian labor wing, whether it operates within the context of a unified labor movement or as an independent organization, could be appreciably enhanced only under two sets of circumstances: (1) if the present parliamentary majority disintegrated to the point of making Christian labor support a vital problem to the CDU-led government, or (2) if a new majority which would include both SPD and CDU should crystallize and make Christian labor an indispensable bonding factor between the two by virtue of both its labor and religious orientations. This possibility of an SPD-CDU majority has figured prominently in the stand taken by Christian labor politicians of independent stature, such as Jakob Kaiser, Federal Minister for All-German Affairs, or Karl Arnold, Minister President of North Rhine-Westphalia. It did not dispel their profound distrust of experiments in dual unionism. Apparently, preservation of a unified DGB also seems more likely to them to provide steppingstones for a political realignment, if one day it should be deemed desirable or inevitable.

Labor's attempts to find enough supporters in the Bundestag for its legislative programs have only been partially successful. Liaison officers on both the DGB and the industrial union level have worked around the clock, and publicity campaigns of considerable magnitude (including, as in the case of labor's 1955 "action program," delivery of copies to all households in the Federal Republic) have been carried through. So far such endeavors have not changed the parliamentary situation: if labor demands concern some question of social policy, such

* H. R. Wagner has analyzed the attitudes of young workers toward religion in his "Social and Religious Outlooks of a Young Labor Elite" (Monograph No. III, under the project *Religion in Germany Today,* Vol. 2, Research Division of the New School for Social Research, New York, 1955). This is an exhaustive study based on both interviews and autobiographic material from students of the Frankfurt Akademie der Arbeit.

as children's allowances or a monthly paid rest period for working women, labor support in the ranks of the CDU will gather strength and collect a nucleus of seventy to eighty socially oriented CDU-CSU members. Either they will be strong enough to force an internal group compromise within the CDU-CSU which, if not completely in line with labor's demands, will be acceptable to the unions, or, in an extreme case, the measure will be carried through the Bundestag with the help of a split CDU and the 151 solid SPD votes. The same kind of thing may happen in the exceptional case when agricultural and labor interests converge, as they might, for example, on the question of allowing special taxation privileges for co-operatives. However, if the issues concern institutional patterns, such as the organization of labor courts or the question of whether the insured (as under the Weimar Republic) should continue to have a two-thirds majority in the administration of the public health benefit fund, labor support within the CDU invariably dwindles.*

The most important vote on the domestic front during the first Bundestag was that on the labor-management law of 1952, which rejected labor's demand for extending "codetermination" beyond the coal and steel industries. On this question, only a handful of CDU members either abstained or voted for SPD amendments. The final roll call records one CDU member voting with the SPD and seven CDU abstentions, as against 122 CDU votes for the majority.[21] After the vote, the unions conceived the idea of showing their dissatisfaction with the political orientation of the first Bundestag openly by intervening in the September 6, 1953, election with the slogan "Elect a Better Bundestag!" This was as close to electioneering on the part of the SPD as is the Catholic clergy's habitual support of the CDU-CSU when it asks Catholics to "vote only for a Christian party." The outcome of the 1953 election was discouraging to the unions: it resulted in a new array of Christian demands for safeguarding the neutrality of the DGB and for giving the Christian minority a firm hold on major positions of power within the Federation.[22] However, neither in 1953 nor in the fall of 1955 (when the same demands were reiterated prior to the founding of the CGD) was the DGB leadership (including the Christian unionists in its ranks) prepared to accede to ultimatums. On the other hand, its success in keeping the strength of its Christian rival to a minimum shows that the DGB went to great lengths to satisfy what it considered the bona fide claims of Christian unionists, as against the demands emanating from Christian labor politicians outside union ranks.

* This was shown in the battle over the law regulating employee representation in government service (cf. Bundestag, 73rd Session, March 17, 1955, p. 4044).

Why have labor's pressure tactics on parliament and parties not been more successful? There are, first, institutional restrictions. It is alleged in union circles that so-called "labor neutrality" did not permit the unions to finance the SPD to a degree comparable to the support given the CDU and other middle-class parties by industry. Under the system prevailing during the Weimar period, when election time came around, the ADGB forwarded to the SPD a contribution significant enough to cover campaign expenditures, so that membership dues in the party were left available for the regular cost of running the party machine. But in 1953 union organizations did not contribute anything directly toward financing the 3.5 million marks which, according to the SPD treasurer, went into the party's federal election campaign.[23] Individual union officers as party members (who regularly pay above-average membership dues according to income) almost certainly contributed to election funds. The union organization as such, however, had nothing to do with that effort. There was some indirect help from union quarters. The DGB contributed the above-mentioned slogan: "Elect a Better Bundestag!" A struggling SPD publishing house here or there may have received some general institutional advertising or some liberal advance on printing orders. A particularly enterprising union laboriously compiled a questionnaire which it sent to all candidates; it asked them their stand on specific issues related to union demands, and publicized both the positive and the negative answers; but it did not dare, in the face of official labor neutrality, to contribute to the campaign fund of the candidates who gave the right answers.

Whatever help labor may have given the SPD was in the form of indirect activity engaged in by the unions themselves, rather than in contributions to the party for campaign purposes. This at best half-hearted and indirect effort, always undertaken with a furtive glance at the neutrality pledge, put both the unions and the SPD at a distinct disadvantage as compared to the CDU and right-wing parties that were liberally financed by industry. The disproportion will probably be still greater in the future, because the second Bundestag has made political contributions tax-deductible. It is this measure that has led SPD and unions to demand repeatedly that publicity be given to party financing in accordance with the requirements of the Basic Law of the Bonn Republic. To date, such information has been made public on a purely voluntary basis only by the SPD.

But even in the unlikely event that party financing should be subjected to effective political control, the unions' ability to influence the minds of the voters would scarcely be equal to that of the industrial community. This then is not a question of equality of conditions under which labor and industry operate; it is rather a question of presentation and audience receptiveness. The unions spend a considerable amount of money, probably close to 5 per cent of their total income, on publications. Every industrial union brings out a periodical, which is furnished free to all members. These sheets, however, share the ills that afflict *Welt der Arbeit,* the official weekly publication of the DGB.* Addressed to all organized workers and their families (some twenty-five million people), they constitute official literature. They are sometimes ponderously written and are given to complaints, exhortations, and indignation; and they often offer narrow, technically conceived social, economic, and legal analyses of conditions, requirements, and achievements. These sheets, therefore, litter the factory floor; they are no match either for the slick plant magazine that weaves the management viewpoint into stories of a happy industrial community, or for the spurious communist plant newspapers, equally interlacing the goals of the Communist Party with matters of interest to the individual worker on a given job. Recently, however, union locals and factory groups have begun to issue plant labor papers in an effort to compete with these other influences.

Workers, along with the rest of the community, tend to go in for light reading; hence the stupendous sales of all types of popular magazines. The more serious general circulation publications, whether local, provincial, or national, follow, by and large, a liberal policy in their political comments. Trying to present the facts objectively, most of them give a more or less impartial coverage to labor news. However, comment and analysis on labor and related economic issues is quite a different story; most of them are more sympathetic to industry than to labor.[24] Some of the authoritative German dailies and weeklies had initially been financed by industry. Most of the dailies with a circulation below 150,000 are closely dependent on the continued favor of both local and institutional advertisers; they shy away from controversial issues. A small number of newspapers close to the SPD, a few of which are popularly written and have a large circulation, are in no position to redress the balance on the national scale. Though the unions could easily afford to do more than they are now doing, they so far have not succeeded either in launching a popular magazine reflecting their viewpoint along with the necessary number of pictures of scantily-clad females, or in establishing a journal of opinion qualified to compete with those which present the views of the industrial community. Moreover, at least as long as prosperity lasts, the coincidence of labor's and industry's interests under a system of liberal economy is widely accepted;

* *Welt der Arbeit,* which, unlike most of the other periodicals, is not given away free, is a heavily subsidized paper with a circulation of about one hundred thousand.

the editorial skill which would sort out the discrepancy between union and industry viewpoints in a nondoctrinaire way is simply not now available to the unions.

While the political neutrality formula lasts, the unions will be less able to help their political friends than is industry. However, labor is not barred, except by lack of initiative and talent, from any effective means of communication. Its appeal is simply not broad enough to overcome the public's (even the union public's) preference for commercial news outlets, whose impartiality of judgment in labor and related issues is limited by financial dependence or expectation of future gain.

The Worker and His Union

A poll was recently taken among some working-class youths in Hamburg, asking them to define their understanding of the term "proletariat." Sixty-seven per cent of the male and 80 per cent of the female interviewees were unable to relate the word to anything whatsoever; 7 and 3 per cent, respectively, thought it to mean "worker"; 12 and 4 per cent thought it meant something degrading; and only 3 and 1 per cent, respectively, related it to traditional class concepts.[25] Though the results might vary somewhat with older age groups, the phenomenon remains the same, as might be seen from the experience of trade-union organizers at traditional May Day festivals; not only are they very poorly attended, but those who do attend have difficulty understanding what they symbolize. Those who organize them, old-timers of the German labor movement, are always relieved when the day approaches its close.

All this confirms a state of affairs apparent during recent years.[26] Workers in general have ceased to consider themselves a specific class with a specific mission. This does not mean that caste distinctions have disappeared, especially between manual and white-collar workers. But these distinctions no longer congeal into total political ideologies. Many factors have contributed to this. The prosperity of the fifties, while multiplying group claims, has not been a favorable soil for the rebuilding of class ideologies. The experience of East Germany, known to all and personally lived through by many, has had a similar effect. Memories of Weimar days are dim and, at best, confused. Only 18 per cent of today's union members belonged to unions in 1933. The good old times, when socialism still attracted the minds and hearts of the members, may still live in the memories of the old-timers, but they live only there. The bureaucratic patterns of present-day unionism, with their inevitable concomitant of low rank-and-file interest in union affairs, may compare unfavorably in their eyes with the situation during the Weimar period.

However, severance of ties between unions and political parties has lessened the chance for the re-emergence of a militant image of the history and tradition of German working-class organization in the minds of the rank-and-filers.

This devaluation or sheer absence of tradition is a contributing cause to the workers' concentration on the concrete situation of the day, and their tendency to interpret their situation in strictly personal terms. Marxist critics dub this state of affairs the *Verbürgerlichung* ("middle-class mental set"), but in applying this term to the workers, they presuppose a class-consciousness on the part of the workers—an awareness of an alternative and better order and a need on their part to dissociate their claims from those of other groups by way of an elaborate theory—which simply does not exist. The workers' attempts to do the best they can under prevailing circumstances, which is characteristic of other social groups as well, may contain an element of resignation, but it scarcely carries the germs of a systematic attempt to set oneself apart from the rest of the community.

Resignation and complaints concern concrete working conditions. The workers often express these with a certain feeling of helplessness, of being exposed to the dictates of anonymous persons and processes, whose workings remain mysterious and beyond their reach. The tendency prevails to translate remote and unintelligible processes and command structures into proximate and approachable ones; problems revolving around working conditions in relation to authorities within reach are tackled on a concrete, personalized level. Improvements are visualized in terms of personal standing; widening or narrowing possibilities are seen within the present organization of work. Satisfaction and dissatisfaction with wages are related to a colleague's remuneration rather than to general principles or abstract standards. The workers' disillusionment with the poor results of codetermination schemes does not derive from the failure, obvious by now, to shift power relations between management and the unions, but from the fact that the hierarchical structure of the shop and the worker's daily work experience have been but little affected by the attempts.[27]

The complex structure of authority faced by the individual at work includes management, works council, and the union. From the viewpoint of the worker, none of these is either completely inimical or unreservedly friendly. To a varying degree, the actions of all of them confine his freedom, but they also contribute to his well-being.

Two of these authorities, management and the works council, often appear to the worker as complementary rather than competing institutions. Management provides the direction and the frame of his daily work; details and possible adaptation of his interests to those of the shop are determined by negotiations between management and works council.[28] Yet the works councils, and especially those in the so-called "co-determination" plants of the coal and steel industries, are plant- rather than union-oriented. With the management of the plant, the works council debates problems of job description and individual performance which determine the actual content of the pay envelope within the wide and loose framework of collective agreements. The manifold voluntary social services which German industry prefers to higher wages, and which also help to lower corporation taxes, remain within the province of management and, much to the discomfiture of the union, outside the sphere of the union-negotiated contract. The works council, however, may have a say in the details of the matter. The works council becomes a harmonizing agency, a sort of buffer between management and the worker, rather than an organ which takes an initiative of its own. That is why the worker will remember a favorable measure initiated by the management more often than a plan submitted by the works council.[29]

Wherever codetermination privileges bring members of the works council still more closely together with management, by virtue of statutory representation on the board of directors, a new stratum of industrial functionaries, to some extent sharing management prerogatives, makes its appearance. The sphere of management may thus tend to include a privileged upper stratum of the working class.[30] To what extent such privileged groups can be effectively controlled by their constituents, the workers, is a matter of conjecture. Workers' complaints about lack of information from the full-time member of the works council are frequent.[31] The possibility of exercising control over elected officers is limited. The workers can hardly do more than refuse to renew the officers' mandates when they come up for re-election at the biennial works-council elections. They have made frequent use of this prerogative in recent years; the turnover among works-council members has been heavy.*

Within this authority structure, the union has come to hold the last and the most uncertain place. Of the elements involved, it is the only one that does not operate within the plant. Union efforts to remedy this shortcoming by invading management's sphere have left but few marks. In the coal and steel industries, there are, of course, the union-nominated "labor directors," a function that corresponds closely to that of vice-president in charge of labor relations in an American corporation.

* Within the jurisdiction of the metal workers union, 43.8 per cent of those elected to the works councils in 1953, and 43.9 per cent of those elected in 1955, were new members (cf. *Gewerkschafter*, 1955, No. 8, p. 38).

But since the unions have not succeeded in establishing industry-wide bodies to co-ordinate this participation in management, they have lost all hold over their nominees. From the workers' viewpoint, the labor director is just another member of the upper hierarchy. Though he may be better known to the workers than are other members of management, few of the workers ever have direct contact with him. Lately, union spokesmen have gone out of their way to say that this new managerial element, which has risen from its ranks, should be regarded as representing management rather than the union.[32]

There are also, as we have seen, union members on the boards of directors of corporations. However, under the 1952 labor-management law (*Betriebsverfassungsgesetz*) applicable to the majority of enterprises other than coal and steel, only few of the union representatives on the boards of directors come from outside the plants. Within the narrow confines in which the worker may choose between a union officeholder and a fellow worker, he prefers to entrust his mandate on the board of directors to a man from the shop. By 1954, of 116 directors' seats in the metal industry which the law permitted to union nominees not on the payroll of the corporation affected, only 37 had actually gone to outsiders.[33] It is doubtful whether this practice is likely to contribute to a more effective representation of the workers' interests; but it does at least permit the chosen rank-and-filers to add to their wages the handsome remuneration that frequently goes with the director's seat.

Another avenue of establishing contact with the affairs of the individual enterprise looks more promising. The unions see to it that union members in every individual shop elect union shop delegates. Unlike the works-council elections, this is not a public election, but generally an informal affair regulated by the bylaws of the individual unions. The delegate gives the unionized worker the feeling of having a person to turn to with his personal difficulties; the delegate will represent the worker both on the works council and to management. The works council—if its members care to be re-elected—usually will prefer not to turn down requests insisted upon by the union delegates. At the same time, the shop delegate, who has no legal standing so far as management is concerned, will have to rely more closely on the support of the union than the works council does. The delegate serves as a link between the factory worker and the union. To what extent this voluntary institution becomes an important factor in the daily life of the workers depends on both the energy of the local union officials and the intensity of interest among the workers themselves.[34] To some extent the works council, shop delegates, and lower-level supervisors compete with each other for the confidence of the worker. The latter's closeness to or estrangement from the union or the works council is indicated by how often he turns for advice or information to the shop delegate, the member of the council, or his immediate supervisors.[35]

The question has sometimes been raised why workers adhere to unions. Union benefits, membership as a precondition for a desirable job, family tradition, antagonism to management practices, or simply the fact that the unions are regarded as representatives of the workingman all figured in the answers.[36] It might be argued that many of these reasons are weaker than they once were in the light of the present generation's distrust of ideologies, and its rational calculation of its interests; but there remain the closely interrelated problems of solidarity and anxiety if present jobs and good times should vanish. Recent studies have shown not only that job security is the most important determinant in the worker's attitude toward his job, but also that the feeling of job insecurity is more widespread among younger workers than among old-timers.[37] This does not imply that the worker specifically expects the union to help him stay on the job; he knows that this, apart from seniority, will be determined by his standing within the factory organization. His joining is the outcome of a much more primitive and undifferentiated feeling. Whatever the future may bring will be easier to face without the additional hardship of isolation.

What permits the unions to retain a place, however ill-defined, in the workers' system of allegiance is this unspecified feeling of solidarity against the possibility of an uncertain future, rather than the concrete objectives advocated or the union movement's practical successes. The unions' chance of commanding obedience among their members has been greatest whenever the issue at stake involved pure questions of political and organizational power. They were able to mobilize the workers for a program of codetermination, which, as the employers pointed out, was neither well understood nor always approved by the workers. One of the reasons was that the unions' authority remained unimpaired in this particular field, since works councils and workers agree that political questions can be solved only on a higher level. Moreover, the immediate stake of the worker in a political issue is somewhat smaller than it is in a wage dispute. Any political strike, since it is on a wider front, is not likely to last as long as a strike for higher pay. A political strike does not endanger the worker's labor contract; one way or another, it is resolved on the governmental level.

Allegiance to the more remote union organization hinges on the attitudes of groups that have first claim on the worker's loyalties. Existing precedents make uncertain, for example, the extent to which a union can rely on worker allegiance in a wage dispute if an agreement over the issue has been reached between management, works council, and shop delegate which the union has not approved. Not only have there been instances when a union's attempt to carry on a *Land*-wide strike has met with only partial success, but also a number of wildcat strikes in individual plants were conducted with the approval of the works council against the express wishes of the union involved. On the other hand, it should be pointed out that the workers' response to the union campaign for a shorter work week was both positive and disciplined— though it was not enthusiastic, since it implied possible loss of cherished overtime pay. In the long and bitter Schleswig-Holstein metal workers strike of 1956–1957, the rank and file was less prepared to make concessions than was the union management.

When a new works council is elected in an individual plant, the union's influence in that plant increases if the incoming works-council members are all unionized. While, in general, the unions still carry most of the works-council seats, the number of nonunion works-council members has recently been on the increase: between 1953 and 1955, it rose from 19.6 per cent to 21.4 per cent in industries that had contracts with the metal workers union.[38] As works-council members are not elected according to political preference, their political affiliations are not always known; it may be assumed that 40 to 50 per cent are close to the SPD. However, recent increases in members without known political affiliation indicate a certain increase in communist strength more clearly than do some of the spectacular victories of avowed Communists, since Communists often go out of their way to describe themselves as politically unaffiliated. A Communist's chances of being elected to the works council depend on his and his noncommunist predecessor's personal qualities, rather than on his politics. There is evidence to show that workers try to distinguish between an individual's politics and his fitness for a works-council job.[39] There have been cases when the entire Communist Party, in a particular locality, drew fewer votes in a political election than did a single communist candidate for works council in a local factory election. To the union, however, the election of a Communist, even though he be a union member in good standing, means that its position on the factory level is weakened and that a competing center of authority has begun to operate.*

Prosperity, the decline of labor militancy, concentration on personal pursuits, and the rise of the plant-oriented works council as the focal point of the laboring man's orientation in industrial relations have all

---

* The recent ban of the Communist Party does not change this situation essentially. If a local Communist, running as an independent, has managed to retain the confidence of the workers, he will, as a rule, be re-elected.

loosened the workers' ties to the union. So far, there are few signs to indicate that the beginning of manpower shortages, and the tactical advantages derived therefrom by the unions, will reverse the present situation and enhance union influence. An intelligent union officer recently called the German trade-unions "a fleet in being"; that is, it is not the present activities of the unions, but expectations of their possible radius of action under changed economic circumstances, that count with the worker. Prosperity may continue; and paternalism, local understandings on the working level, and some union prodding may go on making for an economic pattern acceptable to labor. But if prosperity should not last, or if an economy bursting at the seams and threatened by inflation should produce acute problems of allocating the social product, then the worker may present his draft on the union. The decisive trial of German labor organizations lies in the future. The patterns which have developed during the last decade may not persist; they may even cease to be meaningful.

Foreign Policy: The Status Quo

Neither the DGB nor the industrial union leadership follows closely the day-to-day operations of foreign policy. Nor is there much membership pressure on them to take a definite stand on most issues of foreign policy. In some few fields, it is true, the DGB and the industrial unions have developed definite policies. Even in the absence of pressure from the membership, they supported the stand of the German parties in the Saar, which aimed at the defeat of the Saar statute.

During the Böckler era, the DGB, with the full consent of the industrial unions, also supported Adenauer's Western integration policies, especially the Petersberg Agreement between Bonn and the Western allies in 1949 and, later on, the setting up and implementation of the Coal-Steel Community. A number of reasons made such support possible at that time in the face of SPD opposition. Böckler's unquestioned authority was a prime factor. Secondly, the matters under negotiation were complex, and they involved no immediate disadvantage to the social and economic situation of the workers. Thirdly, in return for labor support on these issues, the government granted a number of domestic advantages to the unions. Labor's stand, therefore, aroused some token opposition only among those unionists who at that time felt particularly close to the policies of the late SPD leader Kurt Schumacher.

In spite of recent changes in the atmosphere surrounding government-union relations, the DGB and especially the two unions most immediately concerned—the metal workers and the miners—have continued to support the CSC. They have done so in spite of some misgivings resulting either from insufficient consideration of the workers' interests by the Community's international authorities, or from the special concern of the miners unions over the effect of CSC policies on the continued operation of a unified German coal-sales organization.[40]

Together with other unions affiliated with the European regional organization of the ICFTU, German labor has recently raised its voice to revive the lagging progress of European integration. It has requested the extension of European integration to new fields, particularly transportation, electric power, and atomic energy.[41] And since the Social Democratic Party also has now come to share these viewpoints, German labor is unanimous in its stand for a policy of speedy and maximum European integration.[42] It has therefore been able to become a positive (rather than a retarding) force in this field, in contrast to tendencies presently observable in the international industrial community and among the governments concerned.

The current rearmament debate in Germany has, for the first time, shifted the locus of discussion of broad and closely interconnected national and international problems from the level of the political and public-opinion specialist to that of the general population. The union opponents of rearmament have had, from the very beginning, two definite advantages in the debate: the lack of enthusiasm for, and often the expressed opposition to, rearmament on the part of minor officials and union members in general; and (2) the apparent unwillingness, or inability, of the government to follow precedent by offering labor domestic concessions in return for its co-operation in the foreign policy field. Therefore, when the top DGB leaders, Fette and Vom Hoff, nevertheless tried to throw union support to the side of the administration, a crisis of confidence arose, which led, among other things, to a change in leadership at the 1952 DGB convention in Berlin.

The slightly reshuffled leadership under Walter Freitag, exposed as it was to a variety of different pressures, tried its best to straddle the issue. It insisted that rearmament was a purely political issue, which therefore came under the exclusive jurisdiction of the political parties. In spite of the militant temper of the membership against rearmament, the resolution on the issue that was originally submitted to the 1954 DGB convention in Frankfurt was couched in vague terms; it gave vent to prevailing moods and unspecified fears, but did not take a definite stand in opposition to administration policies. The resolution did take a stand against competitive rearmament; it also emphasized the threat implicit in the poverty and social injustice existing in many parts of the world, and the need for German unification as a precondition for world peace. It proclaimed the urgent need and the union's readiness to take a stand against all threats to democracy. The resolution ended with a statement that neither cannons nor tank divisions could protect freedom unless social justice and labor participation in the social and economic process first created a popular readiness to protect it.

But, after only a very short and perfunctory discussion, this resolution was rejected, and a supplementary one was adopted almost unanimously. The substitute was to some extent literally lifted from the unanimously adopted text of the DGB youth conference that preceded the convention, and was circulated on the convention floor in advance of the vote. It gave vent to fears that the London Agreements on EDC were tantamount to committing Germany to participation in a system of power pacts, thus endangering both the relaxation of international tensions and the possibility of reunification. On the domestic scene, the new resolution argued, such a system would make for a rebirth of militarism, which would signify the end of German working-class efforts to create political, social, and economic democracy.

The Frankfurt resolution did not go along with the outright rejection of rearmament that was voted by the youth conference, however. Its final paragraph, as proposed by Otto Brenner, cochairman of the metal workers union, was patterned after the corresponding resolution that the SPD adopted at its Berlin convention that same summer. This paragraph put the DGB convention on record as opposed to "any rearmament contribution so long as all possibilities for negotiation have not been exhausted with the goal of obtaining international reconciliation, and so long as the unity of Germany can not be obtained." [43] Identical, or very similar, resolutions were adopted also by subsequent industrial union conventions.

In the wake of these resolutions, the DGB, under the leadership of its vice-chairman, Georg Reuter, also participated "unofficially" in the *Pauls-Kirche Manifesto* of the spring of 1955. (The Pauls-Kirche meeting was followed up by mass meetings throughout Germany under the joint auspices of SPD, DGB, and various church-connected groups.) This was a proclamation that was signed, among others, by all industrial union chairmen, by the DGB district chairmen (except for Scharnowski from Berlin), and by the SPD leaders. The manifesto demanded speedy reunification through negotiation rather than through a policy of military integration with the West.

The DGB, in such official utterances, speaks for a multitude of varying attitudes, personalities, and groups in its ranks. This variety of opinion came into the open during the SPD convention that preceded the DGB meeting at Frankfurt.

No separate trade-union attitude exists toward the closely connected issues of rearmament, unification, and foreign policy. The trade-union official, the active works-council member, or the shop delegate will pick up his arguments in the general public discussion, or, more probably, in the discussions of those questions that take place within the ranks of the SPD. The variety of views that characterizes these discussions also dominates internal union attitudes, be it on the question of the enforced pacifism of the hydrogen age, on the absolute priority of reunification over any other consideration, on the priority of U.S. protection and the consequent need for rearmament, or on the purely domestic question of the danger of a new militarism.

Among members of the older generation, the Weimar parallel is of decisive importance for the question of a German contribution to the defense of Western Europe. In their opinion, the situation, in which military protection is furnished by the Western allies and the civilian establishment is run by the German authorities, provides the most convenient device for handling both foreign and domestic problems. This attitude is rarely voiced openly, partly because it is believed to go counter to still-ingrained national traditions of sovereignty and, more importantly, because under prevailing circumstances it might be considered, at least by unfriendly observers, as an acknowledgment of the semifinality of German partition. Yet a number of German trade-union leaders will often say that "German sovereignty has no meaning"; this remark expresses their attitude exactly. German rearmament, they fear, would do away with the rather satisfactory division of labor between Western military forces and autonomous German government, which not only has prevented war in Europe for ten years, but which has also, in their opinion, created the conditions for domestic stability and internal democratic development.

According to this viewpoint, establishment of a German military force now would be premature by years, if not by decades. As DGB Vice-Chairman Georg Reuter—among others interviewed—expressed it, such an establishment would "destroy the chances of a democratic development in Germany." The older generation of union leaders is almost unanimous in believing that present institutions would not be able to cope with the job of organizing an army under effective civilian control. They fear that, as previously, the army, possibly in conjunction with other domestic political forces, might subvert the political regime and deprive the working class of its legitimate share in the government setup, as happened during the Weimar period. None of those interviewed recognized the crucial difference between Weimar and Bonn: the preponderant role of the military under the Weimar Republic derived largely from the polarization of domestic political forces and the consequent failure of the parliamentary regime. But since there is not, in present-day Germany, either a "radical left" or a "militant right," and since there prevails a general lack of intense political interest, it is not likely that the Weimar experience can be repeated under the conditions of the Bonn establishment.

Recurrent assertions that a German army would contribute little of military value, now that the two great powers are thought by many to have achieved equality in nuclear weapons, reinforce domestic labor opposition to rearmament. But since this opposition has existed ever since the early fifties—before the Soviet Union had demonstrated an atomic capability—the argument from nuclear parity at best only adds support to already established opinions.

This almost universal revulsion against rearmament on labor's part does not, however, take the form of open resistance to, or defiance of, measures to implement rearmament. Neither the temperament of the rank and file nor the attitudes or plans of the leaders lend themselves to such an interpretation. The unanimous opposition rather signifies that, as was the case under the Weimar Republic, German labor will, on the whole, remain on the sidelines when the army build-up takes place.

The present political configuration of the Bonn government will facilitate pursuit of such a noncommittal policy on the part of labor. The SPD is excluded from the cabinet, and the unions are neither emotionally nor politically bound by the presence in the cabinet of some of their former colleagues. Thus, no question of divided loyalty or policy conflict is likely to plague labor, as the rank and file of the SPD and the unions were plagued in 1929, for example, at the height of the parliamentary debate over the building of the so-called "Battleship A." But few labor people will openly counsel defiance of induction orders. The argument that almost certainly will carry the day is that the unions, as law-abiding organizations, will have to respect the laws voted by the duly-elected legislative assembly. Adolf Kummernuss, the chairman of the public works union, has several times said that failure to obey the measures taken in pursuance of such legislation might lead to seizure of trade-union headquarters. His statement seems characteristic in two ways: it shows both the union leaders' concern to avoid a head-on collision with the authorities and the essentially negative and grudging basis on which their obedience to the government rests.

Attempts have been made, by both reformist and radical groups within the unions, to have labor play more than a passive role in rearmament, and such attempts are likely to continue. There is a smattering of union leaders on all levels who would have wanted to participate in the officers' selection committee and who want to help with recruiting efforts and administrative implementation of the rearmament program in general, if only to prevent repetition of the Weimar experience. The white-collar DAG has gone so far as to allow one of its representatives to sit on the officers' selection committee. But both the complexion of the present administration and the fear that a negative rank-and-file reaction may occur and may be exploited by the Communists are likely to keep collaboration attempts within narrow confines.

At the other end of the spectrum are some more radical, younger functionaries and a few union-connected intellectuals, who see in the rearmament issue a chance to combat the prevailing lethargy among workers and to reawaken something of the fighting spirit of former times. According to this group, all possibilities of widening opposition to rearmament should be exploited to the limit. They argue that the ambiguous formula of the Frankfurt resolution, the participation of union leaders in the Pauls-Kirche movement, and the resolutions adopted at the recent textile- and mine-workers convention to grant legal aid to conscientious objectors are all to be interpreted as pointing to a more active opposition to rearmament. In this way, they try to make the best of both the present situation and the willingness of the leadership to consent under pressure to adoption of some measure of radical phraseology in convention resolutions.

Both those who favor more active participation in rearmament, however, and those who urge stronger opposition to it know quite well that DGB leadership will not allow itself to be pushed very far in either direction. There is little prospect that either the DGB-affiliated unions or the DAG will swerve from their somewhat ambiguous line. They are likely to continue asserting that questions pertaining to army matters are of a political nature and therefore outside their jurisdiction.

This withdrawal from political responsibility, however, is not likely to prevent the unions (particularly their most uncompromisingly anti-rearmament youth groups) from being constantly on the lookout to see that labor's social and economic interests are safeguarded during the process of rearmament. There will be technical, though not political, consultations with the government. To the extent that labor's position is not sufficiently taken into consideration, lateral attacks on the rearmament program on purely social and economic grounds may be the order of the day. This policy of semi-abstentionism—rather than of outright opposition—corresponds rather closely to the frame of mind of the majority of union members. It also parallels closely the line taken by the SPD on the occasion of the March, 1956, Bundestag votes on the military questions. The great majority of the SPD members voted for the changes in the Basic Law necessary for the organization of the federal army, but then they voted against the Soldier's Law, designed to implement the new military organization, because they saw in it "a link in the chain leading to the organization of two German armies, integrated into mutually hostile military blocs."[44]

Such policies, however, will not prevent the union members from reaping whatever economic benefits the continuation of the present boom may still hold in store for them. Nor do these policies imply a conflict between union and national loyalties. Yet the union attitude gives cautious support and expression to a vague but persistent feeling of dissatisfaction with the military policies of the administration.

We have seen that labor's attitude toward a new German army is determined largely by concern with the domestic implications of rearmament. It is grounded, further, on the widespread conviction that there exists no danger of a Soviet military attack against Western Europe in the foreseeable future. Sometimes this conviction is based on arguments drawn from Russia's failure to attack shortly after the war, in the middle forties, when her clear superiority in ground troops would have made a conquest of continental Europe relatively easy.

But the argument for the unlikelihood of a Russian attack derives its strongest support from a widespread assumption about the nature of the Soviet opponent. Communism is viewed not as a system intent on military conquest, but as an alternative social system which feeds primarily on the failures and incapacities of the capitalist powers, and uses military force only coincidentally or as a last resort. The Soviet Union is believed unlikely to resort to force because, unlike Hitler, it is seen as calculating its risks rather closely before engaging in any type of action.

Those who thus see the Soviet Union as primarily a competing social system argue that it can not be meaningfully opposed by a display of military force. Official union arguments that emphasize the element of social competition between the West and the East are accepted by all unionists. Even those who admit the need for some sort of military force, such as an enlarged border-police organization to counteract the East German *Volkspolizei,* still put the emphasis on the element of social competition between the two systems. Obviously, this belief fits neatly the propaganda needs of a group that feels itself excluded from political power. It uses the prospect of a largely nonmilitary East-West competition to cajole other domestic groups into supporting social and economic measures that will increase the chances of the German social system to emerge as superior to that of the East.

This tendency of labor to allow its domestic concerns to determine its views on military and foreign policy issues is strengthened by the universally shared belief that the United States is bound to maintain military—or, at least, air—forces in Europe or North Africa as a means of guaranteeing its own security; since America will carry the defense burden, domestic issues remain the really crucial ones for labor to concern itself with. There is little concern with the question of whether this American military establishment will operate with the help of German facilities and supporting troops. Many would clearly prefer to see it based farther West than Germany. Some believe that Allied troops and facilities might be withdrawn from West Germany without impairing their deterrent function, relieving the Federal Republic of direct participation in the Atlantic system while at the same time guaranteeing continued U.S. protection against the possibility of Soviet aggression. In this way, it is believed, it would be easier for the Federal Republic to seek agreement with Russia on some form of unification, while at the same time enjoying the unsolicited, but effective, protection of the United States.

The dual assumption that there is no Soviet *military* threat and that the United States will continue to guarantee the safety of Europe in any case dispenses, according to this view, with the need for the Germans to decide on active participation in Western defense. Military and foreign problems can be largely considered in the light of their domestic implications. Moreover, it is believed, the continued presence of American power in Europe or North Africa will facilitate the envisioned social competition between East and West by providing some guarantee that the Soviet Union will not break the rules of the competitive game. It is clear that this attitude toward issues of foreign policy stands or falls with the assumption that self-interest will prevent United States withdrawal from Europe and North Africa; and few indeed go so far as to argue that modern missile developments would allow the United States to protect European territory efficiently from its own shores. But German labor discusses foreign policy in terms of real alternatives only when this assumption of continued U.S. military protection is questioned and grudging acknowledgment given to the interdependence of European attitudes and U.S. defense policies.

When the assumption of a permanent United States–European military establishment is questioned, two major attitudes emerge as characteristic of labor's thinking on foreign policy. One group supports, somewhat uneasily, the *status quo* that sees West Germany in the framework of the Western alliance. Another group, probably smaller than the first, espouses a more activist policy and argues for socialist renovation through speedy reunification, even if this should involve abandoning U.S. protection. The dividing lines between the two groups are not very distinct, and attempts to harmonize the two attitudes are common.

The first group starts from the premise that the Federal Republic is the only presently obtainable frame for labor's political and social action. Some members of this group have, realistically, put out of their minds any hope of speedy reunification, though they may ardently desire it. Others may have a stronger attachment to the present political fabric, though they would never admit it; they may doubt their ability to control the movements involved in the creation of an all-German state, and therefore prefer the more circumscribed, but much safer, cadre of the Federal Republic. Whatever the individual motivations, the conclusion arrived at by members of this group is the same: the Federal Republic is, for the time being, an integral part of the Western system, and its security rests on continued U.S. protection. This protection could best be ensured purely and simply by prolonging the present system. The Federal Republic would continue to pay, in cash, for military protection. It would either pay for the upkeep of troops actually stationed on German soil, or the system might function equally well if troops were withdrawn from Germany and stationed in other Western countries. Some of those interviewed said they would feel safer if Western troops continued to be physically stationed on German territory, because, they argued, that would provide better protection against communist "Korean-type mistakes."

The great advantage of such paid protection is that it would dispense with the unwelcome and embarrassing necessity of furnishing German troop contingents. This is not to say that German union leaders do not recognize that the pressure for a German military contribution derives from more than exclusively security considerations. They know that the French, and especially the British, want to counter German industrial competition by forcing on Germany a military burden equivalent to theirs. Trade-unionists acknowledge the justice of this argument, but they suggest that politically less perilous methods be employed to achieve the desired goal, such as, for example, a major rise in the German wage level.

As we have seen, the attainment of atomic equilibrium—with no thought so far given to the consequences of possible dispersion of atomic power among a multitude of hitherto second-rank nations—is supposed to have made meaningless any German military build-up. As the recently deceased Hamburg trade-union chairman put it, "These troops could under present circumstances anyhow not help us in getting our former territories back." But this formulation is exceptional. The Hamburg official was, at least for the fleeting moment needed to dismiss the idea as meaningless, thinking of the national goal that a military establishment could serve. The rest of the trade-union community sees any German military force, whether within the Western framework or as an independent establishment, only as providing an additional possibility of conflagration.* German troops might start some Eastern action on their own initiative, and thus involve Germany in a meaningless carnage, or they might ally themselves with the Russians, and thus endanger both the existence of German democracy and the peace of the Western world.

Nevertheless, German unionists would not oppose rearmament if it were the price of continued American support. They prefer a continuation of the Atlantic defense community to some neutralization scheme that would involve American withdrawal from the continent. In the last analysis, as the recently-elected CDU vice-chairman of the DGB put it, since the Federal Republic is an integral part of the Western system, the initiative for specific policies lies with the major partner, the United States. Minor partners such as the Federal Republic can not but follow suit.

Among the labor leaders interviewed, most of those who indicated a preference for continued German participation in the Western alliance stated their preference not in terms of personal choice, but in the form of acquiescence to the choice made by Adenauer. They first minimized the element of choice open to labor by speaking rather in terms of the disinclination of the majority of the country to oppose the policy followed by the government, and then they made it quite clear that that policy was in any event at best the lesser of two evils.

Yet there are doubts about how long the present policies can continue in view of the impasse supposedly created by attainment of an atomic stalemate, the resulting meaninglessness of a major war, and the difficulty of defending rearmament as a contribution toward German reunification. A great number of union officials simply shy away from any discussion of foreign policy, emphasizing the unions' need to concentrate on social and economic issues. Union leaders rationalize their concentration on domestic issues by arguing, in line with the East-West

* Among the 36 per cent of male youths, interviewed in 1954 by EMNID, who declared their conditional willingness to serve in the army, somewhat fewer than 10 per cent mentioned the liberation of the Soviet zone as motivation for such a decision. Nearly all of these had a refugee background, and none of them had what the interviewers call "a positive attitude" toward the present West German state (*Jugend zwischen 15 und 24,* Bielefeld, 1955, pp. 256–268).

social competition theory, that a good social policy is really the best front-line defense against communism. Others seize on the possibility of disarmament as the straw of hope for a rational solution of major problems of a world otherwise seemingly bent on its own destruction. None of them, if pressed, would openly challenge the need to live up to rearmament obligations as part of the German partnership in the Atlantic alliance, but few consider rearmament as a positive contribution to the solution of Germany's foreign policy problems.

These attitudes of the union leaders in favor of maintenance of the *status quo* and of a German contribution to Western defense, if that should prove unavoidable, as well as their doubts about the meaningfulness of a German army; their passive acceptance of the government's decisions; and their inclination to shy away from a foreign policy stand of their own are so many diverse manifestations of a by now well-established conviction that the initiative for a change in the position of Germany remains outside German hands.

The results of Adenauer's 1955 visit to Moscow have served to support this belief. According to an analysis commonly made in trade-union and SPD circles, the U.S.S.R. has profited from the intensive West German propaganda for the release of the German prisoners of war. Once their liberation was blown up into a major foreign policy goal, the U.S.S.R. could use this issue to force the hands of the German government into establishing diplomatic relations at a time when Russia's main interest was concentrated on legitimizing the *status quo*, and, with it, the position of the East German government. According to this analysis, then, it is the U.S.S.R. that determines the pace of any move which might change the present impasse. Soviet policy need do no more than keep constantly before German eyes the anomalous character of the present state of affairs, where Germany has achieved neither full integration with the West nor re-establishment of German unity.

This analysis of the international situation makes little impression on those who simply accept the Federal Republic and its close liaison with the U.S. military establishment as a given and indispensable framework of national existence, and as something more than a provisional solution. Yet the number of those who, while not willing to abandon the Western alliance right now, are constantly scanning the horizon for signs of the great thaw that could produce a definite change in the German situation is growing. This increase is partly the result of the universal conviction that the United States, while able to give Germany protection against further Soviet encroachments, has no means (many would even say no real desire) to effect Germany's reunification. Consequently, the initiative for reunification rests more than ever with the U.S.S.R.

The Search for Alternatives

The extent of real change that the Soviet structure may be undergoing since Stalin's death therefore emerges as an important question in connection with the possibility of German reunification. German union leaders' guesses about the impact on Germany of the changes in Soviet Russia's command structure vary widely. However, the main emphasis lies on the international consequences of changes in Soviet economic policies. If the U.S.S.R. decides to shelve its cold-war policies, some say, this might allow it to concentrate on the production of consumer goods and reorganize its agricultural system, thus not only improving the population's attitude toward the regime but also paving the way for a healthier relation between the U.S.S.R. and the Satellite states, hitherto forcibly oriented toward unilateral support for the Soviet economy.

One of the most astute observers of communist policies among German unionists thought that Soviet policy changes were not likely to be as clear-cut as others expected them to be. He saw Soviet policies as safely anchored to old-fashioned security considerations, and as evolving at best along traditional compromise patterns. Essential Satellite and (equally important) Western Communist Party controls would be maintained, while more responsibility and initiative might be granted in restricted fields. This man believed that the U.S.S.R. was likely to change and liberalize its domestic production patterns only to the extent deemed feasible in the light of continuing intense military East-West competition. Moreover, any new policy, even if viewed in the most optimistic terms, would, for the time being, be aimed only at legalizing the *status quo*. It would therefore not be tantamount to Soviet abandonment of its East German Satellite, especially after the new military situation resulting from achievement of atomic equilibrium had diminished the attractiveness of all-German neutrality in the eyes of the U.S.S.R.

Similarly, there would be no great change in Europe if the great opportunity for communist expansion were seen to lie in amelioration of the fate of the rural masses of Asia. The Soviet Union's confidence that its future lay in Asia might then lead it, under the much more complicated conditions of European politics, to plan a holding operation in the West, calling for a sincere desire for nonaggression, peace, and coexistence.[45] For Germany the results would be the same: the eternalization of the *status quo*.

There is one set of considerations under which Soviet self-interest is seen as leading to long-range changes that will upset the *status quo*. It consists in what one might call the "Chinese projection game," which has become quite fashionable in labor circles, as elsewhere in Germany, since the publication and wide public discussion of Wilhelm Starlinger's *Grenzen der Sovietmacht* (Würzburg, 1954). Starlinger's thesis is that the stupendous rise in the Chinese birth rate, and the consequent Chinese population pressure on the much less densely populated Siberian territories of the U.S.S.R., will result in an increasing Soviet need to arrive at some *modus vivendi* with the Western powers—and especially with the United States—and will therefore necessarily include finding an acceptable solution to the East German problem. This line of argument has two interesting corollaries: (1) in view of the eventual conflict of interest between the U.S.S.R. and China, it is both unnecessary and undesirable for the United States to fight China over the maintenance of the present Formosa regime, and (2) Soviet Russia will seek an accommodation with the United States when its relations with China become strained enough to require some assurance of stability on its Western front. This, in turn, will force the U.S.S.R. to discuss the future of its now firmly-held mortgages on European territory. Until then, a German discussion with the U.S.S.R. would be worse than useless; it would worsen Germany's chances for reunification because those chances now rest on America's continued espousal of Germany's demands on the U.S.S.R.[46]

The manifold and intensive speculations on the future course of China which occupy the minds of DGB officials, from the national chairman to the humblest youth secretary, show that the subject holds a particular fascination within union circles. The reason lies in the close relation between the course of Chinese-Russian relations and the fate of East Germany, which the Starlinger book tries to demonstrate. The urgent necessity of unification has been consistently and continuously reiterated by all factions in the German labor movement. Not all German labor leaders would go so far as to pay a symbolic installment fee against the day of unification by, say, acquiring now a building site in Berlin for their future national headquarters. But no responsible labor leader would ever dare officially to visualize the future of the German labor movement otherwise than within the framework of a united Germany. However, the discrepancy between the official credo and the sharply limited means of realizing it has constituted an increasing drawback for the vitality and sincerity of all official German programs, including that of labor.

It is the particular attraction of the "Chinese projection game" that it allows the reintegration of the Eastern lands into an all-German state without requiring any action beyond remaining passively within the protective orbit of the United States. When foreign policy becomes dependent on vast population movements and on the policy decisions of powers completely out of the reach of German politics, concentration on the nearer tasks can no longer be attacked as an ostrich policy, but becomes the better part of wisdom and of national perseverance. The "Chinese projection game" thus stands as a somewhat complicated attempt to turn the incapacity for present action into the positive assertion of future, if remote, success.

Whatever justification of present attitudes or remote hopes of future unity such considerations may furnish, they do not advance the course of unification. Yet reunification remains a constant preoccupation of German labor. Quite a number of the most active labor functionaries are convinced that the unsatisfactory state of the labor movement is more than a consequence of widespread political apathy and the prevailing boom conditions. They think of it also in terms of Germany's political geography; they see it as the result partly of the shift in the Protestant-Catholic population ratio brought about by the establishment of the Federal Republic, and the resulting greater weight of Catholicism, and partly of the location of many traditional working-class strongholds in the present Soviet zone. In their minds, both of these factors carry a heavy share in the rise and success of the Adenauer regime in the Federal Republic, and they tend to ensure continuation of the regime so long as Germany remains confined within the frontiers of the present Federal Republic. Hence their conclusion that a renovation of the German working-class movement into one that would have a chance to be more than a sort of fire department (as is the present DGB) or a company of old soldiers (as is the SPD) would be possible only within the framework of a unified Germany.

Few unionists are under the illusion that reunification carried through via democratic all-German elections would automatically lead to a reversal of present political trends. Many would agree that, depending on the circumstances under which reunification took place, the present administration might be confirmed in the first free all-German elections. Yet, thinking in terms of renovation of the labor movement rather than in terms of immediate election chances, such a prospect would not necessarily deter the union leadership. There is a widespread belief that the mere fact of reunification, and the great new task which a reunified German labor movement would have to face, would help it to overcome its present stagnation.

These convictions carry two corollaries. First is the expectation that the present administration, even if confirmed in the first all-German elections, would be unable to solve the socioeconomic problems of reunification within the framework of present-day West German economic institutions and policies. Secondly, it is believed that the East

German workers, though cherishing the return of political freedom, would not want to change their present taskmasters for a return to the old owners, but would want to preserve a regime of public ownership.

These assumptions are widespread among labor union and works-council functionaries, though, to judge from a 1953 poll, they are not necessarily shared by the majority of union members. They are assumptions that imply the ascendancy of labor as the predominant force in a reunified Germany.* At the least, they imply that labor would have to be called upon to become an indispensable partner in any German post-reunification regime. The more intensive the belief that unification would lead to such development, the greater the readiness—sometimes even the impatience—of union leaders to do away with foreign policy impediments that might stand in their way. The more minds are directed to labor's future in a reunified Germany, rather than toward the modalities and guarantees of its present existence, the greater the insistence on leaving no stone unturned to effect German unity.

That is why unionists often say that the Western powers and West Germany missed a major opportunity when they failed to follow up the Soviet reunification and neutralization offers of 1952–1953. This allegedly missed opportunity is held as an eternal reproach against the Adenauer regime. The fact that now, when circumstances have changed, there is no way either to prove or to disprove the sincerity of the earlier Soviet offer only serves to turn these reproaches into a convenient political weapon.

Thus the activists, though as much interested as their more cautious brethren in American willingness to keep its European military establishment, would put the accent on renovation of the German labor movement through reunification rather than on the need for security. If forced to make a choice, they would choose neutrality, if it were a precondition for reunification. Expanding on the old theme of social and economic competition between East and West, they profess not to be afraid of the new and enlarged infiltration possibilities created by the existence of a neutralized Germany. They admit that Soviet pressure on a united Germany after the withdrawal of the United States might increase, but, in their opinion, so would the social cohesion and internal stability of a unified Germany remade in the image of German labor. They dwell heavily on the moral and social cohesion of a unified Ger-

* E. P. Neumann and E. Noelle, *Antworten,* Allensbach, 1954, pp. 125–126, report an August, 1953, poll in which it was asked whether after reunification East German factories should remain public enterprises or be returned to their owners. Thirteen per cent of the trade-unionists polled voted for public ownership, as against only 6 per cent of the entire sample; and 71 per cent of the trade-unionists, as against 84 per cent of the entire sample, were for surrender to the former owners.

many as a deterrent to communist attempts to take over the country and on the security advantages which a middle position between two giant power blocs would procure for them.

This middle position, with neither bloc able to take over the German prize, would give Germany some chance to disengage herself completely from the present power configuration. The prospect of such disengagement from international politics is analogous to the individual German's endeavor to disengage himself from the surrounding social world and to lead his own private life; it is a prospect that seems to fascinate a large number of people. Almost all would concede that this disengagement at the same time involves some risks. But, they argue, there is no situation or action that does not involve some risk; and the alternative—continuation of United States protection and a split Germany—bars the chance for reunification and may involve the same degree of risk: Western ground troops would be no match for the U.S.S.R. if the latter should decide to take over Western Europe for good.

So long as the Soviet Union refuses to make any concessions that would allow for free reunification in exchange for West German abandonment of its Western commitments, the chances of a more activist policy are limited, unless its adherents were prepared to sacrifice Western freedoms and institutions entirely. In spite of all reservations about the character of the present West German regime, few, if any, would be willing to go that far. The actual battleground between the various foreign policy schools in the labor camp therefore narrows down considerably. The certainties within which the cautious majority is content to rest solve neither labor's particular problem nor Germany's national troubles. The activists may stress the impasse to which the official position of labor and government has brought Germany. But their own, more audacious, proposals so far have failed to point the way to a concrete avenue of approach to acceptable solutions. Moreover, their own analysis of the present situation and of labor's chances may contain a number of incorrect assumptions. It may overestimate labor's own dissatisfation with the Adenauer regime. It may underestimate the willingness of the East German population to embrace West German social and economic institutions. In all likelihood, it overestimates the confidence which Soviet Russia might have in the ability of a unified German labor movement to exercise what the Soviet Union would call a moderating influence on German policies. This analysis, therefore, may arrive at faulty conclusions as to both the chances of reunification and the nature of the regime in a reunified Germany.

However that may be, renovation through reunification, at the present moment, expresses less a definite policy than some widespread moods and states of mind, brought into sharper focus by some labor theoreticians and especially some younger labor officials. It is conceived as a protest against the middle-class government's dodging, and the SPD's obfuscating, of the reunification issue.

Actual differences of policy in the labor camp are at the moment limited to the one area where German labor has a possibility of forging a policy of its own—the field of East-West contacts. To what extent should contacts be established or upheld, not only with the East German population at large but with the East German government and its unrepresentative labor unions? So far, these labor contacts have followed a stereotyped course. Official East German delegations composed of both bona fide East German trade-unionists and communist political instructors have tried to establish contact with West German union organizations on all levels, and have attempted to engage in discussions with them. Following the general policy line of the DGB laid down at the 1954 convention, the majority of German trade-union leaders have either refused to receive these delegations, or they have broken off the discussions after the preliminary talks showed the uselessness of discussions held under the supervision of SED functionaries.* Only a very few West German union officials, motivated by tactical considerations of their own, have pursued such conversations further. Official invitations tendered to trade-union leaders to visit East Germany have all been rejected. However, many works-council members and shop delegates, over whom the union has but slender control, have recently accepted such invitations, and have visited East Germany, Russia, and even China; in some instances, their reports upon returning have furnished good copy for communist propaganda.

Adherents of "productive coexistence" [47] as a more active policy aimed at reunification would favor sending trade-union delegations to the East zone to establish contacts both with the population and, if necessary, with the official East zone authorities. They hold that contacts do and will take place whether the unions like it or not, and that it would be better to make them official in order to be able to exercise at least some control over them. The resumption of diplomatic relations between West Germany and the U.S.S.R. seems to have reinforced these arguments, but subsequent events in Hungary weakened them.** A vote taken

* The resolution passed at the 1954 convention read: "The FDGB presently is not a free union, and unless a number of prerequisites are met, including especially release of political prisoners, re-establishment of the right to strike, and admission of truly independent unions, no relations with the FDGB are possible."

** In the fall of 1956, the convention of the printers union voted 104 to 97 to recommend the establishment of untrammeled East-West union contacts. Following the events in Hungary, however, the union's executive committee adjourned the implementation of the resolution sine die.

at the Munich construction workers convention in September, 1955, reconfirmed the official line by a vote of 166 to 53 (the vote was taken before the communist-led Rhineland district was ejected from the union), but it showed nevertheless that the official line met with some opposition.

This issue of East-West contacts thus might later become a divisive element. This in itself constitutes a victory for the Communist Party, which is trying to foster and exploit sentiment for increased East-West contact both for its own propaganda purposes and in order to expand its foothold in the Western unions. Yet in doing so, the Communists inevitably cast suspicion on the activities of those who, however sincerely, labor for liberalization of East-West contacts. The circumstances of the objective situation thus restrict the possibility of an alternative foreign policy in labor ranks.

Youth Problems

Co-ordination of the views of labor youth with those of their elders is not at a very advanced stage. Whether questions addressed to them pertain to their own social and economic role or to some institutional pattern, the young workers have few competent answers. They are not quite sure about the need for and the function of political parties.* There is a strong minority who feel that, rather than show interest in and responsibility for the politics of their own country, it is better to leave political power in the hands of the man who is now exercising it.[48] Interest and understanding are lacking in their attitudes toward works councils and trade-unions in their own work experience. A recent survey among Cologne apprentices found that the workers' organizations have to compete strongly for authority with the word of the boss or foreman.**

This situation is not simply the result of lack of communication between age groups. German youth is growing to maturity at a time when institutions as well as traditions show an almost total break of continuity. A very alert trade-union youth functionary in a big Rhineland city, when asked about characteristic differences between middle-class and

* In a Hamburg sample, 40 per cent of the male youth thought one party would be enough, and 44 per cent had no answer to the question of why one joins a political party (cf. H. K. Lüth, et al., Arbeiterjugend gestern und heute, Heidelberg, 1955, pp. 257–258, and 348; and Jugend zwischen 15 und 24, op. cit., pp. 227 ff.).

** Forty-two per cent of the working youths polled in Cologne affirmed the necessity of unions; 52 per cent had no opinion on the subject. When in need of advice, 26 per cent would turn to colleagues or members of the works council, and 50 per cent would turn to their bosses. (Cf. Karl-Heinz Sohn, "Jugend—Betriebsrat—Gewerkschaft," G.M., November, 1955, p. 664.)

working-class attitudes, could think only of varying attitudes toward churchgoing: middle-class people care if their neighbors stay away from church, whereas working-class people do not pay attention to that. It is not surprising, therefore, that 77 per cent of the youths interviewed in the course of a recent poll had no answer when they were asked about the characteristics of bourgeois versus socialist living patterns.[49]

There is also, among the younger age group, a quite conscious re-evaluation of the role of the group in social living. It is no longer the group which in its victory carries its loyal members to a higher station in life; it is rather the individual who plans his own life and who uses the group as a steppingstone toward his own advancement.

The deflation of the group, concentration on individual careers, and the general low intensity of political interest do not remain abstract questions of social psychology; they become primary political factors in the ideological war between East and West Germany. As West German youth profess the same interest in reunification as their Eastern counterparts, contacts between them, which are fairly frequent in West Germany and almost unavoidable in Berlin, turn quickly into political discussions, revealing differences in the respective patterns of life experience. At the same time, they show that the West Germans are no match in a discussion for youths who have been brought up in a system that provides a ready frame of political and social references, and a definite sense of direction.

Seen in the context of this lack of political awareness, the rearmament controversy came as a godsend to the trade-union and socialist youth groups, who had found it much more difficult to capture the imagination of the younger workers than had denominational or sport youth groups.* Having to work with young people who, in 1955, still showed a higher degree of aversion to, and unfamiliarity with, politics than any other youth group, trade-union youth leaders found in the rearmament debate an opportunity to act as spokesmen for the entire working-class youth. Recent polls have confirmed that working-class youth shows the highest resistance to rearmament policies. Only 24 per cent of the working youths polled would like to become soldiers, as against 36 per cent among youth with a farm background. Conditional acceptance of rearmament brings working youth willingness only up to 34 per cent, as against a maximum of 42 per cent among those with a civil service background.[50]

* Asked by EMNID about their personal preferences among youth organizations, only 2 per cent mentioned trade-union youth groups, and 4 per cent mentioned political youth groups; 24 per cent mentioned sport clubs, and 12 per cent, denominational youth groups. Forty-two per cent of the sample gave no indication of preference. (Cf. EMNID Institute, *Jugend zwischen 15 und 24,* Bielefeld, 1955, p. 130.)

Labor youth opposition to rearmament rests primarily on the unwelcome interruption of otherwise promising career prospects, coming in the wake of the introduction of compulsory military service. The traditional image of a German military organization with all its brutality and repression of personality—which has to a large extent dominated the discussion of the possibilities and limits of military reform, and which Kirst's books and movies under the title *0815* have popularized so widely—has increased this aversion. For a youth to whom freedom to follow personal pursuits has become an all-important consideration, military service holds few attractions. Among the more thoughtful members of the younger generation, consciousness of how badly the last generation compromised Germany's existence, and how needlessly it allowed the whole of Europe to be thrown into turmoil, forms an additional strong motive for rejecting rearmament. The conclusion that emerges from most discussions among youth groups, then, is: "We do not want to become guilty again."

While the rearmament debate has clearly captured the interest of labor youth and increased the intensity of contact with trade-union organizations, many working youths nevertheless seem to be aware that rearmament, whatever one's attitude toward it, has to be visualized in a larger frame of reference. Asked to define the most important future political task, those polled cited: reunification (41 per cent); guaranteeing the peace (24 per cent); economic and social tasks (14 per cent); European understanding (7 per cent). Only 2 per cent named the need for rearmament first, and only 1 per cent started out with opposition to rearmament as the most important consideration.[51] It would be far-fetched to argue that this order of concern, with its rather vague and partly overlapping categories, indicates lack of intense concern over the rearmament issue. The most one can say is that a societal organization created, as one youth leader expressed it, "for the self-interest of the Americans," and heretofore accepted as a mere "datum," is now raising problems which most youths would rather not have to face. What the results will be of this head-on collision with an unwanted reality remains to be seen.

Trade-Union Attitudes toward the United States

There are many, often contradictory, images of the United States in the minds of German trade-unionists. There is probably not one of them who has not had some personal experience, and who has not established some form of contact, with Americans during the past two decades. The bomb that fell on his house; the CARE package that he received from his American relatives; the competition with a GI for a girl's favor; the aid his union received from a fraternal organization in the United States; or his various impressions, both favorable and negative, received on a visit to America in connection with the trade-union exchange program—all contribute to a very personalized experience and form an integral, sometimes even a determining, factor in his present attitude toward the United States.

In addition to these personal experiences, there are other, constant factors that have had some weight in the formation of attitudes in trade-union circles, such as the ambivalent experience of the occupation period and the re-establishment of political freedom and the right to organize workers' associations, which, in a sense, came as a gift from the Western occupation powers. But the denazification experience also came from the West, and it left a bad taste with the German labor official, for two reasons. He bitterly regrets having been associated with the unfortunate American denazification policies, which made him incur the enmity of many members of the community; he also criticizes U.S. policy for its timidity and lack of efficacy.[52] His aims and the American aims, so far, have never coincided. The unionist saw in denazification an opportunity to revamp Germany's social system and its social elite, but he detected no social meaning behind the American denazification trials.

The American occupation regime under General Lucius Clay is also held responsible, by militant trade-unionists, for nipping in the bud both the beginnings of socialization and the spread of codetermination directly in South Germany and, through its powerful influence with the British, in Rhineland-Westphalia.[53] These have become stock reproaches with many old-time unionists. The probably much more incisive American contribution to the present German property structure and the implementation of currency reform, without a simultaneous attempt to equalize burdens through some form of property levy, are less vividly remembered, despite the fact that they could not have been to labor's liking. To what degree this aspect of American occupation policy is emphasized depends on how strongly it is felt that socialist institutional patterns are superior to the ones upheld and restored in West Germany since 1945.

If the economic policy of recent years had not turned out so well— by conscious design, as its originators would hold; by sheer luck or coincidence, as most trade-unionists believe—the question of American responsibility for the present economic institutions would have been examined more critically than it has. But unless the economic climate changes tomorrow, criticism of the United States on this score is not very meaningful from the viewpoint of the majority of union members. Though a constant element in the writings of union theoreticians, it is less in evidence than are recommendations that German labor imitate American unions in constructing a union establishment that is committed neither to other social institutions nor to a particular economic theory or political philosophy, and that profits from the experience of American business unionism. Sometimes both the critical and the imitative are present in the top councils of a union, in which case the likely result is that both are quickly and decisively subordinated to the factors seen to be more immediately relevant to the newly-created German experience of the current local situation.

There is among German unionists in general much less of the nationalistic reaction against the United States than is evident, for example, in France. German labor viewed foreign, and especially United States, troops not only as liberators turned occupiers but also as guarantors against the possibility that the U.S.S.R. might take over the whole country—a danger which, against the background of the East German experience, always looked much more real to West Germany than to other Western countries. Further, the absence of any significant communist movement in Germany, and the general mistrust of communist propaganda, have made it comparatively difficult for the Communists to capitalize on German popular resentment of specific American policies, such as the mining of bridges as a measure against the possibility of invasion, or the health and social problems arising out of the concentration of U.S. troops in relatively small areas like the Palatinate. While grievances against the United States may still loom large in the individual worker's picture of America, these grievances do not spark an anti-American neonationalism to the extent prevalent in other Western countries.

During the last five years the Germans have participated in the making of their own history to a probably greater degree than have other European nations. Their attitudes toward this history have tended to take the place either of impotent criticism or of the urge to imitate the occupation powers that the war foisted on Germany in the mid-forties. The substitution of native for American authority has occasioned a shift in the basis of both criticism and appreciation of the United States. German-American relations have become policy matters rather than aspects of personal experience.

What remains is the difficult choice that trade-unionists, as members of the national community, have to make in the field of foreign policy. The experience of the last decade, if taken as a whole, weighs in favor of continued reliance on the United States. While some of the actions of the United States have been criticized, there is no pattern of total rejection and complete mistrust, as there is in regard to the Soviet Union. Therefore, with very few exceptions, even the most critical unionist, whatever else his ideas on American capitalism, would put his trust in the United States if he were asked to make a choice on the basis of the total record of the United States and the U.S.S.R. Yet some insist that any choice must be made "in cold blood and without sentimentality." The experience of the past might mean little in the light of present power relations. A member of a Berlin works council interviewed by the author said:

> If the Russians offer bread, survival and servitude, and the West offers a chance of uncertain freedom, but connected with a great likelihood of universal destruction, there is little doubt where we would turn. Obviously, if the chances of survival on either side are more even, and if the Americans offer twenty dollars a day and the Russians only Kascha and socialist competition, we gladly stick to the Americans.

Such cynicism, based on a somewhat artificial choice, may be illustrative, but it is not typical. Most unionists would think of the United States in somewhat broader terms. In the lower ranks, especially among the works-council members, who are closest to the rank and file, political considerations weigh much less heavily than do expectations and fears concerning the course of U.S. economic development. With the widespread belief in and acknowledgment of the interdependence of the various Western economies, the course of the American economy as a determinant of prosperity or crisis looms very large in the minds of the more active among the industrial workers. In their thinking, such problems are likely to take precedence over the military course of American-Soviet rivalry; in any event, so far as they are concerned, the latter question is beyond the scope of their influence. As members of the Heilbronn works council expressed it: "War is simply a ghastly and utterly meaningless thing; it would mean complete ruin for Germany, and would turn it into one vast cemetery."

In a somewhat simplified yet effective way, the course of the present prosperity, the appreciation of the U.S. economy, and the future course of the whole Western system have all coalesced into a single question in the minds of German workers. They would find it difficult to believe that the present prosperity might give way to a new crisis without at the same time endangering the might of the United States and the cohesion of the Western political system. That is why there is great interest on the part of the better-educated workers in conjectures and prognoses about the course of the American economy, and especially in the stabilizing factors which make improbable a repetition of the great depression of the thirties. Thus, while German labor in general accepts and approves of the good things usually associated with American influence in Europe, there remains a certain undertone of apprehension. Will they last? Can these things be relied on as permanent? But, so long as the great majority of unionists are not unduly apprehensive over the proximity of a war, it is the totality of American social and economic development, with its expected influence on Germany, that remains the decisive factor in the German worker's ultimate image of the United States.

Conclusions

Although it is probably exaggerated to call German labor, as some in its ranks would have it, the only democratic potential in German society, it is by all standards the most important one. Even labor's ardent desire for reunification will scarcely deflect it from its democratic convictions and practices.

But what is labor's impact on the present political scene? Its self-confidence is not overly developed. The organizational connections of the unions with their members are not built on too firm a ground. Relations with industry are based on mutual distrust of each other's intentions rather than on a spirit of collaboration. Finally, in the present official configuration of West German society, labor's representatives do not loom very large.

These weaknesses of German labor inevitably reflect on the over-all strength of present-day German political institutions, which remain narrowly circumscribed and official. Universally acknowledged by the overwhelming majority of German citizens as the external frame of reference for their existence, democracy still has not developed into an instinctive way of life. The Federal Republic forms a huge and admirably organized agglomeration of private citizens, who happen to live on West Germany's present territory. Each citizen watches jealously over his still expanding share of the social product. Germany's forums resound with the zeal and squabbles of technicians and officials, the lusty efforts of lobbyists, and the faint and muffled noises of professional politicians. The public at large deposits its ballots every four years; it then quickly sheds the attire of citizen and sinks back to the level of private individual.

Would it have been different if the workers and their representatives had been associated more closely with the course of public affairs? The answer is in doubt. Withdrawal into private life has by now become an established, and so far rewarding, pattern of existence. But still, there exists in German labor a largely untapped reservoir of potential good will and political common sense.

The mixture of defeat, U.S. protection, cold war, and prosperity has brought some element of stability to the German scene, a sort of "normalcy" growing from a thoroughly abnormal set of circumstances. Labor is assuredly not among those who are prepared to forego this stability, however precarious. Labor thus contributes to the larger course of German policy a steady hand, mistrust of adventure—whether leftist, rightist, or a combination of the two—a realistic evaluation of the advantages of the Atlantic alliance and its purely defensive implications, and a desire to obtain unification by way of persistent negotiations and, if necessary, concessions, which, however, should not endanger the prospects of continued U.S. protection.

The vicious circle implicit in the last proposition has not escaped attention, even if labor's representatives for the record's sake sometimes are inclined to glide over it.* But the labor official's hopes, or, if one wishes, illusions, about the ultimate character of a unified Germany explain his continued search for solutions that will create a unified, protected, and nonaggressive Germany. German rearmament, at best grudgingly acknowledged as the none-too-meaningful price of U.S. alliance and protection, is viewed both as a psychological and political burden, and as the source of many new fears and uncertainties. Given the continuation of present prosperity, the dangers of rearmament are seen to lie less in the likelihood of communist advances among the labor rank and file than in the widening cleavage between what the French used to call the *"pays légal"* and the *"pays réel."*

POSTSCRIPT

Major social trends run too deep to be decisively influenced by current policies in the relatively short span of one year. However, as of the latter half of 1956, it is possible to discern an element of new hopefulness in the expectations of German labor. This mood arises in part from the beginnings of a thaw in the East, from the continuing prosperity, and from signs of a slowly-rising membership—the latter probably not un-related to the general recognition that attempts at founding a rival,

---

*E. Schwarz ("Die Problematik der Wiedervereinigung," *G.M.,* February, 1956) says: "We should not overlook the fact that we fool ourselves and attempt to square the circle when we ask for unity in the same breath with a U.S.-guaranteed security, and when we aspire to freedom without admitting any restrictions on our sovereignty." The author continues to the effect that Germany's choice rests between concessions and restrictions as the price of unity on the one hand, and the maintenance of the *status quo* on the other. He is not certain, however, whether the U.S.S.R. is still willing to consider a compromise ar-rangement.

Christian labor organization are proving a dismal failure. But it is due also to a brighter political picture: enough German voters have apparently shifted their allegiance from the present administration to allow the unions to detect, on the 1957 horizon, the contours of a domestic development that may lead, if not to a labor government, at least to a government that will prove more active in labor's cause. However, since the causes of this popular switch may be multiple, and its reversal well within the realm of possibility, the reaction of the unions has been restrained, as can be seen from the attitude and findings of the Hamburg DGB congress of October, 1956.

The unions' tendency has been to encourage their adherents about the future, while impressing the wider public with their present sense of responsibility and reliability. This policy is apparent in the unions' stand on both domestic and foreign affairs. The long-range goals of a planned economy under active union participation are not forgotten, and the apparent willingness of the government to establish a harmless Federal Economic Council is brushed off as the desire to create "a resting place for supernumerary cabinet ministers and members of parliament who fail of re-election." But the main emphasis is on such immediate goals as the further shortening of the work week, speedy enactment of satisfactory social security legislation, and joint control by government and union of automation and the development of atomic energy facilities. Since the goals are shared by all those who are gainfully employed in dependent positions, such programs have a momentum of their own, and the unions are risking little in espousing them, regardless of what the future may bring. The same caution determines labor's foreign policy stand. The DGB was reflecting the mood of the great majority of its members when it declared itself prepared to support those forces that are willing and able, by democratic means, to repeal rearmament legislation and compulsory military service in a split Germany. Thus, the DGB convention enjoined its newly-elected executives to set up immediately a committee which is to work out and submit by May 1, 1957, proposals for German reunification that will be in accord with the ideals of peace and freedom.

But there remains a clear-cut boundary line between hopes and expectations on the one hand, and the realm of action on the other. Thus, the convention went so far as to say that conscientious objectors should be allowed to invoke not only moral and religious but also political reasons for their attitude, but it did not recommend that its constituent unions furnish legal counsel to such objectors. Nor did it reverse its stand on contacts with East German labor authorities, but, on the contrary, reiterated its previous stand that any resumption of such contacts would presuppose the revival of free German labor organizations in East Germany and the re-establishment of civil liberties.

Organizationally, the top level of the DGB has experienced a drastic rejuvenation. The nine-man executive committee has six new members, and the forty-to-fifty-year-old group, rather than the survivors of Weimar days, is now the dominant element. The new chairman, Willy Richter, previously the committee's social policy expert and chairman of the Bundestag's social policy committee, is a man inclined to compromise; he is thus in step with a DGB in which power may continue to rest with the major constituent unions. But at least three or four of the members of the new executive committee—possibly among them the new vice-chairman, Bernhard Tacke (one of the two representatives of the Christian wing on the executive committee)—are unlikely to condone such passivity for very long, especially in view of the continued urgency of two problems: the gap between the wage structures of the stronger unions and their weaker brethren—the "sickly footsoldiers" of the unions; and the need to establish closer contact with the factory level.

Meanwhile, at the crest of the prosperity wave, employers' resistance to union demands is stiffening. At the same time, the general public is beginning to relate its own desires and grievances to a conscious evaluation of the wider political scene. Growing criticism of the prevailing "middle course" goes hand in hand with a mixture of hope and fear about Germany's active role on the international scene. In 1956 unionism was still dedicated primarily to solid social and economic achievements, reserving an attitude of watchful waiting, albeit a rather hopeful one, for the realm of politics. The year 1957, by contrast, has begun in the shadow of many uncertainties, which seem not only to allow but to demand that German unions increase their radius of action.

The Politics of German Business

Gabriel A. Almond

The German middle classes never fully developed a political style of their own. Impulses toward liberalism and constitutionalism were fairly strong among all sectors of the middle classes in the first half of the nineteenth century; but in the dominant political pattern which emerged after the unification of the Reich, these tendencies had only a weak and peripheral representation. Unlike the case of England, where the crown and aristocracy in the nineteenth century became assimilated in a middle-class ethos, the German middle classes were assimilated into the authoritarian and bureaucratic pattern of the Prussian monarchy.

Heavy industry bore this Prussian imprint to a greater extent than did the rest of the middle classes, because its period of rapid expansion coincided with the consolidation of the Bismarck Reich and was made possible in considerable part by the protectionist and armament policies of that regime. The formative period of heavy industry occurred in an era when those who had political power were not responsible to parliamentary control or to an effective party system, and when the ideal of political leadership and statesmanship tended to emphasize authority and national power. What discredited liberalism and cosmopolitanism among the middle classes were the facts that the Prussian monarchy

EDS. NOTE.—In the summer of 1954, the author interviewed some fifty members of the West German business community, as well as German government and political party officials who were familiar with business interests and activities. The report presented here is based on those conversations and on published materials. It first appeared, in somewhat longer form, as RAND Corporation Research Memorandum (RM-1506-RC), on June 20, 1955. The author has revised the material for inclusion in this symposium, removing some dated observations and adding footnote references to the most pertinent recent literature.

Dr. Almond is Professor of Politics, and Faculty Associate of the Center for International Studies, at Princeton University. He has written extensively on international affairs in general and on Germany in particular.

had fashioned an efficient army and bureaucracy, that in Bismarck it had a ruthless and prudent statesman, and that as a consequence it was able to attain national unity, internal order, and international prestige on its own terms.

On the condition that it accept a subordinate role in this authoritarian bureaucratic regime, heavy industry was given the advantages of a large, protected internal market, the prospect of social acceptance by the aristocracy and court, and gratification of national pride through the rapid rise to power of the Second Reich.[1] Out of this social situation and historical experience there emerged among the middle classes as a whole, and particularly among the big-business elite, an attitude toward politics which had the following ingredients.

First, effective political power was viewed as in large measure beyond the control and responsibility of the individual. The appropriate attitude toward the bureaucratic and authoritarian order was a deferential one, conditioned upon the expectation that the autonomy of industry would be respected. The political parties which heavy industry tended to favor were those which supported the authoritarian, bureaucratic regime.

Second, there were two types of favors which businessmen sought to obtain from government and politico-social authority: interest advantages and social recognition. For the first type of favor, a bargaining and "pressure politics" attitude was appropriate; the second called for the various forms of social lobbying; marriage into the legitimate orders of the landed aristocracy, the army, or the higher bureaucracy; purchase of estates; zealous performance of services; and imitation of the style of living of the ruling groups.

Third, a distinction was made between the legitimate, effective institutions of government, which were largely beyond popular control, and parliament and the political parties. For the latter institutions, there were mixed feelings of lack of confidence (at certain times and among certain groups even contempt) and fear. The lack of confidence resulted from the ambiguity in the power position of the parliament and its lack of dignity as compared with the traditional authoritarian institutions such as the monarchy, the bureaucracy, and the army. The fear resulted from the rapid emergence of the Social Democratic movement with its program of democratization and socialization. In a negative sense, the middle classes and heavy industry failed to develop in any adequate sense a tradition of rational political discussion and of political participation, and the organizational and communications structure necessary to support such a tradition.

Fourth, in this general atmosphere of an authoritarian bureaucratic society, the sense of duty and obligation among the industrialists and businessmen took the form—beyond the requirements of obedience and patriotism—of a narrow concern with the conduct of the business enterprise, a kind of "enterprise fanaticism" (*Betriebsfanatismus*). This involved a specialized intelligence of a high order, but it was an intelligence that did not spill over into the political sphere. In politics, the attitude was one of submissiveness to the authoritarian order, or a sometimes cynical attempt to buy security by making contributions to all the parties to the right of the socialists. This latter pattern became especially marked in the Weimar period.

Finally, as far as attitudes toward international politics were concerned, the Bismarck experience suggested that scrupulousness over means was highly inappropriate in the international sphere. German nationalism was a rather massive and crude ideology, relatively unaffected by Christianity, liberalism, and cosmopolitanism. The bulk of the German middle classes, and particularly heavy industry, was strongly influenced by this nationalist ideology with its rational-ethical primitivism, and it supported the political parties and institutions that advocated it.

The above characterization of the political attitudes of German industrialists and businessmen is, of course, both generalized and oversimplified. There were significant differences of a regional nature, and there were significant fluctuations in attitudes through time. Perhaps the big industrialists in the Ruhr came closest to conforming to the model sketched above, while the industrialists in Southwest Germany and the Hanseatic cities had a more liberal and internationalist orientation. Similarly, the political attitudes of the business community changed through time. In the early years after the shock of the defeat in World War I, a substantial part of the middle classes were ready to support the democratic, liberal parties; but as early as 1921, the middle class began to revert to a nationalist, authoritarian orientation. Again, after World War II, the middle classes have tended to swing their support to parties of a democratic and Christian coloring, but there is no evidence to indicate that this attitude is based on an internalized ideology and conviction; the simplest calculations of power and interest suggest it as the only safe attitude to entertain.

These considerations suggest an interpretation of the relationship of German industry, and particularly heavy industry, to National Socialism. If industry's characteristic attitudes toward politics arose out of a pattern of calculation of interest, use of pressure techniques through trade associations, and an "insurance policy" relationship to the political parties, then the financial contributions made by industrialists to the Nazi party, with noteworthy exceptions, may be evidence not of Nazi conviction but of the same kind of narrow security calculation. There were relatively few industrialists who were thoroughgoing Nazis, just as there were relatively few industrialists who were courageous anti-Nazis. The industrialists in the early years saw in Nazism not its revolutionary and nihilistic features but a means of security from the political left and an instrument of national vindication. In the years of Nazi diplomatic and military successes, the industrialists were swept by the same enthusiasm and fascination which affected most Germans, the same fascination with primitive power and success which had swept their fathers in earlier generations.

The evidence, thus, will not support those who attribute to German industrialists (again with noteworthy exceptions) a dynamic role in the advent of National Socialism, just as it will not support those who seek to attribute a liberal and democratic dynamism to the German industrialists of today. The number of industrialists, bankers, and businessmen involved in the plot of July 20, 1944, and the other anti-Nazi resistance movements was small indeed.[2] These movements stemmed not from the business community but from the left, from the more enlightened representatives of the traditional orders of German society— the army, the bureaucracy, and the churches—and from the free professions. More typical of the business attitude toward resistance to Nazism was the reply of a prominent German industrialist to the invitation of the *Kreisau Kreis* to join their group: "It would be inconsistent with my obligations to the firm."

Though the defeat in World War II and the disorganizing experiences of the occupation have had an undeniable impact on the mentality of German businessmen, it does not appear that their basic pattern of political irresponsibility has been fundamentally changed. In the analysis which follows, it will be shown that the German business community of today is not nationalist, militaristic, or authoritarian in its political views; but, at the same time, the evidence does not point to the emergence of a democratic ideology, or to any widespread readiness to participate in politics and political discussion.

The physical and personal losses of the war, and the difficult and painful readjustments of the postwar era have indeed produced a kind of ideological sobriety, but this is essentially a kind of negative learning, a rejection of political romanticism and enthusiasm. No positive ideology has as yet emerged to take the place of the older patterns, although there are a number of efforts in this direction. The striking achievements of German industry in the few short years since the end of the war— the rebuilding of the German industrial plant and the attainment of a level of productivity higher than that of the prewar years—represent primarily an economic achievement. While some progress has been made in the political sphere, it would be a great exaggeration to speak of a political transformation in the business community.

The main influences which have affected the attitudes of German businessmen in the postwar period may be summarized under five headings: (1) the effect of the defeat and of the immediate postwar occupation policies and decisions; (2) the efforts at indoctrination by the occupation powers; (3) the efforts at reorientation made by the churches and by voluntary associations of one kind or another; (4) the cold war and the division of Germany; and (5) the German economic achievement.

Effects of Defeat and of Occupation Policy

The military collapse of Germany, the extent of physical destruction, and the occupation by the Allied powers shook the confidence of German businessmen in all their prior political attitudes. Nazism, nationalism, and militarism were widely discredited. But the postwar period was hardly one in which opportunities for changes in attitude could be consolidated in any substantial way. The version of German guilt for the Nazi war crimes presented by the occupying powers was unassimilated and unassimilable. It was too oversimplified to be reconcilable with what had been the actual behavior of most Germans. Its net effect, therefore, was that it tended to discredit the very idea of guilt itself, particularly in view of German sufferings from 1944 through the immediate postwar inflationary period. The combination of an unacceptable version of German guilt, German suffering in air raids, postwar imprisonment, and personal losses and suffering in the inflation produced the rather widespread tendency among Germans—which still persists—to dwell only on the period from 1944 on, when they suffered, and to suppress the events of the Nazi period, when they imposed enormous sufferings on others. Thus most Germans, including most German businessmen, have not, in a moral-psychological sense, "worked through" their experiences of the last twenty years. They have discarded the explicit doctrines of the Nazi period, but they have failed to penetrate into the institutional, political, and moral factors which had been responsible for the developments of that period.

One of the most interesting symptoms of this moral condition is that both Nazism and anti-Nazism are in a state of moral suspension as far as a very large part of the German public is concerned. They are unable to reject the Nazi experience in any integral way, and they are unable to take to themselves unequivocally the moral credit of those few Germans who stood out against the regime. Most Germans still see some good features in the Nazi record; and a substantial proportion of them are unable to absolve the anti-Nazi resistance completely from the taint of treason. The typical pattern is to evade both issues, and escape into everyday work and the loyalties of primary relationships and activities.

What has been said about the attitudes of Germans as a whole is largely true of the German business community as well. There were in addition, however, a number of postwar experiences specific to the business community. The combination of denazification, decentralization, and rapid economic expansion since 1948 has changed the structure and composition of the German industrial elite. While former Nazi affiliation no longer constitutes a bar to high position in German industry, there was a period of several years during which many industrialists were removed from their posts. Deconcentration measures, particularly in the iron and steel industry, destroyed some of the older industrial power concentrations and brought to the top of the new industrial units many individuals who had formerly held lower positions, or who came from the outside.[3] Finally, the postwar inflation and the rapid rate of industrial expansion since 1948 have thrown up a class of industrial parvenus who do not share the traditions and patterns of the prewar elite. That is why it is often said of present-day German heavy industry that it has not acquired a political style. The older networks of political and personal ties have not yet been replaced by new ones.

Another development which affected the attitudes of industrialists was the dismantling of certain industries, and the prohibition or limitation of certain types of industrial production. This not only created resentment among industrialists but it also gave them a common cause with their workers. This, in addition to the shared experience of working together in order to get production started, has had a large part in creating an atmosphere of labor peace in the postwar period.

A final special influence was the introduction of the "codetermination law." As applied in the coal and steel industries in the Ruhr, this law calls for one worker representative in the management of an enterprise and a number of seats on the board of directors equal to that of the representatives selected by the shareholders. Outside the Ruhr, the *Betriebsverfassungsgesetz* gives only one-third the seats on the board of directors to representatives of the employees, and gives labor no representation in management. But in either case the power of industrial management has been somewhat reduced, and industrial decisions now have to be made in an atmosphere that is more public than heretofore. Not only has the political style of heavy industry not yet been determined, but also its freedom to use economic power for political purposes has been somewhat reduced.

Efforts at Indoctrination by the Occupation Powers

What actual impact the occupation has had on German life is most difficult to appraise. Not least among the difficulties is the problem of separating the effects of those actions which were intended to "reorient" from the unintended consequences of having American, British, and French civilian administrators and soldiers in such large numbers in contact with Germans for almost a decade. The aim of increasing the extent of political interest, involvement, and participation among all elements of the population has been only partially successful at best. The dreams, cherished by some of the planners of the American reorientation effort, that it might be possible to reproduce in Germany a pattern of voluntary associations—leagues of women voters, parent-teachers associations, and a variety of other types of civic associations—have been fulfilled only on a most limited scale. Now, as before, there is largely lacking in German political life that structure of local civic associations and activities which makes possible a genuine decentralization of political participation and discussion. There is little that lies between the great organizations of the interest-groups, such as the parties, the churches, and the government, on the one hand, and the intimate ties of family and friendship, on the other hand.[4] Not even among the middle classes— the typical soil in England and the United States in which civic organizations have taken root—has there been any significant development of such associations. This is not meant to depreciate efforts in this direction that are being made in the business community and elsewhere, but only to suggest that these efforts are as yet insufficient to create an atmosphere of political involvement and responsibility.

A more specific American influence on the German business community has resulted from the effort to introduce American industrial management practices. This effort appears to have been more successful, since the main goal of increased productivity had obvious appeal to German management. American influence in this area has been continuous since the beginning of the occupation, at first through the economic sections of military government, then through the ECA and MSA missions and the sponsored exchange visits of German and American industrialists. It is difficult to say to what extent the pattern of employer-employee relations in German industry has actually changed under the influence of the American model, but certainly the language typical of the American scene has seeped into the literature of the German business associations and of the economic press. The term "human relations" (along with "public relations") has been taken over untranslated into the German businessman's vocabulary. The spirit of this American industrial model, which involves a relaxed and informal relationship between management and labor and a decentralization of decision-making among the middle management level, comes into conflict with the more authoritarian and paternalistic pattern of German industrial organization.[5] But American efforts have at least introduced a leaven, and it is possible that new practices which develop within the industrial organization may have some influence in other types of relationship.

The Influence of the Churches and Voluntary Associations

In the immediate aftermath of the German collapse there was a substantial turn to religion. The churches were among the few German institutions which survived the Nazi era and the defeat, and businessmen, like other groups, turned to them, and to some extent to religious ideas, as a stabilizing factor in the postwar chaos. But as one prominent religious lay leader put it, there were quite a few industrialists who took off their Nazi party buttons and went to church primarily because it gave them a certain safety. Since the currency reform, according to reliable reports, there has been a swing of the pendulum in the other direction, and participation in church activities on the part of businessmen is now no greater than it was before the war.

However, both the Catholic and Lutheran churches have established lay movements which are especially active among businessmen. The Catholic organization is called the *Bund katholischer Unternehmer,* and has its headquarters in Cologne. It has some eighteen local organizations in different parts of Germany, and a total membership of three to four hundred. Its aim is not to have a mass membership, but rather to reach and indoctrinate a business elite in the social doctrine of the Catholic Church. It is assumed that this small group of business leaders, in their own businesses and in their activities in trade associations, employers' organizations, and in politics, will propagate the doctrine further and advocate a program of labor welfare and employer responsibility consistent with the Papal encyclicals. The *Bund* is opposed to the codetermination law, because in its opinion it violates the "Natural Law" right of private property and conflicts with the requirements of efficient management.

Some elements among the Evangelical clergy and laity have formed an "Evangelical Academy" movement among leading Protestant laymen.

It has a number of "retreats" to which businessmen and other lay leaders are periodically invited in order to discuss pressing social and moral problems. The best-known of these academies is the one located at Kloster Loccum near Hannover, which has a clientele among Ruhr industrialists. Both the Catholic and the Evangelical lay movements have as objectives the development of social and political responsibility among industrialists. The kinds of topics most frequently discussed, however, deal with welfare and labor-relations problems, rather than with general political and foreign policy questions.

In addition to these Catholic and Protestant lay organizations, there are a number of others which are especially active among businessmen. The main organizations of German business (which are treated in detail below) are the Federation of German Industries, the Diet of German Industry and Commerce (equivalent to our Chamber of Commerce), and the Union of German Employers Organizations (which specializes in industrial relations). The conventions and meetings of these central organizations as well as those of their constituent organizations frequently provide forums for lectures or discussions on political, social, and foreign policy problems. In addition, the Federation of German Industries and the Union of German Employers Organizations together finance the German Industry Institute, which carries on an enormous program of public information directed at the business community by means of periodicals, radio broadcasts, lecture services, etc. Much of the output of the Industry Institute deals with questions of public policy, and sometimes with foreign policy. Finally, the Association of Independent Entrepreneurs (smaller, family-owned enterprises) also engages in some activities of this kind.

It must always be borne in mind, however, that, while members of these interest-groups are exposed to some broad political discussion by virtue of their membership in the groups and their attendance at conventions and meetings, the primary purpose of these organizations is to defend specialized business interests. Indeed, it is traditional with German (and European) business associations to confine themselves to representation of interest, and to avoid taking sides publicly on broad public questions such as foreign policy. For example, in late June of 1954, after the speech of former German Chancellor Brüning before the *Rhein-Ruhr Klub* advocating a return to a Rapallo type of diplomacy, the president of the Federation of German Industry, Fritz Berg, gave an interview to the newspaper *Die Welt* in which he stated that German industry was fully in support of Adenauer's foreign policy and was not influenced in the slightest by Brüning.[6] Berg was promptly scolded by the press service of the Free Democratic Party on the grounds that he had no right to set himself up as a spokesman for the foreign policy position of German business.

But the convention limiting the political interests of German business does not appear to have much effect. An examination of the literature of the Federation of German Industry published in the last few years demonstrates that it has been a consistent supporter of Adenauer's foreign policy. It has favored European integration, elimination of trade barriers, participation in EDC and later in WEU, and the European common market. It has also continually propagated the idea of a socially and politically responsible entrepreneurial and managerial class.

In addition to these pressure-groups, there are a number of specialized organizations which are active among, and have support from, business circles. Examples include the *Europa Union,* which is the German branch of the European Union of Federalists (UEF), a German branch of the League for European Economic Co-operation (LECE), and a German group affiliated with the European Committee for Economic and Social Development (CEPES). This last organization is patterned after the Committee for Economic Development (CED) in the United States; it has a German membership which includes some fifty prominent industrialists and businessmen. Finally, there are such organizations as the Institute for European Economics and Politics, and the Economic Policy Association of 1947. The latter holds meetings and conferences attended by businessmen, professional men, and political leaders, at which economic and foreign policy problems are discussed.[7] A recent development of some significance is the formation of the *Gesellschaft für Aussenpolitik,* with branches in Frankfurt on Main and Munich, which carries on a program of foreign policy education similar to that of the American Council on Foreign Relations.

Almost all these organizations are nationwide; they have no local units which can carry on regular discussion and lecture programs. At best they may be viewed as in process of training a civic elite among business and professional men capable of taking a broad view of social and political problems. They can not be said to have sparked off a continual political discussion as yet, or to have created an attentive public of any depth. At the same time it may be pointed out that these organizations are aware of this problem, and are making efforts to extend their scope and increase their impact.

The Cold War and the Division of Germany

A number of consequences of the cold war and the divided and exposed position of Germany call for comment. In the first place, the sudden shift in Allied policy toward Germany after the beginning of East-West tension has tended to divert attention from the original re-orientation goals of the occupation. As one German industrialist put it, after the brief pedagogic phase of the Allied occupation, the United States had turned to Germany and asked her to join in a concert of "Allies and Associated Enemies." This tended to demoralize those Germans who were sympathetic to the aims of the orientation program, and gave some encouragement to those who felt that Hitler was right in his policy toward Bolshevism. Anticommunism in the United States was cited as evidence of the soundness of National Socialism.

Whatever the merits of recent American policy toward Germany, it has provided a certain support for those Germans eager to escape the moral burden of their history. But perhaps more important than this reaction is the atmosphere of risk and tentativeness which the cold war and the division of the country have created. There is a widespread reluctance to view the West German Republic as the permanent form of the German nation. In addition, the vulnerability of Germany in the East-West conflict, the division of the country and the presence of Soviet troops on German soil, and the widespread conviction that Germany would be occupied in a war—all these factors, compounded by the heavy moral burden of the German past, create an unwillingness among all groups, including businessmen, to identify themselves too prominently with politics.

The German Economic Achievement

The state of the German industrial plant and economy at the time of the currency reform confronted the business leadership with an enormous challenge. The magnitude of the problem of physical reconstruction was only part of the picture. The West German economy had to absorb millions of refugees and expellees. Many of these individuals, if they had business experience and small sums of capital, went into business and thereby intensified competition, particularly in small industry and trade. And since war casualties had their greatest impact on the generation which might now be moving into positions of responsibility in industry, the period of intense activity since 1948 has placed an additional heavy burden on the older men, leaving them little time for anything else. Finally, the war meant a heavy destruction of capital, with the result that most industrial establishments are capital-poor. This has tended to place an extraordinary emphasis on quick turnover, which makes great demands on the energies and time of managers and entrepreneurs.

A disinclination to become involved in politics has reinforced the impulse to concentrate on business. In the last decade or so, politics has borne the double burden of the disillusionment attendant upon the collapse of Nazism, and the limited discretion available to the German government under the occupation. By contrast, economic activity has offered an arena where great accomplishments are possible, where material success is attainable, and where a kind of redemption can be sought.

The success of the German recovery effort—like the conditions which it was intended to meet—has also tended to reinforce the business tradition of avoiding political commitments and activity. German recovery has rehabilitated the prestige of the German industrial leadership, after its immediate postwar low. And economic prosperity has placed in power a coalition of parties with wide popular backing, which follows a course favored by the business community. Thus the present atmosphere is one in which German business has high prestige in large parts of the society and can carry on its activities in political safety.

The Political Influence of German Business

Konrad Adenauer's coalition government has been, on the whole, quite satisfactory to German businessmen. Policies which it has followed have encouraged industrial expansion and foreign trade, and have cut short the trends toward regulation and nationalization that characterized the years immediately after the end of the war. While most businessmen are critical of current tax policy and the "anti-trust" line of the German finance ministry, and would prefer a more aggressive position on East-West trade, these are, on the whole, the only significant discordant notes. It would be inaccurate, however, to refer to West Germany under the coalition as an *Unternehmerstaat,* as some Germans do; it is not an entrepreneurs' society. The agricultural bloc has great power in the Christian Democratic Union (particularly in the Bavarian CSU), and working-class support in the Rhineland and the Ruhr is crucial for the maintenance of the dominant position of the CDU.[8] In other words, the governing coalition is dependent on broad support from all the major interest-groups in West Germany, although its most enthusiastic, and financially most rewarding, support comes from the business community.

The business community has excellent channels of communication to the coalition parties, Chancellor Adenauer, the Bundestag, the ministries, and most of the *Länder* governments. It is these connections between business and government that we now wish to examine in detail.

The first Bundestag elected after the adoption of the West German Basic Law had a representation from the business community, broadly defined, of some 15 per cent. This included industrial and financial proprietors and managers (8.7 per cent), officials of industrial and business associations (1.2 per cent), artisans, businessmen in retail and wholesale trade, and officers of interest-groups in these fields (4.5 per cent).[9] The Bundestag elected in 1953 had a representation of approximately 25 per cent from these business groups.[10] Of these, approximately 3 per cent were SPD deputies, with the remainder being deputies of the coalition parties, and particularly the CDU. Thus, the direct representation of business elements in the Bundestag has increased. It has also changed in another respect. In the 1953 Bundestag it is business-group functionaries and elected interest-group officials who constitute a large component of the business representation. The 1953 Bundestag has 24 full-time paid employees of business interest-groups and 20 businessmen who hold elective positions in these organizations. These constitute 9 per cent of the total membership of the Bundestag, 13 per cent of the deputies of the coalition parties, and 44 per cent of the coalition party deputies recruited from the business community. In other words, direct representation in the Bundestag from the business community has a heavy concentration of representatives of pressure-groups. A large percentage of the remaining business representatives are from small industry, handicraft, and retail and wholesale trade. Since some of these are party functionaries, it is difficult to escape the conclusion that a very great part of the business representation in the Bundestag is made up of pressure-group or party functionaries, just as on the side of the SPD the great bulk of the representatives are trade-union and party functionaries, or officials from the state and local governments. There were only 12 deputies from medium and big industry and banking; and even of these, half were simply higher-ranking employees, rather than top managers or proprietors. Outstanding businessmen such as Robert Pferdmenges of the Oppenheim Bank, Wolfgang Pohle of the *Mannesmann-Röhrenwerke,* and Martin Blank of the *Gutehoffnungshütte* are rare exceptions.

The above breakdown suggests that, in so far as direct participation of business in the Bundestag is concerned, it tends to take the form of special interest representation; it thus continues a trend which was pronounced in the Reichstag of the Weimar Republic and of the Second Reich, and which contributed to the rigidity and unimaginativeness of those institutions.[11] This large contingent of pressure-group representatives, when combined with the essentially functionary character of the SPD representation, may account in part for the inadequacy of communication in the Bundestag, and for the resulting impoverishment of political discussion in the countryside. In national politics, as within the political parties and the pressure-groups themselves, one has the impression of a pattern of political discussion in which a few giants speak from the heights of the government ministries, the central party organs, and the *Spitzenverbände,* while very few voices are heard from the constituencies.

According to a survey [12] made immediately after the 1953 elections, the vote of German businessmen went heavily to the Christian Democratic Union. Fifty-eight per cent of the businessmen interviewed reported that they had voted for the CDU, as compared with 8 per cent for the FDP, 5 per cent for the *Deutsche Partei,* and 7 per cent for the Social Democrats. The same pattern of party preference came out of the analysis of voting on the basis of income groups. What is most interesting, however, is that, according to the survey, all the occupation and income groups voted in roughly equal proportions for the CDU, while the FDP and DP were more dependent on the upper occupational and income groups. Thus, 32 per cent of the respondents who reported voting for the FDP, and an equal percentage of those voting for the DP, earned incomes of 500 DM per month or more; only 19 per cent of the CDU respondents were in that income group. Similarly, 45 per cent of the CDU respondents reported incomes of under 300 DM per month, while only 29 per cent of the FDP and 22 per cent of the DP voters made under 300 DM monthly. What this makes clear is that, while the great majority of businessmen voted CDU, a larger proportion of FDP and DP support comes from businessmen and the upper-income groups. The almost equal proportions of the various occupational and income groupings in the CDU tend to make a moderate center party of that organization, while the heavier weighting of the FDP and DP with the upper-income and business groups makes the latter two organizations the more specialized voices of industry and business interests. Both the CDU and FDP are dependent for their financing on the contributions of German industry, and, in both parties, the industrial trade associations play an important role in the collection of funds. But, the mixed social composition of the CDU constituencies makes it more difficult for that party to yield to pressure from business groups. The FDP, on the other hand, more dependent upon business groups, tends to express its point of view more directly and explicitly in the Bundestag. In questions involving industrial policy such as decartelization, business taxation, labor-management relations, and the like, it is the FDP which takes a sharp pro-business position and is most sharply pitted against the welfare and "socialist" measures of the SPD.[13] Nevertheless, businessmen vote in largest numbers for the CDU, because, were they to move to the FDP, they would commit themselves to a minority party and would lose their influence in the dominant CDU. Their present distribution gives them a crucial but not dominant position in the CDU, and a more explicit spokesman in the FDP.

This characterization of the FDP should not give the impression of a unified party. It is anything but that, as events since 1952 reveal. There are at least three wings in the FDP. The right-wing group has sought to bring into the party all right-wing elements. It is led by Middelhauve and has its main strength in North Rhine-Westphalia. There is a "left-wing" group of old-style German liberals, led by Reinhold Maier, which is strongest in Hamburg and Southwest Germany. A middle group seeks to avoid extreme commitments in either direction and prefers to maintain a position of *Koalitionsfähigkeit,* in other words a policy which would enable the FDP to form a coalition with the CDU or the SPD, depending on the election returns. Even though Maier is now chairman of the FDP, the official party position reflects the middle-of-the-road point of view regarding the 1957 election, which is to conduct an independent campaign and to reserve its position on coalition policy until the returns are in.

Despite these differences in ideology and tactics, the FDP everywhere in Germany favors a middle-class business orientation. The different tendencies in the FDP are related to ideological differences in the business point of view. The liberal, cosmopolitan businessman of the Hanseatic cities and Southwest Germany supports the Maier wing. The nationalist industrialists of the Rhineland-Ruhr area support the Middelhauve wing.[14]

The political parties of the center and the right are dependent almost entirely on the business community for their financing. Membership dues are by no means sufficient to cover even the costs of party maintenance between elections. This can be seen from the membership figures. The CDU has an approximate membership of 350,000,[15] or less than 5 per cent of the CDU vote; and the FDP has a membership of approximately 80,000,[16] or under 3 per cent of its vote. In contrast, the Social Democratic Party has almost 700,000 members,[17] more than 10 per cent of the Social Democratic vote. Also, because of the dominant position of the Social Democrats in the trade-union movement, they have a ready supply of paid trade-union functionaries to carry on canvassing activities during elections.

At the present time there is no effective legislative control over party financing. Article 21 of the Basic Law requires that ". . . the parties must give an open accounting as to the sources of their income."[18]

But in the absence of enabling legislation this clause has at the most a slight inhibiting effect. As a consequence, the pattern of center and right-wing party financing is simple and crude.

The Social Democratic Party (SPD) has issued a report, with substantial documentation, describing the methods used in the financing of the coalition parties.[19] According to this report, for the first Bundestag election in 1949, a committee was formed under the chairmanship of Robert Pferdmenges, a partner of the Oppenheim Bank in Cologne.

Pferdmenges is one of the founders of the CDU in the Rhineland, and one of the oldest and most trusted associates of Chancellor Adenauer. Pferdmenges occupies an unusual position in the governing coalition and among the elements which compose it; he combines the roles of a leading Protestant layman, one of the bankers most trusted by Rhine-Ruhr industry, and one of the key figures in the CDU. For Adenauer, he is not only a close and trusted friend but also a contact with Protestantism and heavy industry. For industry, he signifies direct contact with Adenauer, with the coalition parties, and with the ministries. Pferdmenges holds fifteen chairmanships or deputy chairmanships in industrial and insurance corporations, and a total of more than twenty directorships. He is a member of the board of directors of the *Allgemeine Elektrizitäts-Gesellschaft,* the biggest electrical manufacturing concern in Germany; chairman of the board of *Demag,* the largest machine-manufacturing concern in Germany; and deputy chairman of the board of the *Klöckner-Werke AG,* one of the largest iron and steel manufacturing combines in the Ruhr.[20]

According to the SPD report referred to above, Pferdmenges' committee of industrial leaders assigned to each trade association a quota of funds to be collected for the 1949 Bundestag election. The construction industry, it was said, was asked to contribute 600,000 marks. Correspondence published in the SPD report suggests that one characteristic method of collecting funds was to have the trade associations assign contributions to individual firms on a "per employee" basis. The funds collected through the trade associations and industry were prorated among the coalition parties according to a prearranged formula: 60 to 65 per cent for the CDU, 25 to 30 per cent for the FDP, and 5 to 10 per cent for the *Deutsche Partei.*

The SPD Executive wrote Pferdmenges in July, 1949, asking whether the facts reported above were true. Pferdmenges did not, in his reply, admit to the specific details of the SPD description of coalition financing, but stated: "Of course, I have asked my friends to contribute to the campaign funds of the CDU, of which I am a member. In addition, I am collecting funds for the coming election for that part of the German people who see disaster in a planned economy. . . . I assume that everyone has the right to ask for campaign contributions from politically like-minded people." [21]

In all likelihood the neatness of the pattern of party financing described in the SPD report was exaggerated; the plan seems to have worked differently in different parts of Germany. But a number of aspects are clear. The per capita tax for employees was used in some cases; the trade associations unquestionably did play an important role; and a formula for distributing funds collected from these sources among the parties was used at least in certain industries. It is also clear, by the admission of responsible officials of the Federation of German Industry, that that organization was involved in the collection of funds.

There is evidence which suggests that there was a good deal of confusion in campaign financing in the *Länder* elections after 1949. Dissatisfaction with this condition resulted in a more systematic organization of election financing for the Bundestag election of 1953. The SPD report cites correspondence showing that the Federation of German Industry and the Union of Employers Associations decided to organize "promotional associations" (*Fördergesellschaften*) in each of the *Länder,* which would have the job of collecting funds for those political parties supporting the economic policies of Erhard. In North Rhine-Westphalia the organization was called *Verein zur Förderung der sozialen Marktwirtschaft in Nordrhein-Westphalen* ("Association for the Promotion of a Social Market Economy in North Rhine-Westphalia"). These organizations appear to have been most effective fund-raising instruments.[22]

Pressure-Groups

What has been striking in the foregoing analysis of the structure of business influence in German politics and government is not the mere fact that the business community has a degree of influence disproportionate to its size. This is a pattern which is familiar in the United States, England, and indeed in any country with a capitalistic economy and a democratic government. What is unusual in the German pattern, as compared to the American, is the direct and massive involvement of business pressure-groups in representation in the Bundestag and in the financing of the parties. By virtue of their penetration of the middle-class parties and their delegations in the Bundestag, these pressure-group organizations acquire a crucial political importance, influencing in important ways both spirit and content of German politics.

This is not only a consequence of the effective organization and financial power of the pressure-groups, but also a result of the poverty and weakness of other types of organization. Unlike the civic organizations described above, the pressure-groups of German industry are effectively organized both on the national level and on the *Land* level, as well as on a functional basis. Unlike the regional and local units of the political parties of the center and right, which are poorly organized and financed in between elections, the regional units of the pressure-groups have sustained financing and organization at those levels.[23]

The organization of German business is roughly the same as it was in the Weimar period.[24] In addition to the three main *Spitzenverbände* —the Federation of German Industry (BDI), the Diet of German Industry and Commerce (DIH), and the Federal Union of German Employers Associations (BDA)—there are separate associations for banking, insurance, wholesale and foreign trade, retail trade, shipping, transportation, handicrafts, and the like. All of these central organizations are associated in a co-ordinating committee called the *Gemeinschaftsausschuss der deutschen gewerblichen Wirtschaft*. The main function of the co-ordinating committee is to iron out difficulties that may arise among the constituent business organizations, and to provide public representation for the business community as a whole. The committee has only a small staff and is directed by Dr. Paul Beyer, who is also managing director of the Diet of German Industry and Commerce.

Federation of German Industries (BDI). Of the three main *Spitzenverbände,* the most important from the points of view of wealth and influence is the BDI. The membership of the BDI is limited to industrial trade associations at the national level. There are 36 constituent members; these are, in turn, subdivided into more specialized organizations. There are 12 regional offices which co-ordinate activities of the trade associations at the *Land* level, and which carry out the functions of public representation and lobbying vis-à-vis the *Land* government. These organizations, however, have been set up by, and are under the control of, the central headquarters.

The main policy-making organ of the BDI is the Assembly (*Mitgliederversammlung*), the membership of which is chosen by the 36 constituent trade associations. Voting strength is proportionate to the total number of employees represented by the member associations. Trade associations representing firms employing 50,000 persons or less are entitled to two votes. For each additional 50,000 employees, the vote increases by two until a total of six is reached, after which voting strength increases by one vote for each additional 50,000 employees. Given the structure and regional distribution of German industry, it is quite clear that heavy industry—and particularly the heavy industry of the Rhine-Ruhr—has the heaviest voting strength in the BDI Assembly.

The governing organs of the BDI include the Central Committee (*Hauptausschuss*), the Executive Committee (*Vorstand*), the *Präsidium,* and the management (*Geschäftsführung*). The Central Committee and the Executive Committee appear to have mainly supervisory functions, and to be electoral bodies for the selection of the higher organs. The Central Committee elects the Executive Committee, and the Executive Committee elects the *Präsidium*. The *Präsidium* consists of 16 members and has the most regular responsibility of all the elective organs. It is the agency which can make decisions for the Federation in an emergency.

Just as in the case of the National Association of Manufacturers in the United States, the Federation has a large full-time professional staff; this staff operates under the direction of a general manager and Fritz Berg, the Federation's president since its founding in 1949. The professional staff is organized in departments roughly corresponding to the committee structure of the Federation. Thus, most committees work closely with individual departments and receive from them reports for approval and proposals for action.

If one compares the BDI with the American NAM, it is quite apparent that the German organization is far more inclusive and centralized. The electoral units in the NAM, for instance, are the individual member firms (of which there are some 16,000) rather than constituent trade associations. In the election of NAM directors each member company has one vote, and the member firms participate directly in the selection of two-thirds of the board of directors. In the BDI, the selection of the governing organs begins with the trade associations and involves several stages of indirection. The regional units of the BDI are simple instrumentalities of the central organization, while in the NAM the state manufacturing associations and the trade associations are independent and are not directly represented in the national organization.

The net effect of the Federation's structure is to concentrate influence in its central organs, in the permanent bureaucracy, and in the constituent 36 trade associations, which are themselves highly centralized. The prominence of the trade associations and the absence of regional autonomy and of direct contact with the member firms suggest an even narrower expression of special interest in the BDI than in the NAM.[25] David Truman points out, in his discussion of the NAM, that the organization is actually centralized despite its mass individual member-firm base. Actual policy-making is lodged in the Board of Directors, the Executive Committee and the professional staff, and in the hundred or so larger firms which dominate the membership of the elective organs.

At the same time, he points out, the state and functional associations are independent of the NAM, and the "democratic mold" of American society exercises very real limits on the authority of the NAM leadership and bureaucracy. Consider for a moment the fact that, in Germany, individual industrial firms are represented directly only in their own craft or trade associations; that the regional organizations of the BDI and the trade associations have little if any autonomy; and that German society lacks the "democratic mold" of which Truman speaks—and the differences between the BDI and the NAM become clear.

Since its formation in 1949, the BDI has been under the control of a moderate, pro-Adenauer leadership. The BDI has supported the government on most general issues of domestic and foreign policy. There is, however, a group of industrialists in the Ruhr that inclines to a more nationalistic line in foreign policy and to a stronger line toward labor. Perhaps the most powerful exponent of this position is Hermann Reusch, of the *Gutehoffnungshütte*. Reusch holds positions on all the governing organs of the BDI and is viewed as a contender for the presidency.

Given the present-day political composition of the German government, the contacts of the BDI are direct and effective. The various committees and their corresponding departments have direct access to their opposite numbers in the Bundestag committees and the ministries. The volume of communications which passes from the BDI to the Bundestag and the ministries is impressive. In the fiscal year 1954–1955, around two hundred formal communications were submitted to these agencies from the BDI.[26] This does not include the direct communications of the individual trade associations to the appropriate ministries, or the communications of the regional units of the BDI, or of the trade associations, to the *Länder* ministries. One can not escape the impression, in a governmental situation so favorably disposed to industry, that there is a constant stream of influence from the professional staffs of the BDI and the trade associations directly into the appropriate units in the ministerial bureaucracies charged with the recommendation of legislative policy, the formulation of regulations, and the execution of public policy.

Even if much of the influence of business takes the form of direct communication from pressure-group to ministry, the BDI is also effectively organized to exercise influence in the Bundestag and in the *Länder* parliaments. One of the units in the Cologne headquarters of the BDI has the special responsibility of maintaining a file of information on the members of the Bundestag and the *Länder* parliaments. Communication with the Bundestag is centralized through this office, which operates directly under the control of the managing director. The BDI also maintains a contact man in Bonn who handles direct communications with the headquarters of the political parties, the Bundestag committees, and individual Bundestag members. Furthermore, each of the regional offices of the BDI maintains similar contacts in the *Länder*. By virtue of the centralized organization of the BDI and its excellent communications, the resources of the organization can be quickly mobilized and deployed at the national or regional level against parliament or the ministries.

The German Industry Institute (DII). While contact with government is handled by the BDI, only a small part of its public relations is carried on by the organization itself. For the larger tasks of public relations, the BDI, in collaboration with the Federal Union of Employers Associations, employs a separate organization, the German Industry Institute.

The Institute has four departments. One is a research unit which has the job of preparing studies and reports on matters of economic and industrial policy. A second unit specializes on research dealing with labor and welfare policy. The research of both the foregoing is primarily polemical in nature. Thus, if the research organization of the trade-unions prepares a report on wage policy, the Institute will issue one stating the position of industry. It provides this research service for the central organization of the BDI and for the Employers Association, as well as for the constituent units of both these groups. A third department of the Institute has the job of getting industry's point of view across in the various media of communication. The fourth department prepares lectures for businessmen and trade association representatives, and maintains a speakers' bureau.

The volume and variety of publications of the DII are impressive. It puts out a daily sheet for radio stations, a *Schnelldienst* (semiweekly) for the press, three weeklies, and two semimonthlies. It also publishes books giving the position of industry on economic, social, and political problems.

Two of the publications of the DII are directed toward businessmen rather than the public; these are the *Unternehmerbrief* ("Businessman's Letter") and the *Vortragsreihe* ("Lecture Series"). Like the BDI, the Industry Institute favors the Adenauer foreign policy and constantly stresses the need for a politically active managerial and entrepreneurial class. Many of its lectures and letters attack the reasoning behind the "unpolitical" orientation of German industrialists. One of the slogans of the *Unternehmerbrief* in the months before the 1953 election was *"Keine Angst vor der Politik!"* ("Don't be afraid of politics!") While there is a strong emphasis in these publications on the importance of business participation in politics on straightforward interest grounds, the DII frequently stresses the obligations of democratic citizenship and the importance of avoiding fanaticism and political romanticism, and it encourages an active political discussion at the grass roots.

Die Waage. A more specialized public relations organization is *Die Waage, Gemeinschaft zur Förderung des sozialen Ausgleichs.* The name of this organization is rather difficult to translate. In free rendition it might go something like this: "The Balance Wheel; A League for the Promotion of Social Equity." The main purpose of the organization is to spread the virtues of a "free and responsible economy." It works solely through paid advertising in the daily press, which it buys on a very large scale. According to official claims, as of the summer of 1954 (less than two years after the founding of the organization), *Die Waage* had had advertisements published in 70 per cent of the German newspapers with 90 per cent of the total newspaper circulation. With some pride, the head of the organization claimed that, since its formation, advertisements had appeared in newspapers whose combined circulation totaled 270 million. The ads are uniform and are published in times of labor difficulty or impending "collectivist" legislation. During election campaigns, *Die Waage* is able to bring additional resources to the support of the middle-class political parties by taking large advertising space and publishing brief statements in support of the position of the coalition parties without mentioning their names.

The Diet of German Industry and Commerce. There are 80 local chambers of commerce in Germany organized loosely in regional federations and in a central organization called *Deutscher Industrie und Handelstag* (DIH). Chambers of commerce in Germany in the past have been compulsory organizations. All businesses were required under law to be members and pay dues. In the postwar period, the occupation authorities in the American zone eliminated the compulsory features, though that was not done in the British and French zones. Each business firm now has one vote in the local chamber, without regard to size. The central organization of the DIH is quite simple. It has an executive committee consisting of some forty-five representatives of local chambers, a president, and professional staff. Committees deal with such questions as internal trade, foreign trade, transportation, fiscal and tax policy, commercial law, occupational training, general economic policy, public relations, and the like.

The DIH also maintains contact with the Bundestag and the federal ministries, but as compared with the BDI it is a less active and aggressive organization. Also, because it represents all business firms on an equal basis, it takes a more moderate and liberal position on matters of public policy than does the BDI. In this respect, the German pattern of business organization is very much like that in the United States. The DIH-BDI relationship is similar to that of the U.S. Chamber of Commerce and the National Association of Manufacturers in the United States; the former in each case is more liberally oriented on labor and welfare policy, foreign trade policy, and policy affecting industrial concentration.

Other organizations. Two other business organizations call for comment. One of these, the Federal Union of Employers Associations, has already been referred to. This group also is organized on a regional and functional basis, and concentrates almost entirely on problems of labor and welfare policy. While the units in the organization do not themselves engage in collective bargaining, they play an important role in developing the employer position for these purposes, and in mobilizing support for the industries affected in the event of a strike. The central organization and the regional units attempt to influence legislative policy at the federal and *Länder* levels, with special emphasis on industrial relations and social legislation.

Another organization of some interest is *Die Arbeitsgemeinschaft selbständiger Unternehmer* (Association of Independent Entrepreneurs). This is an organization mainly of middle- and small-size family-owned and -operated firms. Its main purpose is to protect the small firm from the triple threat of "big business," "big trade-unions," and "big government." It does not appear to be a powerful organization. One of its major goals is to obtain more favorable tax legislation from the federal and *Länder* governments.

Political Involvement and Participation

Shortly after the West German election of 1953, the Evaluation Staff of the Office of Public Affairs of HICOG issued a report analyzing the election results.[27] One of the questions asked in the survey upon which the report was based was as follows: "How do you feel personally about the outcome and result of these elections in West Germany?" The classification of responses according to income and occupation makes it clear that the upper-income groups, businessmen, and the professions were the most enthusiastic about the results. Sixty per cent of those earning 800 DM or more per month described themselves as very pleased with the outcome. The degree of enthusiasm tended to decrease as income decreased. Among those earning under 150 DM per month, only 38 per cent were very pleased. The occupation breakdown showed that 56 per cent of the businessmen respondents and 62 per cent of the professionals described themselves as reacting very favorably to the election outcome.

This favorable attitude toward the outcome of the election appears to be an aspect of a more general optimistic business mood toward government and politics in West Germany. Responses to a question about the progress of democratization in Germany brought out the same pattern even more strikingly. Seventy-four per cent of the respondents earning 800 DM or over were of the opinion that "democracy in West Germany has become stronger in the course of the past few years." [28] Sixty-four per cent of the professionals, and 58 per cent of the businessmen, also recorded favorable reactions. A number of other questions of the same type reinforced the pattern of high optimism among the upper-income groups and businessmen.

In the same survey, questions were asked about the degree of interest which respondents had toward politics, and about any increase in their interest in the past few years. The higher-income groups, businessmen, and professionals manifested the highest degree of interest, and also claimed most frequently that their interest had increased.

A number of considerations suggest that these findings should be viewed with caution. The questions were asked immediately after the 1953 elections and were affected by the unexpectedly powerful trend toward the moderate parties and away from the extremes. Then, too, most of the questions were so worded as to get at "increases" or "decreases" in certain attitudes and feelings, and did not specify what the base was from which this "progress" had been made; nor did they go into the content and structure of these attitudes.

For answers to questions of base, content, and structure we may turn to interviews conducted by the present author, which, while they do not constitute a representative sample, do offer certain other advantages. For example, in our interviews, such topics as political involvement were often discussed in depth with respondents who were officials of businessmen's organizations, and with political leaders whose contacts with the business community were constant and intimate and who could, therefore, qualify as experts on business opinion. Also, these interviews were made later than the HICOG survey, and they took place during a period of difficulties in foreign policy rather than shortly after an exciting and successful election.

The picture that emerges from an analysis of these interviews suggests that German businessmen continue to take a straightforward interest approach to politics, and that their optimism about the political situation is based on the fact that the Adenauer government has been favorably disposed to the business interests and has been successful in both its internal and external policies. Only a small minority of those who were interviewed spoke with any confidence of a trend toward political involvement and responsibility among businessmen. And these were, in the main, men who were themselves politically active, or who were engaged in efforts to raise the level of political discussion and participation.

With only one or two exceptions, the Ruhr industrialists who were interviewed described themselves and their colleagues as "nonpolitical." Several commented on the fact that, with the breakup of the old iron and steel combines in the Ruhr, the old corporate feeling among the "Ruhr barons" had been destroyed, and the new heads of the successor industrial units had not as yet developed a political style. The young managing director of one of the biggest steel-processing plants in the Ruhr remarked that there was very little political discussion and interest in the business community, and that his associates continued to be rather nonpolitical and indifferent. A colleague of his who participated in the same interview cited as an exception those Ruhr industrialists who attended the sessions of the Evangelical Academy at Loccum. But he admitted that, even so, this activity was atypical.

Another industrial leader commented in general on the intellectual and cultural life of Duisburg. Duisburg is essentially a workers' city with a small elite of industrial managers, big merchants, and professional men. The leading family of the city sponsors an annual "university week," at which university professors are invited to lecture on philosophical, historical, and aesthetic subjects. Political subjects are not discussed. There is heavy emphasis on cultural themes, but none on "political culture." The publisher of one of the most important business newspapers in the Ruhr remarked that at the end of the war there had been a good deal of uneasiness among the Ruhr industrialists, but that now they were fully involved in business and had no time for political discussion. One of the most successful new entrants into the Ruhr iron and steel industry, who was himself extremely well informed about political problems, observed somewhat cynically that "politics isn't good for the character."

These appraisals of the attitudes of the Ruhr industrialists were confirmed and elaborated in interviews with the officers of businessmen's associations, leaders of the coalition parties, trade-union leaders, and intellectuals. A young textile manufacturer in the Rhineland, a leading spokesman for the consumer-goods industry in the Federation of German Industries, referred to German heavy industry as politically indifferent, except when it came to questions of immediate business interests. While the old pattern of nationalism had not re-established itself, no liberal style had as yet emerged to take its place. The director of one of the most important businessmen's associations spoke of the new managers in Ruhr industry as having the mentality of "factory functionaries," as being "industrial fanatics," with few interests outside their work. One of the leading figures in the German Chamber of Commerce commented on the conditions of life of the Ruhr industrialists. Their industrial function of producing coke from coal, iron from ore, and steel from iron was a primitive and violent kind of operation. Their characters were molded after this pattern. The Rhinelander drinks wine, and Germans in general drink beer in moderate quantities. But the Ruhr barons drink either strong liquors or large quantities of beer. He concluded his portrait of the Ruhr industrialists by asking: "Did you ever think what it would be like to spend your whole life in Oberhausen?" Nationalism and narrow, tough, interest politics, in his opinion, were the inevitable consequences of this way of life.

Interviews with leading trade-union functionaries and labor representatives in the management of these Ruhr industries confirmed this appraisal. One official of the main trade-union in the iron and steel industry, *I. G. Metall,* said that he didn't expect the Ruhr industrialists to join the SPD, but believed that they should have some affiliation and involvement with those political parties which represented their interests. But as a group they still continued to be nonpolitical. A group interview with a number of labor directors in Ruhr firms supported the same pattern. One trade-union leader, in a mood of frankness, commented bitterly on the state of political discussion in both labor and management. He said that there was no political discussion among trade-union leaders or among industrial leaders, and no real communication between them. What you had in the labor-management relations field was trade-union and management functionaries confronting one another and trading slogans. He concluded by saying that Germans have forgotten what little they ever knew about political discussion.

While most observers attributed this pattern of political indifference and narrow interest to the industrialists of the Ruhr, the patterns described in other parts of Germany and in other industrial fields were not strikingly different. The argument was often advanced that, by tradition, the South German industrialist, the Catholic Rhinelander, and the industrialist and merchant of the Hanseatic cities were more liberal and cosmopolitan than their counterparts in other sections of the country. While there is undoubtedly truth in this distinction, businessmen interviewed in these three areas did not claim to be politically involved and active. A Rhineland clothing manufacturer described his associates in the textile industry as being poorly informed and politically apathetic. This was an almost inescapable consequence of the conditions under which they carried on their business, he said. Almost all of them were capital-poor. Their products had to move fast if they were to keep their enterprises operating. There was little, if any, time for reading, or for political interest to develop and be expressed. They looked to their trade associations to protect their interests. A South German leather-goods manufacturer argued that the same kind of situation obtained in the luxury goods field. Here the necessity always to have something new, the rapid obsolescence of patterns and styles, kept the typical business-man on his toes and left him no time to develop other interests. One of the leading exporters in Hamburg, who had for some time after the war served as a senator in the administration of that city, had had to give up his political career, since it meant sacrificing his business. He complained: "In business you can do something and earn something; in politics there are only risks."

Some stirrings are noticeable, among the younger industrialists espe-cially. In a number of German cities there are junior organizations affiliated with the senior chambers of commerce. This movement, which has been encouraged by the Junior Chamber of Commerce of the United States, has as one of its goals encouraging young men in the business world to interest themselves in political and community affairs. It also hopes to change the gerontocratic pattern of German industrial or-ganization, and to encourage the participation of younger executives in policy-making. Similar in purpose to the junior chamber of commerce movement is the organization of "Young Entrepreneurs," an affiliate of the Association of Independent Entrepreneurs. This group has about five hundred members, organized in eleven regional associations. It puts out a monthly publication in co-operation with the junior chambers. The organization stresses political responsibility, training for leadership, Europeanism, and internationalism.

One of the leaders of the Junior Chamber of Düsseldorf spoke of the attitudes of the young businessmen of his acquaintance as being "skepti-cal and empirical." They kept political ideas at a distance. They were distrustful of enthusiasm. They wanted to keep their heads, protect themselves. Many of them knew, from their own experience, what the costs of mistaken idealism could be. They were inclined to look things over carefully, and to avoid hasty and unqualified commitments. He cited these attitudes as the reason why the Junior Chamber began its political educational process with the *Gemeinde,* the community. Here they could see what politics and government meant in terms of traffic regulations, streets, sewers, lighting systems, transportation. They knew how these things affected business, as well as the safety and conven-ience of their private lives.

There is a certain ferment among the older generations of German business as well, if the comments of Carl Neumann, Chairman of the Board of the Industry Institute, are accurate.

Democracy can only be successful among intellectually advanced peoples. The danger of tyranny can only be warded off through the resistance of free personalities. This is of decisive importance, the development from *mass* to *person*. And this is promoted through the free exchange of opinions. In business circles this kind of activity is observable everywhere. "Discussion evenings" and conferences between employers and employees are no longer a new thing. We must extend and consolidate these tendencies.[29]

There can be little question that such movements among businessmen have a certain impact, and are tending to produce a nucleus of political leaders in the business community. But by admission of industrialists themselves, this trend has not acquired significant momentum even among the younger age groups. In an interview in Frankfurt on Main, six young businessmen in a variety of fields discussed the problem of political activity and interest in their own generation with great frankness. They all agreed that the typical pattern involved avoidance of political commitment and activity. The reasons advanced differed. One rather hard-bitten son of a famous Ruhr family gave simple economic reasons. Politicians are poorly paid and have no security of tenure. At the same time, high taxation makes it impossible for the businessman to accumulate a reserve. Hence, it means an economic sacrifice to go into a political career, and no one with good sense would do so. Another participant in the discussion thought the reasons were mainly psychological. German businessmen are traditionally so bound up with their jobs that they can't turn readily to the insecure arena of politics. Another argued that the risks were too high in German politics. Germans couldn't forget what happened to liberal political leaders when the Nazis came in, what happened to the Nazis when the Allies came in; and they couldn't help but be troubled about what might happen to noncommunist political leaders if the Russians came in. They couldn't conceive of politics as a game in which an individual could have fun and still work for good causes. What impulses and energies were available after the end of the day's work they turned to aesthetic interests, or to simple family obligations, friends, recreations, and enjoyments.

Nationalism

This picture of massive and highly centralized pressure-groups, of political indifference and narrow-interest mentality, should not lead one to the conclusion that Germans or German businessmen have learned nothing from their experiences. It would be more accurate to say that the learning has been incomplete, the lessons are undigested, and present responses to the political situation are based upon simple power calculations and situational adjustments. The life of the spirit and of the imagination is at a low ebb in Germany, in politics as well as the arts. For politics, this has a positive as well as a negative implication. While there is no significant effort at ideological reconstruction, there are also no significant adventurist and extremist tendencies.

The reasons for this are simple and compelling. The disasters of the Hitler regime and the war are evident in the physical, biological, sociological, political, and military facts of German life. Despite the economic reconstruction of the postwar period, war ruins are inescapable, and they will continue to serve as physical reminders for years to come. The heavy incidence of casualties among the males now in the thirty to forty-five age group leaves an extraordinarily large proportion of the population without the full protections and satisfactions of family life. And if one considers also the other sociological and psychological consequences of the war—the number of Germans who fled, or were expelled from, their homes, the number who were prisoners of war, the number who were bombed out—it is hard to see how any adult German can escape having the most vivid memories of the war and political disaster. At the same time, the facts of the German political and strategic situation provide no realistic grounds for hopes of vindication or revenge. The occupation of East Germany by the Russians and the dependence of West Germany on the protection of the Western powers and the United States limit the possible range of German foreign policy; even though they do permit a range of choice, an adventurous nationalism is hardly included within it.

It is in some such framework as this that one must appraise the evidence as to the persistence of Nazi and nationalist attitudes among the German people. There is a large collection of public opinion surveys bearing on these problems. What they suggest is that some 30 per cent of the German adult population appraise the Nazi experience favorably, roughly another 30 per cent appraise it unfavorably, while the remaining 40 per cent have mixed views. The size of this middle, "uncommitted" group reflects the extent to which there is conflict and ambivalence in the German mind with regard to the Nazi past. As occupation controls have been relaxed, there has been increasing readiness on the part of Germans to express favorable or mixed attitudes toward the Nazis. Business respondents do not display patterns consistently different from those of most of the other occupational groups.

Only in the professional occupations are the respondents consistently more critical of the Nazi past, more in favor of democratic institutions, and less nationalistic in their foreign policy attitudes.[30]

While it would be a serious error to conclude that Germans are unregenerate and ready to revert to Nazism and extreme nationalism at the first opportunity, the evidence does suggest that there are nationalist trends in German public opinion which favor an assertive and independent foreign policy course. At the present time, this trend toward independence and assertiveness is overtly reflected in more or less acute dissatisfaction with a number of specific situations and limitations. Some of these dissatisfactions are distributed generally among the population; others are more specific to particular groups in the population. What is apparent among all groups is a demand, that varies in degree, for more independence in the conduct of foreign policy. In its milder form, this demand is based on the reasonable argument that, though Germany is bound to the West, Germans are better exponents of German interests than are the occupation powers. Thus, it is felt that rather than follow the American lead, the German government should take the diplomatic initiative and follow a more direct and aggressive course in pursuit of Germany's own interests. Such a course, according to its proponents, would continue to be within the framework of a basic identity of interest and alliance with the West, and particularly with the United States.

The extreme form of the demand for independence calls for a return to the *Schaukelpolitik* ("see-saw policy") of the Rapallo era. But this extreme point of view, which has been expressed in speeches by former Chancellor Brüning, has the support of only a small minority of German businessmen.

Related to this pressure for independence and full rehabilitation is a general demand for equality of treatment in diplomatic and military arrangements. Among industrialists and businessmen, this pressure for independence and equality is more specifically directed against economic restrictions. There is a practically universal demand in these circles that Germany have the same opportunities to trade with the communist bloc that all other powers have. Another evidence of this pressure is the dissatisfaction with those features of the European Coal and Steel Community that are alleged to be discriminatory against Germany. Finally, there is increasing pressure among businessmen against certain economic reforms introduced by the occupation powers, in particular the deconcentration and decartelization policies. The attack on these policies often stresses the fact that they are of foreign origin and hence not in the interests of Germany.

Reunification

Of all the political issues confronting Germany today, that of reunification appears to provoke the strongest feelings; and at the same time it is the only one that seems to be the least capable of solution by any acceptable means, short of a radical change in the international situation. It is sometimes viewed as the issue around which latent resentments might, under certain circumstances, combine to shake the internal political balance in Germany, and perhaps provoke foreign policy adventurism. The public opinion polls suggest that reunification is the most urgent political question confronting the German public. They also suggest that the German public feels that more could and should be done about it. Other survey evidence indicates that Germans are largely convinced that France is opposed to reunification of Germany. Also, they are skeptical of British intentions, and they feel that even the United States could do more toward attaining German unity. It is of interest that businessmen and professionals, more frequently than other groups, feel that the Western powers could do more to attain German unity.

A wave of optimism about the possibilities of reunification swept West Germany in the wake of shifts in Russian policy after 1953. The Austrian peace settlement brought those hopes to a peak. The change in expectations was reflected in public opinion polls on foreign policy issues, and particularly on prospects of reunification. In the years of frustrating negotiations which followed, this optimism subsided, and it showed a particularly sharp decline after the suppression of Hungary. This disillusionment may have taken some of the intensity out of the reunification issue. While a large proportion of Germans still describe it as the most urgent German foreign policy issue, the majority appear to be increasingly vague and doubtful about its prospects.[31]

The intensity of feeling among German businessmen about reunification came out in a number of interviews, conducted by the present author, during which the respondents brought the issue up spontaneously and with especial emphasis. One young Ruhr manager thought that the main basis for a possible revived German nationalism was the concern over regaining the East zone and the territories incorporated into Russia and Poland. He said that the division of Germany and the fact that certain parts of it now are Russian and Polish are matters close to the heart of many Germans. A Hamburg shipbuilder agreed that the issue was "close to the heart," but that at the moment there was nothing that could be done about it. A South German drug manufacturer also spoke of it as a real issue, but said that most Germans were resigned to the fact that nothing could be done about it now. He expressed the fear that the longer the East zone was occupied by Russia the more communist it would become. Given a few more years of Russian occupation, even a free election might not produce a noncommunist majority, he said.

In a conference of young businessmen in Düsseldorf, the view was expressed that there was no question of "lip service" to the issue of reunification. Feelings were genuine and strong. The problem of East Germany was on the conscience of most West Germans. They did not talk about it, because there was nothing that could be done about it under present circumstances. One of the participants broke in to say that, if anyone were to get up in public and say that the division of Germany was a permanent thing, there would be a public explosion, and that man's political career would be over. At the same time, nobody wanted to risk war to reunite Germany. The question was then turned on the interviewer; he was asked how he would feel if California, Oregon, and Washington were separated from the rest of the United States and were ruled and oppressed by a hostile power.

In a conference of senior industrialists and bankers in Frankfurt on Main, similar views were expressed. The head of a large chemical concern stated that Germans will never forget the problem of reunification, and that German acceptance of Western integration should never be construed to mean that they have accepted the division of Germany. It was also pointed out that Germans expect the Western powers to support Germany's desire for unification. These views were expressed with great feeling and with general agreement. Yet, at the same time, the feeling was expressed that Germany could not be reunited without a general settlement with the Soviet Union.

There were a number of different approaches to the problem of reunification. The largest group favored a policy of building strength in Germany and the West, and then carrying on pressure diplomacy from such a position of strength. One of the respondents argued that the Russians were conservative when it came to a direct threat to their power structure. Once the Western alliance were established and Germany had an army, it was suggested, the Russians might yield to pressure and permit reunification. A Ruhr "baron" known for his nationalist views argued that there were two ways of attaining German unification. First, the West might start a preventive war. He did not oppose the idea, but he thought it unlikely that such a policy would be followed. The second method was to rearm Germany thoroughly with American help and then "put the pressure on." He thought the Russians might really react to tough pressure from the outside during the next ten years while they were still weak and unready to accept a war. He was of the opinion that this policy should be carried out on the basis of an American-German alliance. A Western European alliance would, if anything, hamper such a policy, he said.

Another group of businessmen argued that negotiation with Russia regarding reunification ought to be continuous. This was a minority view based upon the criticism that the resources of diplomacy were not being fully exploited. If the West failed to do this, it was suggested, the initiative on the reunification question would be left to the Social Democrats and the Russians. And if the Social Democrats came into power, they might really be willing to sacrifice the security of the West for the sake of reunification. One respondent took the position that, if Germany were permitted to normalize her relations with the East zone and with Russia, such normalization might spread, ultimately, from technical and trade questions to the political level, and might produce a diplomatic atmosphere in which reunification would become possible. This emphasis on diplomacy as a means to unification was not generally treated as an alternative to Western integration, but as a line of action that should be carried on simultaneously with it.

A third view pictured trade as a way to reconciliation and reunification. The most extreme exponent of this point of view described Germany as uniquely qualified to serve as "a bridge to the East." There was a terrific ground swell of demand for consumer goods from the East, he said. The communists could not escape this pressure, and they were prepared to go far to improve trade relations. With improved trade relations would go increased cultural contact. Thus, consumer demand and cultural contact would gradually transform communist policy and make possible not only reunification but also a general reconciliation between East and West. In his opinion, German integration in Western security arrangements and German rearmament were fatal mistakes which would postpone reunification indefinitely, and would inevitably lead to war.

In its more common and milder form, this argument for renewal of trade with the East, like the argument for renewing diplomatic communication, was not advanced as an alternative to integration with the West, but as a line to be followed simultaneously with the development of Western European integration.

Most of the respondents were quite pessimistic about the prospects of reunification. They could not see how any reasonable measures now being undertaken could lead to it. Perhaps a long build-up of strength in the West, along with a slow process of change in the attitudes and policies of the communist orbit, might lead to the desired result. One highly-placed official of a business organization put it as follows: He did not know what methods would be necessary to attain German reunification, but he felt in his bones that in the long run it would come. He referred to Bismarck who, he said, never made blueprints. Bismarck always believed in taking things as they came; performance of day-to-day tasks eventually added up to a plan. Therefore, there was no point in laying out a grand strategy as to how to reunite Germany. Our respondent thought that, if Germany and the West continued to build their unity and strength, Russia might in the end give way, since Russia historically responds only to strength. He did not think that a reunification of Germany was attainable on acceptable terms at the present time, but in the long run, he felt, Russia would give way to pressure.

Remilitarization

For the last five or six years, the question of German rearmament has been widely discussed both in Germany and abroad. Until the summer of 1954, the proposal was for German participation in a European army within the European Defense Community; the adoption of EDC by the participating powers was to be the signal for the end of the occupation. The rejection of EDC by the French in 1954 terminated this phase of the rearmament debate. The second proposal for German rearmament, in the Paris treaty, involved the admission of Germany into NATO, with limits on the size and composition of her armed forces.

A series of surveys made by the *Institut für Demoskopie* during the controversy over EDC showed that opposition to German participation in an integrated European army varied between 50 per cent in 1951 and 36 per cent in the months immediately preceding the French rejection. Support for EDC ranged from 22 per cent in 1950 to 33 per cent in the summer of 1954. Roughly 30 per cent either were undecided, or their approval was subject to certain conditions.[32]

The German opposition to EDC was composed of several elements. In addition to the antimilitarist bloc, there was another, perhaps equally significant group, which was chiefly afraid that, in an integrated army, German military units would not be accorded equal treatment with the forces of the other nations. Hence, 48 per cent of Germans who were asked to make a choice between an integrated and an independent German army favored the latter, as against 20 per cent who preferred integration. But when the qualification was added that, in an integrated army, full equality of treatment would be guaranteed, the proportions were just about reversed, with 40 per cent of the respondents for an integrated army and 27 per cent in favor of national forces.[33] These latter findings should be viewed in the light of the fact that most Germans, as shown by other surveys, were convinced that only in an integrated form could rearmament be attained.[34]

When it came to approving the Paris treaty, which provided for German inclusion in NATO, the proportion of those in favor was somewhat higher than it had been in the case of EDC. But opposition was still substantial (around 35 per cent), and it continued to comprise both the antimilitarist and the somewhat smaller nationalist elements.[35] These findings suggest that there was little homogeneity in either the pro-rearmament or the anti-rearmament group. Our own interviews with German businessmen during the summer of 1954 were suggestive of the conflicting currents among both supporters and opponents of rearmament. For example, there were those who opposed EDC on the grounds that it would restrict Germany's freedom of action. This point of view prompted the following remark by a member of a prominent Ruhr industrialist family: "We're the only anticommunist country the United States can rely on in Europe. What kinds of allies are France and Italy with their communist parties? America needs us. We can afford to wait. We don't have to jump at the first invitation." At the other extreme, on the side of Europeanism and internationalism, there were those who opposed EDC on the grounds that German remilitarization in any form was a threat to the development of European unity, that it provoked French anxiety, and that military integration should follow rather than precede economic and moral integration. Both of these, however, were minority points of view.

Proponents of EDC also were variously motivated. There were those who favored it because they thought it the only way to get Germany rearmed; these constituted a substantial part of the pro-EDC support. As for the greater part of the internationalists among businessmen, EDC was favored not so much because it promised to improve German security, but primarily because it was a part of a pattern of integration of Germany into a European community.

The particular complex of attitudes which lay behind the various positions on EDC came out clearly at the moment when it was defeated. The "Europeans" and internationalists were sunk in pessimism. This was particularly true of the Rhineland businessmen who were the closest friends and supporters of Adenauer. Many of these were shattered by the collapse of their hopes. One of Adenauer's business friends sat in his office the morning after the news of the action of the French Assembly, and repeated, more to himself than to the interviewer, "Now we won't have Europe. We will have sovereignty and soldiers in NATO or somehow, but we won't have Europe." Another businessman, who had devoted himself since the end of the war to efforts at French reconciliation, could not find words strong enough to express his hatred for Mendès-France and his contempt for the French. A journalist spoke of the "icy wind" blowing from the West.

Those who had opposed EDC on nationalist grounds, or who had favored it because they viewed it as the only possible way of getting security for Germany, expressed views either of actual satisfaction or of only mild disappointment. One young Ruhr entrepreneur said that he took no satisfaction from the defeat which Adenauer had experienced. He was genuinely sorry for the "old man." He said he had a lawyer friend with whom he often played cards, and with whom he often went out to have a drink. His friend was a loyal CDU man who supported Adenauer and was strongly identified with EDC. After the action of the French Assembly, he got together with his friend, and while it was an occasion on which he could quite properly have said "I told you so," he had actually refrained from doing so. He thought his friend and Adenauer had been tragically misled by their idealism, that the world was a hard place to live in, and that one had to be tough to survive.

A similar division of view obtained with regard to alternatives to EDC. The internationalist-minded businessmen tended to favor the inclusion of Germany in the NATO structure as the best alternative. They also urged a policy of understanding and patience vis-à-vis France. The nationalists, on the other hand, either took a skeptical view of the NATO solution, and favored it only because they thought it was the best Germany could get, or they opposed such a solution, and argued that Germany "ought to sit tight and wait" for rearmament on more favorable terms, perhaps in alliance with the United States and without the disadvantages of being tied to and hampered by the French.

But among the large majority of German businessmen who favored EDC or the NATO alternative—whether from nationalist or "European" motives—there was a significant internal conflict over the question of what consequences the inclusion of Germany in the military arrangements of the West would have for German reunification. Those operating from nationalist premises inclined toward an alternative that would give Germany a maximum of freedom in remilitarization, one that would assure that German arms would be used for German interests; in particular, they sought a military arrangement that would enhance the likelihood of reunification, or at least not make it more remote. The internationalists, on the other hand, had their faces turned toward the West; they sought to escape from all the difficulties and the "provisionality" of the West German Republic into a higher European unity. Europeanism tended to be more important to them than reunification.

What was particularly striking among the businessmen interviewed was the fact that so few of them had given any thought to the question of what consequences the development of a German army might have for German foreign policy and for German domestic politics. The collapse of EDC left them up in the air. Only a few of the most thoughtful individuals interviewed had speculated about the internal political consequences of re-establishing a German army. One of these argued that the civil political structure in Germany was still so weak and so without roots that the existence of an army would almost unavoidably involve a setback in German democratic development. This articulately pessimistic view was not typical of the disappointed supporters of EDC. The typical reaction was one of anxiety and helplessness.

But again, the majority point of view regarding the consequences of a German army was one of indifference. Most German businessmen had not thought about it. When they were confronted with the specific question about what the consequences might be for internal political stability and for foreign policy, most of them expressed the opinion that an army would not significantly affect internal politics and would not produce an aggressive foreign policy. The main argument advanced was that the Germans had had their fill of militarism.[36] One young businessman remarked that, in 1914, German troops had fought with enthusiasm; in 1939, they were serious and anxious, but not enthusiastic. In a third war, he thought they would fight for their land, their homes, and their families, but in desperation, not with enthusiasm. It was also argued that a foreign policy of aggression was out of the question, since it was clear to everyone that Germany would be the battlefield of the next war.

There were few businessmen who took the position that German troops would be generally unreliable or wouldn't fight hard in the event of war. It was pointed out that much would depend on how they were used or treated, whether they were used to defend German soil or not, and whether or not they were commanded by German officers. German troops so deployed that they could be discriminated against, or used to defend the French or other peoples rather than the Germans, might not be reliable. But to permit German troops to be used in such a manner was politically unthinkable, according to these informants. If equally treated, and intelligently used in relation to German interests, the view was that they would be good troops. One young Frankfurt banker put it this way: "If it's a question of mastering a new weapon, adapting to new tactics or new types of military organization, the Germans would say to themselves: '*Wir machen es besser*' ['We can do it better']."

While only a small number of the businessmen were opposed to re-armament, or were doubtful of the morale of German troops, none of the younger men interviewed was himself ready to volunteer for service. The opinion was widely shared among these younger businessmen, with regard to both themselves and their peers, that very few of the men in their age range and class would volunteer for service in the first phases of reconstitution of the army. It had taken so long to establish a satisfactory existence after the difficulties of the war and the immediate postwar period that only those who had been unsuccessful in making an adjustment to civilian life would volunteer. One young banker in Düsseldorf, who had served in the air force during World War II, observed that he personally knew the air force officers of his former unit who had volunteered to serve in the cadres of the new German air force. He stated that in every case they were the poorer officers, who had been unable to make a go of it since the end of the war.

European Integration

Survey evidence indicates that a majority of Germans favor partici-pation in a Western European union.[37] Pro-integration sentiment appeared to be more widespread and intense in Germany than in France, Italy, or England.[38] When Germans were asked whether they would favor such a union even if it should prove to be disadvantageous at times, the percentage in favor dropped but the decrease in Germany was far smaller than similar shifts in opinion in France, Italy, and England. This predominantly pro-European attitude in Germany was also reflected in support of the Schuman Plan and of the EDC.[39] Earlier surveys also suggested that a large proportion of Germans felt that Germany had most to gain from the integration of Western Europe.[40] Another survey showed that almost half of the German respondents thought that Germans were entitled to play a leading role in Europe in the future. The opinions of businessmen did not deviate in any striking way from the responses of other occupational groups.

While these findings show substantial support for specific plans for European integration, they also suggest that this is not a homogeneous attitude among Germans in general, or among German businessmen in particular, and they leave open the long-run question of the stability of these pro-European tendencies. If we can understand the basic composition of these attitudes, our capacity to predict may be somewhat improved.

Our interviews with German businessmen suggest that pro-European sentiment has been fed from a number of different streams. In the first place, there is a genuine European current based upon one or a combination of religious, cultural, economic, and political considerations. Secondly, there is a phenomenon which may be appropriately characterized as an "escape into Europe."[41] And, finally, there is a kind of "crypto-nationalist" Europeanism, a belief that German economic and political dominance may be attained through European integration. These attitudes occur most typically in combination, but it is possible to distinguish among individuals according to the type of attitude that predominates in the thinking of each.

The genuine Europeans in the business community were attracted to the *mystique* of European unity, the hope that, after more than a millennium of conflict and warfare, the underlying unity of the Christian ethos and of the European cultural tradition would finally express itself in a political form. This European impulse was frequently religious in its content. It was often accompanied by the conviction that, regardless of the costs and sacrifices which they might be called upon to incur for European unification, Germans could gain their redemption only by such action. This attitude was most often found among leading Catholic and Protestant laymen and among the leaders of the various German European movements. The dynamism in this attitude was the impulse for redemption, and it sometimes occurred without any further calculation of economic and political consequences.

More frequently, however, the pro-European businessman had given some thought to the economic and political consequences of European unification. The president of a machine-tool manufacturing company in the Ruhr had for years been tempted with the vision of a Europe which ". . . might become a common market with European industry and 250,000,000 consumers and skilled laborers." If this vision could become a reality, ". . . then it might have been possible to do something, make the workers happy, give them something to work for, and create in Europe a happy and secure land. In an integrated Europe prices might have sunk and one might have been able to do something about the bitterness and the feelings of injustice that create the basis for communism." He believed that it was the French sense of inferiority and anxiety that made it impossible for France to accept such an integrated Europe. Hence everything must be done, he thought, to strengthen France and to remove French anxiety over German power and aggressiveness. One young Catholic textile manufacturer argued that the Ruhr ought to work for France, help her with capital goods, and accept arrangements which discriminated against Germany in the French interest, in order to create a stronger and more confident France.

There were a number of German businessmen who argued that it had been a mistake to press for EDC, that it would have been sounder to proceed gradually with economic measures of integration, instead of frightening the French with the prospect of German rearmament, even in an integrated form. The ground should first have been thoroughly prepared, and the way to prepare it was by economic collaboration and the creation of a European sense of community.

The impulse to escape into Europe, to find in Europe the security and the identity that could not be found in Germany, was typically a shallower, a less structured attitude than the genuine European current described above. And it is impossible to avoid the conclusion that this type of escapist Europeanism was more widespread among businessmen than was the more genuine Europeanism. There has been and continues to be a rather widespread impulse to escape from all the liabilities of being German in the postwar era, to escape from the division of Germany, from her moral isolation, from the moral burden of German history, and from the dangers consequent on the presence of Russian military power on German soil. Since this escapism is more of a mood than it is an attitude based upon intellectual and moral conviction, it is unstable, and it may flow in other directions in response to other opportunities or other conditions. This mood is fed by powerful impulses toward security, stability, and a satisfying identity. If it appears that these needs can be satisfied in a reunited and revalidated Germany, the European trend will be stemmed, and the relatively small number of genuine Europeans may find themselves in isolation. We have already seen how strong the drive toward reunification is, and how strong, also, the drive to revalidate the German past.

The immediate aftermath of the French rejection of EDC in the summer of 1954 was a deflation of European hopes. Among German businessmen, the first target in this period was the European Coal and Steel Community (CSC). A Hamburg shipbuilder pointed out that his firm could buy sheet steel more cheaply from Japan and the United States than from the Ruhr, because of the artificially high prices set by the CSC. A steel manufacturer asked: "Does the *Montan-Union* make sense now?" In his opinion it had made sense only so long as it was to be a part of a larger union, a currency union, a free market, and a military and political union. By itself, its faults became glaring. He cited his own case. He has to charge the same price for steel whether it is sold in thousand- or in twenty-ton quantities. He said that CSC was becoming a government-controlled cartel, and would come increasingly under attack. The restrictions which it imposed made the iron and steel business uninteresting. Another young Ruhr manager pointed out how CSC gave the French access to cheap Ruhr coal and made it possible, because of the shorter freight haul, for the French to sell steel more cheaply in the South German market than the Ruhr industries could. He too felt that there would be increasing criticism and attack against the *Montan-Union,* since it was no longer a part of a general European integration, but was now vulnerable to attack on straightforward economic grounds.

The Europeanism of the crypto-nationalist variety was a cynical attitude, infrequently expressed, in which the expectation was that, whichever way things went, Germany had a good "card hand." If Europe were integrated, Germany's economic power and energy would be such as to gain her the position of dominance in Europe to which she was entitled. While those holding these attitudes refrained from attacking European institutions and plans, they were in no way committed to these hopes. It was a strictly expediential Europeanism. The individuals who held it were those who, after the collapse of EDC, found it difficult to conceal a certain satisfaction. The prospect of being integrated with France and Italy had not been an attractive one. If there had been any other way of attaining military security, they would have preferred it. Their real preference was for an alliance with the United States, and for the use of German military capacity for German purposes such as reunification and the regaining of the lost territories in the East.

Most recently, German opinion about European integration has been affected mainly by apparent shifts in the prospects for German reunification. The period immediately following the collapse of EDC was one in which many Germans favored probing the "new Soviet course." Expectations ran particularly high after the Austrian treaty. They began to subside with the failure of German negotiations with Moscow, and ended abruptly with the suppression of the Hungarian revolt. The current negotiations about the European atomic pool and the common European market have again directed German attention toward European integration. But one may doubt that Germans today are as optimistic of achieving major results as they were prior to the collapse of EDC.[42]

East-West Trade

Before World War II, German foreign trade with the countries now under communist domination (including China) averaged some 16 per cent of the total of German imports and exports. In 1953–1954, German trade with the communist countries (Alabania, Bulgaria, China, Poland, Rumania, Czechoslovakia, Hungary, and Russia) stood at approximately 2.5 per cent.[43]

The dependence of the German economy on foreign trade, and the concern of German industrialists over the present complete dependence on Western markets, have led to increasing pressure on the part of industry for an aggressive exploration of trade possibilities with the East.

It is of some interest that the pressure for an aggressive exploration of trade possibilities with communist countries is not based on immediate economic needs. With only a few exceptions, German industry has a heavy backlog of domestic and foreign orders and would not be in a position to fill orders from the East for some time to come. The resentment among German industrialists appeared to be of two kinds. There was, first, a realistic anxiety over the fragility of the German economic position, because of its heavy dependence on foreign markets which might be lost to Germany. Hence it was prudent to seek other opportunities for foreign trade and to have as diversified a foreign trade position as possible.

The second type of resentment was political, and a part of the general trend toward national assertiveness. It was pointed out again and again in interviews with German businessmen that the embargo restrictions against the communist bloc were more rigorously applied against Germany than against other countries, and that the Eastern markets were traditional purchasers of the products of German industry. The demand was for equality of treatment, and freedom for Germany to find its own level of foreign trade.

Common to most German businessmen is, on the one hand, a more or less serious overestimation of the trade possibilities with the communist areas, and, on the other hand, a failure to consider the possible political consequences of substantially heavier trade relations with those areas. There is an interesting nostalgia among many German businessmen, which is their own special version of the "Rapallo memories" revived by such German leaders as former Chancellor Brüning. Just as some former German diplomats recall with longing Germany's diplomatic independence in the Rapallo era and convince themselves that it is possible to carry on such a policy today, so do German businessmen vividly recall the great contracts and bulk orders from the Soviet Union during the 1920's and 1930's. It is sometimes argued that, precisely because the communist bloc has a planned economy, it is a reliable trade partner, a kind of stabilizing ace-in-the-hole in the event of an economic crisis in the West. Many German businessmen remembered that in the depression it was Russian demand for machine tools and industrial products that mitigated the general economic disaster.

One German leather-goods manufacturer who had returned from discussions with Russian and Chinese trade representatives in Moscow spoke with dreamy eyes of the enormous backlog of consumer needs in

Russia and China. He said: "Russian women have no handbags, and they are just as vain as women anywhere. Just imagine what an order for a million handbags would do for Offenbach! In China, the peasants have no flashlights to use when returning from the fields after dark, and no bicycles to cover the big distances from the fields to their homes. Just imagine what an order for millions of bicycles and flashlights would do for Bielefeld!" The dreams of this manufacturer were a good deal richer than those of most of his colleagues, and yet they reflect in extreme form the extent to which memory and a kind of apolitical thinking affect judgments and expectations. Little consideration is given to the fact that the economic structure of the communist-controlled areas is in process of radical change, that consumer demand is repressed in the interests of capital investment. One better-informed businessman pointed out that the kinds of orders now placed by the Eastern bloc are of a pilot variety. They will import foreign machine tools, or industrial products in small number, only to imitate and produce these items themselves.

Similarly, most German businessmen fail to take into account the priority of political over economic calculation in the communist areas. If the communist bloc were to open up large trade possibilities with Germany, this might very well be the result of a political motive based on either domestic or foreign considerations. Very few businessmen interviewed had considered the possibility that Russia might offer attractive trade possibilities to German industry as a means of attaining a certain political leverage in Germany. Once a substantial proportion of German trade was dependent on the communist areas, it might be possible to create pressure among German business circles—now the most pro-Western of all groupings in Germany—against too complete an involvement in the West. This does not appear to be an immediate possibility, but, in the event of a decline in the level of foreign trade with the areas outside the communist orbit, it may become a factor of some significance. Just as the Russians have a trump card in offers of reunification which all Germany would find it difficult to resist, so also do they hold a more specialized trump card in offers of attractive trade possibilities particularly directed at the business community.

While, given present circumstances, these are only possibilities, it remains interesting that the business community in Germany is relatively unaware of the priority of political factors in communist policy-making. Only government officials and some leaders of business pressure-groups seem to see this point. Few of the industrialists, even in the largest establishments, are aware of it. Their thinking about the possibilities of the communist market is dominated by simple, apolitical economic calculation.

Conclusions

The foregoing analysis suggests the conclusion that, despite the tragedies of her recent history, Germany has not yet begun to exhibit a pattern
of political involvement and responsibility. The tragedies are in some
part attributable to the historic failure of the German middle classes to
develop a liberal spirit, and to impose this spirit on their political competitors. Thus the historic failure of German democracy is inseparable
from the historic failure of the German middle classes, and the fragility
of the democratic institutions in contemporary Germany is inseparable
from the spiritual poverty of the German business and professional
classes.

When criticism of German politics is put in such massive terms, it
may incorrectly suggest by comparison that in such successful democracies as England and the United States there is a pattern of universal
political involvement and participation. This is obviously not the case.
The crucial differences may be put as follows. In Germany, there is a
sharp break between the public and the private spheres. Political and
social responsibility is an attribute of office, whether in the parliaments,
the ministries, the churches, the trade-unions, or the interest-groups.
What is more, within these various political structures a strong hierarchical spirit dominates, so that political responsibility and communication tend to be confined to the very heights of these institutions.

In England and the United States, on the other hand, there is a
gradation from public to private. Private association for public purposes
is not confined to political parties and interest-groups, but includes a
variety of general and special public-interest groups concerned with
policy issues of all kinds at all levels of the governmental process. Power
and communication are more or less decentralized within these organizations. Finally, in England and in the United States there is an attentive public, a discriminating audience, which tends to limit the
pressures of special interest, and which subjects the holders of office to
regular and frequent accounting.

Thus, English and American political society has what is still lacking
in Germany: a broad and relatively decentralized elite which extends
beyond governmental office and the specifically political formations of
party and pressure-groups, and an attentive and involved stratum in
the general population.

Both of these political phenomena of the English-speaking nations
have grown and are nourished in middle-class soil. They are the
products of the professional and business classes. Quantitatively they
represent only a small proportion of the total population: a few tens of

thousands of people who are active in community associations, in the grass-roots party organizations, in church groups, humanitarian organizations, and foreign policy associations. Small as they are, these two political formations—a decentralized elite and an attentive public—affect the political tone of the society at large in most significant ways. They provide centers of policy initiative outside the governmental, party, and special-interest systems, and a discriminating audience for public policy discussion. They are sustained by an educational system which at least makes an effort at citizenship training, by a system of communication which feeds information into these groupings, and by a network of civic and public-interest organizations which offer part of the population opportunities to assume public responsibilities.

The shortcomings of democratic society in Germany result from absence of such institutional pluralism. When that is recognized, the problem of overcoming the difficulties becomes more manageable. More limited and attainable goals can be set, and points of leverage suggested. Despite their lack of a tradition of political responsibility, the professional and business classes in Germany are the best-informed stratum of the population. There are already small elite groups aware of these problems of political communication. A relatively small allocation of resources in the educational system, in the press and communication field, and in support of voluntary civic associations may make some progress toward producing the beginnings of a pattern of broad and continuous political discussion, and may thereby provide more depth and stability in the German political process.

This, of course, is not to argue that the American or British political pattern can be exported to Germany. Political cultures are governed by something like a law of inertia. They change slowly and in terms of the past. And yet there are points in their development when the range of choice is suddenly broadened, when a change of direction becomes possible. The present juncture of German political development appears to offer such a range of choice, and there is evidence—to be sure on a most limited scale—of a will to take advantage of these opportunities.

But these possibilities are clearly of a long-run order. At the present juncture, Germany will have to rely on a rather shallow political foundation, which includes the governmental structure, the political parties, and the pressure-groups. And here it would be a great mistake to overlook a number of positive and stabilizing developments. The structure of government in Germany and the electoral system tend to discourage political irresponsibility and extremism. The party leaders appear to have assimilated some of the lessons of the Weimar period and seem to be able to operate more effectively in a parliamentary framework. The pressure-groups and the trade-unions have also assimilated in some measure the lessons of the past and are now less ready to press special interest to extremes. All of these political elements are at present constrained by a mood of political sobriety.

If we use our findings about the present state of political thinking among the German business classes as clues to their possible political behavior in the kinds of situations which may confront them, we arrive at a number of speculative conclusions. In the first place, it is a serious error to describe the changing trend of opinion in Germany today as moving in a neo-Nazi direction. There are few neo-Nazis, and they have little influence among the population. There is, however, an increasing tendency toward national assertiveness, which in most Germans stops short of any form of extremism or adventurism. The destructive past is too much with Germans today and the risks of adventurism and aggressiveness too compellingly obvious. Perhaps no group inclines more strongly away from adventurism than do the business leaders, who have gained so much in the postwar period and who have so much to lose in the event of another war.

Among businessmen, as well as among the general population, the strongest and most authentic political impulse is the search for a secure political framework. Until the collapse of EDC, this impulse was largely engaged in the effort of European integration. With the collapse of EDC in the summer of 1954, however, the integration trend began to ebb.

German reunification is another popular formula for increased political stability, but recent events have demonstrated the unlikelihood of reunification in acceptable terms, and may have somewhat reduced the salience of the entire issue. Successive Soviet rebuffs may also have created a greater willingness on the part of businessmen to accept the present West Germany as a stable form of the German state.

Finally, one must consider the probable effects of the development of a German army. The main question is whether the introduction of such an institution in Germany will overwhelm a weak civilian society and its moderate foreign policy. The threat arises from the possibility not only that an army may become a contender for political power, but also that the existence of such an army may constitute a temptation for political movements to gain control of it and use it for aggressive purposes. Even excluding these possibilities, the existence of a German army will broaden and complicate the problem of foreign policy-making. Whatever may turn out to be the strength of the German military establishment, it is bound to be dwarfed by communist strength, what with the continued development of unconventional weapons and the means for their delivery. Given present as well as probable future conditions, German military strength can be significant only in the over-all structure of Western security. Even if Germany were ever tempted to take the initiative in aggressive action, she would no doubt be deterred by the knowledge that she would be the first to be overrun in the event of war.

SEVEN

The Mass Media in West German Political Life

W. Phillips Davison

Within a generation, the German media of mass communication have flourished under the Weimar Republic, experienced "co-ordination" by the Nazis, and been banned and then reconstituted by Allied military governments. Since 1949 they have developed freely within the framework of the German Federal Republic and now, once again, occupy an important position in a democratic German society.

This paper attempts to describe the part which these media and the individuals who direct them play in the formation of West German domestic and foreign policies. The discussion includes newspapers, news agencies, periodicals, and radio, but does not extend to books, motion pictures, or the still relatively undeveloped medium of television.

It may be useful at this point to outline the four main conclusions which emerge from the study. First, it is apparent that those who control the mass media do not function as an interest-group in the manner of industry or organized labor; as a group, publishers and radio executives have no political philosophy which they are trying to promote. Nor do the mass media, either singly or collectively, ordinarily exercise very much effect on major domestic or foreign policy decisions.

Second, the West German mass media provide communication facilities

EDS. NOTE.—Information for this report was obtained from published sources and from conversations in 1953 and 1954 with some forty journalists, newspaper publishers, radio executives, and others familiar with the West German information services. The manuscript was completed in 1956 and revised in the spring of 1957.

The author is a staff member of The RAND Corporation's Social Science Division and for several years has been concerned with problems of public opinion and international communication.

without which German democracy would be unable to function, and thus exercise an important indirect influence on both foreign and domestic policy. They enable groups of almost all political shades to reach their own adherents and also to appeal to the public at large. They make a substantial amount of political information available to the ordinary voter, if he wishes to avail himself of it, and they also provide facilities for the exchange of views among specialists.

Third, relatively great freedom is accorded the press in the Federal Republic, and this freedom appears gradually to be becoming more firmly anchored. There are, however, a number of forces which, if they gain in strength, may curtail freedom of the press in the coming years, with consequent damage to democratic institutions.

Finally, the influence of the mass media as a whole bolsters the *status quo* and reinforces the preoccupation of the mass of West Germans with domestic, nonpolitical affairs.

Limited Media Influence on Specific Issues

Press and radio personnel, and also students of the German press, are nearly unanimous in agreeing that the mass media have relatively little influence on individual political issues.* Such influences as the mass media do exercise tend to be greatest at the level of local politics, and become smaller as one enters the realm of national politics. As far as foreign policy is concerned, the role of the press and radio is minimal. At most, the mass media are credited with being able to embarrass the government in the conduct of foreign relations. Dr. Dolf Sternberger of Heidelberg University has suggested that the expression "fourth estate," and references to the press as a great power, belong to a period which is past.[1]

Numerous reasons are cited for the modest political role played by radio and print. One is that these media, taken as a whole, devote relatively little attention to propagating political viewpoints; their focus is usually on the cultural field, on providing entertainment, or on conveying professionally useful information. A closely related reason is that, as far as the printed media are concerned, editorial policies are frequently determined not by the political sympathies of the publisher, if indeed he has any, but by the desire to maximize circulation and profits.

Students of the German mass media point out further that the Federal Republic, unlike England and France, has as yet no national press. In-

---

* The following discussion is not intended to imply either that the mass media *should* influence specific political decisions or that they *should not*. The present paper aims merely to describe the existing situation.

stead, it has large numbers of local organs and several regional papers with national aspirations. The German radio, likewise, is regionally oriented. There are very few nationally-known press or radio personalities. Syndicated columnists with well-defined points of view on political subjects, or radio commentators who speak over national hookups, have not developed since the war, and the political pundits of Weimar days who used to have the ear of top policymakers have not reappeared.

Finally, relations between mass media and government are not such as to encourage press and radio influence on political decisions. Most high governmental officials do not feel that views expressed in the mass media should influence official policy. And many, perhaps most, of the major publishers would have little interest in trying to influence political policies even if they had a better opportunity to do so. As for radio, it rarely takes an editorial stand on controversial issues, since it is charged with providing opportunity for expression to all major points of view.

In the following pages these factors, which tend to limit the influence of each of the major categories of mass media in molding specific political decisions, will be discussed in more detail.

Politics and the Daily Press

Of the media of communication, the daily newspaper is usually thought of as the one most concerned with political affairs. West Germany is well covered with dailies: in 1955 there were slightly over fourteen hundred of them, with a total circulation of about sixteen million.* Furthermore, these papers, taken together, reach almost the entire West German population. In repeated surveys between 1949 and 1955, only from 5 to 7 per cent of the West Germans told interviewers that they were not newspaper readers.[2]

All these papers report political news, but relatively few have a well-defined political viewpoint or take stands on major political questions. While one can not determine, on the basis of available information, precisely how many may be regarded as frequently expressing a view on controversial political issues, it is possible to say with a fair degree of confidence that, of the sixteen million total circulation, about three-quarters is accounted for by organs without a well-defined editorial viewpoint.[3]

One group of daily papers that seldom raise political issues is composed of what Germans often call "boulevard sheets." One of these, and

---

* Unless otherwise specified, all circulation figures are taken from *Die Deutsche Presse 1956*, a handbook issued in 1956 by the *Institut für Publizistik* ("Institute for Communication Research") of the Free University of Berlin. Figures cited do not include West Berlin unless this is specifically stated.

by far the largest daily in Germany, is the *Bild-Zeitung,* a tabloid with a circulation of nearly two-and-a-half million. It sells for the equivalent of 2.5 cents, and was described to an American newspaperman by an irate German as "ten pfennigs worth of blood and bosom." [4] Roughly another half-million circulation is accounted for by competing smaller boulevard papers of a slightly higher intellectual level.

A second category of newspapers which skirt political issues is made up of politically colorless city organs, often referred to in German as *Generalanzeiger.* The *Generalanzeiger* in its purest form attempts to avoid giving offense to anybody, while seeking to interest as many people as possible. Editorial campaigns favoring kindness to animals, or better care for city parks, are characteristic of such papers. Stands on controversial political issues are rare, although not entirely unknown. Since classification of any given organ as a *Generalanzeiger* in this somewhat invidious sense is a matter of individual opinion, it is difficult to give an exact figure for the circulation of papers of this type, but it would be safe to say that it is on the order of four to five million.

Third, a very large proportion of West Germany's newspapers are small organs. Indeed, three-quarters of them have press runs of under ten thousand, but their combined circulation is about five million. Most of these are small-town papers, heavily oriented toward local matters. While they carry some international news, they do not often take editorial stands on foreign policy problems or even on major problems of national policy. Many papers of this type are referred to as *Heimatzeitungen* ("home-town papers").

The remaining daily newspapers, with a combined circulation of some four million, often do take editorial stands on controversial issues of domestic and foreign policy. They are of two classes: those which reflect, either formally or informally, the views of a political party or interest-group; and those which are independent and often outspoken in their editorial comment. The views of the papers in the second class, of course, sometimes run parallel to those of one or another political party.

It is in both subdivisions of this last category that the outstanding newspapers of present-day Germany must be sought. Of those which speak for political parties, the *Rheinische Post* (circulation 219,000 in 1955) identifies itself as "democratic and Christian," and is usually regarded as following the lead of the Adenauer government, while the *Westfälische Rundschau* (circulation 248,000 in 1955) identifies itself as "independent; close to the SPD."

The newspaper editorials most often quoted are those in the papers that speak primarily for themselves. Of these, the "big three" are *Die Welt* of Hamburg, the *Frankfurter Allgemeine Zeitung,* and the

Süddeutsche Zeitung of Munich. The first and last have circulations of over 200,000; the Frankfurt paper has over 160,000.

Today the majority of newspapers seek to avoid political controversy or even association with a political viewpoint. But before 1933, according to Professor Dovifat, one of the senior students of the German press, nearly half of the country's papers identified themselves with some political philosophy. At the present time, only about 12 per cent associate themselves with a particular party, and another 12 per cent acknowledge a general political viewpoint, such as "liberal," "middle-class," or "Christian." [5]

Most dailies, even the small ones, have editorials on political subjects, but in the majority of cases these are phrased so as not to give offense to any major group. Such editorials are often dull and usually receive relatively little attention. In 1955 a public opinion poll found that 26 per cent of those interviewed usually read newspaper editorials, 72 per cent local news, and 51 per cent the advertisements.[6] Several editors of rather colorless mass-circulation papers remarked to the writer that they really didn't believe their readers paid any attention to editorials at all. On the other hand, the editor of a paper distinguished by its articulate political views said that he had been greatly impressed by readers' interest in his editorials.

The numerical dominance of politically neutral newspapers is explained by publishers and editors in several ways. First, the postwar German public as a whole is suspicious of identification with any group or ideology. People are much more likely to be against than for something. Between 1945 and 1951, this negativism, including a certain impatience with political institutions, was noted repeatedly by American authorities who conducted opinion polls in Germany, and many manifestations of it still persist.

A second and possibly more important reason for the dominating position of unaffiliated papers is the economic necessity for newspaper publishers to achieve as large a circulation as possible within a limited geographic area. National advertising and national circulation contribute a relatively small share of the incomes of most German newspapers, which must live largely on income from subscribers and from local advertisers. Furthermore, in view of increased publishing costs, they must achieve a fairly large circulation in order to break even. A newspaper which, before 1939, could show a profit on a circulation of three to four thousand copies must now sell thirty to forty thousand. A publisher therefore can not afford to identify his paper with any one group if this would mean driving away potential subscribers or advertisers.

In a Hessian city on the border of the Soviet zone of Germany, a leading publisher described the policy of the local paper in a neighboring town as that of "moving far enough to the right to attract the refugees, but not so far as to lose the Social Democrats." A German official whose work brought him in contact with large numbers of newspaper publishers declared: "Most papers try to steer a straight line down the center of every issue, because if they don't they will lose circulation."

Many of the larger publications conduct periodic opinion polls in their communities in order to keep track of public reactions to their content. Indeed, the writer was impressed by the frequency with which opinion poll results were mentioned by the editors and publishers with whom he talked.

The policy of appealing to everyone and antagonizing nobody also affects the agencies which sell centrally-prepared news stories, editorials, or features to the smaller newspapers. When controversial issues are concerned, these agencies must be cautious in the extreme. It is only on matters about which most people are agreed that they can take a definite stand: the desirability of reunification, the virtues of economic progress, or the superiority of German culture.

A number of devices which enable the thousand or more very small papers to survive and, in some cases, to prosper reinforce the tendency to editorial colorlessness. Many outwardly independent papers are actually satellites of a larger newspaper. They are printed at a central point and share the news and feature content of the larger paper. Only the name and the local news and advertising vary. Other small papers are in fact independent enterprises, but they buy nearly their entire content from a central agency in a form ready to print, leaving only local news and local advertising to be collected by the paper's own staff. A third common device is for several small papers to band together and share editorial, business, or mechanical facilities. In this way the expense incurred by each is reduced to manageable proportions.

The penalty for these money-saving devices is usually loss of editorial color, especially on national and international issues. A very small paper may occasionally be able to carry a locally-written editorial on some village issue, but for discussions of more complex political affairs it must rely on editorials prepared elsewhere and probably destined to be used by a number of different papers.

For all these reasons, vigorously expressed political viewpoints are found in very few (some say in less than a hundred) of the approximately fourteen hundred papers published in West Germany. It is not difficult to see that a press whose editorial policies are, in general, so timid is unlikely to exercise more than a modest influence on specific political issues.

But what of the influence of the vigorous and outspoken minority? It is true that these papers are not read by the masses, but they are carefully perused by those in positions of authority, the very people whom one might expect to give practical effect to the policies advocated by their favorite newspapers. Moreover the vigorous minority comprises many large papers, some of which have circulations of over 200,000.

Contrary to what one might expect, it is the almost unanimous opinion of both newspaper personnel and government officials who deal with the press that even the best newspapers have little influence on specific political decisions. Such an influence, they say, was possible in the days of the Weimar Republic, when the prestige of certain newspapers was so high and the authority of some journalists so great that the press was able to take part in the highest councils of the state, but the situation has changed.

Most informed Germans cite the lack of complete news coverage and authoritative analysis as the chief limitation on the influence of the present-day German press. They point out that no West German paper can afford an adequate world-wide network of correspondents. Most of the leading dailies have a handful of correspondents in principal capitals, but many of these are shared among several papers, and others are "stringers." There have been numerous complaints about the quality of postwar reporting from abroad.[7] Even when correspondents are highly qualified, the inability of their papers to pay large cable charges limits the amount and type of reporting they can do. The number of foreign correspondents has increased steadily since the war, but is still far from satisfactory. In 1952 only ten correspondents represented individual German newspapers abroad.[8] The press handbook published two years later listed nearly 150, although all but 29 of these were concentrated in nearby Western European capitals, and many combined newspaper reporting with other work.[9] The result is that very heavy reliance must be placed on standardized wire-agency reports for most foreign news.

It is frequently observed that even the best West German papers do not attain the high standards of political analysis reached by the outstanding papers of the Weimar Republic, and their influence is correspondingly lower. Editorials on political subjects may be seriously and competently written, but they are neither stylistically nor analytically the equal of those which could be found in the *Frankfurter Zeitung* during the 1920's. Journalists and students of the press give a number of persuasive reasons for this decrease in quality. Economic circumstances of present-day German newspapers do not allow editors to reflect at length on a single article or editorial; they are forced to rush into print with one piece of writing after another. Moreover, there is a severe shortage of well-qualified political journalists. Those few who were trained during Weimar days and are now back in newspaper work are spread too thinly. The Nazis trained no capable political journalists, and those newsmen trained since the war have yet to develop their full stature.

The impressive erudition and expertness which made it possible for the journalists of the 1920's to influence policy through the weight of their ideas had as a corollary the fact that their audience was very small. Although they sometimes published in newspapers with large circulations, the number of people who could understand what they were writing about was usually quite limited. A prominent Weimar journalist once stated privately that he often wrote editorials intended to influence one specific government official. Others have mentioned that articles intended for one or more members of the government, or for a specific party official, were often misunderstood by general readers who did not know enough of the background.* A modern-day journalist, describing the profundity which was a characteristic of the most expert journalism of Weimar days, recalled that one often had to spend four or five minutes on an editorial in the *Frankfurter Zeitung* before one knew what it was about. Journalism of this type made great demands on the reader and thus kept the audience small, but it also influenced the policy of the nation.

Some students believe that the lower quality of postwar journalism stems from the fact that the reading public has changed. Those newspaper readers who previously had been able to study at leisure the editorials in the *Hamburger Fremdenblatt* or the *Berliner Tageblatt* have now disappeared, and have been replaced by readers who would like their day's news and views in ten-minute capsules.

Finally, it is pointed out, Germany's present divided state and lack of a real national capital mean that there is no focus for political, economic, and cultural activities. The resulting provincialism is reflected in the press. There is no truly national newspaper in West Germany.

Because even the best of Germany's contemporary newspapers do not meet the standards of news coverage and political analysis shared by such giants of the press world as *Le Monde, The Times* of London, or the *New York Times,* one frequently hears it said by West Germans: "We have no newspaper of international stature in present-day Germany." [10] The best newspaper in the German language is usually identi-

* The writer is indebted for these examples, as well as for helpful criticism at many points, to Dr. Dietrich Mende, formerly of the *Institut für Europäische Politik und Wirtschaft,* Frankfurt on Main.

fied by politically interested intellectuals, not without bitterness, as the Swiss *Neue Zürcher Zeitung,* and there is remarkable unanimity among intellectuals and political leaders that, if one wishes to be sure of complete coverage of the news, combined with authoritative interpretation, it is advisable to read the *"Neue Zürcher."* *

It may be that lack of comprehensive coverage and authoritative analysis tends to limit the influence of the press on political decisions, but influence is also limited by the attitude of editors and publishers toward government and the attitude of government officials toward the press.

While it is difficult to generalize about the attitudes of press personnel toward government, one receives the impression that in Germany the fourth estate does not feel as strongly about its political role as does the press in other Western democracies, although it feels more strongly about its cultural role. Journalists are less likely to see themselves as protectors of the individual against the state, or as spokesmen for the public interest, except where cultural matters are concerned. One result of this attitude is that the German press does not, by and large, emphasize the task of newsmen to go out and dig up political information; it is more apt to be content to accept handouts from governmental or party authorities. Consequently, the press is less likely to inspire political action based on information it has ferreted out itself than are mass media in countries where journalistic inquisitiveness is a more highly regarded professional trait. And when the press does uncover new facts about political matters, party or official agencies are often reluctant to take action on the basis of this information. These generalizations have, of course, many exceptions, some of which will be mentioned below.

When asked whether they frequently had occasion to call up leading executive officials, or to discuss political matters with them informally, publishers and chief editors usually said that they preferred to leave such dealings to their correspondents in Bonn. Indeed, one of West Germany's most prominent and successful editors maintained that he intentionally avoided contact with political leaders because he wished to preserve his reputation for political independence. Newspapermen who became too closely identified with governmental officials, he said, were often considered "personal mouthpieces." While these views are rarely expressed in such extreme form, one receives the impression that those who control the press, as a whole, are content to keep government at arm's length and to report on its activities from a distance.

---

* In presenting these criticisms, the writer has acted as a reporter of opinions which he does not fully share. It is his impression that present-day German journalists have a tendency to criticize their own products somewhat more harshly than the facts warrant.

Governmental officials likewise tend to see the press as having a limited political role. Chancellor Adenauer, in an address before the annual meeting of the German Journalists' Association in 1954, recognized the right of the press to criticize policy, but asked that this be positive criticism. Editors should try to explain policy to the people and to present better proposals instead of merely tearing down existing ones.[11]

These remarks aroused predominantly unfavorable reactions among journalists, who recalled that the Nazi government had also expected the press to "educate" the people.[12] Others observed that a similar role had been assigned the press by postwar military governments. A few complained that inability to cook did not disqualify one for criticizing the preparation of meals.

Other government officials have indicated a desire to see the press and radio function as a means of explaining policy to the masses and gaining support for it. They seem to think of the press primarily as a public-address system which enables state authorities to speak to the population as a whole, but they are reluctant to see the media talk back. Officials do not ordinarily concede a legitimate role in policy formulation to the mass media, except in rare cases where one or another journalist can qualify as a political expert. The conception of the mass media as an alternative channel for the expression of the desires of the public is rarely encountered.

These attitudes are reflected in the procedures governing press conferences. There tends to be little give-and-take between top governmental personnel and reporters. On the federal level, press-government relations are rather formal, and the official who grants a journalist an interview is likely to feel that he is doing a favor rather than performing an official duty. The Chancellor usually answers questions from the press only if they are written out and submitted in advance.

In searching for factors that limit the influence of the press on political decisions, one is tempted to suggest also that the nature of political issues themselves has changed during the past generation, so that the press is unable to speak about them with the authoritative assurance that was possible thirty years ago. However this may be, it is certain that West German mass media personnel believe almost universally that the influence of even the most highly-regarded daily papers on specific political decisions is small.

Politics and the Periodical Press

In number of titles and in circulation the periodical press far overshadows the daily newspaper. The press handbook issued by the Free

University of Berlin lists for 1955 over five thousand periodical titles in West Germany, excluding Berlin. These had a total circulation of well over one hundred million. Like the daily press, periodicals seldom take a strong stand on political issues, though a few, most of them with rather small circulations, can be included among the world's best political journals.

Of the total periodical circulation, approximately one-third is made up of trade and technical journals, and magazines published for the guidance of consumers. For instance, 17 periodicals, with a circulation of almost two million, are devoted to retail trade; another 23, with a circulation of one million, deal with medicine and pharmacy; and so on. These, of course, rarely discuss political issues unless the latter directly concern the economic group for which a magazine is published.

Another 10 per cent of the total periodical circulation is accounted for by 90 illustrated magazines, short-story magazines, and others devoted to entertainment. They ordinarily avoid taking stands on political issues, but from time to time give attention to politically explosive subjects. In the early fifties the illustrated magazines published a series of articles about the lives of former Nazi leaders, and caused many students of the press to condemn them for exerting a baleful influence on political life. The purpose of these articles was merely to build circulation, and when public interest in them subsided, the illustrated periodicals returned to the doings of the heads of royal houses, sensational court cases, popular medical discussions, and other subjects of wide appeal but little intellectual or political content. Dr. Friedrich Medebach of the Free University of Berlin, an authority on German periodicals, speaks of these journals as being directed toward the individual's primitive interests.[13] Readership per copy of the illustrated magazines is high, and one can estimate conservatively on the basis of poll results that more than half of the population reads them regularly. German journalists and academic students of the press frequently express apprehension that these periodicals might exert a large and unfortunate influence if they became the instrument of unscrupulous political forces.

Other categories of large-circulation periodicals include women's magazines (four million), religious periodicals (nearly seventeen million), and radio and television journals (five million).

In this flood of print, periodicals devoted primarily to political questions occupy a very modest place. The Free University of Berlin's *Institut für Publizistik* has classified 211 magazines published in West Germany and West Berlin, with a total circulation of somewhat over three million, as falling within the category of "politics and cultural policy." Dr. Medebach concludes from the relatively small number and modest circulation of the periodicals in this group that large segments of the public are not interested in serious political discussions.[14]

More than a million of the total political periodical circulation is accounted for by weekly newspapers. Periodicals published by the political parties have a total press run of almost another million. The remainder are highly diverse.

The names of many of the weekly newspapers soon become familiar to anyone concerned with German politics. Although their press runs are relatively small, they are read by influential groups. The *Deutsche Zeitung und Wirtschafts Zeitung,* with a circulation of only 48,000 a week in 1955, is regarded by many students of German politics as one of the very best sources for current political analysis. In spite of its excellent reputation, its circulation declined by three thousand between 1953 and 1955. Its views often parallel those of the more liberal industrialists. There are three well-known weeklies with a religious orientation: the *Allgemeine Sonntagszeitung* (circulation 68,000), *Sonntagsblatt* (circulation 69,000), and *Christ und Welt* (circulation 72,000). The first represents German Catholic views; the latter two Protestant views. *Rheinischer Merkur* (circulation 69,000) usually parallels the position of Chancellor Adenauer. *Welt der Arbeit* (circulation 109,000) is an organ of the German Trade-Union Federation. *Die Zeit* (circulation 63,000) is a vigorous weekly journal of commentary, which often presents the views of the North German CDU. *Der Spiegel* is a sensational news magazine, modeled in its external appearance on *Time,* and has a circulation of 230,000. These, and a few titles which are mentioned somewhat less often, almost exhaust the list of leading political weeklies and semiweeklies.

At least four other journals, however, are repeatedly mentioned by both journalists and political leaders as politically significant. They appear less frequently and have smaller circulations. The smallest is *Aussenpolitik* (circulation 2,200 a month), which carries serious articles on foreign policy problems. Slightly larger are *Die Gegenwart* (circulation 14,000 twice a month), which offers a broad coverage of politics, economics, and cultural questions; *Frankfurter Hefte* (circulation 15,000 a month), which covers a similar field; and *Der Monat* (circulation 25,000 a month), which is more heavily oriented toward the arts and rarely takes a stand on political issues but does include some excellent political analyses.

When one asks German students of the press to mention the "politically most influential" media in Germany, it is striking to see how frequently these weekly, twice-monthly, and monthly publications are named. Fairly often they are thought of as overshadowing even the best of the daily papers in the effect they have on policy determination. References to the same small group of periodicals are also found frequently in the remarks of political leaders and in governmental publications concerned with press opinion. For instance, a check of the magazine digest prepared by the Press and Information Office of the Federal Republic for six months during 1956 showed that the *Deutsche Zeitung und Wirtschafts Zeitung* was cited more often than any other publication, while nearly all the other weeklies mentioned above figured prominently as well. *Die Gegenwart* also received attention out of all proportion to the size of its circulation.

The influence of the smaller publications may be attributed to several factors. First, they are able to fulfill the requirement of expertness more easily than the large dailies. They can present carefully-considered articles on complicated subjects written by outstanding authorities, while, with rare exceptions, the dailies could not afford to devote the necessary space to such articles even if they were willing to do so. Moreover, many political leaders themselves write for the serious journals and take time to read them. Thus it might be said that these periodicals serve as a more efficient means of communication within the governing group than do the larger dailies.

A number of the weeklies speak for powerful groups in the population. *Welt der Arbeit,* for instance, presents the trade-union position, and there are various periodicals which comment on politics from the standpoint of religious groups, industrial groups, or organized political groups. All these organs may be expected to exert influence upon the groups they represent, if not upon others as well. By presenting a clear viewpoint, they escape the colorlessness which afflicts all but a few of the daily papers.

Politics and the Radio

Radio reaches at least as wide an audience in West Germany as do newspapers and periodicals. At the end of 1954, there were almost exactly 12 million radio receivers. Since an average of four listeners are served by each receiver, the total radio audience approximates 48 million, or almost the entire population of West Germany.[15] Public opinion surveys indicated that, in 1955, 92 per cent of the adult population listened to the radio.[16]

Seven independent broadcasting organizations cover the Federal Republic. In addition, there are two in West Berlin, one of which is operated by U.S. authorities. Most of the West German stations are primarily devoted to serving a particular *Land,* or state, although some include more than one state in their area of responsibility. Several of the stations are able to offer two programs, since they broadcast in both the medium- and the ultra-short–wave bands. Most radio owners can also tune in on stations outside the Federal Republic.

The seven broadcasting organizations in West Germany are all organized as "public-law institutions." [17] As such they are not owned or controlled by government, but neither do they have private owners. To finance the stations, each owner of a radio receiver is required by law to pay two marks a month for the privilege of operating his receiver. This fee is collected by the postman, and most of it goes directly to the station which serves the listener's place of residence. The rest goes to the Post Office Department to cover costs of collection and certain technical services. The charters of the seven radio organizations specify that they be administered in such a manner as to afford a fair hearing to all principal points of view and that no one political tendency shall dominate their output. To ensure this independent standpoint, various mechanisms have been adopted in different regions.

Typical of the organization of the majority of the stations is that of the South German Radio, with headquarters in Stuttgart. It is directed by a Radio Council of 33 members, each of whom is designated by an agency or organization concerned with the public welfare. Such agencies include the churches, educational organizations, trade-unions, chambers of commerce, and journalists' and publishers' associations. In addition, the Baden-Württemberg State Assembly elects five members of the Radio Council, which remains independent of the state government. The principal tasks of the Council are to exercise control over program policy and to hire the station director. He can be removed only for "major cause." Alongside of the Radio Council is an Administrative Council of nine members, five of whom are elected by the Radio Council and four by the state assembly. It is concerned primarily with supervising the financial practices of the station. This organizational setup was established by *Land* legislation and can be altered by the *Land* assembly.

The two stations in the former British zone of Germany are organized so as to allow a far larger degree of governmental influence, although it can not be said that they are arms of the state.*

The West German Radio, with headquarters in Cologne, is governed by a Radio Council of 21 members elected by the state assembly of North Rhine-Westphalia so as to give proportional representation to each political party having deputies in the assembly. This Radio Council, in turn, elects a seven-member Administrative Council and a Program Ad-

---

* Following World War II, British Military Government set up a single broadcasting organization, the North-West German Radio (NWDR), in its zone of occupation. In 1955, this was divided by the German authorities, and two independent stations started operation in April, 1956.

visory Board. The Administrative Council then appoints the *Intendant* (or "station director"), who performs the actual work of running the station. According to the station charter, not only the state government but also the federal government may demand time on the air to make official announcements. Furthermore, the state government is vested with authority to review the legality of actions by the radio organization and to intervene if an allegedly illegal action is not corrected.[18]

A similar organization exists for the North German Radio, with headquarters in Hamburg, although here power in the last analysis is vested in the assemblies and governments of three political units: the states of Lower Saxony and Schleswig-Holstein, and the City of Hamburg. Of the 24 members of the North German Radio Council, three are appointed by the three governments, and the other 21 are elected by the three parliaments.[19]

The South German Radio, then, differs from those of the West and North in that citizens' groups as well as state authorities are represented on its governing council. Both these systems of organization have been strongly criticized. A number of outstanding journalists have attacked the representation of civic organizations in the South German system on the ground that one can not equate the public interest with the sum of private interests. Others have expressed the fear that continual compromise among the representatives of various groups will lead to mediocrity and colorlessness. One leading journalist expressed this viewpoint by saying that the listener would be treated as a poor devil as long as the Radio Council played at being a parliament.[20] A leading legal commentator went so far as to express the opinion that the "neutralization" of radio, as far as parties and interest-groups were concerned, violated Article 21 of the Basic Law, which was intended to protect free formation of political opinion.[21]

The stress of opposing forces in the South German system was illustrated in 1956 when the post of station director in Bavaria became vacant, owing to the death of the incumbent. Analyzing the situation, a writer in the *Deutsche Zeitung und Wirtschafts Zeitung* observed that the CSU (Bavarian counterpart of the Christian Democratic Union) controlled a bare majority of votes in the Radio Council and could push through its favorite candidate if it wished to do so. On the other hand, the Social Democrats, senior partners in the state's governing coalition, strongly opposed the favorite CSU candidate. If the majority in the Radio Council pushed through the CSU candidate, the Social Democrats might use their majority in the state assembly to change the law governing the composition of the Radio Council, and thus destroy the CSU majority. A second candidate for the position, Walter von Cube, the station's able and controversial chief editor for Politics, Economics, and Culture, was unlikely to be selected because he had antagonized the politically powerful refugee groups. The *Deutsche Zeitung* correctly predicted the victory of a third candidate, Mayor Stadelmayer of Würzburg, because he was known to be sympathetic to the CSU but was not opposed by the Social Democrats.[22]

While the South German system clearly has not excluded politics from radio, critics of the more recently inaugurated North German system point out that it threatens radio with domination by a political party or government. Helmut Cron, one of Germany's most respected journalists and former chairman of the German Journalists' Association, wrote in 1955 that the new charters for the North German and West German stations virtually threw away chances for an independent radio by giving the political parties and state governments the influence over radio which they had long sought.[23]

As far as can be determined, however, the new status of the North German radio stations so far has not led to domination of their output by any one political group. Nowhere does one find a single political viewpoint permeating all or most of a station's programs. And under the South German system well-defined political views are by no means excluded from the air; to this extent the critics' charge of "political colorlessness" is unfounded. All stations provide time for the expression of principal political viewpoints, and most of them provide "live" broadcasts of certain political events, such as Bundestag sessions in Bonn. Some also include on their programs political commentators with well-defined viewpoints.

Most of the news analysts are known only within the limited areas served by their stations. A notable exception is Walter von Cube of Radio Munich, who is known to most radio listeners in part because his views have shocked many people (he has suggested that the stream of refugees from East Germany be denied entry to the Federal Republic); and in part because he is recognized as a vigorously independent commentator. Another exception is Peter von Zahn, who since 1951 has been the Washington correspondent of the North-West German Radio and of its two successor stations. His commentaries are less dramatic than those of Walter von Cube, but he also can be said to have a national following.

In general, however, German radio programs, while they have a substantial and vigorous political content and a number of strong radio personalities, have rarely exercised a direct influence on specific political decisions. This is at least partially because they must be oriented toward a mass audience rather than toward the relatively small number who determine political policy.

Examples of Influence: The Exceptions That Prove the Rule

When those who are most familiar with the German mass media are asked to mention instances in which the press or radio has influenced decisions on specific issues, they are usually able to do so, although sometimes only after a period of reflection. There is general agreement that the mass media have something to say about decisions in the realm of cultural policy: the nature and quality of the music or drama offered by city or state cultural institutions may depend in part on the views of authoritative publicists.

Most press and radio personnel can also mention one or more instances in which action by municipal or state authorities has been brought about or inhibited by the mass media: these include installation of traffic lights, policies governing parks and playgrounds, and sometimes local government personnel policies. The editor of a powerful South German newspaper remarked in this connection that his newspaper, in co-operation with other local organs, had finally been able to force one particularly incompetent official out of office. To bring about this single action, however, had taken weeks of research and repeated editorials over a series of months. This editor, and also several other mass media personnel, remarked that, when one bureaucrat was attacked, the other bureaucrats all rallied to protect him.

Another type of influence, mentioned fairly often, appears when governmental authorities at various levels are induced to take action after the press has publicized some abuse or other. Several editors and publishers cited cases in which injustices to individuals had been corrected following publicity in the mass media.

It is more difficult to find clear examples of the effects of mass media influence on national and international affairs, but they do exist. Several years ago, when the number of former Nazis in the new German Foreign Office became known, combined attacks of press and radio brought about a parliamentary inquiry which induced the Foreign Office to make some adjustments in its personnel policy. Several high governmental officials expressed the opinion that this was an improper use of the power of the press. They were supported in this view by a number of conservative journalists.[24]

It is also generally conceded that the press can embarrass the government in both its domestic and foreign relations. The "Schmeisser Affair," in which Chancellor Adenauer was accused of having been involved during the early postwar period in secret operations on behalf of France, was built up by some of the more sensational organs, and the publicity it received undoubtedly caused considerable discomfiture in Bonn. A

German periodical which publicized alleged difficulties in the royal house of the Netherlands was said to have contributed to tension in relations between the two countries. The mass media—especially their more sensationalist elements—can also embarrass individual officials and others in prominent places by making them look ridiculous; by publicizing alleged wrongdoing; and by reviving or distorting inconvenient incidents from the past. *Der Spiegel* has shown itself particularly adept at this. Since most members of German officialdom never have developed the thick skins which those prominent in the political life of the United States have found so useful, attacks of this sort often cause explosive reactions on the part of the officials concerned, and may also have an important cumulative effect on the way policies are formulated or administered. For instance, they may cause officials to be more cautious or more discreet. Nevertheless, attacks of this sort were never cited by those interviewed as having influenced a decision on a major political issue.

An incident in which the sensationalist press showed its ability not only to embarrass the German government but also to cause at least limited political action occurred in the summer of 1956. At that time, a number of mass-circulation newspapers and periodicals publicized a series of crimes committed by U.S. military personnel stationed in Germany. Although, as it later turned out, the "crime wave" was statistically insignificant and represented no more than the number of such incidents which normally plagued German and American authorities, the treatment given them in the mass media aroused popular emotions to a high pitch, and the town council of Bamberg passed a resolution asking that U.S. forces be withdrawn from the area. At this point, German press personnel became alarmed at the extent of the storm which they had helped to whip up and began trying to calm popular emotions. Even the tabloid *Bild-Zeitung* carried a front-page editorial asking for restraint.[25] While this incident is the only outstanding one of its kind in the past few years, and appears not to have had any long-term effects, it suggests alarming possibilities.

The only area in which the mass media can be said to have consistently exerted a strong effect on political decisions is in connection with governmental policies affecting freedom of information. Several proposals emanating from officials very close to Chancellor Adenauer—and looking toward the establishment of bodies resembling a propaganda ministry in some of their proposed functions—were withdrawn, in part because they ran into strong opposition from press and radio. A similar fate overtook the draft of a highly restrictive press law prepared by the Ministry of the Interior. Proposals to subject the radio to closer governmental control have also been defeated, largely as a result of consistent opposition by the mass media. The only law affecting freedom of information passed over the objections of the mass media to date is a statute intended to protect youth against pornography and trash. Hans Wallenberg, editor of the U.S.-sponsored *Neue Zeitung* until its discontinuance in 1953, has concluded that the German press has so far watched jealously and effectively over its regained freedom.[26]

The Mass Media and Democratic Institutions

While the influence of the mass media on specific political decisions is relatively slight, the indirect political impact of press and radio is very great. The mass media afford all major points of view an opportunity for expression; they allow political interest-groups of all shades (except the farthest extremes of left and right) to reach and organize potential supporters; they make it possible for almost any voter to obtain the basic minimum of information about political events which he needs to make his decisions at the polls; they provide the political expert with specialized information on which to base his decisions; they make known major governmental actions to the citizenry. In short, the mass media provide communication facilities which enable the democratic system to function.

One may argue with justice that the communication facilities afforded by the German mass media are far from perfect; that they devote far more space and time to entertainment than to enlightenment; that they are more hospitable to the views of some groups than to those of others; that various types of politically important information are provided only sparingly and other types not at all; and that political leaders must, on occasion, look to non-German publications, such as the *Neue Zürcher Zeitung* or the London *Economist,* for the specialized information they need. Nevertheless, it would be a serious mistake to allow the obvious shortcomings of the German mass communications system to obscure its less striking but far more important virtues.

As far as the daily press is concerned, it is apparent that a majority of newspapers offer only indifferent facilities for the expression of political views. Most of them are in the hands of small and large businessmen, who are not primarily interested in educating people or in convincing them of anything. Their first aim is to operate profitable enterprises and to produce newspapers which will sell. As has been pointed out above, papers of this type take few political stands, and include nothing that is likely to antagonize the reader.

By far the largest press concentration in Germany is that of the Hamburg publisher Axel Springer. Daily newspapers operated by the Springer enterprises include the tabloid *Bild-Zeitung,* the *Hamburger Abendblatt* (approximately 300,000), and *Die Welt* (about 200,000). In 1956 Springer bought a 26 per cent interest in the large Ullstein publishing house in Berlin. In addition, he controls a number of weekly periodicals with a total circulation of about three million, the largest of which is primarily devoted to presenting radio program schedules. Some German students of the mass media feel that the large size of the Springer enterprises makes for a high concentration of ownership in the German mass media. One should note, however, that no locality in Germany is restricted to one of the Springer newspapers, as many localities in the United States are restricted to the output of one publisher, and also that the Springer enterprises are the only really large publishing concentration in the country.

Numerous persons have attempted to find out what Springer's political sympathies are. None, so far as the writer is aware, has succeeded, and Springer has stated that he has no interest in becoming a political influence.[27] One experienced observer of German politics expressed the opinion that, if democracy in West Germany were ever seriously threatened, Springer would be found among its defenders, but that, until then, he would continue to operate his enterprises in the most profitable manner possible, without a great deal of attention to political issues. He does, however, allow his "prestige" paper, *Die Welt,* to take editorial stands, and these are often opposed to the policy of the Adenauer government.

Even though as much as three-quarters of the daily press is inhospitable to vigorously expressed political viewpoints, the remaining quarter, with a total circulation of some four million, provides an appreciable outlet for political opinion. According to the *Institut für Publizistik* of the Free University of Berlin, 2.7 per cent of the press (by circulation) was identified with the views of the CDU in 1955; 4.5 per cent with the SPD; and slightly less than one-half of 1 per cent with the Communist Party.* In most major cities there is at least one paper which identifies itself with one or another political point of view, even if not with a specific party. Furthermore, because of the relatively small geographical size of the Federal Republic, with its well-developed distribution mechanisms and mail system, the inhabitants of most localities have in fact a fairly large choice of daily papers. There are few towns of any size where socialist, liberal, conservative, and other political views do not find expression in locally-available, even if not locally-published, dailies.

* The Communist Party press was subsequently outlawed by a decision of the Constitutional Court in 1956.

The German radio is established in such a manner that access of all principal points of view to the airwaves is expressly guaranteed, and it thus supplements the daily press by offering another avenue for political expression. Nevertheless, existing radio stations find it impossible to satisfy all the various interest-groups' requests for time. Radio executives report continuous pressure from parties, unions, industrial groups, and many others for more time on the air. Nevertheless, since there are only a limited number of frequencies available, and the broadcast day must also include entertainment, news, and cultural material, the time available for the presentation of political views must, of necessity, be limited.

Off the record, radio executives sometimes argue that limited radio time does not in fact tend to inhibit expression of political views. They say that their principal problem is to find spokesmen for political interest-groups who are not so dull as to cause radio listeners to turn off their sets. They maintain vigorously that no group which really has anything of general interest to say is ever denied time in which to say it, and that the principal effect of time limitations is to exclude from the air boring speakers to whom nobody would listen anyway. It is a fair conclusion that no major point of view is denied access to radio, even if all must be brief.

Periodicals offer more adequate means of expression for diverse political views than either the daily press or the radio, as the proliferation of weekly and less frequent publications testifies. Cost factors, which make it difficult for smaller groups to maintain daily papers, are less restrictive here, and the number of shades of opinion which find expression is impressive. In addition to more than thirty periodicals associated with the CDU, SPD, and FDP, at least a dozen are affiliated with smaller parties, and there are publications speaking for monarchists, pacifists, anarchists, those who are "against corruption, mismanagement, and dishonest currency," and numerous others.

At the same time, one must also recognize that by far the largest portion of the periodical press excludes political viewpoints or presents them in greatly watered-down form. The publishers of general-circulation magazines, just like the publishers of the boulevard press, are convinced that the public does not wish to read serious political discussions. The fact that politically-oriented periodicals do not enjoy a larger circulation (most of them have to be subsidized in one way or another), or that general-circulation magazines do not contain more expressions of political views, is thus due largely to lack of demand on the part of the public.

When all the major mass media are taken together, the public does in fact receive a large dose of political views, and these are fairly well distributed throughout the political spectrum. There is no group of "press and radio tycoons" who can be said to dominate the airwaves and the printed page to such a degree that other groups have difficulty in communicating with their own supporters or with the public at large. At the most, one could say that those whose views are to the right-of-center have somewhat easier access to the media of communication than those to the left-of-center.

Political News in the Media of Communication

To say that many shades of opinion have access to the West German media of communication does not necessarily mean that these media make political information of sufficient quantity and quality available to their various audiences. Anyone in West Germany who is determined to secure full information about national and international political affairs will be able to do so, but the amount of determination required may be considerable, and it may be necessary to read several publications of diverse viewpoints.

For the bulk of their news on national and international events, most mass media must rely principally on news agencies. It is, therefore, relevant to inquire briefly into the structure and operation of the German news-gathering and disseminating industry.

There are approximately five hundred news, photographic, and feature services in the Federal Republic.[28] Of these, by far the most important is the *Deutsche Presse-Agentur* ("German Press Agency"), whose dispatches are slugged "DPA." This agency is owned co-operatively by approximately 190 German newspapers and radio stations. As of 1952, it had 29 offices in Germany and was represented in another 22 locations abroad. DPA provides a full news file of twenty-five to thirty thousand words a day, and also issues a number of specialized background-news and feature services.[29]

In addition to subscribing to DPA, many West German press enterprises buy foreign services, such as that of the Associated Press or the United Press. In 1954, both AP and UP were reported to have more than three hundred customers in West Germany and West Berlin.[30]

Since DPA must compete not only with these world-wide agencies but also with Soviet zone news sources (in the sense that any glaring gaps or biases in its coverage would probably be exploited by the East German radio), it is forced to maintain high professional standards of news coverage. There are some who allege that DPA is dominated by a group of Social Democrats who very subtly inject socialist propaganda into their news file. Other critics point out that, since the majority of the German newspapers that own DPA are controlled by conservative interests, the agency's dispatches are bound to be slanted in a conservative direction. Neither allegation appears to have any weight. DPA provides a solid and fairly thorough news file, from which those who buy the service can take their choice.

In addition to DPA, there are several agencies which supply smaller papers with canned news material. In preparing this material, they seem to be governed by the tastes of those toward the political right rather than the left, probably because most of their newspaper clients are in rural districts, where conservative views outweigh liberal or leftist ones. DIMITAG (the anagram comes from a German title meaning "Service for Middle-Sized Dailies"), the largest of these services, insists strenuously on its complete independence and political neutrality.[31] Most of DIMITAG's raw news comes from DPA and is tailored according to the requirements of the subscribers, who receive the material by teleprinter or by mats sent through the mails. Other agencies of this type are much smaller and offer more limited news and feature services.

A third category includes agencies which represent the views of various interest-groups—religious, labor, employer, political, and so on. The material they prepare is often given away free; in other cases a small charge is made. Many interest-groups operate such news services in order to ensure that their views reach the mass media and key individuals. An officer of one political group told the writer that his organization was planning to try to sell a news service to home-town newspapers. He didn't really expect to find many buyers, he conceded, but the process of canvassing would enable his salesmen to acquaint country editors with the ideas of the group.

Finally, there are large numbers of "confidential" newsletters. These are mostly published by very small enterprises and reflect a wide variety of views. Since they are directed largely to business, however, it may be assumed that the majority of them present material which the publishers think businessmen will be willing to buy.

In spite of the wide range of news sources available to the German newspapers, opinions vary widely as to the adequacy of the press's coverage of political news in general and foreign news in particular. A substantial number of observers hold that political coverage is poor. As one high government official put it, ". . . the press, with few exceptions, is utterly provincial; it does not even provide sufficient information on national events, and with respect to world news falls down on its job altogether."

On the other hand, when the Bonn correspondent of *Le Monde* criticized foreign coverage in the German press, his judgment was vigorously contested by a German expert, who replied that, on the basis of a comparative study, he had found that German papers did about as well as the press in other countries. He admitted, however, that the quality of news coverage needed further improvement.[32]

Coverage of course varies widely according to the type of paper in question. The "boulevard press" gives little political news of any kind. Mass-oriented dailies, such as the *Hamburger Abendblatt,* present a substantial number of political news items every day, but each in extremely brief form. The smaller home-town papers usually carry few individual political news items and rely for their coverage on "roundup" stories of mixed news and commentary, which are prepared at a central point (either at a consolidated editorial office or by a news agency) and distributed to using newspapers in ready-to-print form. The author of a work on the German press published in 1951 reported that, of about eighty recently established home-town papers in Bavaria, only fifteen received a regular news service; he added that, in "normal" times, it was taken as a matter of course that every daily paper subscribed to such a service.[33] Although these figures are several years old, it is unlikely that the situation has changed appreciably in the interim.

Some of the news roundups carried by these small papers appear to be written by qualified experts on political matters and, if given careful reading, make it possible to build up a fairly adequate picture of political affairs. This material has, however, two characteristics which combine to make it dull—and thus to reduce its readership. First, because it must be suitable for subscribers of various shades of political preference, it usually avoids controversial material and hews to a broadly "national" point of view. Second, it is usually written in a ponderous style, which would offer few problems to an intellectual but is difficult for the rural or small-town elementary-school graduate to follow.

The best big-city papers offer a national and international news coverage which is inferior in scope only to that of the most outstanding foreign papers. Nevertheless, they, too, often fail to present political material in a manner that will arouse public interest. Former State Secretary Dr. Otto Lenz, among others, has complained that almost all the best newspapers and periodicals affect a style so academically fastidious as to make their political content incomprehensible to the broad mass of the population.[34]

An exception to this general rule is offered by the *Glossen,* or brief commentaries, which sometimes deal with political subjects. Often incisive and easy to read, these *Glossen* receive wide attention. The editor of one large and respected newspaper stated that opinion surveys commissioned by his paper showed the *Glossen* to have more readers than any other part of the paper dealing with politics.

Even the best papers, however, occasionally leave important gaps in the news, partly for lack of space (they feel they must devote a large part of their available space to cultural matters), and partly because there rarely is a sense of obligation to present "all the news that's fit to print." During the early fifties, for instance, it was common for newspapers to omit items on atomic tests and the development of atomic energy, even though these were included in the DPA news file. Several editors, when asked why this was, replied that, in their judgment, these items would only have disturbed people.

The segment of the periodical press which includes political material supplements the news coverage of the daily press, but it does so in a highly selective fashion, since most politically-oriented periodicals are devoted to analyses of a limited number of major developments. There is no periodical publication that offers even a reasonably complete coverage of political news. *Der Spiegel,* which identifies itself as a news magazine, concentrates on those stories which it apparently regards as likely to arouse the widest reader-interest. As a result, it does not mention some of the most important but less lurid national and international events. On the other hand, *Der Spiegel* has developed to a high degree the art of making political news readable, and may well interest in political matters a substantial number of persons who otherwise would give little attention to them.

West German radio stations give substantial time to political news. Each station differs slightly in its approach, but the policy of the North-West German Radio, which, until its recent division into two organizations, served approximately half of the Federal Republic, offers an example. As of 1953, this network carried ten news broadcasts a day on its medium-wave program and six on its ultra-short-wave program. These newscasts took up a total broadcast time of three hours. Their content of approximately fifteen thousand words was distilled from some three hundred thousand words of incoming news.[35] In addition to newscasts, each station carries several other types of programs dealing with political matters. These include roundups of newspaper opinion, analyses by political commentators, talks by public figures, and "live" coverage of such events as Bundestag debates in Bonn.

News reporting is one of the most popular services performed by the various stations, as repeated public opinion surveys have shown. According to a study made by the North-West German Radio in 1955, for example, newscasts ranked second in popularity among the various types of programs offered by radio.

INTEREST IN VARIOUS PROGRAM TYPES INDICATED
BY NWDR LISTENERS *

Type of Program	Per Cent Indicating Interest
Variety shows; prize contests	86
News	78
Folk music	69
Radio plays	68
Dance music	67
Sport broadcasts	41
Political talks	36
Cultural talks	28
Serious, contemporary music	12

A number of efforts have been made by radio stations to promote listener interest in political matters, and to widen the ranks of the politically sophisticated in the audience. The present director of the West German Radio, in the course of a discussion at the NWDR radio school in 1952, stated that it was the function of radio to bring the listener out of his passive and indifferent attitude and lead him in the direction of reflection and action on political matters.[36] Radio Stuttgart has for several years conducted an evening program entitled "From Day to Day," the purpose of which, according to one of the personnel concerned, has been to introduce the listener to the jargon of politics and to close the gap between news and commentary.[37] Radio research has shown that the number of listeners attracted by this program compares favorably with the number attracted by the program of light music that usually follows immediately. On Fridays, however, the quiz program which comes after "From Day to Day" enjoys an audience approximately twice as large.

West German radio thus provides good, general coverage of political information, and has a very large audience for its news broadcasts. Most stations make a conscious effort to present their political information in an interesting manner, and to draw more and more listeners into the circle of those who are able to follow political developments with understanding. At the same time, the limitations of radio as a medium for providing political information are obvious. It can devote only a small

---

* Compiled from a mimeographed report entitled "Das Hörspiel und seine Hörer" and designated as "NWDR-Studie 1955." The data were obtained by oral interviews with a cross section of listeners to the North-West German Radio.

portion of the program day to news, and most of its material must be framed with a mass audience, rather than specialized users, in mind.

When viewed as a single communications system, the West German mass media offer a good elementary coverage of basic news facts for members of the general public who wish to keep abreast of principal political events; and the periodical press, in particular, contains a rich diet of commentary for the political expert. Sufficient information is made available to allow almost anyone to play a simple political role: namely, to vote in national or local elections. The information require-ments of those who take a more active part in politics are also largely satisfied; where they are not, specialized foreign publications are ob-tainable. German critics of the mass media are certainly correct in pointing out that coverage of political information is more often poor than good. But the proliferation of the communications system is so great that even the relatively small segment of the mass media which give more than cursory attention to politics provides an information service adequate to the functioning of German democracy.

Threats to Freedom of Information

If the mass media are to fulfill their part in the democratic process, they must have freedom to present as wide a spectrum of views and as full political news as possible. In particular, they must be free to report the functioning of governmental and nongovernmental institutions, so that citizens can work for whatever changes they think are necessary.

Persons familiar with the West German mass media see this freedom of information threatened from several directions. The fear that is ex-pressed most frequently is that government, by restricting sources of news and by imposing regulatory legislation, will be able gradually to turn the information media into an arm of state authority. A second threat is seen in the power of business interests to control the flow of advertising and thus to exercise economic pressure on the information media, many of which are financially weak. A third threat is the ability of interest-groups, such as trade associations, labor unions, or religious bodies to limit the freedom of press and radio to discuss certain subjects.

The attitude of the West German government to freedom of informa-tion has been ambivalent. On the one hand, nearly all leading personali-ties in the government have repeatedly expressed themselves as favoring freedom of the press. In speaking to the International Press Institute in London, for instance, Adenauer said: "I am convinced that the freedom of the press as defined in your statutes has indeed become an essential criterion of the democratic order."[38] Foreign Minister Brentano told the

International Federation of Journalists in Baden-Baden that the state needed a "truly free and independent press." [39]

On the other hand, federal agencies have repeatedly proposed measures which would give the government widespread powers to control both press and radio. These measures have never been represented as moves to limit freedom of communications, but have been advocated as helping to protect the public welfare and ensure order and decency. The four major measures of this type proposed since 1950 include a federal press law, a law to regulate radio, the establishment of a central body to co-ordinate government information, and a law for the protection of youth against pornography and trash. Only the last of these has been passed, and its administration has been subjected to numerous criticisms. For instance, one magazine was confiscated under the provisions of this law because it had printed a cheesecake picture of Jane Russell. Journalists hastened to point out, however, that it also contained a story attacking the federal government for lavish expenditures at Bonn, thus suggesting that Jane Russell may merely have offered a pretext.[40] About half a year later, a prominent representative of the book trade resigned from the central body administering the law for the protection of youth saying: "It smells suspiciously like censorship." [41]

The proposed press law was never actually submitted to the federal parliament, apparently because of the storm of protest it aroused when the text—as drafted in the Ministry of the Interior—became known. It would have given the federal government grounds to proceed against almost any newspaper which it found objectionable, since the law contained such elastic provisions as one forbidding the press to publish anything which "damaged the reputation of the Federal Republic" or "was directed against the idea of international peace." One of the publishers' associations complained bitterly that, in some respects, the proposed press law was even more restrictive than Nazi legislation, and concluded that its tendency was to bind the press to the state.[42]

A law providing for federal regulation of radio came closer to passing, but was defeated at the last minute. Two proposals for the establishment of a central information office or committee in Bonn—one in 1953 and one in 1954—were withdrawn as soon as a strong negative reaction to them became evident in the Bundestag and among the public. The opposition of both the Social Democrats and the Free Democrats played an important part in defeating these measures.[43]

The interest of the Bundestag in public information media is shown by the fact that for several years it has maintained a committee for press, radio, and film, and it is here that some of the proposals for government regulation and control have been discussed. Not all the members of this committee have shown a consistent interest in maintaining freedom of information. At one point, the committee chairman, noting that a book sharply critical of German military tradition (Walter Kirst's *0815*) was being displayed in the Bundestag bookstore, asked the bookstore management to remove the book. This brought protests not only from the Social Democratic opposition members on the committee but also from some members of the CDU. The dynamic Bavarian deputy who later on became Minister of Defense, Franz Josef Strauss, although strongly in favor of German rearmament, informed the bookstore management that in his opinion the book should remain on display, since "limitation of sale is not the way to solve an argument about a book." [44]

Review of the history of relations between the government and the media of information under the Federal Republic strongly suggests that most governmental officials, whether in the executive or the legislature, start with the assumption that it is the proper function of government to exercise a rather extensive degree of control over the content of press and radio. In many cases, however, officials who have frequent contacts with the mass media have adopted a more liberal attitude. In a brief biography of Paul Bausch, chairman of the press, radio, and film committee in the second Bundestag, a publication of the Federal Press and Information Office had this to say:

. . . previously he had been at loggerheads with a number of journalists who in his opinion had been lacking in discretion and against whose activities he had expressed himself. However, his intensified relations with the "Fourth Estate" now have led him to the conclusion that government interference with the freedom of the press must in every case be avoided. [45]

Nevertheless, the tendency of many governmental officials, including Chancellor Adenauer, is to rattle the saber of the law when some conflict between officialdom and the press or radio occurs. In castigating the statements of a news analyst of the former North-West German Radio, Adenauer said: "A station which infringes this principle of non-partisanship thereby loses its right to existence. . . ." [46] And several months later, an official governmental release, which protested the way in which sensationalist German periodicals were airing alleged scandals in European royal houses, concluded that "if necessary the federal government will resort to the law" to protect the honor of the leaders of friendly nations. [47]

In spite of governmental tendencies to encroach on freedom of information, no serious limitations have been imposed since 1949. Under existing law, however, a number of practices are possible which constitute serious annoyances to the press and which might, in the future, be expanded to throttle organs to which the government objected. These include court-ordered confiscations in connection with criminal proceedings, restriction of information at the source by governmental officials, limitations on the flow of information to West Germany from other areas, and governmental action pursuant to legislation governing official secrets.

Among these annoyances, confiscating of single issues of publications is the most severe. Just how many numbers of various publications are ordered confiscated by the courts is impossible to determine, but a month rarely goes by without at least one being reported by the trade journals. A few examples will suffice to show how far authority to confiscate can extend. In August, 1954, the Hamburg District Court suddenly ordered police in the entire Federal Republic to seize the current issue of *Der Stern,* an illustrated weekly with a circulation of about 750,000. The editors of the magazine were not told what it was to which the court objected until a day later, when it appeared that the action had been instigated by the city administration of Würzburg, which felt itself insulted by an article entitled "Bureaucracy Ruins a Citizen." The following day, the court released the issue on condition that the offending article be cut out. The police, therefore, removed it from each copy with scissors, and the subscribers received the mutilated issue.[48]

An even more egregious example was the conduct of a District Judge in Hannover-Münden. On seeing an SPD political poster, which in his opinion implied that Chancellor Adenauer had knowingly made false statements, the judge ordered the poster confiscated. Neither Dr. Adenauer nor his party had raised any objections to the poster.[49] While the judge's action was speedily reversed, it indicated the lengths to which official interference could go.

The legislation on which such confiscations are based is intended to protect individuals and groups from false statements which would have the effect of sullying their honor. Few voices are raised in Germany against the principle of this law, but the manner in which it is administered is often questioned.

A second way in which governmental authorities can restrict freedom of information is to suppress news about their activities. From time to time, various mayors and other political figures have attempted to punish papers of which they disapproved by denying reporters from these publications access to information. A number of attempts have also been made to restrict the flow of news to all media of information. Ordinarily, when restrictions of this character have been clearly unreasonable, they have been broken down by protests from press and public. Harmony between governmental authorities and the press is now the rule rather than the exception, although public officials are still much more tight-lipped than their English or American counterparts. Attempts to impose sweeping restrictions on the flow of news at the federal level have been fairly rare. For a time, the newly-established Defense Ministry offered an extremely difficult nut for newsmen to crack. Not only was the information released by the ministry at first extremely meager, but former Defense Minister Blank, when requested to hold a press conference, replied that he was too busy.[50] Since those early days, however, a somewhat more generous news flow has been established.

A third governmental restriction on freedom of information is the practice of prohibiting or making difficult the flow of certain types of information into West Germany. Soviet zone publications addressed to West German journalists, for instance, have been stopped at the border. Another restriction on incoming information was finally abandoned in the summer of 1955. Journalists had frequently protested that press photographs from abroad were taxed on entering the Federal Republic. While this tax was not high, newsmen feared that it might be raised at any time that the government wished to find a club with which to beat the press. According to new tariff regulations of June 30, 1955, however, up to three prints of each photograph can be imported free of duty.[51]

Another highly controversial restriction on freedom of information is the law governing official secrets. This law can be so interpreted as to subject to severe harassment anyone who discloses information which the government regards as secret. The most notorious case of the use of this legislation involved a highly respected economic journalist, Dr. Robert Platow, a strong supporter of the Adenauer government, who issues an economic newsletter. In 1952 Dr. Platow obtained, and published in his newsletter, information about an agreement with Israel which had not yet been officially released in Germany. Soon afterwards, the police descended on his office, turned his files upside down, seized some of his records, and threw him into jail. The press rallied to his defense, holding that he had not engaged in any activities beyond those of legitimate news-gathering, and the indictment against him was withdrawn. A so-called "Platow-Amnesty Law" was passed in the summer of 1953, but Justice Minister Dehler refused to sign it. Dr. Platow resumed his journalistic activities, but the basic principle involved was not clarified.[52]

A different type of incident, which also hinged on the principle of official secrecy, involved a journalist who demanded a new trial for an Oldenburg man who had been convicted of murdering his wife and sentenced to ten years' imprisonment. The journalist was convinced that this was a miscarriage of justice, and in 1954 published an article on the case in an illustrated magazine. A new trial was granted and the defendant was acquitted, but the Oldenburg Attorney's Office then instituted proceedings against the journalist, because he allegedly had used material from official documents.[53]

It is often said that the German government can interfere with freedom of information through its use of the secret fund which the Chancellor is granted each year for "information tasks" in Germany and abroad. This fund started at 4.5 million marks, but has grown to over ten million. Both journalists and members of the political opposition tend to show alarm at the very mention of this fund. They allege that it is used to subsidize publications favorable to the government, and sometimes hint at even more unorthodox uses.

Finally, there are some who believe that the federal government has been able to bring indirect pressure on even outstanding newspapers, sufficient not only to slant their news stories but even to influence their personnel policies. It was rumored, for instance, that the *Neue Zürcher Zeitung* had been forced to withdraw its Bonn correspondent as a result of German government demands. This rumor was denied by the Swiss paper. Another story was to the effect that Bonn had induced the *Frankfurter Allgemeine Zeitung* to dispense with the services of the well-known editor Paul Sethe, whose foreign policy views were opposed to those of the Adenauer government. Sethe was, however, immediately employed by the Hamburg newspaper *Die Welt,* indicating that even if governmental pressure had been sufficient to force him out of one paper it could not prevent him from being taken on by an even larger one.

Pressure exerted by business interests is frequently mentioned by mass media personnel as another force limiting freedom of information. Small-town newspapers, especially, are often influenced by advertisers or trade groups. A recent German dissertation has assembled some striking examples.[54] One newspaper was allegedly denied advertising by the German automobile industry because it expressed the opinion that driving was dangerous. Another was boycotted by the local merchants' association because it had suggested that some items could be bought more cheaply in a neighboring town. The writer was told a number of similar stories by editors of small-town papers.

In addition to cases which can be fairly well documented, there are innumerable rather vague allegations about the pressure of economic interests on the press. Central trade associations have reportedly rationed national advertising to various papers according to the latter's political views. Anonymous industrialists are said to have bought into this or that newspaper and to be influencing wide circles of readers by subtly slanting the contents. Among the more unusual allegations is the suggestion that some publications receive a subsidy from people who covertly buy—not one, but several—copies of each issue at the newsstands. There are, without question, some attempts to influence the press by devices such as these,[55] but it is striking that those students of the mass media who are best informed usually attach the least importance to them. It is among the less well informed that suspicion of hidden influence is greatest.*

Actually, the close attention given by the German public to any indication whatsoever that a publication or radio personality is covertly speaking for an interest-group tends to make secret attempts to acquire influence over the mass media both difficult and unrewarding. A few newspapers are generally believed to receive, or to have recently received, financial assistance from industrial circles, and hence are expected to represent substantially the views of those circles. But this subsidization is regarded as an open secret, and little if any opprobrium attaches to it. Indeed, some semi-openly subsidized papers have been among the most respected in the country for their quality and impartiality. The *Frankfurter Zeitung* in Weimar days was a case in point.

Some journalists and students of the press see business influence as a greater threat to freedom of information than government intervention. They believe that purchase of some publications, combined with the alleged covert control of others, will ultimately result in a mass communications system from which all nonbusiness viewpoints will be excluded. But such a course of development is difficult to envisage as long as there exists a reasonably extensive SPD press and a trade-union press, and as long as radio remains outside the area of business control. To obtain a position of dominance or even near-dominance over the mass media, business would have to enlist government aid to stamp out opposing viewpoints.

Some limitations on freedom of expression are imposed by groups of subscribers, who threaten to boycott a paper unless it publishes, or refrains from publishing, certain items. A journalism trade periodical has complained that this practice is becoming so widespread as seriously to inhibit local reporting. If a small paper publishes anything derogatory to "a cattle dealer, a professor, or, for that matter, a bicycle rider," then all cattle dealers, professors, and cyclists feel insulted. They threaten to can-

---

* Mountebanks have attempted to take advantage of this generalized public suspicion. For example, the publisher of a "confidential" news service advised his clients that most of the West German press had sold out to anonymous interests, the implication presumably being that one should subscribe to his news service to learn what was really going on. (Cf. *Zeitungs-Verlag*, March 1, 1955, p. 126.) One editor, wishing to turn his inability to sell advertising space into a virtue, told the writer that his paper did not accept very much advertising because it wished to protect its reputation for independence.

cel their subscriptions and agitate against the paper.[56] Even more sweeping was the action taken by a farmers' association in the Rhineland, which instructed its members to cease delivering agricultural products to the subscribers of a pro-socialist paper.[57]

Radio's legal position and administrative structure protect it from many of the pressures to which newspapers and periodicals are exposed, especially the economic pressures. On the other hand, radio is more directly exposed to political pressures. In one *Land*, for example, radio personnel reported that there was a local politician whom the local station could not afford to refuse when he requested air time. In other instances, interest-groups represented on the radio councils were said to have been able to prevent discussions of certain subjects. It is the writer's opinion, however, that such limitations have had a very small aggregate effect on radio's ability to speak freely. Up to the present time, no station has been robbed of its independence. The most severe tests of radio's freedom may be expected to come in the future. If, over a period of years, the same party controls the *Land* government in Düsseldorf and the federal government in Bonn, for example, the Cologne radio may find it difficult to avoid becoming an official mouthpiece.

On the whole, one can say with considerable confidence that, since the establishment of the Federal Republic, a relatively high degree of freedom of information has existed in Germany. While some media have been limited in their ability to discuss certain subjects, other media have been able to give attention to them. Thus, business interests can hardly succeed in influencing publications supported by trade-unions; official pressure is unlikely to intimidate an organ of the opposition; and items that are successfully excluded from the press may be carried on the radio. Few news items of any significance can be suppressed successfully.

Nevertheless, one must recognize that the forces tending to limit freedom of information are strong. It is, therefore, relevant to examine the forces that are helping to preserve the independence of the mass media.

Forces Sustaining Freedom of Information

The near-unanimity with which the mass media oppose attempts on the part of governmental authorities to limit their freedom is one safeguard of freedom of information. This solidarity among publishers and journalists is something new in Germany. During the Weimar Republic, when a substantial segment of the press was controlled by political parties, these newspapers were likely to split along party lines on any issue, while the rest of the press disregarded politics almost entirely.

Press and radio personnel also have shown that they can work to-

gether in guarding their freedoms. Numerous papers warned that freedom of the radio was endangered when the North-West German Radio
was broken up into two stations.[58] At the 1955 convention of the German Journalists' Association, a resolution was passed pledging opposition to "any attempt to restrict the independence and editorial freedom
of the radio." [59] When the government backed down in the case of Dr.
Platow, this was at least partly due to the vigorous support he had received from large segments of the press.* Similarly, when a governmental plan to create a co-ordinating committee for information became
known, the journalists' organization in the German Trade-Union Federation protested to each party fraction in the Bundestag.[60] Examples
could be multiplied. The overwhelming defeat of the proposed federal
press law is often attributed largely to the pressure of journalists and
publishers.

Even more important in preserving freedom of information is the role
of the opposition. With few exceptions, the SPD has fought every effort
by the Bonn government to pass legislation for additional controls on
press and radio. In addition, the SPD has been on the watch to detect
and nip in the bud anything that looks like an attempt by the federal
authorities to gain special influence for themselves over the content of
the press and radio. On May 21, 1954, a question submitted by the SPD
parliamentary fraction precipitated a major debate on freedom of information in the Bundestag. An SPD spokesman charged that the government was subsidizing publications which supported the regime, had
plans to set up a government information service, was bringing pressure
on the DPA news agency, and was using unethical means to influence
the dispatches of press correspondents. The SPD also protested against
the widespread practice of confiscation by court order.[61]

Government and CDU spokesmen denied nearly all these charges, and
from the debate it is difficult to determine which party had the greater
weight of the argument on its side. More important than the correctness
or incorrectness of each detail are two general points which emerged
from the debate. The first was that, except for the conservative German
Party, the smaller coalition parties half-supported the SPD. The spokesman for the Free Democratic Party, in particular, while not supporting
the SPD's charges in detail, took the opportunity to advocate greater
freedom of the mass media from government influence.

* This judgment is based on the statements of several journalists, both German and American, who were closely acquainted with the case. That the press support for Dr. Platow was
by no means unanimous, however, is shown by the statement of an experienced journalist,
H. G. von Studnitz: "The Platow case showed in a terrifying fashion that all is not well
with the solidarity, with the professional self-consciousness within the press." ("Erlaubt ist
was gefällt," *Zeitungs-Verlag*, February 29, 1952.)

The second general point was that spokesmen of all parties, including the SPD, acknowledged—either explicitly or implicitly—that the West German press was quite free at that time. The SPD saw tendencies toward limitations on this freedom, the CDU denied them, and the German Party advocated increased governmental influence on the media of information.

There are some indications that the jealousy with which the SPD guards freedom of information in Bonn arises more from its position as opposition party than from doctrinal commitments. In *Länder* where the SPD controls the machinery of government, the position tends to be reversed. In Bavaria, for instance, Christian Socialists in the state legislature have protested against efforts on the part of the SPD-led government to limit statements of *Land* officials to the press.[62] Numerous journalists have expressed the opinion that a so-called "great coalition" in Bonn, uniting Christian Democrats and Social Democrats, would present the press and radio with the greatest threat to free expression that they have faced since the beginning of the Federal Republic. Without a large and vigorous opposition party to defend them, the information media would find themselves cut off from their most important source of support.

A third major force in the preservation of freedom of information is the division of authority between federal and state government. Efforts of the Bonn government to bring about a central jurisdiction over radio, for instance, have been opposed by the *Land* authorities, who now enjoy appreciable influence over their local stations even if they do not control them. The fact that the same party is unlikely to hold the reins of power in Bonn and in all the state capitals at the same time tends to rule out any nationwide regimentation of press and radio.

Two sources from which one might expect powerful support for freedom of information are, in fact, relatively unimportant at present. One is public opinion, and the other is constitutional law.

In 1953, an American professor of journalism, who had just returned from studying the press in Germany, concluded: "No substantial segment of the public can be counted upon to identify with the press in case of a fight between the press and the government." This judgment is supported by the opinion of numerous German journalists and publishers, who feel that the traditional public respect accorded governmental authority is still so strong that little support from the masses could be expected if ever the state sought to coerce the information media.[63] A professional public opinion researcher observed that respondents frequently considered radio more reliable than the newspaper press because radio received more governmental supervision.

One reason, although by no means the only one, that the press does not enjoy more public support is probably that most newspapers and journals do not really trust the public. Editors with whom the author talked mentioned repeatedly various categories of news which, for one reason or another, they withheld from the public. The publisher of one of West Germany's most respected dailies said that there was a local politician whose name was never allowed in the columns of his paper, because this man was a demagogue who thrived on publicity. Personnel on the better newspapers revealed an attitude of something approaching condescension toward their readers, a lack of respect for public tastes, a feeling that the public had to be protected and improved.

Those publishers who were attempting to cater to public tastes felt that this was something to apologize for. The most striking exception to this generalization is *Der Spiegel,* which makes no apologies for giving the masses what they want. Perhaps this is one reason that *Der Spiegel,* when it is exposed to governmental or other pressure, can count on appreciable public support (although not, as a rule, from the more highly educated).

An unwillingness to allow disputes to be settled in the realm of public opinion, and a strong tendency to carry them into court, can be observed on the part of nearly all publications. For instance, when an irate reader called up a local newspaper reporter and hurled a string of insults at him, the reporter, instead of considering this part of the day's work, went to court and won a judgment of 100 marks.[64]

Similarly, when a religious publication called one of the illustrated weekly journals a "swamp flower," the pictorial magazine went to court.[65] Such examples could be multiplied almost indefinitely. A great many matters which might be left to the judgment of individual readers, or to public opinion as a whole, are taken to the courts by the publishers themselves. In doing so, the latter recognize the competence of the judiciary to function as a public conscience, and thereby weaken their own public support in any conflict with state authority.

This is not to say that there is no public support for a free press. There certainly are those who would defend it to the end, and it is the writer's impression that their number is growing. In addition, more and more voices of those who are professionally concerned with the media of information are being raised in favor of a comprehensive interpretation of press freedom. Professor Dovifat recently formulated this point of view in the publishers' trade journal: "Freedom of the press is something so priceless—this we know after twelve difficult years—that for it we must accept freedom of bad taste, freedom of stupidity, and freedom of meanness." [66] This formulation is entirely incompatible with the principles of an authoritarian, paternalistic state and tends, in the last analysis, to make the public rather than the government the judge of what information may or may not be disseminated.

Nevertheless, it is a minority formulation, and freedom of the press and radio in West Germany still rests on a narrow popular base. The conception that the primary function of the mass media is to improve the population culturally rather than to perform a political role is so strongly held by the better-educated West Germans that a publication which offends against the canons of good taste is likely to forfeit the support of those elements which otherwise are strong defenders of press freedom.*

The other somewhat shaky support for a free press is constitutional law. The Basic Law of the Federal Republic, which serves as a constitution, explicitly recognizes the freedom of press and radio—although without defining it—and it forbids censorship.[67] The Basic Law also recognizes the right of the public to have access to political information. The constitution provides, however, that freedom of the press may be limited by "general law," ** and that, under certain conditions, constitutional protection for the press may be withdrawn by the Federal Constitutional Court. Freedom of the press is, therefore, assured only as long as the federal legislature does not pass any general laws abridging it, and as long as the interpretations of the Constitutional Court are favorable to the press. It is true that, according to the constitution, a basic right such as freedom of the press can never "be affected in its basic content," but this protective clause is in itself subject to interpretation. An American student of press freedom in West Germany concludes that "at bottom, the basic rights of the Bonn republic rest on as fragile a basis as those of its predecessor." [68] In general, German legal experts take a somewhat more optimistic view.[69]

* One of West Germany's most distinguished students of the press, Professor Walter Hagemann of the University of Münster, has suggested that freedom of information be guaranteed in areas and on subjects "which actually affect and influence public affairs," but that such guarantees should not be extended to publicity about private affairs serving only curiosity and the desire for sensationalism, and appealing to the lower instincts of the readers. ("Abhilfe gegen Missbrauch der Pressefreiheit," *Zeitschrift für Politik,* Heft 3, 1956.)

In an effort to avoid the official controls which the excesses of the sensationalist press would almost inevitably bring down on the press as a whole, publishers and journalists have recently formed a private Press Council, through which the profession itself will attempt to check journalistic irresponsibility. It is too early to predict how successful this body will be. This approach is in accord with one advocated by Professor Hagemann in a recent book (*Dankt die Presse ab?* Munich, 1957), in which he concludes that the best way to improve the press is not to subject it to restrictive legislation but to eliminate instances in which freedom is misused.

** A "general law" is one which regulates a total field of activity and does not apply solely to an individual case. Neither can a "general law" inhibit the "purely intellectual impact" (*rein geistige Wirkung*) of expressions of opinion.

If constitutional guarantees for freedom of information in the Bonn constitution are not absolutely firm, it must not be assumed that the framers of the Basic Law were opposed to the principle of such freedom. Rather, they apparently sought to secure freedom of the press at the same time that they tried to guard against the destructive influences which an irresponsible and demagogic press might exert on the new democracy. Even now there are signs that, as the mass media prove themselves responsible institutions, a body of legal interpretation may grow up to anchor the freedom of information more securely.[70]

Mass Media and the Status Quo

The German mass media constitute a force tending to preserve the *status quo* rather than a force for change. The most influential press and radio personnel are committed to the prevailing political and economic order; and both the political and nonpolitical content of the mass media, viewed as a whole, support the existence of things as they are.

As we have seen, the percentage of total mass media output devoted to political matters is small. Responding to what they find to be the public demand, publishers (and to a lesser extent radio executives) devote the lion's share of their space or time to material designed to entertain; to help people improve themselves culturally, financially, or socially; or to provide information necessary for the operation of the West German economic system. The principal social function of the mass media seems to be to help people to live in and enjoy the prosperous postwar German society.

In the political realm also, the mass media tend to preserve the existing order. This does not mean that they are devoted to maintaining any particular party in power. More of them lean toward the political right than toward the left, it is true, but there is no lack of channels through which any political group (except very small minorities at the extreme right and left) can reach the public. The press and radio support the prevailing constitutional system by providing communication facilities which are necessary for its efficient operation. These facilities not only enable the leaders of the state to reach the people, but also facilitate the orderly replacement of one party by another in government.

The very limitations of the mass media—including the political colorlessness of many publications and radio broadcasts, and the inability of most political writers to present material in a manner comprehensible and interesting to more than a small minority—tend to support the present political order in West Germany. Active participation in German politics is, as a rule, reserved for a fairly well-educated minority, while the political role of the masses is limited. Although press and radio have made some efforts to involve a broader sector of the population more deeply in political affairs, these efforts have not been strenuous. Whenever a publication does involve the masses directly in politics (usually through sensationalism), one hears protests that this is a misuse of the power of the press. In general, the mass media do little to change the existing situation whereby political decisions are made by the group that has traditionally made them.

The men who control the mass media recognize that their own interests are best served by the present constitutional order. As Hans A. Kluthe, chairman of the Association of German Magazine Publishers, stated at the association's annual meeting in 1954,

The Association of German Magazine Publishers is, of course, absolutely neutral as far as the political parties are concerned. But we clearly and unequivocally declare our devotion to democracy, because we can thrive only in the atmosphere of freedom, which is guaranteed solely by this form of government. . . .[71]

Among press and radio personnel one can identify only a tiny minority which is interested in changing the form of government, and these extremists exercise an insignificant influence. There is a larger group of those who appear to have no political sympathies at all and to be concerned only with profits, but even they are far from being in the majority. Though mass media personnel may, in their professional activity, make concessions to popular preferences and avoid political discussions, in their personal opinions they appear to be among the strongest supporters of German democracy.

The West German mass media, as they now exist, are an expression of general satisfaction with the present state of affairs. If popular discontent with the *status quo* were to grow during the coming years, this discontent would likewise be reflected in the mass media, but it could scarcely be attributed to their editorial policies.

EIGHT

Trends in West German Public Opinion, 1946–1956

W. Phillips Davison

This paper seeks to provide a brief, nontechnical survey of information obtained by opinion polls in West Germany during the postwar period in order to shed light on three questions: How firmly is democracy established in Germany? With what political and economic problems are West Germans most concerned? What is the relative strength of the principal political parties in West Germany?

There are four principal sources of quantitative information on West German public opinion during the period 1946-1956. U.S. Military Government started polling civilians in the U.S. zone shortly after World War II, and expanded these activities in 1949 to cover all of West Germany. When Military Government was terminated later in 1949, the surveys were continued by the Office of the U.S. High Commissioner. Many of the results of these surveys have been made public.[1]

Three excellent domestic centers of opinion research developed in West Germany during the time that the American surveys were taking place. The Institute for Market and Opinion Research (EMNID) was established in Bielefeld shortly after the war, and has since published a weekly bulletin (*EMNID Informationen*) with increasingly comprehensive reports on political and economic opinion. Erich Peter Neumann and Elisabeth Noelle, a talented husband-wife team, founded the *Institut für Demoskopie* in Allensbach at about the same time, and have published results of their public opinion research extending as far back as 1947.[2] The third major center, *Deutsches Institut für Volksumfragen* (DIVO), is located in Frankfurt and makes some of its results available in the form of periodic press releases. There are at least fourteen additional polling organizations in the Federal Republic, but those are concerned primarily with specialized subjects or with limited geographical areas.[3]

Fragmentary information on German public opinion is also available from a number of other sources, including government publications, general-circulation magazines, advertising copy, and occasional specialized studies.[4] During the early postwar period, British Military Government conducted opinion surveys in North and West Germany, but, to the best of the author's knowledge, only small portions of that research have ever been published.

The observations about German public opinion made in the present paper are based almost entirely on work done by the former U.S. opinion research agencies, EMNID, the *Institut für Demoskopie,* and DIVO, and the writer is thus heavily indebted to the work of those organizations.

Nearly all the subjects discussed have been explored independently by two or more research groups, and while there are inevitably slight differences in the precise figures obtained by the different polls, substantial agreement is the rule rather than the exception. Consequently, proportions are usually cited below in gross terms—as thirds, quarters, or tenths—rather than as percentages.* This makes it possible to concentrate on larger shifts in opinion rather than on smaller variations which may be the result of differences in sampling techniques or wording of questions.

A Statistical Picture of the West German Population [5]

What is the composition of the West German public, miniature replicas of which are repeatedly questioned by public-opinion-poll interviewers? ** First of all, it is a population heavily overweighted with women and with older people. According to the 1950 census, there were 117 women for every 100 men in the population, and almost exactly half of the population was over forty-five years of age.

* In reading opinion poll results it should be kept in mind that some people are usually undecided on any given issue. Therefore the proportions of those answering "yes" to a question and those answering "no" rarely add up to 100 per cent. It is, for example, quite common to find one-third "for," one-third "against," and one-third undecided or refusing to answer. Except in cases where the size of the undecided group of respondents is particularly relevant to the point at issue, they have been omitted from consideration below in the interest of brevity.

** More precisely, it is a replica of the adult population, usually defined as those over eighteen, which is questioned by opinion pollers.

Of the almost fifty million persons living in West Germany (*not* including West Berlin) in 1954, about eleven million were expellees or refugees from East Germany or Eastern Europe.* Many of these eventually crowded into the cities of West Germany after the war, as did many people who had been born in the West German countryside. Thus, from 1946 to 1952, towns under 5,000 actually lost population, in spite of the heavy influx of refugees, while cities of more than 100,000 increased in size by nearly 35 per cent.

As the movement to the cities would suggest, industry provides occupation for a large proportion of the population. Almost half of all West Germans gainfully employed are skilled or unskilled industrial workers. The next-largest group is composed of white-collar workers, who make up approximately 15 per cent of the labor force. Independent farmers and small businessmen, each with some 12 per cent, and farm laborers and government officials, each with about 5 per cent, make up the other principal categories. Practitioners of the free professions account for only about 1 or 2 per cent of the working population. In addition to those who are engaged in some kind of gainful work—about 85 per cent of the total adult population if one includes their families—some 15 per cent are retired, students, or unemployed.

West Germany is dominated by the middle-income groups. Only about 10 per cent of the households have incomes below 150 DM a month, but less than a quarter have incomes of more than 500 DM a month. Median household income falls at about 400 marks. Even though the buying power of the mark is almost equal to that of the dollar in respect to personal services, food, and shelter, it is far below the dollar when it comes to clothes and most other commodities. The average West German can afford necessities but relatively few luxuries. About one family in ten has an automobile, and one in eight has an electric refrigerator. Nearly half the households have vacuum cleaners.

Slightly more than 50 per cent of the inhabitants of the Federal Republic are Protestants. About 45 per cent are Roman Catholic, and the remainder are divided up among smaller religious groups or profess no religion.

Nearly all West German adults have had some schooling, and about 15 per cent have reached the *Abitur,* which corresponds roughly to completion of junior college in the United States.

* Sources differ widely on the number of expellees and refugees in West Germany. Figures vary according to what definitions of "refugee" and "expellee" were used; they depend further on whether or not the compilers included the city of Berlin, the persons who have not received official permission to reside in West Germany, etc. The figure given here, taken from the official *Statistisches Jahrbuch für die Bundesrepublik Deutschland,* 1955, p. 21, is a conservative one. Some sources give a figure as high as sixteen million.

Chief Concerns of the Population

Ever since U.S. Military Government started systematic polling operations in 1946, interviewers have been asking the West Germans to name their principal problems: their main hopes and fears. In addition, respondents were sometimes asked to mention what they thought were the chief problems facing the German government.

During most of the postwar period, people tended to mention one or more of the following: national or personal economic matters, the reunification of Germany, Germany's orientation in the East-West struggle, restoration of Germany's sovereignty and status as a great power, and rearmament. The order of priority accorded each of these problem areas changed from time to time during the period 1946–1956, and also varied somewhat depending on the technical procedures used in any given poll: whether "open" questions were asked, or whether respondents were given a list of alternatives; whether people were requested to name the most important problem facing the "federal government," or whether they were asked to mention what they thought was the most important question facing "West Germany"; and so on. Nevertheless, all the polls agree on the over-all picture.

During the first year following the war it was quite obvious which problem was bothering West Germans most. They couldn't get enough to eat. When U.S. Military Goverment tried to ascertain the extent of the hunger in May, 1946, by asking people whether they were getting enough food to do their work efficiently, almost 90 per cent said that they were not. The proportion of respondents who complained about insufficient nourishment declined steadily after that, however, and by November, 1949, it was only 15 per cent. EMNID obtained similar results when it asked people whether they were most in need of improvement in their food, clothing, or shelter. Until 1949, more than half the respondents mentioned food; but, after that, concern with food diminished, and clothing and shelter were mentioned more frequently.

Even after the food problem was solved for the overwhelming majority, personal economic concerns quite naturally remained in the forefront of attention, although the nature of these concerns tended to vary over the years. In 1950, for instance, more people were worried about unemployment than about any other economic issue, and housing came next. In 1956, worry about unemployment had almost vanished, and housing was mentioned by only half as many respondents as in 1950. Now people were more concerned about high taxes, low pensions, and the problem of controlling price increases.

From 1946 to 1956, the proportion of West Germans who said that their living conditions had improved in the recent past, or who expressed satisfaction with the economic progress the country was making, increased steadily. By 1954, the *Institut für Demoskopie* found that three out of ten people said that they were better off than they had been the previous year, and five out of ten said there was no difference. In the following year, EMNID interviewers reported that well over half the people they had questioned said they were better off than they had been before the war, or that they were just as well off. Only a third thought they were worse off.

The picture varied with each population group. Most satisfied with their lot in 1955 were the businessmen and members of the free professions. Least satisfied were the pensioners and agricultural workers. Two-thirds of the pensioners reported that their living standard was lower than it had been before the war. In general, one receives the impression that most West Germans were satisfied with the economic progress the country was making—at least until late in 1955 or early in 1956, when a number of indicators of dissatisfaction began to be visible.

Satisfaction with the economic progress of the country as a whole does not mean that people as individuals are satisfied with the income which they personally are receiving. Their attitude toward their personal economic situation seems to depend much more on what they think they ought to be receiving and what they are able to do with their money. For instance, after the 1948 currency reform had brought a sudden economic upsurge to West Germany, many more people said that their incomes were not sufficient to cover necessary expenses than had said so during the lean days before currency reform. According to U.S. High Commission researchers, the reason was that more goods were on sale and people had higher standards of "necessary expense."

After this drop in satisfaction with *personal* income in 1948, the proportion of those who felt that their own economic situation was improving increased steadily, although with numerous fluctuations, until about 1955. During 1956, however, there were indications that more and more people did not feel that they were receiving their proper share of the national product.

EMNID has asked respondents periodically whether they were getting more, less, or just the basic minimum of income required to run their households. During 1956 the proportion saying "more" decreased to a point where it was about the same size as the proportion saying "less" (slightly over 25 per cent in each case). The proportion saying "just enough" increased proportionately. The trend toward *more* satisfaction with one's personal economic situation thus appears to have halted, at least for the time being. DIVO has found that the proportion of those who say they are satisfied with their own economic situation increased from less than half the population in 1951 to almost 80 per cent at the end of 1954. But then the curve of subjective economic satisfaction began to level off, and even declined slightly during 1956.

The reasons for this decline in satisfaction are certainly complex. But they include at least two developments. One is that many people's estimates of the amount of income they require increased more rapidly than the amount they actually took in. EMNID found that the average estimation of minimum income requirements per household increased from 365 marks in 1954 to 442 marks in 1956. The other reason is that prices also rose during the period in question, although not nearly so rapidly as estimations of minimum income requirements. If prices for 1950 are taken as a base, the price index for the normal household rose only from 107 in January, 1954, to 117 in December, 1955.

The way in which a dichotomy has grown up between attitudes toward the economy as a whole and attitudes toward one's own share in it is shown by another question EMNID asked during 1956. Respondents were requested to indicate areas in which developments had been especially favorable since the war, and those in which they had been especially unfavorable. As areas which had developed favorably, respondents mentioned industry, export, reconstruction, and the economy as a whole. As areas which had developed unfavorably, respondents tended to name living standards, prices, wages, and the social order in general.

Germany between East and West

The partition of Germany and her position between East and West are mentioned repeatedly by respondents as the chief political problems facing both the government and themselves as individuals. Nearly all Germans would like to see their country reunited, yet they fear the Soviet Union and would oppose any concession that would be likely to increase communism in West Germany.

Ever since the end of the war, when asked to choose between the two power blocs, respondents have indicated a preference for the West. The proportions expressing this preference have been rather stable, but the pro-Western views appear to be based more on fear of the Soviet Union than on love for the democracies. For instance, DIVO asked respondents in 1951 which country was more often right in East-West disputes, America or Russia. Over half said that they thought America was in the right, and only 3 per cent chose Russia; but over one-third said both countries were equally in the right, or else expressed no opinion. Subsequent surveys have produced similar results, and suggest that, as long as the cold war lasts, West Germans will prefer to side with the West.

By the same token, ever since 1948 a majority of respondents has almost always opposed withdrawal of Western military forces from Germany (unless some other military guarantee were given), because of fear of the Soviets. People who express these views have mentioned that the Bolshevization of all Germany would follow withdrawal, or that communism would be strengthened, or that the Russians can not be trusted. In 1952, when the *Institut für Demoskopie* asked respondents whether they felt threatened by the Russians, two-thirds said they did feel threatened, and only 15 per cent said they did not. Three-quarters of the respondents opposed cutting Germany loose from the Western powers and concluding a security pact with the Russians. Following the death of Stalin in 1953, and the more friendly approaches to West Germany by the Soviets, fear of Russia diminished slightly, but most people never abandoned their deep-seated distrust.

At the same time that fear and distrust of the Soviet Union dominated opinion on the East-West struggle, a popular majority has (at least for the last few years) been willing to trade with the East. People apparently do not feel that economic relationships with the Soviet Union and its satellites carry a danger of political domination.

Although fear of Russia and communism has remained, West German fears of war have gradually been quieted. From 1946 to 1949, approximately one-half of the population consistently expected the outbreak of another world war within ten years. Fears surged even higher at the outbreak of the Korean conflict, but diminished steadily from that point on until temporarily revived again by the Hungarian and Suez crises. In 1956, prior to those crises, only one West German in twenty thought that a war was probable in the near future, although a third thought it was "possible."

Yet there remains a deep-seated fear of war, and of what it would mean for each individual if it came. Almost two-thirds of the West Germans think that, if war came, their area of residence would be threatened. One in ten mentions atomic war as something about which he is most worried. This proportion may not seem high, but it is just as large as the percentage of those who are most worried by the prospect of sickness and accidents, or about future uncertainty and death. Atomic war has taken its place as one of the great causes of human apprehension. It occasions far more worry than the prospect of poverty, inflation, storm, or flood.

Until 1955 or 1956, West Germans were fairly certain that, if a world war came, the Western powers would win it in the end. Now they are not so sure. From 1946 to 1948 a large majority was confident that the United States was stronger than the Soviet Union, but starting in 1949 the proportion saying that both nations were of approximately equal strength grew rapidly. At the present time, about two-fifths have adopted that point of view, as opposed to approximately one-third who still think that the United States is stronger and one-quarter who think Russia is now ahead.

Fear of atomic war makes people want to avoid involvement in the East-West struggle, while fear of Russia tends to make them seek safety in close association with the West. Since the beginning of the West German state, popular opinion has been divided on which is the preferable course. In 1950 U.S.-sponsored surveys found the division of opinion was five to four in favor of siding with the West. By 1956 EMNID found that over half of their respondents preferred a policy of neutrality in the East-West struggle, as opposed to slightly over a third who favored identification with the West. An increase in neutralism was particularly strong from 1955 to 1956, and could be noted in every major population group except agricultural labor, which became more pro-Western. DIVO, using a question which avoided the word "neutrality," found a considerably higher proportion of respondents in favor of siding with the West, although from 1953 to 1956 those in favor of "not taking sides" increased from about two in ten to about three in ten. Early in 1957—probably as a result of Soviet intervention in Hungary—the size of this group fell back to about two in ten.*

To say that many people favor neutralism or "not taking sides," however, is to oversimplify the story. Opinion researchers have noted that, when respondents talk about neutrality, they usually mean neutrality which is guaranteed by both sides. If people are asked to choose between a neutral Germany guaranteed only by Russia and a Germany in association with the West, a majority chooses association with the West. Asked why they prefer this alternative, people tend to say: "Russia can't be trusted," or "I am opposed to communism." No research organization has been able to find more than 1 or 2 per cent of any West German cross section in favor of siding with the East.

Nationalism and European Union

The issue of a strong national state versus a Germany which is a part of a European union cuts across the question of neutralism versus association with the West. That is, a strong national state can either follow a policy of neutrality or maintain the Western alliance. By the same token, a united Europe can function either as a third force or as a part of a larger

---

* In its release of March 1, 1957, DIVO explained that it intentionally avoided the word "neutrality" in its question because many people identified "neutrality" with "independence."

alliance which includes the United States. Poll questions on sentiment for and against a united Europe do not, therefore, throw as much light on sentiments in the East-West struggle as they do on the character and degree of nationalism in West Germany.

All the polling organizations which have asked for a statement of preferences on this subject have found a powerful sentiment in favor of European union, although not always a majority sentiment. U.S.-sponsored polls from 1946 to 1949 found that, on the average, six out of ten respondents supported the idea of European union; nearly all of the rest said they had no opinion on the subject. When German survey organizations, starting in 1949, asked people whether they preferred an independent national state or a European union, the proportions of people favoring each alternative tended to be about the same (approximately 40 per cent on each side, with 20 per cent undecided). In 1950 and 1951, however, presumably because of the influence of the Korean war, the proportion of persons favoring an independent national state declined sharply, with a proportionate increase in those favoring European union. By 1956 (but prior to the Hungary and Suez crises), the advocates of a national state had regained some of their lost ground, and the proportions of respondents favoring each of the alternatives was again about equal. It is significant, however, that in 1956 only about one person in twenty had no opinion on the subject. That is a very low proportion, and it is usually regarded by opinion researchers as indicating that most members of the population have at least some information on the subject and that their opinions are relatively stable.

Extreme nationalism has little currency in the Germany of today. When people are asked about the likelihood that Germany will again achieve her prewar power, most of them are inclined to be skeptical. However, between a third and a half do believe that Germany will take its place as *one* of the stronger powers in Western Europe, and a majority of respondents say they would *like* to see Germany play a more active role in West European affairs. When asked how Germany is to achieve such a position, most people say that it should be won through hard work or through co-operation with other countries; very few mention armed strength.

It is not necessary to cite public opinion polls to show that extreme nationalism has found little support in postwar Germany. The election results speak fairly clearly on that question. On a national basis, extreme right-wing parties have never received as much as 5 per cent of the vote. Even if one defines the right wing very broadly, so as to include the German Party and part of the Free Democratic Party, the proportion of voters involved is still not more than 15 per cent. Communism has attracted even less support than the extreme right wing. Communist candidates received slightly over 2 per cent of the vote in the 1953 elections, and the Communist Party rarely is given as a political preference by more than 1 per cent of respondents in opinion polls.

Reunification

More than nine out of ten West Germans are in favor of the reunification of their country, but relatively few are willing to sacrifice their form of government, their economic system, their security, or their peaceful existence in order to attain it. Most people are willing to pay *some* price in order to achieve reunification, but few are willing to pay what they feel is an exorbitant price.

One attitude toward reunification which has been prominently displayed ever since 1946 is that every peaceful avenue of achieving it ought to be explored. A majority has consistently been in favor of negotiating with the Soviets or with the East German government about reunification even if, at the same time, they expressed the belief that no substantial prospect of achieving a satisfactory agreement was in sight. When interviewers have asked respondents why they support this point of view, the most common answers have been: "You can't make any progress if you don't try," and "Perhaps the Russians will change their attitude." It is possible that attitudes on this question changed during 1956 but, unfortunately, recent information is not available. There had been no substantial change through 1955.

While approving negotiation, most people are opposed to making basic concessions in order to achieve reunification. Again and again, substantial numbers of respondents (usually about 75 per cent of those giving an opinion) say that they would oppose reunification if it meant taking the communist leaders of the East German government into an all-German cabinet, or even if it meant that communism would win a substantial influence in West Germany. Even larger majorities oppose leaving the East German economic system as it is in the event of reunification. The land, in particular, should be given back to its former owners, they feel. These attitudes, expressed in 1953 and 1954, appear to resemble those of an earlier period. In 1948 and 1949, when U.S. Military Government–sponsored polls asked U.S. zone Germans which was more important—to check the spread of communism or to unite Germany—the proportions in both years were about the same: 70 per cent said "check communism," 25 per cent said "unite Germany," and 5 per cent had no opinion.

Just as security should not be compromised to achieve reunification, so should Germany not seek unification at the price of renouncing her Eastern territories; these include Silesia, East Prussia, and the other areas which were part of Germany in 1939, but were placed under Polish administration or incorporated into the Soviet Union after the war. If the Soviet Union were to support German reunification on condition that Germany renounce her claim to these Eastern territories, the offer—according to polls during 1949-1953—would probably be rejected by a substantial majority of West Germans. Some observers feel that popular willingness to renounce the Eastern territories in exchange for reunification grew during 1955 and 1956, but the author was unable to find poll results sufficiently recent to confirm or deny this impression.

One should not conclude that the West Germans are not anxious for reunification or that they are not willing to pay a substantial price for it. The only thing they ask is that the price be within reason and not compromise the very base of their current prosperity and freedom. In 1953 the *Institut für Demoskopie* asked respondents whether they would be in favor of paying three billion marks to the Soviets if that would lead to reunification. Substantially more than half of the respondents who had an opinion said they would support payment of the sum, which was equal to about 15 per cent of the 1953 federal budget, even though payment would mean a substantial rise in taxes.

Another way of gauging attitudes in favor of reunification is to compare them with sentiments on other issues. Many West Germans are for some kind of European union. When they are asked, however, whether they consider European union or German reunification more urgent, substantial majorities say that reunification is the more urgent. In 1956 approximately three-quarters of all respondents agreed on the greater urgency of reunification.

Two further aspects of attitudes toward reunification should be noted. One is that people are confident that reunification is inevitable. The other is that the relative importance attached to reunification appears to be growing.

Hopefulness about reunification has existed almost from the end of World War II. Interviewers found in 1948 and 1949 that about two-thirds of the respondents in the U.S. zone of Germany thought that there would once again be a unified government for all Germany. In 1952 a substantial majority of those with an opinion believed that peaceful reunification would take place within a few years. Subsequent polls have revealed similar views.

The degree of popular interest in reunification has been rising steadily since 1949. The precise proportion of the population which cites unification as the "most important issue facing the West German government," or as "the question with which Germans should be most concerned," varies according to the way the question is asked and the answers are tabulated, but all polls agree that interest is rising. Some surveys even indicate that interest in reunification has outstripped that in economic improvement. A DIVO survey toward the end of 1956 showed that reunification, price stabilization, and improvement of old-age care were each mentioned by a quarter of the respondents as "the most pressing problem of the Federal Government." An EMNID survey early in 1957 found a somewhat higher proportion mentioning reunification as the government's most pressing problem, while fewer people than in 1956 referred to economic problems.

The Lost Territories

West German attitudes toward the "lost territories" are similar in many ways to their attitudes about reunification. When they speak of lost territories, incidentally, many people include not only Silesia, East Prussia, and the other Eastern portions of 1939 Germany, but also Danzig, the Sudetenland, and (until the recent agreement with France) the Saar.

Most West Germans definitely expect that the lost territories will some day be a part of Germany again, but they are vague about the date, and they are not in favor of going to war to regain them. In 1949 nearly half the respondents in the U.S. zone said Silesia and East Prussia would have to be returned eventually "even if this could be accomplished only by war," but more recent polls have indicated that only about one of every ten West Germans favors going to war for this purpose, although most people say they would reserve the right to use force in the future if all other means failed.

At the present time, a large majority of Germans favor the use of all instruments of negotiation and all other peaceful means to recover the lost territories. Presumably, the fact that the Saar was returned to Germany through negotiation (and substantial economic concessions to France) will further swell the proportion of those favoring the peaceful approach to the recovery of the Eastern territories.

Confidence that the lost territories will eventually be regained is perhaps one reason that West Germans are willing to negotiate for them patiently, and that they are opposed to major concessions to communism or the Soviet Union as the price for their recovery. A vast majority is confident of the justice of Germany's legal claims to these territories which were included in her 1939 boundaries, and nearly half add that Germany has a legal claim to the Sudetenland.

As long as East and West Germany remain separated, however, discussion of the lost territories has a certain unreality, and expressions of popular opinion on the subject at the present time can scarcely be taken as indications of what popular reactions would be if the return of Germany's Eastern lands were imminent.

Rearmament

Rearmament is the final issue which respondents usually mention as among the chief concerns of both the individual and the government of West Germany. It does not compare in urgency with reunification and economic questions, however. Several polls indicate that rearmament has been considered a pressing issue by about one respondent in ten ever since 1951. A recent DIVO survey found that 12 per cent of one sample mentioned rearmament as "one of the most pressing problems of the Federal Government," but only 2 per cent said that it was *the* most pressing.

The proportion of respondents in favor of a German defense force has increased markedly since 1950, when somewhat fewer than half of those queried expressed themselves in favor of it. By 1956, nearly two-thirds of all respondents indicated that they believed Germany needed a defense establishment, and a quarter were opposed. It is striking, however, that those opposed to a German defense establishment have not appreciably decreased in number during the last few years. About a quarter of the population was opposed in 1950 and 1951, and about a quarter is still opposed. The increase in the number favoring a defense force has come primarily from the ranks of those who were previously undecided.

While a substantial majority of Germans now approve rearmament, opinion is more evenly split on the question of a professional army composed of volunteers as opposed to an army based on universal military service. Most respondents favor a professional army. In May, 1956, EMNID reported that 49 per cent of its respondents were in favor of a volunteer army of professionals, and 39 per cent were for universal military service, with 12 per cent undecided. That division of opinion has been substantially the same since 1949. The 1956 Bundestag decision in favor of universal military service was an unpopular one at the time it was made.

The proportion of West Germans who would *like* to become soldiers, or, in the case of women, who would like to see their husbands or sons become soldiers, is very small. Only 5 to 10 per cent of West Germans would accept military service "gladly." About another 25 per cent would accept it as a necessary duty, and almost all the rest would serve only reluctantly or not at all. The sentiments of young men under thirty do not diverge appreciably from the national average. EMNID surveys early in 1957, following the start of conscription, found that opposition to service had diminished somewhat, although slightly more than half of the male respondents still said they would serve very reluctantly or not at all.

Popular Interest in Politics

In 1950 about one out of twenty West Germans mentioned politics as a field of particular interest, according to the *Institut für Demoskopie*. That contrasted with one out of five interested in sports, and about one out of six interested in music and singing. As of 1954, about a third of the adult population had at one time or another attended a political meeting. In the previous year, over half the population had said that they discussed politics frequently or occasionally, although the remainder discussed political matters "scarcely ever." It may be significant that a substantial majority of men and nearly half of the women said that they would prefer a spouse who was *not* interested in politics. On the other hand, a quarter of the men and a third of the women expressed a preference for a partner who was willing to work on behalf of a party or a trade-union.

Whether these bits of information indicate a relatively great or an abnormally low interest in politics is difficult to say.* It is possible, nevertheless, to make two statements with a fair degree of certainty. One is that the German electorate is gradually becoming better informed about politics. The other is that, as a group, German women are far less interested in politics than the men are.

In 1949 a report of the U.S. High Commissioner concluded, on the basis of opinion polls, that U.S. zone Germans lacked confidence in their own ability to manage their affairs in a democratic way. Less than two-fifths of the population claimed to have any interest in politics, and a majority of respondents in each survey since 1946 had claimed to be insufficiently informed on political matters. That this represented apathy rather than intellectual modesty was indicated by the fact that most of those who said that they were insufficiently informed also said that they had no wish for any more information.

The situation started to change shortly after the establishment of a federal government in Bonn. By the end of 1949, surveys conducted

* The difficulty lies in establishing the level of interest in political matters one should expect in a democracy. While the author is not aware of directly comparable data from other countries, a number of studies made in the United States have found a degree of interest in politics roughly similar to that in West Germany. Cf. Paul F. Lazarsfeld *et al.*, *The People's Choice*, Columbia University Press, New York, 1948, p. 44; also Martin Kriesberg, "Dark Areas of Ignorance," in Lester Markel (ed.), *Public Opinion and Foreign Policy*, Council on Foreign Relations, Inc., New York, 1949.

by the office of the U.S. High Commissioner found that the proportion of those claiming not to know enough about politics had dropped ten percentage points. Factual questions about the Bundestag and the federal government as a whole, asked by the *Institut für Demoskopie* and EMNID, have shown a fairly consistent (although not a rapid) shift in the direction of better information. For instance, in 1951 only slightly more than a third of West Germans knew that each election district had a representative in the Bundestag; by 1954, half of them knew it.

A related phenomenon can be observed when attitudes toward politics revealed by early U.S. Military Government surveys are compared with those reflected by recent polls. In 1946 a very large majority of West Germans consistently indicated that they wished to have as little as possible to do with politics. By contrast, a sentence-completion test administered by DIVO in 1956 showed a relatively favorable attitude toward politics.

The differences between the sexes on the subject of politics are striking. In a 1952 poll, over half the men told the *Institut für Demoskopie* that they were interested in politics, while fewer than a fifth of the women said they were interested. This difference shows up in almost every survey on political matters; two-thirds to three-quarters of the respondents who say "don't know," or who have no opinion, are women. As we have seen, the adult population of West Germany is heavily overweighted with women at the present time. Women comprise well over half of the electorate; and consequently the extent of political apathy among women has been worrisome to those who are concerned with the functioning of democracy in Germany.

Democracy versus Authoritarianism

Since the establishment of the West German state, and even before, numerous questions have been raised about the future of democracy in Germany. The polls can not answer any of these questions completely, but they shed light on several of them.

One can say with confidence that there has been a slow but steady growth of sentiment in favor of democracy in Germany. Surveys do not reveal how strongly-rooted these prodemocratic attitudes are. On several occasions in 1948 and 1949, the U.S. opinion survey unit asked respondents what rights they would be willing to give up if the state would promise them economic security. Up through January, 1949, a majority of respondents indicated that, in exchange for such a promise, they would be willing to give up the right to vote; and nearly half of those having an opinion were willing to give up freedom of the press. On the other hand, almost nobody was willing to give up the right to express his opinion freely or to bring up his children according to his own views. When asked whether they would prefer a government which would assure civil liberties or one offering economic security, six out of ten U.S. zone residents consistently indicated, until 1949, that they would prefer the latter.

During 1949, however, came the first indications that democracy and the rights associated with it were attaining greater popular support. The percentage of those willing to give up the right to vote in favor of economic security dropped from 55 to 38, and the number of those willing to give up other freedoms declined proportionately.

Although questions asked by EMNID and by the *Institut für Demoskopie* are not directly comparable to those asked by the U.S. survey unit, they show similar trends. During the past four years, EMNID has asked respondents which form of government they consider best for Germans. Over half chose democracy in 1953, and by 1956 the proportion had risen to over two-thirds. During the same period, those favoring monarchy or "an authoritarian regime" dropped from one in five to slightly more than one in ten. There are, however, a great many people (20 per cent in 1956) who have no opinion. When asked what they mean by democracy, increasing proportions of respondents are likely to say "freedom," or "government by the people." These two answers accounted for nearly all the definitions given in 1956.

Since 1951, the *Institut für Demoskopie* has been asking West Germans whether they think it is better for a country to have several parties, so that various points of view can be freely represented, or only one party, in order to assure the greatest possible unity. In 1951, six out of ten respondents favored having several parties, and, by 1955, the proportion was better than seven out of ten. During the same period, the numbers of those in favor of only one party declined proportionately. A 1950 survey by the U.S. High Commissioner's office, using substantially the same question, obtained almost exactly the same results as did the *Institut für Demoskopie* in 1951.

Recent questions by a number of survey organizations have indicated that the freedoms assured the individual by democracy have gained increasing appreciation during the past few years. People were asked by the *Institut* in 1953, and again in 1955, whether one could really talk about politics freely in Germany, or whether it was better to be careful. The proportion believing that one could talk freely increased from slightly more than half in 1953 to seven out of ten in 1955, while the proportion of respondents who thought it was better to be careful decreased from one-third to one-fifth.

Attitudes toward the German government, as contrasted with attitudes toward democracy in the abstract, are much more ambivalent. On the one hand, there is evidence of strong resentment toward Bonn and the principal officials of government as a class. On the other hand, the various branches of the Bonn government are receiving increasing acceptance; and knowledge about the detailed working of the system, although still relatively small, is increasing.

Resentment is indicated by several questions asked periodically by the *Institut für Demoskopie*. One is: "What costs the state the most money?" The two most popular answers to this question by far are "occupation costs" and "ministerial salaries." Farther down the list come such items as "buildings in Bonn," "salaries for civil servants," "social welfare expenditures," and "German defense contribution." The fact that "ministerial salaries" have been mentioned by three to four out of ten respondents as the major item of government expense every year since 1951—when a moment's reflection would indicate that this must be one of the smallest items in the government budget—seems to be indicative of a stubborn resentment toward holders of high office. The fact that occupation costs were mentioned still more often, even after the occupation had ceased to exist, probably indicates a mixture of resentment and misunderstanding. Similarly, a substantial majority of respondents has consistently said that the Bonn government was wasteful in its fiscal policies, although this proportion has declined sharply since 1951, when three-quarters of a cross section reproached the government for wastefulness.

Another question which seems to elicit expressions of resentment concerns the motivations attributed to Bundestag deputies in Bonn. In 1951 a third of the *Institut's* respondents thought that the behavior of those men and women was governed primarily by their personal interests, that the deputies were concerned first of all with obtaining money and publicity for themselves, while only a quarter said that the deputies thought first of all of the interests of their constituents. Each succeeding year showed a slightly more favorable popular judgment of the deputies, and by 1954 fewer than 20 per cent of the respondents thought that their representatives in Bonn were governed primarily by personal interests, while approximately 40 per cent saw them as representatives of the public. A similar shift in favor of the deputies is indicated by answers to another *Institut für Demoskopie* question used several times in the years 1951–1954. When people were asked in 1951 whether they thought one had to have great ability to become a Bundestag deputy, fewer than four in ten replied that great ability was necessary. Each year showed a slightly higher proportion with this opinion, however; and, by 1954, about half of the respondents replied that great ability was necessary to become a deputy.

While acceptance of democracy and democratic institutions has been growing slowly, sentiments which might be interpreted as favorable to Nazism have been receding. The status of Nazis and neo-Nazism in Germany, being a subject charged with emotion, has occasioned some rather extreme statements. Nevertheless, available poll results are entirely consistent with the thesis that acceptance of a democratic system of government is growing. To summarize in a few words the results of many questions asked by four survey organizations, it might be said that one-third to one-half of the population, when asked to look back on National Socialism, remember it as a phenomenon in which the good outweighed the bad. Hitler himself is remembered favorably by about a quarter of the population. The numbers of those favoring either a revival of a system similar to Nazism or the resurgence of a man like Hitler are small, however, and appear to be declining.

To understand the way in which the German public looks at Nazism (which is very different from the way it is regarded abroad), one must examine it as one in a series of periods in German history which most respondents experienced themselves. A rough (although somewhat outdated) indication of the way in which people look at these various periods is afforded by a question asked by the *Institut für Demoskopie* in 1951: "When in this century did, in your opinion, things go best in Germany?" The answers may be surprising to foreigners. Nearly half the respondents said things went best during the old imperial Reich of the Kaiser; four out of ten said things went best during the Nazi period; and only a scattering mentioned the Weimar Republic, World War II, or the period after the Second World War.

One key to the relatively favorable attitudes toward the Nazi period may be the highly unfavorable recollections of the Weimar period. Older respondents still mention the Weimar period with vehemence. They remember it as a time when everything was confused, when there seemed to be no leadership in the country, when money wouldn't buy anything, and when weakness, unemployment, injustice, and corruption were the hallmarks of Germany. These answers may be unfair, from the point of view of the historian, but they are real to those who give them, i.e., to almost 90 per cent of the respondents who lived through the period.

Then came the Nazi era. To the individual German this meant that order emerged out of chaos. He was able to find a job. He was no longer baffled by the political confusion of the Weimar period. The government seemed to be able to do something for him. When people were asked, in a U.S.-sponsored survey in 1952, what they liked about National Socialism, nearly half the respondents mentioned job opportunities and a decent standard of living; more than a third mentioned the social welfare policies of the state; and a tenth spoke of good organization and discipline. Nobody recalled the Nazi racial policies or the warlike posture of the Third Reich. A slightly earlier, German-sponsored survey revealed substantially the same set of opinions.

Hitler himself is regarded less favorably. A survey by the *Institut für Demoskopie* in 1952 shows that, at that time, he was regarded by more than two-thirds of the West Germans as a man who accomplished a number of very good things, but who personally was either an unmitigated scoundrel or else a man whose ugly deeds and characteristics far outweighed the good that was in him. The rest, however, remembered him either as a very great statesman or else as a man who, although he made mistakes, was on balance an excellent chief of state.

If Hitler were to return to the German political scene now, he would probably fare poorly. During the past four years, EMNID has asked respondents whether they would vote for or against "a man like Hitler" if they had the opportunity to do so. The proportion who said they would vote *for* such a man has ranged from 12 to 15 per cent; but the proportion who said they would vote against a new Hitler has increased fairly steadily from nearly seven out of ten to more than eight out of ten. This increase has been achieved at the expense of the undecided. However, not all those who say they are in favor of a "man like Hitler" are conscious enemies of democracy or even advocates of an authoritarian system. Some say only, "I had a better life then"; others are chronic malcontents.

Hitler would apparently not have a chance if pitted against the present German Chancellor. In 1954 the *Institut für Demoskopie* asked respondents who they thought was the greater statesman—Adenauer or Hitler. Nearly half the respondents mentioned Adenauer, and only 14 per cent chose Hitler; a few said there was no difference; and the rest had no opinion. It should be noted in passing, however, that, although Adenauer easily outdistanced Hitler in this contest, he was himself snowed under by a vote of five to one when people were asked to choose between him and Otto von Bismarck.

A number of survey organizations have attempted to determine among which population groups the greatest support for National Socialism or a man like Hitler still exists. They all reveal substantially the same picture. It is not surprising that Nazi sentiments are most likely to be found among people who are adherents of one of the right-wing splinter parties. Also showing a relatively large proportion of Nazi advocates are former professional soldiers and the inhabitants of small towns and villages. It is striking that neither of the two major political parties shows a substantial proportion of adherents who would vote again for a man like Hitler—about one out of ten in each case. The incidence of Nazi sentiments is substantially the same among Catholics and Protestants, and there is little difference among age groups.

Current Party Preferences

Several general characteristics of postwar German political life have become apparent since 1946. One is that the trend in Germany is toward a two-party system rather than a multi-party system. Another is that the two big parties, instead of drawing their adherents from one population group, or even from two or three population groups with closely related interests, now tend to attract support from all major groups. This trend toward bigness and toward heterogeneous composition undoubtedly has repercussions on party programs and activities. Finally, the total constituencies of the political parties as a whole are growing. Those who say "don't know" when asked which political party they prefer have steadily declined in number.

As far as the popularity of the two big parties is concerned, there have been rather large fluctuations during the postwar period. Until 1953 the number of those who said they preferred the SPD was greater than the number who favored the CDU. In 1953, however, the CDU forged ahead, and maintained its lead until 1956, when the SPD resumed its position as the party with the most adherents. Early in 1957 the popularity of the CDU began to increase again, and the two parties then appeared to command about equal allegiance; each was mentioned by about 40 per cent of the voters who were willing to state a preference.

The trend toward a two-party rather than a multi-party system is clear from both election and poll results. In 1949, at the time of the first federal elections, the CDU and SPD together received 60 per cent of the votes cast. The Free Democratic Party was a poor third, with about 12 per cent. In the elections of 1953 the two big parties accounted for 74 per cent of the valid votes, and the Free Democrats and the groups affiliated with them received slightly less than 10 per cent. Five other parties each received 1 per cent of the vote or more. They were:

League of Refugees and Expellees	6%
German Party	3%
Communist Party	2%
Bavarian Party	2%
All-German People's Party	1%

The polls show a similar picture. In 1950 the *Institut für Demoskopie* found that over two-thirds of those who stated a party preference mentioned the CDU or the SPD. By 1955 this proportion had risen to almost eight out of ten. EMNID, although using a slightly different question wording, has obtained very similar results. The trend continued in 1956.

Since 1946 the proportion of the total population that is willing or able to name a political party preference, when asked to do so by an interviewer, has been growing steadily. At times, during the 1949–1950 period, almost half of the respondents refused or were unable to make a choice. This figure has declined consistently, although with minor periodic fluctuations; it now ordinarily amounts to less than a quarter of the population.

At least until 1956, the heterogeneity of the supporters of the two big political parties was striking, although it was possible to generalize to a limited degree about the make-up of each. For instance, it has been found repeatedly that labor union members are very likely to vote for the SPD, but that members of all other population groups, especially farmers and civil servants, are more likely to vote for the CDU. Regular churchgoers (whether Protestant or Catholic) are likely to vote for the CDU. As of 1955, almost 60 per cent of the adherents of the CDU were women, and 60 per cent of the supporters of the SPD were men. Adherents of the FDP are likely to be very much better educated than the supporters of the other parties, and are to be found among farmers and independent businessmen. Young people are more likely to prefer the SPD, and older people the CDU.

While these varying proportions are important indicators of the differences among the parties, it is perhaps more significant to note the degree to which both major parties tend to represent the entire population, rather than the degree to which they represent different groups. Both parties usually enjoy about equal strength in the North, West, Middle, and South of the Federal Republic, although there are, of course, periodic fluctuations. Income groups are split fairly evenly by parties. Those in the very lowest (under 250 DM per month) and those in the highest income brackets (over 600 DM per month) prefer the CDU, while those with incomes in between prefer the SPD; but no income group chooses one party by an overwhelming proportion. While unionized labor is generally in favor of the SPD, about two out of ten union members are likely to be opposed to it. All other occupation groups, although their members tend to favor the CDU, also contribute significantly to the SPD. Similarly, while Roman Catholics are more likely to prefer the CDU than any other political party, approximately three out of ten choose the SPD. Protestants are usually divided about equally between the two. Thus, although each of the major parties has a distinguishing composition, each of them also draws for its support on appreciable segments of all principal population groups.

Since party composition is far from homogeneous with respect to personal characteristics and occupational and social groupings, one would scarcely expect to find that the adherents of either of the major parties agree overwhelmingly on any issue which divides the German population generally. At least as far as foreign policy is concerned, differences *within* parties are scarcely less marked than differences *among* parties. For instance, a thin majority of CDU adherents has consistently been in favor of giving priority to European defense over reunification with East Germany, but a good third of those who mention the CDU as their party preference think reunification is more urgent.

Similarly, slightly over half of the SPD supporters have consistently advocated giving priority to reunification over European defense, but more than a third would prefer defense. When people are asked whether they think reunification or security is more important, a majority of the adherents of both political parties choose security. When attitudes toward communism are tested, both CDU and SPD supporters are likely to express a negative attitude. For instance, when respondents were asked whether they would be in favor of reunification if communism were to win a substantial influence as a result, eight out of ten adherents of both parties said that they would be opposed to reunification under those conditions. A majority of CDU supporters has consistently been in favor of German rearmament, and a majority of SPD supporters has consistently been opposed, but strong minorities in both parties differ with the opinion of the majorities. Thus, particularly on issues of foreign policy, party leaders are unlikely to represent the opinions of more than half to three-quarters of those who vote for them at the polls.

The divergence between party position and the views of party adherents on foreign policy issues appears to have increased during 1956. For instance, according to a recent EMNID survey, neutralism among workers increased sharply after 1955, while at the same time neutralism among adherents of the SPD decreased. Yet, at precisely the same time, the proportion of workers identifying themselves with the SPD has increased. Apparent contradictions of this sort can sometimes be explained by the fact that party preference is determined principally by domestic issues; it is not unusual for a person to support a party with the foreign policy stand of which he is in disagreement.

Some Ten-Year Trends

While ten years is not a long enough period for enduring patterns of thought and behavior to become established in a whole people, a number of trends shown by opinion polls from 1946 to 1956 are sufficiently well outlined to suggest likely courses of future development.

Economic problems, at first the overriding concern of most Germans, have tended to recede from their position of unquestioned precedence over political problems, and have also changed in character. Rather than worry about unemployment or about obtaining enough food to eat or clothes to wear, people have tended more and more to concern themselves with the value of money, improving their housing, and maintaining their standard of living.

In the political realm, when asked to specify Germany's major problem, people are increasingly likely to mention reunification. While there appear to be fairly well-defined limits to what Germans are willing to sacrifice for reunification, they do spend more time thinking about the issue. Pressure for reunification is likely to be greater in the future than it has been in the past.

As for the future of German democracy, the trend is mildly encouraging. Popular interest in political life is still not overwhelming, but it appears to be rising. Democracy is an increasingly popular symbol, even though thoroughgoing defenders of it are still rare. There are few who would favor a return to something like Nazism, but there are indications that substantial numbers of voters believe that democracy should be tempered by some measure of authoritarianism. However, they are now thinking of the authoritarianism of a Bismarck or an Adenauer, not of a Hitler.

Finally, the trend is fairly strong toward a two-party system in which a large majority of the whole population participates. Not only have the minor parties tended consistently to become smaller of late, but fewer people are unable or unwilling to give a party preference than was the case earlier. The postwar aversion to political identification, while not yet overcome, appears to be fading.

Notes

ONE: Introduction: The German Political Scene

1. Paul Weymar, *Adenauer,* New York, 1957, p. 457.

2. *Ibid.,* p. 434.

TWO: The Development of German Foreign Policy Institutions

1. "Die völkerrechtliche Stellung Deutschlands, nach seiner bedingungslosen Kapitulation," *Europa Archiv,* Oberursel, 1946, p. 209.

2. Eberhard Menzel, "Zur völkerrechtlichen Lage Deutschlands," *Europa Archiv,* Oberursel, 1947, pp. 1009 ff.

3. Eugen Budde, *Gibt es noch eine deutsche Aussenpolitik?* Hamburg, 1947.

4. "Ansätze einer deutschen Repräsentation," *Europa Archiv,* 1948, pp. 1148 ff.

5. Quoted in *Die Neue Zeitung,* November 14, 1947.

6. Fritz Stricker, *75 Jahre deutscher Aussenpolitik,* Düsseldorf, 1947.

7. Cf. Deutsches Institut für Wirtschaftsforschung, *Wirtschaftsprobleme der Besatzungszonen,* Berlin, 1948; also Institut für Besatzungsfragen, *Einwirkungen der Besatzungsmächte auf die westdeutsche Wirtschaft,* Tübingen, 1947.

8. Proclamation of the Parliamentary Council of September 15, 1948, quoted in *Neue Zeitung,* September 16, 1948.

9. Wolfgang Abendroth, "Deutsche Einheit und europäische Integration in der Präambel des Grundgesetzes der Bundesrepublik Deutschland," *Europa Archiv,* 1951, pp. 4385–4392.

10. Werner Kraus, "Die parlamentarische Kontrolle der Aussenpolitik," *Aussenpolitik,* Vol. 6, No. 8.

11. Cf. Ludwig Rosenberg, "Gewerkschaften in der Aussenpolitik," *Aussenpolitik,* Vol. 1, 1949.

12. Rupert Breitling, *Die Verbände in der Bundesrepublik,* Meisheim am Glan, 1952.

13. Karl Arnold, "Bundesstaat und Integration," *Aussenpolitik,* Vol. 3, No. 6, 1952, pp. 345 ff.

14. Cf. *Rheinischer Merkur,* October 28 and November 25, 1955.

THREE: Party Leaders and Foreign Policy

1. Helmut Gollwitzer, *. . . und führen, wohin Du nicht willst,* Munich, 1952.

2. Wilhelm Wolfgang Schütz, *Die Stunde Deutschlands,* Stuttgart, 1954.

3. Second Session of the Consultative Assembly of the Council of Europe, August 7–28, 1950, *Reports,* Part I, p. 238.

4. Schütz, *op. cit.,* p. 83.

5. *Ibid.*

6. Cf. Official Report of Debates of the Consultative Assembly, Council of Europe, Extraordinary Session, January 14–17, 1953, pp. 9–15.

7. SPD Program for Four-Power Negotiations on German Reunification, May 9, 1955.

8. Erich Ollenhauer before the Bundestag, 115th Session, December 2, 1955.

9. Carlo Schmid in *Bonner General-Anzeiger,* Christmas issue, 1955.

10. *Reichsruf,* August 15, 1953.

11. *Ibid.,* July 2, 1955.

FOUR: POLITICAL VIEWS OF THE WEST GERMAN CIVIL SERVICE

1. Cf. Karl Dietrich Bracher, *Die Auflösung der Weimarer Republik—Eine Studie zum Problem des Machtverfalls in der Demokratie,* Stuttgart-Düsseldorf, 1955, pp. 174 ff.

2. Otto Kirchheimer, "Notes on the Political Scene in Western Germany," *World Politics,* Vol. 6, 1954, p. 311.

3. Theodor Eschenburg, *Bemerkungen zur deutschen Bürokratie,* Mannheim, 1955, pp. 17 ff. See also the same author's *Der Beamte in Partei und Parlament,* Frankfurt am Main, 1952.

4. See Bracher, *op. cit.,* p. 178.

5. Cf. *ibid.,* pp. 194 ff.

6. Cf. E. W. Schnitzer, "German Geopolitics Revived," *Journal of Politics,* Vol. 17, 1955, pp. 407 ff.

7. *Christ und Welt,* December 24, 1952. (This is a weekly periodical published in Stuttgart.)

FIVE: WEST GERMAN TRADE-UNIONS: THEIR DOMESTIC AND FOREIGN POLICIES

1. Cf. Ossip K. Flechtheim, *Die KPD in der Weimarer Republik,* Offenbach, 1948.

2. Cf. Ludwig Preller, *Sozialpolitik in der Weimarer Republik,* Stuttgart, 1949.

3. Cf. Wolfgang Abendroth, *Die deutschen Gewerkschaften,* Heidelberg, 1955, p. 34; Evelyn Anderson, *Hammer oder Amboss,* Nürnberg, 1948.

4. Cf. K. D. Bracher, *Die Auflösung der Weimarer Republik,* Stuttgart, 1955, esp. p. 441.

5. Cf. *Gründungskongress des DGB,* 1949, Protokoll, pp. 183 ff.

6. Cf. Götz Briefs, *Das Gewerkschaftsproblem gestern und heute,* Frankfurt, 1955; for a German union criticism of Briefs, cf. Helmuth Wickel, "Gewerkschaften als Gesellschaft," in *Gewerkschaftliche Monatshefte* (hereafter cited as *G.M.*), December, 1955, p. 713. See, also, C. Kerr, "The Trade

Union Movement and the Redistribution of Power in Postwar Germany," in *Quarterly Journal of Economics,* November, 1954, p. 535.

7. Cf. Abendroth, *op. cit.,* pp. 42 ff.

8. Based on figures given by Dr. Viktor Agartz, as quoted in *Wirtschafts- und Steuerpolitik, Referat,* October 4–9, 1954, p. 26.

9. Cf. F. Fricke, "Konstruktive Gewerkschaftspolitik," *G.M.,* June, 1955, p. 337; and the discussion by H. Seeger (chairman of the woodworkers union), *ibid.,* p. 435.

10. Cf. *Protokoll des 2. ordentlichen Bundeskongresses,* Berlin, 1952, p. 34.

11. *Geschäftsbericht Metall 1952–53,* p. 146.

12. *Geschäftsbericht Textil 1955,* p. 277.

13. V. Agartz, *Staat, Wirtschaft und gewerkschaftliche Lohnpolitik,* 1954.

14. Cf. *Gewerkschaften im Staat: Drittes europäisches Gespräch 1952,* 1955, p. 181.

15. Cf. V. Agartz' speech at the 1954 Frankfurt DGB convention, published in *Wirtschaft, Steuerpolitik* . . . ; ÖTV chairman Kummernuss' speech at the 1955 ÖTV convention, reprinted in *Gewerkschaften in Staat und Gesellschaft,* May, 1955; and metal union co-chairman Brenner's speech at his convention in September, 1954, published in *Die Aufgaben unserer Gewerkschaft in der gegenwärtigen Situation.*

16. Kummernuss, *op. cit.,* p. 31.

17. For the labor viewpoint, see Erich Pothoff, *Zur Geschichte der Montan- Mitbestimmung,* Cologne, 1955.

18. For discussions of the codetermination problem, see the literature noted in Kerr, *op. cit.,* p. 522, and Herbert J. Spiro, "Codetermination in Germany," *American Political Science Review,* Vol. 48, 1954; see also H. C. Wallich, *Mainsprings of German Revival,* New Haven, 1955, p. 309.

19. For more detailed data on the KAB, cf. R. Breitling, *Die Verbände in der Bundesrepublik,* Meisenheim, 1955, pp. 153–157.

20. Jörge Simpfendörfer, "Christen und Einheitsgewerkschaft," *G.M.,* November, 1955, p. 649.

21. Cf. the SPD pamphlet *Das Betriebsverfassungsgesetz im Bundestag,* 1952.

22. Cf. *IG Metall Geschäftsbericht 1952–53,* p. 9.

23. *Parteitag Berlin 1954,* SPD Protokoll, p. 219.

24. For a measured view on the state of the German press, see A. Grosser, *The Colossus Again: West Germany from Defeat to Rearmament,* New York, 1955, p. 175.

25. H. K. Lüth, U. Lohmar, and R. Tartler, *Arbeiterjugend gestern und heute,* Heidelberg, 1955, p. 346.

26. For examples of recent interpretations of the state of mind and job attitudes of German workers, see Karl Bednarik, *Der junge Arbeiter von heute,* Stuttgart, 1953; Carl Jantke, *Bergmann und Zeche, die sozialen Verhältnisse einer Schachtanlage des nördlichen Ruhrgebietes in der Sicht der Bergleute,* Tübingen, 1953; and Th. Pirker *et al., Arbeiter, Management, Mitbestimmung,*

Stuttgart and Düsseldorf, 1955. See also *Betriebsklima, eine industriesoziologische Untersuchung im Mannesmann Bereich* (hereafter cited as Mannesmann), mimeographed version, Frankfurt, 1955.

27. Cf. Pirker *et al., op. cit.,* p. 330; and Mannesmann, pp. 207 ff.

28. Cf. *ibid.,* pp. 345–436, and Mannesmann, pp. 287–369.

29. Mannesmann, pp. 134 and 135.

30. Cf. Pirker *et al., op. cit.,* pp. 392 and 422.

31. *Ibid.,* p. 424; Mannesmann, pp. 255 ff.

32. Cf. V. Agartz, *Wirtschaft und Steuerpolitik,* p. 12, and Pirker *et al., op. cit.,* p. 419.

33. *Geschäftsbericht Metall 1952–53,* p. 120.

34. For the union viewpoint on relations between shop delegates and works councils, cf. Georgi, "Gewerkschaft und Betrieb," in *G.M.,* November, 1955, pp. 660–663.

35. Mannesmann, p. 115.

36. A. Mausolff, *Gewerkschaft und Betriebsrat im Urteil der Arbeitnehmer,* Darmstadt, 1952, p. 98; a youth sample is given in Lüth *et al., Arbeiterjugend, op. cit.,* p. 348.

37. Pirker *et al., op. cit.,* p. 267; Mannesmann, p. 71.

38. Cf. *Gewerkschafter,* 1955, No. 8, p. 38.

39. Cf. S. A. Elten, "Die vielbeachtete Betriebsratwahl in der Westfalenhütte," *Stuttgarter Zeitung,* December 9, 1955.

40. *Geschäftsbericht Metall 1952–53,* Frankfurt, pp. 70–76. Cf. *Bergbauindustrie,* August 20, 1955, for the resolution adopted at the August, 1955, convention of the miners union.

41. Cf. resolution reprinted in *Bergbauindustrie,* September 10, 1955.

42. Cf. speech of SPD member Wehner in *Verhandlungen der gemeinsamen Versammlung, Europäische Gemeinschaft für Kohle und Stahl,* No. 11, June 23, 1955, p. 339.

43. For text of resolution and summary of debate, see *Welt der Arbeit,* October 10, 1954; for the SPD rearmament debate of June, 1954, see *Parteitag Berlin . . . ,* pp. 71–148.

44. Cf. F. Erler's official explanation of the SPD vote on the Soldier's Law (132nd session of the Second Bundestag, March 6, 1955) in *Das Parlament,* March 14, 1956, p. 10.

45. Cf. O. Pollack (editor-in-chief of the Vienna *Arbeiterzeitung,* as quoted in *Vorwärts,* November 11, 1955.

46. For a refutation of Starlinger, see Hermann Poerzgen, "Gelbe Gefahr für die Sovietunion" and "Ein fragwürdiges Russlandbild" in *Frankfurter Allgemeine Zeitung,* December 10 and 16, 1955.

47. Werner Vollmer, "Arbeiterschaft und Wiedervereinigung," *G.M.,* April, 1955, p. 208.

48. EMNID Institute, *Jugend zwischen 15 und 24,* Bielefeld, 1955, p. 238.

49. Cf. Lüth *et al., op. cit.,* p. 354.

50. EMNID Institute, *op. cit.,* pp. 263 and 264.

51. *Ibid.,* p. 249.

52. Cf. W. Dirks, "Folgen der Entnazifizierung," in *Sociologica, Festgabe für Max Horkheimer,* Frankfurt, 1955, p. 444.

53. For an indictment of the "socially restorative measures" of the occupation powers, see W. Abendroth, "Kampf für die soziale Demokratie," in *G.M.,* October, 1955, p. 585.

SIX: The Politics of German Business

1. For appraisals of the role of the German middle classes and heavy industry, see Max Weber, "Parlament und Regierung im neugeordneten Deutschland," in *Gesammelte politische Schriften,* Munich, 1921, pp. 164 ff., and *passim;* Sigmund Neumann, "Germany," in Taylor Cole (ed.), *European Political Systems,* New York, 1953, pp. 292 ff.; John Herz, "The Government of Germany," in Carter, Ranney, and Herz, *Major Foreign Powers,* New York, 1952, p. 607; Rudolf Olden, *The History of Liberty in Germany,* London, 1946, pp. 121 ff.; Guido de Ruggiero, *The History of European Liberalism,* London, 1927, pp. 271 ff.; Eugene Anderson, "Freedom and Authoritarianism in German History," in Gabriel A. Almond (ed.), *The Struggle for Democracy in Germany,* Chapel Hill, 1949, pp. 3 ff.; Koppel S. Pinson, *Modern Germany,* New York, 1954, pp. 219 ff.; Wilhelm Mommsen, *Grösse und Versagen des deutschen Bürgertums,* Stuttgart, 1949.

2. See Rudolf Pechel, *Deutscher Widerstand,* Zurich, 1947, pp. 177 ff. and pp. 339 ff.; Günther Weisenborn, *Der lautlose Aufstand,* Hamburg, 1953, pp. 92 ff.

3. See K. H. Herchenröder, Joh. Schäfer, Manfred Zapp, *Die Nachfolger der Ruhrkonzerne,* Düsseldorf, 1953; see, also, Kurt Pritzkoleit, *Männer, Mächte, Monopole,* Düsseldorf, 1953.

4. See Helmut Schelsky, *Wandlungen der deutschen Familie in der Gegenwart,* Stuttgart, 1954, pp. 350 ff.

5. On the organizational pattern of German industry, see Frederick Harbison, "Modern Management in Western Europe," *Quarterly Journal of Economics,* August, 1956, pp. 364–379.

6. *Die Welt,* June 23, 1954.

7. For a description of these and other civic organizations, see Hans Edgar Jahn, *Vertrauen, Verantwortung, Mitarbeit,* Oberlahnstein, 1953.

8. Rudolf Wildenmann, *Partei und Fraktion,* 1954, pp. 61 ff.; Max Gustav Lange, Gerhard Schulz, Klaus Schütz, *Parteien in der Bundesrepublik,* Stuttgart and Düsseldorf, 1955, pp. 117 ff.; and Joseph H. Kaiser, *Die Repräsentation organisierter Interessen,* Berlin, 1956, p. 253.

9. Otto Kirchheimer, "The Composition of the German Bundestag," *Western Political Quarterly,* December, 1950, pp. 590 ff.

10. Adapted from *Zusammensetzung des Bundestages,* 1953, by the Deutsche Industrieinstitut. Cf. Ossip K. Flechtheim, *Die deutschen Parteien seit 1945,* Berlin, 1955, p. 75. See, also, the detailed analysis of the representation of businessmen and representatives of business pressure groups in Rupert Breitling, *Die Verbände in der Bundesrepublik,* Meisenheim am Glan, 1955, pp. 101 ff.

11. For similar views, see Kirchheimer, *op. cit.*, p. 601; Wildenmann, *op. cit.*, pp. 61 ff., pp. 92 ff.; and Weber, "Parlament und Regierung im neugeordneten Deutschland," *op. cit.*, pp. 164 ff.

12. Evaluation Staff, Office of Public Affairs, Office of the U.S. High Commissioner for Germany, *A Survey Analysis of the Factors Underlying the Outcome of the 1953 German Federal Elections,* December 11, 1953; for other survey materials on German elections, see Friedrich Tennstädt, *Der Wähler,* Allensbach, 1957.

13. See Wildenmann, *op. cit.*, pp. 91 ff.

14. For background on the FDP conflicts, see Lange, Schulz, and Schütz, *op. cit.*, pp. 356 ff. For more recent information on FDP developments and policy, see *Der Spiegel,* February 29, 1956, pp. 15 ff., and February 27, 1957, pp. 20 ff.

15. Wildenmann, *op. cit.*, p. 37.

16. *Ibid.,* p. 50.

17. *Ibid.,* p. 98.

18. Friedrich Giese, *Grundgesetz für die Bundesrepublik Deutschland,* Frankfurt on Main, 1953, p. 47; Theodor Eschenburg, *Staat und Gesellschaft in Deutschland,* Stuttgart, 1956, pp. 527 ff.

19. Sozialdemokratische Partei Deutschlands (SPD), *Unternehmermillionen kaufen politische Macht,* Bonn, 1953.

20. Pritzkoleit, *op. cit.*, pp. 39–41.

21. SPD, *op. cit.*, pp. 57–58. See, also, Flechtheim, *op. cit.*, pp. 78 ff.

22. See Bundesverband der Deutschen Industrie, *Kundgebung und Mitgliederversammlung,* Wiesbaden, May 18, 1953, p. 41. For a discussion of these promotional associations, see Friedrich August Freiherr von der Heydte, *Soziologie der deutschen Parteien,* Munich, 1955, pp. 168–169.

23. For general discussions of German interest-groups, see Breitling, *op. cit.;* Kaiser, *op. cit.;* Theodor Eschenburg, *Herrschaft der Verbände?* Stuttgart, 1955; Von der Heydte, *op. cit.*, pp. 166 ff.; and Otto Stammer, "Politische Soziologie," in Gehlen and Schelsky, *Soziologie,* Düsseldorf, 1955, pp. 281 ff.

24. See Franz Neumann, *Behemoth, the Structure and Practice of National Socialism,* New York, 1942, pp. 235 ff.; Robert Brady, "Manufacturing Spitzenverbände," *Political Science Quarterly,* 1941, pp. 199–225. For the Nazi period, see Eberhart Barth, *Wesen und Aufgaben der Organisation der gewerblichen Wirtschaft,* Hamburg, 1939. For brief comments on the current situation, see Pritzkoleit, *op. cit.*, pp. 416 ff.; Kaiser, *op. cit.*, pp. 96 ff.; and Breitling, *op. cit.*, pp. 10 ff.

25. See Alfred S. Cleveland, "NAM: Spokesman for Industry," *Harvard Business Review,* May, 1948; David B. Truman, *The Governmental Process,* New York, 1951, pp. 137 ff.

26. *Jahresbericht des Bundesverbandes der deutschen Industrie,* May 1, 1954, to April 30, 1955, pp. 223 ff.

27. HICOG, *A Survey Analysis of the Factors Underlying the Outcome of the 1953 German Federal Elections,* December 11, 1953. See, also, Erich Peter Neumann and Elisabeth Noelle, *Antworten: Politik im Kraftfeld der öffentli-*

chen Meinung, Allensbach, 1954, pp. 47 ff.; Noelle and Neumann, *Jahrbuch der öffentlichen Meinung,* Allensbach, 1956, pp. 143 ff.; Tennstädt, *op. cit.;* and Heinrich Satter, *Deutschland ohne Feigenblatt,* Munich, 1956, pp. 47 ff.

28. HICOG, *ibid.,* p. 56.

29. Deutsches Industrieinstitut, *Unternehmerbrief,* October 29, 1953. See, also, a lecture by Ernst Joachim Dohany, "Das Ethos des unternehmerischen Standes," *Vortragsreihe des Deutschen Industrieinstituts,* No. 45, November 7, 1955.

30. The surveys summarized in this section were made by HICOG, Reactions Analysis Staff (*A Year End Survey of Rightist and Nationalist Sentiments in West Germany,* January, 1953, and earlier studies in this series); the *Institut für Demoskopie* (reported in Neumann and Noelle, *Antworten,* p. 29, and Noelle and Neumann, *Jahrbuch der öffentlichen Meinung,* pp. 276 ff.); and the EMNID *Institut für Meinungsforschung,* a Gallup affiliate (reported in Satter, *op. cit.,* pp. 42 ff.).

31. HICOG, Office of Public Affairs, *Do the West German People Believe the U.S. Is for German Unity?* May 27, 1952. For later polls, see Satter, *op. cit.,* pp. 61 ff., and Noelle and Neumann, *op. cit.,* pp. 313 ff.

32. See Noelle and Neumann, *op. cit.,* pp. 360 f.; Satter, *op. cit.,* pp. 88 ff.; and HICOG, Office of Public Affairs, *West German Opinion on Defense Participation Following the Formal Bundestag Debate, March 31, 1952,* p. 1. On the attitudes of youth toward military service, see Rolf Fröhner, *Wie stark sind die Halbstarken?* Bielefeld, 1956, pp. 125 ff.

33. HICOG, *West German Opinion on Defense Participation . . . ,* March 31, 1952, p. 8. See, also, Noelle and Neumann, *op. cit.,* p. 366.

34. HICOG, *ibid.,* p. 12.

35. Noelle and Neumann, *op. cit.,* p. 366.

36. Cf. *ibid.,* pp. 374 ff.; and Satter, *op. cit.,* pp. 91 ff.

37. HICOG, Reactions Analysis Staff, *Public Opinion in Western Europe,* January, 1953, p. 10; Noelle and Neumann, *op. cit.,* pp. 389 ff.

38. HICOG, *Public Opinion in Western Europe,* pp. 10, 12.

39. *Ibid.,* pp. 195, 221.

40. HICOG, Reactions Analysis Staff, *West German Thinking on a Federation of Europe,* November 28, 1951.

41. Schelsky, *op. cit.,* pp. 132 ff.

42. For present opinion of organized German business, see *Jahresbericht des Bundesverbandes der deutschen Industrie,* May 1, 1954, to April 30, 1955, pp. 18 ff.

43. *Ibid.,* pp. 120 f.

SEVEN: The Mass Media in West German Political Life

1. "Über die Wirksamkeit der deutschen Presse," *Zeitungs-Verlag,* September 15, 1955.

2. Elisabeth Noelle and Erich Peter Neumann, *Jahrbuch der öffentlichen Meinung 1947–1955,* Allensbach, 1956, p. 55.

3. Cf. an essay by Emil Dovifat in *Die Deutsche Presse 1956,* issued by the

Institut für Publizistik ("Institute for Communication Research"), Berlin, 1956, pp. 27–37; see, also, Claus Jacobi, "The New German Press," *Foreign Affairs,* January, 1954.

4. Joseph Wechsberg in *The New Yorker,* October 9, 1954.

5. Dovifat, *op. cit.,* pp. 34, 124.

6. Noelle and Neumann, *op. cit.,* p. 56.

7. Cf. H. G. von Studnitz, "Der Auslandskorrespondent," *Aussenpolitik,* October, 1953.

8. *Deutschland-Jahrbuch 1953,* p. 584.

9. *Die Deutsche Presse 1954,* Berlin, 1954, p. 86.

10. Cf. Horst Adameitz, "Ein deutsches Weltblatt?" in *Die Deutsche Zeitung,* July, 1952, pp. 7–9; see, also, Otto Stolz, "Eine Klage und ihre Ursache," *Die Feder,* April, 1954.

11. *Die Feder,* April, 1954.

12. For a report on the editorial opinions of numerous newspapers, see *Zeitungs-Verlag,* April 30, 1954.

13. *Die Deutsche Presse 1956,* p. 76.

14. *Ibid.,* p. 50.

15. Kurt Magnus, *Der Rundfunk in der Bundesrepublik und West-Berlin,* Frankfurt, 1955, p. 9.

16. Noelle and Neumann, *op. cit.,* p. 62.

17. Magnus, *op. cit.,* pp. 25 ff.

18. *Ibid.,* pp. 43 ff.

19. *Der Journalist,* January, 1955.

20. Nordwestdeutscher Rundfunk, Rundfunkschule, "Der Rundfunk im politischen und geistigen Raum des Volkes" (Minutes of a meeting of scientists, politicians, and persons in public life), Hamburg, June 6–7, 1952, pp. 46–47.

21. Helmut K. J. Ridder, "Meinungsfreiheit," in Franz L. Neumann *et al.* (eds.), *Die Grundrechte,* Vol. 2, Berlin, 1954, pp. 272–273.

22. *Deutsche Zeitung und Wirtschafts Zeitung,* May 12, 1956.

23. *Der Journalist,* January, 1955, citing the *Deutsche Zeitung.*

24. H. G. von Studnitz, "Gestalt und Aufbau des Auswärtigen Amts," *Aussenpolitik,* December, 1952.

25. Cf. *Deutsche Zeitung und Wirtschafts Zeitung,* July 14, 1956; *The New York Times,* July 25 and 26, 1956.

26. Hans Wallenberg, *Report on Democratic Institutions in Germany,* American Council on Germany, Inc., New York, 1956, p. 79.

27. Wechsberg, *op. cit.*

28. *Zeitungs-Verlag,* July 15, 1955, p. 481.

29. *Deutschland-Jahrbuch 1953,* p. 584; see, also, Max Frhr. von Besserer, "Das deutsche Presse-Nachrichtenwesen nach 1945," *Zeitungs-Verlag,* April 30, 1954, pp. 319 ff.

30. Erwin Weghorn, "Die ausländischen Nachrichtenagenturen in Deutschland," *Zeitungs-Verlag,* April 30, 1954, pp. 330 ff.

31. Federal Press and Information Office, *Bulletin* (English ed.), October 8, 1953; see also Erich Wagner, "Der DIMITAG, Bestimmung und Erreichtes," *Zeitungs-Verlag*, April 30, 1954, pp. 324 ff.

32. Werner G. Krug, "Die Aussenpolitik in der deutschen Presse," *Zeitungs-Verlag*, June 15, 1953, pp. 361–362.

33. Josef März, *Die moderne Zeitung—ihre Einrichtungen und ihre Betriebsweise*, Munich, 1951, p. 45.

34. Federal Press and Information Office, *Bulletin* (English ed.), October 25, 1956.

35. *NWDR Jahrbuch, 1950–1953*, Hamburg, 1953, p. 39.

36. "Der Rundfunk im politischen und geistigen Raum des Volkes," p. 43.

37. Paul Gerhardt, "Die elementare politische Pflicht des Rundfunks," *Rundfunk und Fernsehen*, No. 2, 1953, pp. 22 ff.

38. Federal Press and Information Office, *Bulletin* (English ed.), June 18, 1953.

39. Federal Press and Information Office, *Bulletin* (German ed.), April 28, 1956.

40. *Zeitungs-Verlag*, June 15, 1954, p. 473.

41. *Ibid.*, February 15, 1955, pp. 86–87.

42. "Presserechtsprobleme in Vergangenheit und Gegenwart," printed manuscript by the *Landesverband Schleswig-Holstein und Hamburg im Verein deutscher Zeitungsverleger*, 1952.

43. *Die Feder*, June–July, 1954.

44. *Ibid.*, April, 1954, and *Zeitungs-Verlag*, April 30, 1954.

45. Federal Press and Information Office, *Bulletin* (English ed.), June 3, 1954.

46. *Die Feder*, July–August, 1953.

47. *Der Journalist*, January, 1955.

48. *Zeitungs-Verlag*, September 1, 1954, p. 682.

49. *Die Feder*, March, 1954.

50. *Der Journalist*, July, 1955; and *Die Feder*, July–August, 1955.

51. *Der Journalist*, August, 1955.

52. *Die Feder*, September, 1953.

53. *Zeitungs-Verlag*, November 1, 1954, p. 811.

54. Bernhard Maurer, "Der Anzeigenentzug als wirtschaftliches Druckmittel," *Der Journalist*, May, 1955, pp. 10–12 (one section of a dissertation entitled "Gefahren für die innere Freiheit der Presse," which was published serially by *Der Journalist*).

55. Maurer, "Der Einbruch anonymen Kapitals in die Presse," *ibid.*, February, 1955.

56. *Die Feder*, June, 1953.

57. Maurer, "Private Einflussnahme auf den Zeitungsinhalt," *Der Journalist*, July, 1955, p. 9.

58. *Die Feder*, April, 1954, cites several editorial protests.

59. *Der Journalist*, April, 1955.

60. *Ibid.*, August–September, 1954.

61. Minutes of the Second German Bundestag, 30th Session, Bonn, May 21, 1954, pp. 1378–1380.

62. *Zeitungs-Verlag,* June 1, 1955, p. 371.

63. For a published expression of such views, see Heinz Commer, "Öffentlichkeit, Obrigkeit und Presse," *Zeitungs-Verlag,* November 15, 1954.

64. *Die Feder,* March, 1953.

65. *Zeitungs-Verlag,* March 16, 1953, p. 201.

66. "Deutsche Zeitung—Deutsches Schicksal," *Zeitungs-Verlag,* September 15, 1955.

67. "Pressefreiheit und Selbstkontrolle," *Zeitungs-Verlag,* April 30, 1954, pp. 303 ff.

68. Peter J. Fliess, "Freedom of the Press in the Bonn Republic," *Journal of Politics,* November, 1954, p. 683.

69. See, also, Ridder, *op. cit.,* p. 282, and *passim.*

70. Cf. Fliess, *op. cit.,* p. 673; see, also, *Der Journalist,* July, 1955.

71. *Zeitungs-Verlag,* September 15, 1954, p. 715.

EIGHT: Trends in West German Public Opinion, 1946–1956

1. Cf. *Trends in German Public Opinion 1946 through 1949,* Office of the U.S. High Commissioner for Germany, Office of Public Affairs, Mehlem, 1950; see, also, subsequent reports of the Reactions Analysis Staff, HICOG, listed in Bruce L. Smith and Chitra M. Smith (eds.), *International Communication and Political Opinion: A Guide to the Literature,* Princeton University Press, Princeton, N.J., 1956, pp. 206 ff.

2. Cf. Elisabeth Noelle and Erich Peter Neumann, *Jahrbuch der öffentlichen Meinung 1947–1955,* Allensbach, 1956; E. P. Neumann and E. Noelle, *Antworten: Politik im Kraftfeld der öffentlichen Meinung,* Allensbach, 1954; and E. Noelle, *Auskunft über die Parteien,* Allensbach, 1955. For published EMNID results, see Heinrich Satter, *Deutschland ohne Feigenblatt,* Munich, 1956.

3. Cf. *Directory of Organizations in Opinion, Consumer, and Related Research Outside the United States,* Bureau of Social Science Research, Inc., Washington, D.C., 1956.

4. E.g., *Betriebsklima: Eine industriesoziologische Untersuchung aus dem Ruhrgebiet,* a publication of the Institute for Social Research of the University of Frankfurt, 1955, based in part on interviews conducted by DIVO.

5. These figures were compiled from the following sources: Klaus Mehnert and Heinrich Schulte (eds.), *Deutschland Jahrbuch 1953,* Essen, 1953; *Jahrbuch der öffentlichen Meinung 1947–1955,* pp. xxxv and 3–4; *DIVO Pressedienst,* February 1 and 11, 1957; and *Statistisches Jahrbuch für die Bundesrepublik Deutschland, 1955,* Stuttgart-Cologne, 1955.

List of Abbreviations

ADGB—Trade-union association in the Weimar Republic

BDA—Federal Union of German Employers

BDI—Federation of German Industries

BHE—League of the Refugees and the Dispossessed

CDU—Christian Democratic Union

CED—(U.S.) Committee for Economic Development

CSC—Coal and Steel Community (see *Montan-Union* in Glossary)

CSU—Christian Social Union, Bavarian affiliate of CDU

DAG—German Clerical Workers Association

DGB—West German Trade-Union Federation

DIH—German Chamber of Industry and Commerce

DII—German Industry Institute

DIVO—German Institute for Public Opinion Surveys (Frankfurt a.M.)

DM—Deutsche Mark (about 25 cents at 1957 rates of exchange)

DP—German Party

DPA—German Press Agency

DRP—German Reich Party

EDC—European Defense Community

EMNID—Institute for Market and Opinion Research (Bielefeld)

FDGB—Trade-union association in the Soviet-occupied zone of Germany

FDP—Free Democratic Party

FVP—Free People's Party

GVP—All-German People's Party

HICOG—Office of the U.S. High Commissioner for Germany

ICFTU—International Confederation of Free Trade-Unions

KPD—German Communist Party

LDP—Liberal Democratic Party

NAM—(U.S.) National Association of Manufacturers

NWDR—North-West German Radio

SPD—German Social Democratic Party

UEF—European Union of Federalists

WEU—West European Union

WWI—Economic Research Institute of the West German Trade-Unions

Glossary

Allgemeiner Deutscher Gewerkschaftsbund (ADGB)—Trade-union association in the Weimar Republic.

Bundesrat—Upper house of the West German federal parliament.

Bundestag—Lower house of the federal parliament.

Bundesverband der deutschen Industrie (BDI)—Federation of German Industries.

Christlich-Demokratische Union (CDU)—Christian Democratic Union.

Christlich-Soziale Union (CSU)—Christian Social Union; Bavarian counterpart of the CDU.

Deutsche Angestelltengewerkschaft (DAG)—German Clerical Workers Association.

Deutsche Partei (DP)—German Party.

Deutsche Presse-Agentur (DPA)—German Press Agency.

Deutscher Beamtenbund—Association of German Civil Service Officials.

Deutscher Gewerkschaftsbund (DGB)—West German Trade-Union Federation.

Deutsche Industrie- und Handelskammer (DIH)—German Chamber of Industry and Commerce.

Freie Demokratische Partei (FDP)—Free Democratic Party.

Freier Deutscher Gewerkschaftsbund (FDGB)—Trade-union association in the Soviet-occupied zone of Germany.

Gemeinschaftsausschuss der deutschen gewerblichen Wirtschaft—Co-ordinating Committee for the German Industrial Economy.

Gesamtdeutsche Volkspartei (GVP)—All-German People's Party.

Grundgesetz—Basic Law; a document framed in 1949 which serves as West Germany's constitution.

Kommunistische Partei Deutschlands (KPD)—German Communist Party.

Land—State. West Germany was divided by the occupation powers into eleven *Länder*, two of which were the cities of Hamburg and Bremen. Three southwest German *Länder* were later consolidated into one, leaving a total of nine.

Länderrat—Council of States; a council of the three minister presidents of the states within the U.S. zone, formed in the early postwar period, with headquarters in Stuttgart. The same term was later used to describe the body representing the states of the British and U.S. zones in the bi-zonal administration in Frankfurt during 1948 and 1949.

Landser—"Doughboy"; a German foot-soldier.

Landtag—State legislative assembly or diet.

Liberal-Demokratische Partei Deutschlands (LDP)—German Liberal Democratic Party; merged with other political groups to form the FDP in 1949.

Montan-Union—European Coal and Steel Community; also known as "CSC."

Rapallo—Italian town where a treaty of nonaggression and friendship between Germany and Soviet Russia was signed in 1922. The term "Rapallo policy" as used in Germany usually refers to a policy of establishing closer relations with the Soviet Union in order to play off the East against the West.

Rechtsstaat—A state governed in accordance with established legal principles.

Sozialdemokratische Partei Deutschlands (SPD)—German Social Democratic Party.

Wirtschaftswissenschaftliches Institut der Gewerkschaften (WWI)—Economic Research Institute of the West German Trade-Unions.

Name Index

Name Index